YOUTH & SOCIETY

Exploring the social dynamics of youth experience

SECOND EDITION

Rob WHITE & Johanna WYN

OXFORD
UNIVERSITY PRESS
AUSTRALIA & NEW ZEALAND

253 Normanby Road, South Melbourne, Victoria 3205, Australia

Oxford University Press is a department of the University of Oxford.
It furthers the University's objective of excellence in research,
scholarship, and education by publishing worldwide in

Oxford New York

Auckland Cape Town Dar es Salaam Hong Kong Karachi
Kuala Lumpur Madrid Melbourne Mexico City Nairobi
New Delhi Shanghai Taipei Toronto

With offices in

Argentina Austria Brazil Chile Czech Republic France Greece
Guatemala Hungary Italy Japan Poland Portugal Singapore
South Korea Switzerland Thailand Turkey Ukraine Vietnam

OXFORD is a trademark of Oxford University Press
in the UK and in certain other countries

National Library of Australia Cataloguing-in-Publication data

White, R. D. (Robert Douglas), 1956–
Youth and society : exploring the social dynamics of youth experience.
2nd ed.
Bibliography.
Includes index.
ISBN 978 0 19 555133 4 (pbk)
1. Youth – Social conditions. 2. Youth –Australia – Social conditions.
3. Social values. I. Wyn, Johanna, 1952– . II. Title.
305.23

Edited by Sandra Goldbloom Zurbo
Cover design by Leigh Ashforth, watershed art & design
Text design by Leigh Ashforth, watershed art & design
Typeset by Leigh Ashforth
Proofread by Pete Cruttenden
Indexed by Russell Brooks
Printed in Hong Kong by Sheck Wah Tong Printing Press Ltd

CONTENTS

PART 1: THEORISING YOUTH

PART 2: SOCIAL DIVISIONS

PART 3: SOCIAL INSTITUTIONS

PART 4: SOCIAL IDENTITIES

LIST OF FIGURES AND TABLES

PREFACE

Readers who are familiar with the first edition of *Youth and Society* will be aware that the book aimed to provide a comprehensive analysis of young people's lives in contemporary society in the emerging field of youth studies. This new edition aims to fulfil this goal even more effectively. With the benefit of detailed feedback from our readers, this edition of *Youth and Society* includes three new chapters: 'Youth and Social Change', 'Indigenous Youth and Social Identity' and 'Youth in a Digital Society'; there is also new material in every chapter that takes account of new information and emerging debates. Changes to the format have been included to increase accessibility and to encourage readers to follow up on the key issues. This edition provides a comprehensive overview of young people's lives in the context of significant social change, though it is not the intention to study every aspect of the youth experience. While acknowledging the interrelatedness of young people's experiences, the chapters concentrate on specific domains of young people's lives, drawing on empirical evidence and current theoretical perspectives. In this way we aim to engage the reader in conceptual and substantive explorations of issues that are the leading edge issues confronting youth, youth researchers and policy makers today.

This edition of the book has been restructured to provide a more explicit theoretical introduction to understanding the changing dynamics of youth through two introductory conceptual chapters. The book continues to build on our previous book, *Rethinking Youth*, and other work in which we have argued that the conceptualisation of youth needs to be uncoupled from deterministic frameworks of youth development. We argue that a sociological approach to the concept of youth provides a basis for understanding how the life stages of childhood, youth and adulthood are simultaneously constructed and shaped by institutional processes and social structures and by individuals and groups.

The first chapter, 'Youth and Social Change', provides a theoretical and conceptual overview and an introduction to current debates in the sociology of youth and focuses on the issue of young people and social change. We provide a discussion and analysis of sociological conceptual tools and theoretical frameworks that inform our understanding of the nature and effects of (changing) social processes on young people's lives and the ways in which young people's identities are shaped. This chapter provides an introduction and a critical assessment of the use of frameworks that currently dominate thinking about social and generational change and youth transitions. It explores current debates about the extent of social change and its impact on young people's lives. Terms that will be used throughout the rest of the book are introduced and defined in this chapter, including individualisation, risk, globalisation, subjectivity and responsibility.

The second chapter also provides a theoretical overview, focusing specifically on social class. It is impossible to understand young people's lives and experiences without acknowledging the effects of systematic processes that bring inequalities across many dimensions of young people's lives. While social class is almost inevitably recognised by youth researchers in one way or another, the very issues that we discuss in Chapter 1 (for example, social change and individualisation) have changed the appearance of class relations and many researchers believe that class has become obscured within young people's lives. Chapter 2 provides an overview of the changing and complex ways in which class divisions continue to be a significant feature of life in the twenty-first century, especially in the lives of young people.

The themes of social change, structural processes and identity construction are woven throughout each of the remaining chapters. The next three sections of the book address these issues in different arenas of life. Part 2 focuses on social division and the impact on young people of new and old forms of inequalities. These chapters also explore the experiences of youth and the ways in which they are responding to their circumstances. The chapters in this section explore four areas: gender and sexualities, race, ethnicity and rural location. Each of these chapters discusses key research and thinking about young people and social division, which are recurring themes throughout the book.

Part 3 is devoted to the discussion of the changing relationship of young people to key social institutions: the state, education, the family and criminal justice. Across each of these areas we argue that the assumptions underlying these institutions, and the policies that support them, are frequently out of step with the lives of young people. We describe how policies affecting youth operate, and are contested, at many levels. While youth participation in policy formation is often acknowledged as important, few organisations provide adequate structures to enable this. Education has never been more significant, both as a means of personal development and for the necessity of obtaining qualifications for employment, yet there is evidence that young people do not simply equate learning with formal education. Work experience, travel, leisure and relationships are also a source of learning and education.

We describe in Chapter 7 how the state has played a significant role in re-defining youth through policies that ensure that young people remain in formal education until they are over the age of eighteen, in shaping the nature of that educational experience and in restructuring workplaces.

In Chapters 9 and 11 we identify new patterns of transition, which involve overlaps between study and work, deferment of career outcomes, increases in part-time employment and a decline of opportunity for the uncredentialled.

We discuss the evidence that young people are shaping new understandings of family and education. Young people regard both of these institutions as significant to their lives, but not in traditional ways. Family is an important source of support for many youth, but at the same time, there is a strong trend for young people to remain single, to marry later than did the previous generation and to choose not to have children of their own. In Chapter 10, 'Doing Bad: Juvenile Justice', we focus on the regulation of young people by the state, and how risk and responsibility are translated into particular forms of criminal justice practice.

In Part 4 we analyse the social processes of youth and becoming adult. We argue that in many areas there is evidence that the traditional stages of youth and adulthood have become disrupted. We suggest that there is a need for social analysts to understand the effects of generational *and* social change in shaping the experience of youth today. The chapters focus on young people's active engagement in work, culture, the use of digital communications, health and well-being, and public space. In different ways, these chapters explore what it means to undertake a relational analysis of youth. They contribute a richer understanding of youth through the fine detail of young people's lives in different settings, locations and arenas of life. In each of these chapters, we describe the changing circumstances of young people's lives and the shaping of contemporary identities. In the area of work, for example, we discuss the far-reaching impact for youth of changes to the labour market and in workplace relations. We also discuss the evidence that young people are responding to present circumstances with new approaches to the place that employment has in their lives. Our discussion of youth identities and culture takes seriously the finding by other researchers that the sphere of leisure is emerging as a significant source of identity to young people. Young people are often referred to as 'digital natives', and so we also explore the ways in which young people use digital communications and examine the technology's relationship to young people's identity formation and civic engagement. Chapter 14, 'Defining Well-being and Health', tackles the problem of understanding young people's health by moving beyond an illness-based approach to explore young people's own approaches to health and well-being. Finally, issues pertaining to young people's place and their use of space are analysed.

In taking this approach to the organisation of the book, we have consciously taken the decision to focus on the social processes that constitute youth. We especially wanted to avoid categorising and analysing young people according to one element in their complex lives (for example, drug taking, early school leaving or sexual behaviour). Our approach has enabled us to acknowledge the multidimensional nature of young people's lives. Young workers are also students, partners, have sexual, racial or ethnic identities and are parents. Our understandings of social change are enhanced by taking account of the links between these areas. Acknowledging that students are also workers, for example, enables us to understand how both of these roles are changing. It is also important to have a holistic concept of youth in order to understand how they are shaping their lives across many dimensions. For our analysis, this has meant that several themes recur throughout the chapters. Throughout the book three main themes predominate: inequality, social change and identity. The themes of marginalisation, youth participation and individualisation are also woven through the text.

We have also made a conscious effort to move beyond academic closure by drawing on evidence from diverse sources. The analysis of our own research on Australian youth is informed by the findings of research from other countries, such as New Zealand, Canada, the United Kingdom and the USA. In some of the chapters, and in particular Chapter 6, 'Rural Geographies', the unique nature of the Australian context is central. Even in these chapters, though, comparisons are made with related research and conceptual work from other countries. We make the point that even though young people in these settings experience specific conditions, there are nonetheless themes that resonate with youth in other settings. Through this approach, we have ensured that the text has relevance to international debates about youth and society.

ACKNOWLEDGMENTS

A number of people have been of great assistance in the production of this edition of *Youth and Society*. We would like to thank Anne Hugo and Sue Dilley of the Australian Clearinghouse for Youth Studies for their help in accessing literature and references for the first edition. Debra Tyler, Helen Cahill, Ani Wierenga, Graeme Smith, and Peter Dwyer, colleagues at the Youth Research Centre at the University of Melbourne, have played a role in supporting this project. Collaborative writing projects with Johanna by other colleagues at the Youth Research Centre — Ian Fyfe, Helen Stokes, Dan Woodman, Julie Green, and Hernan Cuervo — have also influenced our approach to the second edition. Many of the insights in this book would not have been possible without funding from the Australian Research Council for the Life-Patterns research program (1998–2000, 2002–04 and 2005–09). Della Clark, Lyn Devereaux, Kevin Tomkins, and Di Heckenberg at the University of Tasmania have also contributed in varying ways to the book's completion, and for this we are grateful.

PART 1

Theorising Youth

YOUTH AND SOCIAL CHANGE

Introduction

This chapter provides an overview of the context in which young people's lives are being negotiated and shaped. It discusses key concepts that are currently used extensively in youth studies literature to understand the stage in life we call 'youth'. From a sociological point of view, youth is a social process (Wyn & White 1997) that describes how groups of young people and individuals experience being young and how this is defined through institutions and policies, and how it is related to social, economic, and political circumstances.

The issue of social change recurs throughout this book. There is no dimension of young people's lives that has not been affected by the processes of social change. However, while youth researchers are agreed that social change has had a significant impact on young people (as it has on all age groups), there is disagreement about the extent of this change, whether it constitutes a fundamental shift in social structures and in what ways it affects young people. Some youth researchers have argued that we are seeing the emergence of a 'new youth' (Leccardi & Ruspini 2006) or a 'new adulthood' (Dwyer & Wyn 2001); others are more cautious, referring instead to 'significant changes in the nature and experience of transition' (Furlong & Cartmel 2007) and caution that the 'rhetoric of new times' can be exaggerated (McLeod & Yates 2006).

Concepts such as 'risk society', 'individualisation', and 'globalisation' are widely used to describe these shifts. We provide an introduction to the use of these terms. We also provide a critical assessment of other terms, such as 'transition', which have widespread use in youth research and policies. We suggest that 'social generation' provides a useful framework that enables researchers to link social conditions with young people's patterns of living and transitions.

Through the concept of social generation we discuss the related concepts of subjectivities and identities. We argue that while evidence about patterns of living is important, we also need to understand how young people's subjectivities are being formed. Material changes in living conditions have had a significant impact on who young people can (and must) become. For this reason, understanding young people's subjective experiences, the meanings that they attribute to their actions and lives, and the ways in which they shape their identities is very important.

To conclude Part 1, we acknowledge that a focus on social change can obscure the extent of continuities with the past and their effects on young people's lives. We have noted that, while subjectivities and identities have become common themes in youth research, most researchers also comment that social class in particular continues to mark the boundaries of identity formation and to influence patterns of living profoundly. Given its importance, we turn to the specific issue of social class in Chapter 2.

SOCIAL CHANGE

The issue of social change is especially relevant to conceptualising youth because of the direct impact that changes in social institutions and relations have on young people's lives. Young people forge their identities through active engagement with the local and global realities they find, and hence make sense of new social realities in ways that are different from the ways of older generations. Shifts in patterns of life are inevitably interwoven with wider social processes that influence the possibilities (or available subject positions) that frame who young people can become (Wexler 1992). For this reason, youth researchers are interested in evidence about patterns of life as well as about the meanings that young people attribute to these patterns and the identities that they shape.

In Chapter 3, in order to illustrate some dimensions of social change, we compare some key trends for young people who were in their early twenties in 2001 with those who were in their early twenties in 1976. The comparison shows that there has been a significant shift in three areas in particular: education, labour markets, and family formation.

Some facts about changing experiences

- At age 21 young men were nearly one and a half times more likely to be in education in 2001 than in 1976, but young women were two and a half times more likely.

- Young men in their early twenties in 2001 were less likely to be in paid employment (87 per cent) than their counterparts in 1976 (92 per cent).

- Young women in their early twenties in 2001 were more likely to be in paid employment (75 per cent) than their counterparts in 1976 (57 per cent) and were working part-time while studying rather than working before having children.

- Nearly one-quarter of young women had their first child when they were over the age of 30 in 2001, compared with only 12 per cent in 1976.

- Young people in their early twenties were more likely to work longer hours in 2001; 28 per cent worked longer than 40 hours per week compared with 22 per cent in 1976.

Source: ABS 2005.

We elaborate further on some of these issues in Chapter 11, where we identify how the labour market has had an impact on young people's lives, affecting the nature of work, the kind of worker who is required, and the forms of employment that are available. In Australia, as in many Western economies, jobs have shifted from manufacturing and primary production to the service sector, which has resulted in the creation of new high-skill jobs in some industries but has also resulted in many low-skill jobs. Across most sectors, the kind of worker who is now required is the part-time worker, who is employed on short-term contracts (opening up many opportunities for school-aged workers). Employers have come to rely on educational credentials and are providing less in the way of on-the-job training.

The features we have described above are identified in many studies of young people across Western countries. There is widespread agreement among social scientists that the last quarter of a century has witnessed significant social changes that affect the experience of youth. Furlong and Cartmel (2007: 138), for example, have recently revisited the question of young people and social change. Their work focuses on young people in the United Kingdom, but they draw on thinking that has emerged from different countries about this issue. They conclude that 'the experiences of young people growing up in the contemporary world are quite different from those encountered by previous generations'. A recent collection edited by Leccardi and Ruspini (2006) documents the impact of these changes on young people in Eastern Europe, Italy, the Netherlands, Finland, Georgia, the USA, the United Kingdom, Germany, and New Zealand. Another collection, by Bagnall (2005), explores changes in young people's transition patterns in Australia, New Zealand, the South Pacific, England, the Netherlands, and France. Bagnall argues that 'social change is occurring at such a rate that traditional forms of transition into adulthood have become increasingly undermined' (2005: 7).

Thus, there is a convergence of evidence that significant social changes have occurred on a global scale, resulting in new social issues, conditions and relationships. There is less agreement about what counts as evidence of change, how these changes should be measured and, most importantly, how they should be interpreted (Wyn & Woodman 2007).

We suggested above that one reason why social change is an especially significant issue for the conceptualisation of youth is that young people forge meaning and make sense of the social conditions in different ways from previous generations. As many youth researchers have pointed out, young people in each age generation have always made their own sense of their worlds. It is commonly argued that in times of relative stability (if, indeed, there have been such times), youthful ideas and projects gave way to fit into established approaches and patterns that were forged by the previous generation. In other words, adulthood offered distinct and reasonably clearly prescribed ways of being compared to the period of youth. This was demonstrably the case for the baby boomer generation (that is, people born between 1946 and 1965). For them, the achievement of adulthood was marked by a clear shift from the status of student to worker, from living in the parental home to living independently. Then, it was the norm for these events to have occurred by the time people were in their mid twenties. However, in times of significant change, such as those we are experiencing at present, adulthood, too, is changed.

This shift has lead to a considerable debate within youth studies about the extent to which youth is a universal stage of life or whether it is a social construct and, like adulthood, gains its parameters and meaning from social conditions. The debate about social change is closely connected to this because, according to some interpretations, both youth and adulthood are changing (Mizen 2004). This means that the new meanings that young people give to education, work, and relationships will not necessarily drop away as they get older, to conform to older patterns and meanings. If the world has changed, their new life patterns may indicate the changing shape of adult life as well. As Wyn and Woodman argue:

> There is significant debate within youth studies about the extent to which youth is a universal stage of life or whether it is a social construct and, like adulthood, gains its parameters and meaning from social conditions.

widespread and significant changes in labour markets; in the relationship between education and employment and in workplace relations; and in the actions of the state have altered the significance of traditional markers of adult status in industrialised countries and brought in new markers (2007: 375).

Individualisation and the risk society

The shifts in the material conditions of life that are described above have been seen as indicators of a shift in modernity—in the conditions under which society functions. Beck and Lau argue that:

> All around the word, society is undergoing radical change—radical in the sense that it poses a challenge to Enlightenment-based modernity and opens up a space in which people choose new and unexpected forms of the social and the political (2005: 525).

They argue that although there has been a 'radical change' there has not been a clear break with modernity. They use the term 'first modernity' to refer to nation-state societies that exist in a clear territorial sense and exercise control over their dominions. A shift to 'second modernity' has involved the fragmentation of collective ways of life based on the nation state and, through globalising processes, on the undermining of the possibilities for nation states to control social conditions (to provide for full employment, for example, or to be able to ensure the value of educational credentials). On the other hand, people are freed from older networks and constraints to negotiate new meanings and social relationships.

As Bauman explains in the foreword to *Individualization* (Beck & Beck-Gernsheim 2002), the fragmentation of traditional structures (including nation states, families, and trade unions) has created a situation where people's identity has become a task rather than a given: 'Needing to *become* what one *is* the hallmark of modern living' (Beck & Beck-Gernsheim 2002: xv). The sources of collective identity that were characteristic of industrial societies have begun to lose their relevance.

BOX 1.2

Some meanings of globalisation

- Transnationalisation—the dissolving of national boundaries.
- Supranationalisation—transcending national limits.
- Internationalisation—exchanges of capital and labour.
- Universalisation—spread of information and cultural phenomena worldwide.
- Neoliberalisation—removal of regulatory barriers to international exchange or transfer.
- Westernisation—homogenisation, driven by advanced industrial economies.
- Anglo-Americanisation—homogenisation driven by the USA.
- Modernisation—the diffusion of managerial economics.

Source: Muncie 2007: 47.

These processes have a number of implications for young people. First, because the world they experience is different, the pathways and approaches used by older people, especially those in the previous generation, do not necessarily provide a reliable guide for action. The Youth Research Centre's Life-Patterns research program, for example, found that young people in the post-1970 generation saw mobility and flexibility as a more effective way to ensure their (financial) security than predictability (Dwyer & Wyn 2001). In other words, whereas their parents had often made a success of their lives by remaining within one occupation or job for the majority of their lives, they learnt that it was best not to become dependent on one job for any length of time. In a precarious labour market, being flexible and mobile are important skills that can provide longer-term security, which means that young people are aware of the need to forge their own pathways. They have learnt to be very proactive.

Second, the decline in control over social processes by nation states has meant that it is individuals who have come to bear increasing responsibility for their lives. The capacity to be proactive in uncertain times relies in part on the ability to be reflexive; that is, to see one's own life and biography as something that does not just unfold, but that is also actively constructed through one's own efforts. This active construction of one's biography is called the 'project of the self' (Beck & Beck-Gernsheim 2002) and involves an active process of personal management, even in circumstances where, objectively, individuals would have little control. In the Life-Patterns study, for example, young people in their mid twenties (in 2002) said that, after the support of their families, their own personal development was the most significant influence on their lives.

The process of individualisation captures the way in which young people come to bear personal responsibility for their lives. They feel that they are responsible for bearing the risks that are actually related to how our society functions. As Beck and Beck-Gernsheim argue, social inequalities in late modernity have become redefined in terms of 'an individualisation of social risks' (2002: 39). They explain that, as a consequence, social problems become perceived through a psychological, and therefore individualising, lens (as personal inadequacies or neuroses, for example). The recent upsurge of concern over obesity among young people could be seen as an illustration of this. The complexities of the role of the marketing and accessibility of (fast) food consumption in globalised economies tend to be underplayed through the overwhelming focus on the responsibility of parents and children to eat only healthy foods. To refer to an older sociological distinction made by Mills (1959), the scale of obesity marks it as a public issue, which is related to the organisation of our society; however, the issue has been treated as a personal trouble to be solved by individuals (see Willis 2004: 18).

Beck and Beck-Gernsheim argue that the 'do-it-yourself biography' is also a 'risk biography' (2002: 3); that is, in a society in which individuals must make choices against a backdrop of uncertainty and impermanence, it is easy to make the wrong choice. The point is that it is seen as both the right and the responsibility of the individual to make choices, and as the failure of the individual if the choice is not a good one. Individualisation, then, is a process that makes risky social processes and structures invisible and vests individuals with the responsibility for bearing these risks.

Individualisation, then, is a process that makes risky social processes and structures invisible, and vests individuals with the responsibility for bearing these risks.

These processes have been supported by shifts in the way in which governments manage youth. In *The Changing State of Youth*, Mizen (2004) discusses a shift in the United Kingdom from Keynesian economic policies (1946 until 1976) to monetarist policies, which extend from 1977 until the present. He analyses how Keynesian state policies involved support for a welfare state, a commitment to full employment, the expansion of secondary schooling, and the inclusion of youth in civic life. Under monetarist policies economic goals have become the primary focus. This has meant the progressive reduction of public support for young people, minimising the provision of social welfare, the development of categories of 'deserving' and 'undeserving' youth, and an emphasis on instrumental, vocationally oriented education (Mizen 2002, pp. 14–16). Monetarist policies have narrowed the fiscal responsibility of the state for young people while at the same time hugely expanding the reach of monitoring, surveillance, and control over young people's lives and the institutions in which they spend their time.

Transitions

The changing patterns of life that have occurred as a result of the social changes described above have created a strong interest in the nature of processes that support youth transitions. In Australia, the concept of youth transitions gained prominence during the early 1980s with the collapse of the youth labour market, a rise in youth unemployment, and increased participation in education (Te Riele & Wyn 2005). As young people responded to changing social conditions, new patterns of transition emerged (Wyn & Dwyer 2000). State policies have had two effects in particular, by:

> defining youth as primarily a human resource for economic development, as students, consumers and 'flexible workers' and heightening inequality between groups of young people (Wyn & Woodman 2006: 504).

Yet despite the evidence of changes in patterns of transition, there is evidence of emerging dissatisfaction with the use of this term to describe and analyse youth (Wyn & Woodman 2006; Mizen 2002; Cohen & Ainley 2000). Most criticism centres on the descriptive nature of the term 'transition' and the ease with which this term is invested with implicit understandings of youth. 'Transition' is, for example, often used uncritically, to measure the patterns of life for contemporary youth against the experiences of the baby boomer generation, who came of age during the late 1960s and 1970s. The generation who were youth in the 1970s have become normative, and it is the contemporary generation that is seen as faulty or lacking, with transition patterns that are 'on hold' (Coté 2000), are 'extended' (Jones & Wallace 1992), 'emerging' (Arnett 2004) and 'lost' (Howe & Strauss 2000).

The concept of transition has been especially prominent in policy documents within the domains of education and employment (Dusseldorp Skills Forum 2006). To paraphrase the arguments made by Wyn and Woodman (2006) and Stokes and Wyn (2006), youth is often implicitly conceptualised as simply a transitional state of life. This approach conflates youth developmental processes with social processes; it generally assumes a linear trajectory and makes normative assumptions about young people's lives.

Transition as development

Because the term transition tends to draw on psychosocial (human emotional development) or biomedical (brain development) theories, it either ignores or underestimates the significance of the social meanings and experiences of age. As Cohen and Ainley (2000) have argued, a focus on transition has become narrowly defined as (vocational) maturity and (nuclear) family formation. This is reiterated by Bagnall (2005), who draws on a descriptive schema of four 'thresholds' that define and pattern the progress of transition into adulthood: completing education, entry into employment, leaving home, and forming a couple. This concept of transitions tends to overlook the blurring of the boundaries between youth–adult and student–worker as young people engage in adult practices incrementally and early, across many dimensions of their lives. Elsewhere, we have argued that we may be witnessing the emergence of a 'new adulthood' that foreshadows complex new patterns of adult life (Dwyer et al. 2003).

> We may be witnessing the emergence of a 'new adulthood' that foreshadows complex new patterns of adult life.

Transition as linear pathways

Uncritical uses of the concept of transition have been integral to neoliberal youth policies that, despite ample evidence to the contrary, are based on the idea of *the* transition from school to work and adult life. Transition carries a notion of linear progress from one clearly defined status to another. While gaining a secure job is a priority that is frequently expressed by young people (Dwyer et al. 2003), policy approaches that focus only on the links between study and work tend to over-emphasise the linearity of this process and its direction. The assumption of linear movement that underpins the metaphor of transition masks the reality of more complex and often chaotic processes in young people's lives.

Transition as the norm

The term transition tends to rest on the assumption that by a particular stage (and age) all young people should have achieved a particular milestone or crossed a defined threshold, an assumption that can send misleading messages to policy makers. In Australia, for example, even as youth research demonstrates the increasing diversity of young people's lives (Te Riele & Wyn 2005), educational policy makers are favourably assessing the idea of raising the compulsory school attendance age to eighteen, which is based on the idea that one normative pattern of transition would be beneficial for all young people. The outcome of such a policy would be to further limit the flexibility and responsiveness of formal schooling to the education–work nexus for young people.

> The term transition tends to assume that by a particular stage (and age) all young people should have achieved a particular milestone or crossed a defined threshold, an assumption can send misleading messages to policy makers.

A further problem with the concept of transition is that it rests on an implicit assumption that the life patterns of one generational group, the baby boomer generation, represent the standard. As argued elsewhere (Wyn & Woodman 2006), contemporary youth transition patterns will inevitably be seen as faulty or failed by comparison with the previous generation. The problem with using the baby boomer generation as the measure of transition is that the conditions of security and predictability that gave rise to their distinctive experiences and patterns no longer exist. The implication of using this generation as the standard is that subsequent generations will always be found wanting.

Our criticisms of the way the term 'transition' is used in each of these examples highlight the tendency for the term to obscure the dynamic relationship between youth and society. As we discussed in our earlier work (Wyn & White 1997), youth is a social process, shaped and defined by social conditions. Yet the term 'transition' tends to be associated with a descriptive and categorical approach to youth. While this approach acknowledges social change, it does not provide an adequate grasp of how social change has affected not only life patterns but also the very meaning of youth—and of adulthood. In the next section we discuss the emerging interest in the concept of generation for understanding youth and for capturing a broader meaning of transition, one that acknowledges that society, as well as young people, is in transition.

Social generation

In contrast to the use of transition as a way of understanding young people's lives, the concept of generation has also emerged within the popular media to make sense of young people's lives. Stereotypes, such as Gens X, Y, and Z, Generation Me, millennials, baby boomers, and baby busters, to name just a few, have appeared in popular writing in order to describe successive generations of young people (Twenge 2006; Sheahan 2005; Foot 1996; Coupland 1991). The popularity of these terms suggests that there are significant, distinctive experiences that link some age cohorts to each other and separate them from others. Although these stereotypical terms are often based on market research, they raise the question of the impact of specific conditions on young people's lives and the distinctive ways in which young people shape their generation. These popular stereotypes assert that generations can be distinguished from each other and imply that they will continue to be distinctive—and to be identified as a social generation—throughout their lives.

Within sociological writing, the concept of social generation has a long history. It is based on the understanding that age is a sociologically significant variable (Pilcher 1994) and the meaning of age is given through social and economic relations (Allen 1968; Finch 1986; Wyn & White 1997; Mizen 2004). Mannheim (1952) proposed the use of social generation as a conceptual tool for the analysis of social change. He argued that people who belong to a common period of history, or whose lives are forged through common conditions, form a 'generational consciousness'. He distinguished social generations from age cohorts and developed an argument about social change in which individuals 'both constitute historical configurations and are constituted historically by them' (Pilcher 1994: 490).

Social generation has emerged in recent literature on social change to provide a conceptual framework for understanding how patterns of transition are linked to specific historical conditions. Edmunds and Turner (2002), for example, argue that social generations develop a 'cultural identity' that they form as a result of 'their particular location in the development of a society or culture' (2002: 7). There is debate about whether the concept of social generation is too general. Some researchers have cautioned against the use of a very abstract concept of social generation, suggesting that the concept needs to be connected to an understanding of class, and of local variation and difference (Jones 2003; Nayak 2003).

Nonetheless, a concept of social generation has value because it overcomes the reliance on age as *the* defining feature of 'youth' (Cohen 1977) and embeds

> Social generation has emerged in recent literature on social change to provide a conceptual framework for understanding how patterns of transition are linked to specific historical conditions.

youth within historical and local conditions. Perhaps most importantly, this concept also has value because it focuses on the meaning of change to young people.

One dimension of the relationship between youth and social context is the shaping of youth by state policies. In understanding this dimension we find Mizen's analysis of youth (2004) useful because it enables us to see the link between the social and material conditions fostered through Keynesian economic policies and the conditions that so powerfully defined the baby boomer generation (Wyn & Woodman 2006). As argued in Wyn (2007), in Australia these features included the expansion of social welfare, a commitment to full employment, and the implementation of universal, free, public education through mass secondary schooling, which were instrumental in creating the conditions that enabled the distinctive educational, labour market, and domestic patterns that marked the baby boomer generation.

The shift to monetarist policies coincides with the post-1970 generation (Dwyer & Wyn 2001) and the emergence of the term 'Generation X'. Under monetarist policies, state support for young people has been reduced as welfare systems were restructured. In Australia, as in other Western countries, reducing state responsibility for young people has been supported at a policy level by using age as a means of exclusion. These policy approaches have also contributed to the creation of distinctive generational experiences for the post-1970 generation, in which uncertainty and insecurity are heightened and reliance on personal cultural and material resources increased.

There is considerable evidence across a number of indicators to suggest that in some Western countries a significant shift in life patterns has occurred between the baby boomer generation and the generation born after 1970 (Bynner 2005; Mizen 2005; Wyn & Woodman 2006). While this is likely to remain disputed territory for some time to come (Roberts 2007), it nonetheless provides a useful conceptual framework for understanding the construction of youth and the diverse experiences of young people within their social contexts. Most importantly, the concept of social generation gives significance to the meanings that young people themselves attribute to their lives. A social generation is constituted through common subjective understandings and orientations as well as material conditions (Wyn & Woodman 2007). Increasingly, the area of subjectivities is of interest to youth researchers as they seek to understand the active role that young people play in constructing the kinds of reflexive subjectivities that will enable them to navigate their way through life.

In the early sections of this chapter we argued that social processes influence the possibilities of who young people can become. In the following section we discuss this in more detail through the concept of subjectivities because young people's subjectivities provide important insights into the effects of social change—and they can also influence change.

> Most importantly, the concept of social generation gives significance to the meanings that young people themselves attribute to their lives.

SUBJECTIVITIES, IDENTITIES, AND SOCIAL CHANGE

Throughout this book we return many times to the concept of subjectivities and to the related concept of identity. We describe how young people draw on a range of influences and experiences in the development of their identities. We provide a more detailed discussion of the emergence of identity as a key concept within youth studies in Chapter 12, but here we introduce the idea of subjectivities and identities and how they are integral to social change.

While the terms 'identity' and 'subjectivity' are sometimes used interchangeably, there is an important distinction between them. The term subjectivity refers to the social, economic, and political frameworks, constraints, and limits within which identities are formed. Social identities are shaped within specific social contexts in which only limited possible subject positions (subjectivities) are given (Davies 2004). In other words, identities are produced by young people but mediated through the experiences they have in schools, the nature of their family relationships, their workplaces, and in all areas of their lives.

> Identities are produced by young people, but mediated through the experiences they have in schools, the nature of their family relationships, their workplaces and in all areas of their lives.

The evidence that supports the claims made by youth researchers for change generally takes the form of statistics comparing the life events of one generation with another. What these statistics do not tell us is what meaning these patterns have for young people. Young people's subjectivities and the ways in which their possibilities for being are framed provide another very important source of information for understanding just how much has changed and what has not. In what ways, for example, is the pattern for later marriage and childbearing related to new subjectivities about womanhood? How does the increase in part-time work, even for graduates, influence how young people see themselves as workers?

In order to answer these questions, a lot of recent youth research has focused on subjectivities, which enables researchers to provide evidence about the new possibilities that are emerging for different groups of young people (for example, for some groups of young women, as argued by Harris (2004) and McLeod and Yates (2006)). The focus on subjectivities also enables researchers to understand how new meanings of career, employment, and family are emerging (Wyn & Woodman 2006). Evidence about young people's subjective understandings of learning and work has begun to challenge the traditional view that learning only happens at school (Smith & Green 2001).

The Life-Patterns research project has explicitly linked social and economic conditions of uncertainty in Australia in the 1990s with the need for young people to become active decision makers who are capable of being flexible in the face of precarious employment and increasing requirements for educational credentials (Dwyer & Wyn 2001). The processes of individualisation (discussed above) have been linked by other researchers to the development of dominant subjectivities. Kelly (2006), for example, has argued that contemporary conditions favour, and in one sense 'require', the performance of an 'entrepreneurial Self' (see Chapter 12). This self, he argues, is one that requires young people to demonstrate considerable autonomy in making decisions, and to take responsibility for the mistakes they make. Similarly, Harris (2004) describes the phenomenon of the 'can-do' girls—young women who believe that they can achieve anything—and McLeod and Yates (2006) describe the emergence of distinctive subjectivities that enable young people to 'self monitor' and adjust their goals and performances. There is a clear link between these ideas about young people's subjectivities and processes such as individualisation.

Summary

This chapter has provided an introduction to many of the ideas and concepts that we make use of throughout this book. Some key concepts that researchers are using to understand the meaning of youth in a context of social change have been discussed. We would conclude that there is now a wealth of research on young people's subjectivities, which serves to highlight young people's active role in making meaning and shaping change, and the diversity and extent of local cultures and individual meanings. This research reveals the complexities of young people's identities across many areas of their lives, and documents their effects on social structures that are fragmenting.

Most of the researchers to whom we have referred in this chapter have, at the same time that they explore these dimensions of social change in young people's lives, cautioned that a focus on social change alone can obscure the extent to which there are continuities with the past.

Change can be superficial and patterns of continuity can be invisible to young people. Young people do not overwhelmingly recognise collective experiences, especially those related to social class, as being a significant dimension in their lives. The obscuring of class relations has been referred to by Furlong and Cartmel (2007) as the 'epistemological fallacy'. Their point is that we can see from statistical surveys just how much young people's lives are still constrained by classed patterns. Despite this, young people (fallaciously) underestimate the impact of social structures on their lives, and hold to views that emphasise their own actions and efforts.

In the next chapter we focus on social class in order to delve more deeply into what we see as important questions about change and continuity in young people's lives.

Questions for further exploration

1   How is the question of social change linked to our understandings of youth?

2   Discuss whether there are any significant events or transition points in young people's lives today that definitively mark the transition to adulthood.

3   Identify some generational stereotypes that are current in the popular media and discuss what they are saying about young people and what they are based on.

4   What are the most significant changes that have occurred between the baby boomer generation and the post-1970 generation?

5   What patterns of life are associated with a 'risk biography'?

QUESTIONS

2

CLASS INEQUALITY AND COMMUNITY RESOURCES

Introduction

The social relations of class play a fundamental role in young people's lives, as they do in everyone's lives. In one way or another, the effects of social class are seen in the choices that young people make, the resources that they have at their disposal, where they live, where they go to school and what they do for their leisure. Research that tracks young people's lives over any extended period reveals the reproduction of class relations, as the children of families that enjoy socioeconomic wealth and security routinely attain more secure lives, higher-paid jobs, and enjoy better health than their peers from lower socioeconomic origins. This chapter provides an overview of the debates concerning social class and young people, and introduces concepts and ideas that will recur throughout the chapters that follow. We have found that, regardless of the dimension of young people's lives being discussed, class relations, intersecting with gender, race, and ethnicity, are central.

Despite its undisputed importance, class is surprisingly complex to talk about and to theorise, in part because class is not a static relationship. As the economic bases of modern societies change, so do the dynamics that drive social class. The social changes that we discussed in the previous chapter, which Beck and Lau (2005) argue have resulted in a shift to 'second modernity', have implications that have a particular impact on young people's experiences of class in two ways. These are the fragmentation of collective experiences and understandings (Furlong & Cartmel 2007), and a shift in the resources that capitalist enterprises exploit to include cultural dimensions (Skeggs 2005).

In this chapter we draw on these ideas to discuss the ways in which social class is being interpreted in the context of social change. We raise questions about new forms of class struggle in which young people are implicated, especially those evident in the conscious and unconscious strategies used by middle-class families to maintain advantage in an uncertain and changing world. Next, we focus our discussion on the effects of contemporary class relations and processes on those who are marginalised and excluded. We highlight the entrenchment of inequalities in access to paid employment and the effects of these inequalities on individual young people, their families and their communities. We conclude that the experience and meaning of social class is changing, and that many young people are more aware of their own efforts and of the risks they must bear than they are of the class-based patterns that structure their lives.

CLASS AND YOUTH

There are many ways to understand class, but most derive from two distinct approaches: categorical (descriptions of static hierarchies or tiers of classed positions) and relational (class as a social process, constituted through relations of production and consumption). These approaches are not mutually exclusive, because at times hierarchies can be used to illustrate the effects of class as a social process (Jamrozik 2001). However, just as we see 'youth' as a social process, constituted through historical conditions, so we see class as most usefully conceptualised in a relational way. As we have argued previously:

> In understanding the relationship between class and youth, it is necessary to go beyond simply assert-
> ing that the structures shaping the social divisions of class, gender and ethnicity/race are simply there,
> to be 'read off' from cultural practices. Class relations are historical and specific, and it is important,
> in understanding the meaning and experience of 'youth' to locate particular young people in their
> specific historical location (Wyn & White 1997: 24).

Yet when we do look at the fine grain of young people's lives, at their specific historical locations, it can seem as if class disappears. As young people are forced to make more choices and their pathways diverge and become complex, the traditional social divisions become more obscure. This is reinforced by the importance in young people's lives of leisure and consumption, creating a sense of diversity and individual choice that blurs class difference (Furlong & Cartmel 2007). It is also reinforced by young people's common experience of precarious labour markets (see Chapter 11).

> When we do look at the fine grain of young people's lives, at their specific historical locations, it can seem as if class disappears. As young people are forced to make more choices and their pathways diverge and become complex, the traditional social divisions become more obscure.

Indeed, McLeod and Yates ask whether it possible to talk about class in countries such as the USA and Australia. They question the utility of a class as a concept that was 'built from nineteenth century industrial England and Germany' (2006: 160). They answer their question in the affirmative, pointing out that a static concept of class has often framed discussion of young people and class, resulting in a limited understanding that 'reads' class off patterns of (educational) success and failure (Yates & McLeod 2006). They opt for a more nuanced conception of class as a relational process within which individuals are aware of the uneven distribution of resources. Their research documents the ways in which class is perpetuated through the efforts of families, schools and young people themselves to forge identities that will be marketable, and conclude that the concept of class is a useful tool for understanding young people today.

Young people in the middle

McLeod and Yates specifically researched young people 'in the middle'—that is, middle-class young people from different types of secondary schools and communities, whose narratives and journeys would reveal how individuals form themselves and how social inequalities are created. Their research has contributed significantly to our understanding of the construction of forms of middle-class identities that would position these young people favourably within new economies and labour markets.

In one sense, the processes identified among the middle-class families studied by McLeod and Yates reveals their awareness of the role that culture plays in contemporary economics. Skeggs (2005) has argued that culture has become commodified, as new markets are sought. She describes how culture is deployed as an economic resource, and how this is shaping our ideas of what class is, through the identification of (class) attributes that are deemed to be morally worthy and unworthy. Understandings about class-based attributes may simmer under the surface, to be fanned by occasional media outbreaks. An example is the negative characterisation by the Australian media of the people involved in and of the small rural community in East Gippsland in Victoria where a toddler was murdered: the media drew on a discourse that linked poverty with questionable morals, bad motherhood and bad style.

Beyond this, Skeggs argues that class has become 'cultural property'—and class struggle becomes not just about the entitlement to the labour of others, but also the entitlement to their culture, feelings, affect and dispositions, which she calls 'a very intimate form of exploitation'. Middle-class viewers find the working-class exploits of *The Royle Family* (in the United Kingdom) and the aspirational middle-class adventures of Kath and Kim (Australia) humorous, but it is a humour tinged with a cautionary tale about taste, disposition, and appearance. When class is also cultural property, we learn how our cultural practices do or do not have a worth and value for others. The research on young people and middle-class families shows that culture and identity formation are also sites of class struggle in contemporary society (Ball 2003; McLeod & Yates 2006).

> When class is also cultural property, we learn how our cultural practices do or do not have a worth and value for others.

The significance of cultural practices in class relations is reinforced through the conditions of uncertainty and the individualisation of risk that we discussed in the previous chapter. This does not mean that young people are completely free to navigate their lives. Structures of inequality have remained quite entrenched. As Furlong and Cartmel argue, 'life chances remain highly structured' (2007: 5). What has changed is the nature of the effort required by young people and their families to ensure security and privilege.

The stability of inequality

Longitudinal research shows that, even though young people across all socioeconomic groups experience the effects of uncertainty about the instrumental uses of education and a precarious labour market, social class continues to be a predictor of success (Furlong & Cartmel 2007; Dwyer et al. 2005). There are intergenerational continuities in terms of employment opportunities, educational experiences, and family culture that together tend to shape the class trajectories of individuals. Class mobility is possible, but this concept is also relatively difficult to pin down in a context where subjective understandings of class position are sometimes at odds with objective indicators. Studies of the general patterns of life have long suggested that 'working-class kids get working-class jobs' (Willis 1977) and that 'the rich get richer, while the poor get prison' (Reiman 1998). The increasing phenomenon of long-term unemployment in many communities suggests the possibility of occupying 'de-classed positions', as in the case of membership of the so-called underclass, or that of a refugee kept in detention.

Community resources are distributed via the market, the state and informal community and family networks. For young people, what happens in each of these spheres has a huge bearing on their class situation: the phenomenon of unemployment remains the biggest single factor in the transformation of young people, their families, and their communities. In a wage-based economy, subsistence is wrapped around having a paid job. If one is not available, then a number of social problems are not far away. There is strong evidence that demonstrates, for example, a positive relationship between long-term unemployment and criminal activity (Chapman, Weatherburn, Kapuscinski, Chilvers & Roussel 2002), and where communities are encumbered by high levels of unemployment, social disorganisation is likely to be highly prominent (Wilson 1996).

In many Western nations, recent years have seen the fragmentation of communities and the emergence of deep social divisions within society. Generally speaking, there have been massive changes to social policy and in the extent and nature of criminal justice intervention in the lives of those suffering most from economic restructuring (see, for example, Males 1996; Miller 1996). Policies are being adopted that are intended to maximise the efficiency of the state in cushioning the community against the impact of social problems, rather than dealing with the generative conditions of these social problems. As Jamrozik (2001: 271–2) puts it:

> Many of the issues that are commonly regarded as 'social problems' are indeed normal conditions in a free-market society. For example, unemployment, poverty, inequality and law-breaking are normal conditions, directly related to and stemming from particular political, economic and social arrangements ... The activities that are provided to ostensibly remedy or alleviate the given problem serve, first and foremost, to legitimise the situation and at the same time alleviate public consciousness by demonstrating that the government cares and aims to remedy the situation. The outcome is usually a demonstration of an inadequacy or fault of the affected population — it is indeed an activity creating a 'blaming the victim' syndrome.

The context within which this is happening is that of the domination of specifically capitalist economic and political relations. The distributive principles of this global phenomenon are evident in the increasing concentration of wealth and power into fewer and fewer hands. Ideologies based upon the free market and economic rationalism (or neoliberalism) have fostered a climate of unfettered competitive individualism, with clear advantages to the already well off. The distributive effects of such economic trends are evident in the luxurious lifestyles and extravagant wealth of the minority, and the simultaneous impoverishment of many communities, neighbourhoods, and families around the globe. This is a Western trend, though its impact is evident in most nations, as well as one that demarcates the divisions between north and south.

There are intergenerational continuities in terms of employment opportunities, educational experiences and family culture that together tend to shape the class trajectories of individuals.

Social exclusion and marginal communities

Research in the USA, Australia and Britain, for example, has pointed to the devastating social impact of high concentrations of unemployment within local areas (Wilson 1996; Gregory & Hunter 1995; Green 1995; Vinson 2004). General youth employment patterns have been marked by high levels of unemployment, dramatic increases in insecure part-time and casual positions, and declines in

In essence, the poor are being locked into poverty-stricken areas with few job prospects and overall declining economic fortunes. Poverty is being entrenched at a spatial level.

real earnings derived from paid work and government benefits. The problems associated with the precarious nature of work and income (a general trend) are multiplied when 'neighbourhood effect' (Reiss 1986) is taken into account.

In essence, the poor are being locked into poverty-stricken areas with few job prospects and overall declining economic fortunes. Poverty is being entrenched at a spatial level. Not only is this affecting the ability of young people in these areas (often inner-city ghettos) to find paid work even when employment is in a growth period, but it also has major ramifications in terms of local community infrastructure. Poor people often live in areas with deteriorating housing, they suffer more profoundly any cutbacks in public amenities and they are more likely to experience declining quality in their health, and in educational and welfare services. These kinds of trends have obvious implications for the employment and educational opportunities of young people, as well as how they perceive themselves and their future prospects.

Research also shows that the most vulnerable, the most dispossessed, the most poor and the most deprived people are being concentrated into increasingly smaller islands of ghettoised neighbourhoods and social housing. Unemployment, disability, and sole parenthood, for example, are prevalent in certain defined geographical and residential locations. The very composition of these areas and housing estates (for example, disproportionately high numbers of those suffering from mental illness) is such that 'nuisance neighbours' are much more likely than might otherwise be the case in more socially heterogeneous neighbourhoods (see Burney 2000). The recent history of public housing has, in essence, been a history of residualisation: the housing of those types of households who have little choice in where they live. As demonstrated in British research, it is the most vulnerable of the vulnerable who are forced into the least attractive accommodation (Goodchild & Cole 2001).

Similar to the wider discourses on the underclass, management practices in the housing arena that implicitly or explicitly adopt a 'moral responsibility' concept, rather than a more structurally oriented 'social justice' perspective, tend to reinforce punitive and restrictive forms of authority (Cowan, Pantazis & Gilroy 2001; Haworth & Manzi 1999). In particular, it has been observed that, increasingly, there is a strong judgmental bias in housing discourse, one that has seen a shift 'from a focus on adding to or improving the housing stock to concern about the behaviour of residents and the introduction of policies designed to control such behaviour' (Haworth & Manzi 1999: 153). This shift has been underscored by the assumptions of the threat to order posed by members of the underclass. One consequence of this type of thinking has been the development of policies such as the imposition of strong normative standards in tenancy agreements, or the use of introductory tenancies as a means of dealing with perceived social problems on housing estates.

Here we see the intersection of broad law-and-order discourses decrying the antisocial and criminal behaviour of young people, with specific institutional discourses, as in the case of public housing, that reinforce the idea that any problems are reducible to bad behaviour on the part of residents. Issues of social marginalisation and inadequate social provision are thus diminished insofar as crime dominates the political and policy agendas. As Jamrozik (2001) noted above, this represents yet another type of blaming the victim on the part of state authorities.

The concentration of poor people in poor areas carries with it a range of implications for social policy and state intervention. In the Australian context, the reality for many such neighbourhoods is that even when job growth and economic fortunes are generally on the rise after a period of economic slump, these areas tend not to benefit; it is the women and children living in better-off or more affluent neighbourhoods who are more likely to gain paid work once a recession is over (see Gregory & Hunter 1995). Poverty is thus spatially entrenched, and this entrenchment persists over time. In describing these kinds of social processes in the USA, Wilson (1996: xiii) makes the point that:

> the consequences of high neighborhood joblessness are more devastating than those of high neighborhood poverty. A neighborhood in which people are poor but employed is different from a neighborhood in which people are poor and jobless. Many of today's problems in the inner-city ghetto neighbourhoods—crime, family dissolution, welfare, low levels of social organization, and so on—are fundamentally a consequence of the disappearance of work.

The disappearance of work is, then, a key condition for the expansion of the underclass. Again, US research has demonstrated that profound place-based disparities in opportunity structures and social and institutional resources affect labour market success (Coulton 2003). Within metropolitan areas, various social and economic processes sort jobs and job seekers geographically and segment their networks. The result is to trap some people in disadvantaged positions within urban labour markets (see also O'Regan & Quigley 1998).

Structural features of the underclass

- It is non-working in the conventional sense (although it might be noted that the expansion of part-time work could be explored as a boundary issue between the underclass and the marginal sectors of the working class).
- The primary source of income lies permanently (or effectively permanently) outside the capital–wage labour relationship.
- The economic conditions of life for this group lie at or below relative subsistence.
- There is a strong intergenerational component, with underclass conditions persisting from one generation to another.
- There are significant cultural, ideological and political factors that reinforce a subworking-class position, associated with such things as ethnicity, race, and so on.

Source: Cunneen & White 2007: 136.

BOX 2.1

Moreover, it is very often those working-class occupations, such as factory work in the manufacturing industry, that are filled by other-than-English-speaking workers and that are most likely to be lost. As economies change, and global economic restructuring leads to shutting down of plants in many Western countries, whole communities are affected, regardless of first language spoken. But, significantly, when these jobs are lost it is particular ethnic minority migrant groups who are most affected (Moss 1993; see also Wilson 1996). As the number of jobs in particular geographical areas decline, so, too, does the amenity of the neighbourhood. In other words, economic transformations (involving, for example, the demise of manufacturing) and economic recession (characterised by, for example, high levels of unemployment) compound the physical deterioration of particular locales and hasten the social homogenisation of specific neighbourhoods. This is due to such things as the flight of capital, including small businesses, from these areas, combined with the inability of residents to afford to either travel from or live outside the area. The net result is a process of ghettoisation, as middle-class people retreat to different suburbs, governments disinvest in public infrastructure (such as schools and hospitals), and neighbourhoods gain the reputation of being 'no go' zones for the rich and the respectable.

For young people in these circumstances life will be hard and legitimate opportunities for social advancement few and far between. Doing it tough may also translate into the creation of alternative social structures at the local level. These may be economic and they may be social. If, for example, no paid work is available in the formal waged sectors of the economy, a new or underground economy may be the only viable option. Here we may see the emergence of what could be called 'lumpen capitalists and outlaw proletarians'—people who subsist through illegal market activity. Davis (1990) illustrates this when discussing how cocaine, once the preserve of the rich, was transformed into a 'fast food' drug known as 'crack cocaine', thereby opening up extensive new markets and entrepreneurial activity at the street level. The emergence of gangs is likewise linked to economic imperatives (if activity is centred on illegal methods of gaining money and goods) and social considerations (methods of gaining a sense of meaning, purpose and belonging).

At the local neighbourhood level new social structures may be based on networks of friends, families, and peers who collectively reconstitute the social in periods witnessing the retreat of the welfare state and the limited availability of charity services relative to need. The family or the gang may represent a turn to subterranean sources of income, emotional support, and sharing and distribution of goods and services when formal market mechanisms and state supports are of negligible assistance. Communal networks of this kind may be reinforced by shared social markers, such as geography, ethnicity, and local history. Coming from a certain area may thus be transposed as a badge of communal membership and territorial identity to counter the stigma pertaining to the area due to its low economic status. In other cases, identity may be constructed in the crucible of conflict. For instance, over time there may be continuous cultural and physical resistance to racist policing, which may be manifest in the language of the streets, in its music and dance, and in police–citizen confrontations, including riots.

> At the local neighbourhood level new social structures may be based on networks of friends, families and peers who collectively reconstitute the social in periods witnessing the retreat of the welfare state and the limited availability of charity services relative to need.

The social status and crime rate of a neighbourhood has been shown to have an effect on a young people's chances of becoming involved in offending behaviour independent of their specific socioeconomic status (Reiss 1986). A young person from a low-income background living in a high crime rate area, for example, is far more likely to engage in offending behaviour than a young person living in a low crime neighbourhood. Community context is therefore an integral part of why some unemployed young people have a greater propensity to commit crime than other young people in a similar social position. This was demonstrated in a Sydney study of unemployed young people living in a socially disadvantaged inner-city suburb (Vinson, Abela & Hutka 1997). The study showed that the young people had a high degree of motivation to work, but were handicapped in pursuing work by having relatively few relatives and friends who could introduce them to job opportunities and prospective employers, because they themselves were unemployed (see also Hunter 1998; Wilson 1996). The young people in the study acknowledged reliance on crime as a way to make ends meet. Similar findings were apparent in a study of young people in Melbourne that examined youth livelihoods in low-income suburbs (White, Aumair, Harris & McDonnell 1997). Each study highlighted the importance of the cash-in-hand and criminal economies in enabling young people to supplement their incomes.

The systematic marginalisation of young people (and their communities) is marked by the disintegration of connections with mainstream social institutions (such as school and work), and a tenuous search for meaning in an uncaring and unforgiving world. The quality and quantity of youth crime is heavily overlaid by geographical location in that local economic resources, social networks, and the spatial organisation of (un)employment shape the choices available for young people. Attempts to engage in alternative productive activity, such as the illegal drug economy, are influenced by existing production and distribution networks, and by the marginal attractiveness of drug dealing relative to the low rewards (poor wages and part-time work) available in the mainstream economy. Making ends meet is, therefore, contingent upon local contacts and local alternative economic structures.

Marginality, as a result of the privatisation of services and the introduction of user-pays services, is constituted through permanent part-time work, seasonal or irregular employment combined with unemployment, minimum or substandard conditions at, near, or even below the poverty line, short-term contract employment, and accelerated reductions in the social wage (for example, education, and health). This describes a condition of existence for an expanding proportion of the working class. It also provides the structural floor upon which rests the underclass proper. The movement between these categories is ultimately shaped by the contours of unemployment and the general status of wage labour in the economy.

Fundamentally, however, the underclass lies outside of the reserve army of labour and therefore has no direct bearing either on the wage structure (because members do not enter the competition between workers for the limited positions available) or political discipline of the working class (since they do not rely upon a wage as such in order to subsist). The underclass is not simply marginal to the labour market; it is excluded from the labour market — by virtue of family history, structural restrictions on education and job choices, geographical location, racial and ethnic segregation, stigmatised individual and community reputation, and so on.

The underclass is not simply marginal to the labour market; it is excluded from the labour market—by virtue of family history, structural restrictions on education and job choices, geographical location, racial and ethnic segregation, stigmatised individual and community reputation, and so on.

PERSPECTIVES ON SOCIAL EXCLUSION

In times of economic polarisation and social division, the penalties of change often first appear in relation to children and young people. As a relatively less powerful section of the working class, young people have neither the knowledge nor the experience to systematically confront state and market institutions that place them in a structurally disadvantaged position vis-à-vis income, employment, and social status. Where large numbers of young working-class people congregate in particular areas, they constitute visible evidence of the failures of capitalism and the threats to social order posed by these failures. The echoes of this class situation are seen in vandalism, making trouble, gathering on the streets together, theft, and generally asserting public spaces as youth spaces. Urban space is transformed into the site where state and private representatives of capital encounter the marginalised layers of the working class. The boundary police of the class structure are evident not only in relation to the regulation of public space, but also in the conflict that takes a variety of other ideological and material forms.

For example, in recent years the issue of poverty, and what to do about and with the poor, has been framed in either the language of underclass or the language of social exclusion. The first is framed within a particular and peculiar form of moral discourse in which members of the underclass are perceived of and portrayed as morally corrupt, a group needing to be disciplined and reformed. Commentators tend to emphasise the antisocial behaviour of young people, and to blame young people directly for this behaviour (for examples and critique, see Schissel 2002; Males 1996). Thus, from a right-wing perspective, it is the habitual and long-term unemployed who are seen as a threat to the economic fibre of the nation; it is the culturally impoverished and socially deviant unemployed who are seen to threaten society's standards of decency and respectability. As a substratum of the working class, the so-called underclass can thus appear as a highly visible blight on the social landscape and an 'unnecessary' drain on public and private resources (see especially Herrnstein & Murray 1994; Murray 1990).

From this perspective, the problem lies with the personal pathologies of many of the underclass, with self-perpetuating 'pathological communities' that are characterised by a 'hand-out' mentality, immorality, and criminality (Jones & Smyth 1999). Thus, this 'underclass' comprises those sections of the poverty-stricken who, through their own volition or choice, or by genetic default, engage in criminal activity, substance abuse, illegitimate births, and deliberate non-engagement in paid employment. To combat social exclusion, therefore, demands adoption of coercive policies to control populations and behaviours.

The introduction and use of the second of these terms, 'social exclusion', has allowed nation states to deal with issues of poverty and unemployment in ways that are less politically charged than underclass terminology, and yet more palatable than traditional poverty discourses. Social exclusion is often a notoriously imprecise term (Arthurson & Jacobs 2003), and the concepts underpinning its use can vary greatly depending upon the perspective and politics of the commentator (see Jones & Smyth 1999).

One point of view on social exclusion concentrates on the issue of poverty. The source of the problem is seen to lie essentially in having little or no money. In this view, it is poverty that leads to disconnection from the social, economic, political, and cultural systems that determine the social integration of a person in society (Jones & Smyth 1999). It is not specific kinds of people who matter so much as the social conditions that they are forced to endure (Rodger 1992). The key issue is, therefore, one of societal resources, and the redistribution of resources, in order to enhance the participation of those who, because of their poverty, exist on the margins of society. The emphasis here is not on condemnation of the poor (in the rhetoric of the underclass), but on social solidarity and collective intervention to reconstitute the relationship between rich and poor. In other words, the agenda is ultimately one of social justice. Young people raised in conditions of poverty are not blamed for their condition; rather, the concern is to develop policies and strategies that will lift them out of poverty, and radically alter the distribution of goods and services across the society.

Social exclusion has also been approached from the perspective of exclusion from work (Jones & Smyth 1999). Here, it is the relationship of a person to the world of paid work that is seen to be determinant. Exclusion from paid work means disconnection from a range of useful activities: from the ability to contribute to the social good via one's labour, and from the social binds that emerge when people work in concert. The crux of the problem, in this view, is on generating sufficient jobs so people are no longer placed in marginal positions outside of work. Job sharing through to public sector job creation are often touted as possible measures to bring the poor into the work experience. For young people, the vital factor is the role of paid work in rekindling morale and spirit through productive interaction; the benefits of work go beyond that of a wage per se to include important social dimensions.

Academic work on the notion of social exclusion points to the ambiguities and difficulties of the concept (see Arthurson & Jacobs 2003). Some of the problems identified include it being used as a catch-all term, that it is more imprecise and harder to measure than other phenomena (such as poverty, itself a hard concept to quantify), and that it necessarily involves many different dimensions (such as social, economic, legal, political, moral, and cultural). One general advantage of the concept, though, is that it does provide for a more dynamic understanding of the processes surrounding inequality than often hitherto was the case in relation to traditional poverty studies. It speaks of social participation and social networks as well as deprivation in material goods and services. It makes the link between diverse types of exclusion (such as from school, from production, from politics), and it allows for consideration of the interface between structural explanations of inequality and social interactions associated with being poor. In some discussions, it is argued that the concept of social exclusion ought to be linked to the concept of social polarisation (Andersen 1999). This is especially so in the light of the growing power of elites. If one considers there is an underclass that exists at the fulcrum of social exclusion, then perhaps attention should also be directed at the overclass that creates the conditions for this to occur.

Dynamics of exclusion

If social exclusion is understood in a holistic way, then action to reduce it must be multi-dimensional and multi-pronged; intrinsic to any discussion of social exclusion is also the idea of inequality. Addressing inequality raises big political questions about the nature of power and wealth in a society. Strategically, few governments have approached problems associated with social exclusion in a systemic, transformative manner, for to do so they would have to challenge many of the structural foundations of inequality—such as individualistic notions of private property, the private accumulation of wealth, monopoly capitalism leading to the further concentration of ownership into fewer hands, the decline of public accountability in favour of reliance upon market forces, and so on. Accordingly, social exclusion is usually dealt with via policies and strategies that combine elements of the carrot and the stick but that rarely broach inequality in its own right.

> If social exclusion is understood in a holistic way, then action to reduce it must be multi-dimensional and multi-pronged; intrinsic to any discussion of social exclusion is also the idea of inequality. Addressing inequality raises big political questions about the nature of power and wealth in a society.

Indeed, the political offensive of the ruling class in periods of high unemployment and low levels of collective labour mobilisation (union militancy) places even greater pressure on 'losers' to either cope with their situation, or to face the coercive penalties of state intervention. One way in which to neutralise the social expense of inequality and disadvantage is to construct official state ideology that reinforces the individual nature of the problem (you are, for example, unemployed because you don't have the right skills, training, attitude, or work ethic) and the responsibility of individuals to the state (in varying forms of, say, mutual obligation welfare requirements). Another response is through state coercive action, generally involving some form of criminalisation of the poor and containment of social difference via geographical segregation of rich and poor.

In effect, welfare and law enforcement policies serve to reinforce the distinction between 'the virtuous poor' (who exhibit positive attitudes towards self-improvement, healthy lifestyle, and ready submission to state criteria for welfare assistance) and the 'vicious poor' (who lack industry and the work ethic, and who are seen as idle, wanderers, and generally unrespectable). It is the 'deserving' poor who are the object of state welfare, while the 'undeserving' poor are left to scramble for resources from the non-government charities and welfare organisations. It is the latter who are also subject to unrelenting state intervention by the directly coercive arms of the state (the police) and of the private sector (security guards). The new 'dangerous classes' of late capitalism generate fear and contempt in ruling class circles—a social attitude that pervades the popular media and political caucuses.

BOX 2.2

Targets of state intervention

■ Those people living off illegal or criminal activities (for example, theft, drug dealing, gambling).

■ Those who work at subsistence wages for those living off the proceeds of the actions of others (for example, extortion, prostitution, gang protection rackets).

■ Those living off subsistence welfare (government and non-government).

■ Those significantly dependent on subsistence-level, non-waged income generation in the underground economy (for example, busking, hawking, begging).

■ Dependants of the above.

The criminalisation industries of the state and the media reflect concern about the growing reality of subsistence criminality driven by an expanding layer of the underclass and unemployed that has emerged out of global political–economic restructuring. Thus, a key site of contemporary class struggles is that of law and order. On the one hand, deprived individuals, families, and communities will organise their own means and forms of subsistence and enjoyment. They will especially do so under circumstances in which they are excluded from desirable areas in which to live and separated from opportunities to find paid work. Moreover, even if work is there to be had, illegality may be far more rewarding, secure, and satisfying as a source of income than is precarious employment, with all its economy insecurities and exploitations, in the formal sectors.

On the other hand, the ideological representation of the poor and deprived as irresponsible underclass is built into the policy apparatus of the state in relation to welfare and criminal justice (see White 1996a). Unemployment and any resistance to enforced participation in poor workplace situations are reduced to bad attitudes and bad families. The response is to impose varying forms of mutual obligation on the poor—below poverty-line benefits and inadequate services in return for work–search obligations and imposition of training and employment programs. For those who do not play the game, there is exclusion from state support. For those who ignore the game and make a living through alternative means, there is state coercion—in the form of increased policing, harsher sentencing, and greater use of imprisonment.

The dilemma of underclasses and what to do about them has been expressed as follows:

> the hypercasualization of the labour market, and fall in opportunities and incentives for formal employment of less skilled workers, has led to an increase in informal activities of many kinds, including crime. It has also generated informal clubs of various sorts, based on the acquisition, consumption and exchange of semi-legal or illegally acquired goods, the sharing of information about informal activities, and the pooling of risks associated with illegality. In this way, poor and excluded people have sought to compensate themselves for the inequities of market-based outcomes, to 'tax' the better-off of the unjustified gains they have made, and to gain revenge on the various authorities that oppress them, as well as on the mainstream population who despise and exclude them (Jordan 1996: 218).

The response in many places to this phenomenon has been to introduce expanded law-enforcement measures (including a wide range of legislation, including youth curfews, intended to deal with antisocial behaviour) and more intensive and extensive regulation of welfare provision (including work-for-the-dole types of schemes and systematic penalisation of any breaches in welfare provision rules). The crux of state intervention is how best to manage the problem of underclass formation and activity, rather than to eradicate it, for to eradicate it would require action to reverse the polarisations in wealth and income—to pit the state directly in opposition to dominant class interests.

CLASS EXPERIENCES AND YOUNG LIVES

Living in a class-divided society means that not all young people have the same resources, experiences, and opportunities. There are gradations of material resources available to young people, just as there are remarkable variations in how young people experience class. That class is experienced

Living in a class-divided society means that not all young people have the same resources, experiences, and opportunities. There are gradations of material resources available to young people, just as there are remarkable variations in how young people experience class.

is well recognised by young people themselves, and is a theme that is evident throughout this book. As will be demonstrated in a range of ways, class is never far from the surface in discussions of schooling, juvenile justice, public policy, and diverse forms of social inequality pertaining to gender, race, and ethnicity. Class-based resources, linked to family and community contexts, are essential parts of how young people negotiate their lives in many different social situations.

Consider, for example, the question of leisure. For marginalised working-class youth, leisure is shaped by lack of money, a strong sense of neighbourhood boundaries, and the stigma attached to geographical and class location. McDonald (1999), for example, describes how the young people in his study encounter two sides to community affirmation: it is both a source of pride and experienced as a form of stigma. This creates a profound and enduring tension among these young people. They tend to stay in their own suburb and contrast the warmth of their neighbourhoods with the coldness and remoteness of the affluent 'other side' (McDonald 1999: 24). The reason why they stay, however, is as much as anything related to lack of resources, such as access to a car, than simple loyalty and familiarity. Meanwhile, the community of which they are a part is subject to major processes of social disorganisation, which the young people experience as threatening and unsettling. The violence of everyday life, of relationships in their immediate living sphere, are random, unpredictable, and unintelligible, and as such a cause of constant worry.

When they do venture out of their suburb, these marginalised youth once again realise the extent of their social exclusion, and the sense of stigmatisation can be amplified by the contrast between their neighbourhood and others more affluent. Meanwhile, nightlife does promise some sense of connection to life outside and beyond that of the suburb. Thus, in relation to one group of young men: 'All have recently been to Melbourne's new casino. Serge affirms that the casino is "grouse—they let you in. I got let in! I went like this—I wore this jacket, just a going-out shirt, jeans, and shoes". It is an opening into the global flow, into an urban experience of movement, pleasure, and visibility' (McDonald 1999: 46).

But the openness of some venues only accentuates the closedness of others. As the young men relate, nightclubs are different. Here they are not welcome. Here they are explicitly and publicly rejected. There are places for them, and places for us. Social exclusion is not only constructed around the economic, but also the cultural and the spatial (Chatterton & Hollands 2003). As British research demonstrates, 'residual youth groupings' that include the young unemployed are left to consume the residual, or 'bottom end', of the nightlife market (Chatterton & Hollands 2003: 188). For many, even these options do not exist in their area. For these young people, the street becomes a central place for socialising.

Exclusion from work carries with it negative consequences that influence what one does and how one does it. It reshapes the experience of time, as well as that of space. While what individual young people do is always somewhat contingent upon personal practice and initiative (see Wyn & White 1997), the wider class setting creates general patterns of disadvantage and alienation that mark whole communities.

What about young working-class people who do work? How is class experienced in these instances? An interesting and insightful study is provided by Lindsay's research involving hairdressers in Melbourne. Leisure, in this case, is intertwined with the work process in particular ways. As a traditional working-class occupation, hairdressing is basically hard, stressful work that is not paid well, is physically and emotionally difficult, and often involves listening to problems and doing emotional work for the clients (Lindsay 2004). But hairdressing is very much 'serious', and seen as an important career choice and/or important means of financial support.

Lindsay's research found that many young hairdressers escape their difficult work conditions by partying hard in their leisure time. It was found that hairdressers drink at more harmful levels than other young workers, and that they were more likely to use illicit drugs. Getting drunk is described as 'conventional practice' for these working-class young people (Lindsay 2004). In this instance, leisure is not constructed so much around questions of access and social exclusion than matters of style and intent. The doing of leisure is overshadowed by the nature of the work experience. The sphere of production bears down upon the sphere of consumption in ways that make unconventional (and often unhealthy) behaviour the norm. It also creates distinctive methods of having fun and participating in consumer culture, based upon class experiences.

Class is basically about how social resources are mobilised in pursuit of one's interests. Middle-class young people can generally lay claim to greater resources than working-class young people, although this will vary depending upon age—the older one gets, the more significant family-related class resources become (see West, Sweeting, Young & Robins 2006). For middle-class youth, these resources are derived from family and from better opportunities to find work in their local labour markets compared with their working-class counterparts (see Gregory & Hunter 1995). Being able to marshal resources leads to very different social experiences and opportunities in the world of leisure, as well as in other spheres of activity. For middle-class youth, the transformed night-time economies of late capitalism present myriad leisure choices.

The corporate commercial entertainment industries do their best to attract custom in the form of standardised, yet variable, venues and attractions. As Chatterton and Hollands (2003: 93) point out:

> the commercial mainstream is a differentiated 'playground' which offers a number of goods and spaces
> for the active production and reproduction of social groupings of young people, keen to refashion their
> night-time consumption identities in relation to their peers and their own labour market positions.

In their research, conducted in the United Kingdom, Chatterton and Hollands (2003) found a correlation between consumer preferences and labour market position. In other words, how particular groups of young people consume in the night-time economy was related to intraclass differences (based on hierarchies of age, gender, and locality) as well as interclass differences (based on elements of yuppie culture, such as cash-rich, time-poor).

The physical environment was shaped by factors such as gentrification, which in turn was contingent upon catering for the increasing numbers of high-spending young professionals and service employees. Commercialisation of night life is accompanied by different types of mass and niche markets. It is also accompanied by segregated social spaces and frequently the exclusion of particular sections of the working class from these spaces altogether. Whereas the young people in Lindsay's study spoke of the use of leisure to escape from and compensate for the pressures of work,

Commercialisation of night life is accompanied by different types of mass and niche markets. It is also accompanied by segregated social spaces—and frequently the exclusion of particular sections of the working class from these spaces altogether.

for many young professionals going to a bar is experienced as an extension of their work. This is acknowledged by employers as well: 'Corporate workplaces are eager to foster a sense of sociability both in the workplace and outside it, by linking up with certain nightlife operators' (Chatterton & Hollands 2003: 122). The world of leisure thus means very different things, depending upon class background and occupational position.

Summary

The dearth of paid employment in a capitalist society is the key reason for heightened social dislocation and disorganisation. When accompanied by neoliberal policies that place great emphasis on individual initiative, along with restraint in the provision of social welfare, this becomes a recipe for the objective expansion of social inequality and social problems. Young people will respond subjectively to changing material circumstances in many different ways. In part, this is due to the ideological and cultural conditions of late capitalism, as well as to changes in political economy.

One consequence of class inequality and transformations in the class structure that deepen this inequality is a sharpening of the class struggle and other social conflicts. It takes the form of conscious resistance by working-class communities to intensive policing (Lee 2006). It takes the form of wide-scale protests against neoliberalism, racism, and capitalism (Healy 1999). It takes the form of gang formations and street fights. It takes the form of engagement in so-called transgressive cultural activities, such as hip hop, graffiti, and drug use (Presdee 2000). In each of these responses and lived expressions of class situation, young people are at the forefront.

But social divisions are also often re-translated from being problems of milieux to dilemmas of the individual. In other words, a central paradox of contemporary Western society is that while class-based inequities and inequalities are sharpening, there is some evidence that class-based identifications for young people are diminishing (see Furlong & Cartmel 2007). Instead, there is a tendency to take an individualistic perspective about aspects of their life circumstances, and thereby to blame themselves for not negotiating the opportunities, and the constraints, as well as they might (Wyn & White 2000). The meaning that young people make of the social forces within which they are positioned is, therefore, of vital importance in understanding their relationship to society generally.

Analysis of class situation and the processes of social exclusion alert us to the continuing importance of inequality in young people's lives. As will be demonstrated throughout this book, class is a dynamic that permeates young people's experiences with a wide variety of social institutions. Young people's class background plays a crucial role in how they negotiate their way through these institutions, how they experience being a young woman or young man, how they constitute themselves in terms of ethnic identity, and so on. The contemporary meanings and experiences of class are best illustrated in the crucibles of everyday practice. To interpret these meanings and experiences requires an acknowledgment of the structural parameters set by class structures in the first place.

Questions for further exploration

1   What are some common sense indicators of class, and of class difference?

2   What are the major influences that affect people's capacities to marshal economic, social, and cultural resources in ways that they want to?

3   The underclass is variously defined in terms of subjective elements (for example, lazy, deviant) and objective elements (for example, poor, unemployed). In what ways do these elements reinforce each other?

4   Class is a lived experience that means much more than simply being in a particular socio-economic position. Yet, social being shapes social consciousness. Discuss.

5   What are some of the ways in which class position and class situation can possibly change for young people as they get older?

QUESTIONS

PART 2

Social Divisions

GENDER, SEXUALITIES, AND SOCIAL DIFFERENCE

3

Introduction

In this chapter we take up three related dimensions of young people's lives—gender, sexualities, and social difference—and draw on contemporary research to introduce and explore some key debates that have emerged in these areas. We are interested in the ways in which changing times have opened up new opportunities and ways of being for young men and women. We explore the evidence of new patterns of living and new subjectivities that have emerged over the last twenty years for young men and women. We are also interested in exploring the question of continuities in gendered patterns that link today's young people with previous generations. In exploring these issues we ask: How much has changed? Are boys the new disadvantaged? To what extent is difference in sexual identity recognised? Our approach focuses on the ways in which young people reinvent and place new meanings on older divisions based on gender. In the final section of this chapter we focus on the issue of social difference, highlighting the ways in which social difference is reinforced through taken-for-granted social practices, everyday language, the media, and institutional processes.

> How much has changed? Are boys the new disadvantaged? Are different sexual identities recognised? How is social difference based on gender and sexual identity reinforced through taken-for-granted social practices, everyday language, the media, and institutional processes?

GENDER

The sociological study of gender involves exploring how masculinities and femininities are constructed by individuals and by institutions, and how meanings of masculinity and femininity are contested. Within sociology gender has traditionally been understood as a social process involving the identification and performance of masculinity and femininity. It refers to the ways in which social groups define these relationships and how individuals themselves identify with them. Gender is, in one respect, a term for the social understandings of sexualities that go well beyond biological understandings of 'male' and 'female'. Gender involves the formation of sexual identities (such as lesbian, gay, heterosexual, bisexual, same-sex attracted, and transgendered identities), as well as the formation of identities on the basis of ethnicity, class, geographical location, and disability. In other words, gender identities are highly differentiated. There is evidence that over the last twenty-five years new definitions and understandings of being male and female have been forged, opening up new opportunities for sexualities to be recognised and expressed.

As a background to discussing the complexity of gender in young people's lives, it is useful to consider some indicators of social change. Table 3.1 shows that there have been some significant changes in gendered patterns of living for young men and women today compared with the generation that grew up in the late 1970s. Young men and women who were in their early twenties in the early 2000s were not marrying until their late twenties, whereas young women and young men of the previous generation were getting married, respectively, by the age of twenty-one and twenty-four. There is a strong trend towards childbearing later than the previous generation, too. By the early 2000s, nearly half of all young women were having their first child over the age of thirty. Patterns of work and educational participation have also changed considerably, especially for young women. Over the twenty-five years that these comparative data span, young men and young women have increased their participation in education, but young women have seen the most significant change. Today, nearly half of all young people are still attending an educational institution in their early twenties, but twenty-five years ago, this was rare for young women; only 9 per cent of young women who were aged twenty-one were attending an educational institution in 1976. The figure was also lower for boys than it is today—but it was at that time nearly double the rate of girls' participation (16 per cent). Over the course of one generation, then, there has been a dramatic shift in the participation in and use of post-compulsory education by young women.

TABLE 3.1   Snapshot of gendered patterns: Young Australians in their twenties in 1976 and 2001

	Baby boomers (aged 20 in 1976)	Gen X (aged 20 in 2001)
Median age at first marriage	Men 24 Women 21	Men 29 Women 27
First birth within current relationship	10 per cent to women aged 30 years+	48 per cent to women aged 30 years+
Attending an educational institution	Men 16 per cent Women 9 per cent	Men 23 per cent Women 24 per cent
Holding a non-school qualification	Men 38 per cent Women 24 per cent	Men 45 per cent Women 45 per cent
Labourforce participation	Men 92 per cent Women 57 per cent (women mainly working before having children)	Men 87 per cent Women 75 per cent (women mainly working part-time while studying)

Source: ABS 2005.

The figures on labourforce participation also reveal change. Here, we see the drop in the proportion of young men aged twenty-one involved in the labourforce compared with the previous generation. But the most remarkable change is in young women's participation: more young women are working at age twenty-one in the 2000s than in the 1970s, and they are working for different reasons. Then, young women were working before having children; now they are mainly working part-time while studying.

While young women have significantly increased their participation in the workforce over the last twenty-five years, the figures show that men and women are working in very different sectors of the labour market and they do not earn the same levels of income. The segmentation of occupations along gender lines reveals that gendered processes are influential in the complex mix of personal decision making and institutional processes that result in who works in what jobs and under what conditions. In this area, too, older patterns of gender division have coalesced with new developments in gendered patterns.

Some facts about gender and the workforce:

- Overall there is a wage gap of 8 per cent between men and women. Women earn less than their male peers in all occupational sectors.
- Women make up:
  - 71 per cent of the workforce in health and community services
  - 65 per cent of the workforce in education
  - 54 per cent of the workforce in finance and insurance.
- Men make up:
  - 73 per cent of the manufacturing workforce
  - 90 per cent of the construction workforce
  - 71 per cent of the wholesale trade workforce.

Source: ABS 2004.

BOX 3.1

These comparative figures provide a snapshot of change as well as of continuity. They show that, despite social change, gendered patterns of living continue to be of significance. The ongoing significance of gender is also reflected in evidence about what issues are important to young people.

Surveys of the views of young people between the ages of fifteen and eighteen reveal that while there are some areas in which young men and young women have very similar perspectives, there are also significant areas of divergence. Young women are more likely than young men to rely on getting a good education in order to secure their future, and place education ahead of keeping fit. Young men are more likely to be concerned about their financial future and securing employment. Young women are slightly more likely to be employed in the part-time labour market while they are students and they rate the importance of friendships more highly than young men. Young men are more concerned about abuse of alcohol and other drugs, while young women are more concerned about physical abuse.

Some facts about young people's views

- The proportion of full-time female students continuing from Year 10 through to Year 12 was 9.6 percentage points higher than for male students in 1994 (80.2 per cent and 70.6 per cent) and 9.8 percentage points higher in 2004 (82.1 per cent and 72.3 per cent) (Dusseldorp Skills Forum 2004).

BOX 3.2

- Percentage of fifteen to nineteen year olds in the labour force 2002–03: males 58.4 per cent, females 60.7 per cent (ABS 2004).

- More females ranked friendships of importance (71.8 per cent) than did males (58.5 per cent), while males ranked financial security (20.9 per cent) higher than did females (13.5 per cent) (Mission Australia 2006).

- Just over 30 per cent of males, compared with around 14 per cent of females, valued getting a job highly.

- A much higher proportion of males than females are significantly concerned about alcohol and other drugs: 34.2 per cent compared with 24.7 per cent (Mission Australia 2006).

- Physical and sexual abuse were major concerns for 30.8 per cent of females compared with 23 per cent of males (Mission Australia 2006).

- The most important current issues for both male and female respondents were keeping fit, getting more education, and having lots of friends, although females considered getting more education to be more important than keeping fit (Australian Institute of Family Studies 2006).

- Male respondents were more likely than female respondents to 'attach high importance to the things that would help them to get ahead in life, such as having a successful career, making a lot of money, and saving and investing' (Australian Institute of Family Studies 2006).

These figures paint a picture of contrasts between the ways in which young women and young men see things. The question is, are these significant issues and how do they affect young people's lives? Do the different labour market outcomes, different uses of education, and different approaches to life mean that some groups are disadvantaged? These questions are difficult to answer on the basis of broad statistical patterns. In the following section, we discuss some sociological analyses of contemporary gender patterns among young people that explore the expression and meaning of gender within particular sites and locations. Following this, we discuss recent debate about gender and disadvantage.

Sites of gendered practices

Research on gender has highlighted the ways in which young people perform gender in different sites and settings. One example, a study of young Italo-Australians in Adelaide city streets found that groups of young men, united around their common Italian heritage, met regularly in the suburbs and in specific Italian areas of the inner city (Foote 1993). The groups essentially formed on a social basis, with 'hanging around' an activity in its own right shared by group members. At times, the hanging around involved conflicts between these young men and other groups, including 'Australians'. Foote comments that these conflicts often involved an affirmation of both their ethnic and gender identities: 'Rivalry and physical conflicts with other racially based groups reinforces their identity both as Italians and as "macho men". In this context, especially as victors in the fight, they can turn their status as "wogs" from a point of derision to something of which they can be proud' (Foote 1993: 127).

The interrelation of practices of masculinity, ethnicity, and class has been noted in other Australian studies. A Sydney study found that there was an intersection of masculinity, ethnicity, and class in such a way as to affirm social presence, ensure mutual protection, and compensate for a generally marginalised economic and social position:

> This performance of the 'gang' functions in several ways: it provides a venue for cultural maintenance, community and identity; and at the same time provides the protection of strength in numbers in the face of physical threats by other youth, and harassment by police and other adults … Central to their partial negotiation of their experience of racialisation, they affirm a masculine and 'ethnic' identity of toughness, danger and respect (Collins, Noble, Poynting & Tabar 2000: 150).

Assertion of gang membership can be interpreted as attempts by the young men to valorise their lives and empower themselves in the face of outside hostility, disrespect, and social marginalisation.

The affirmation of masculinity and femininity is experienced through relationships that are sometimes conflictual, as illustrated in the above examples, and at other times simply oppositional. Lantz, for example, describes how young women in her study of student sex workers felt that the sex work affirmed their femininity because there were times when they were working with clients that they felt desired and appreciated as women (Lantz 2005). Her study demonstrates the importance of understanding the young women's point of view, and at the same time of understanding how their choices inevitably position them as the Other, as unworthy and as victims.

A lot of research on gender has been conducted within school settings that has provided important information about young people aged between twelve and eighteen. A classic longitudinal Australian study by McLeod and Yates (2006) shows how fourteen girls and twelve boys at four different types of schools in four different locations developed and negotiated their identities over a seven-year period (1993–2000). Their study focused on the issue of gender and social change, and especially on changes in how girls saw their lives unfolding compared with girls of their mothers' generation. The results provide an insight into the 'uneven and differentiated impact of contemporary social and gender change, and the profound influence of school community and culture on the shaping of subjectivity' (McLeod & Yates 2006: 2).

Subjectivity has become a common conceptual tool used by researchers to understand the particular ways of being that are required or rewarded in contemporary times. Kelly (2006), for example, argues that the 'entrepreneurial Self' has become a dominant form of subjectivity today, a suggestion that is based on the idea that social conditions provide the possibilities for and limits on what we can become. Kelly is suggesting that, far from being able to become anything they want to, young people in these times are constrained to develop and perform a particular kind of subjectivity that involves demonstrating the capacity to be 'rational, autonomous and responsible' (Kelly 2006: 18). This can be illustrated through McLeod and Yates's study. They comment that many of the young women they interviewed were 'enterprising' and 'strategic', with a clear orientation towards constructing their futures. They comment that: 'Cultivating an enterprising subjectivity signals an ease and sense of purpose in the world, a capacity to imagine and present oneself as "can-do", as able to imagine and make life' (McLeod & Yates, 2006: 199).

The concept of subjectivity focuses attention on the way in which young people are actively and reflexively engaged in the project of producing particular identities over time. Because the concept of subjectivity focuses our attention on the (constant) process of becoming, it enables researchers to understand the difficult and sometimes impossible task that young people face of shaping identities within the constraints of their social context (Youdell 2006).

As McLeod and Yates point out, becoming is a project and a process. It is a project in the sense that young people are developing sets of identifications and a sense of self. It is also a process through which subjectivities are shaped (by individuals) through social location and social and economic processes, and through state policies (Mizen 2004). The important point is that identities are not seen as fixed, essential properties of individuals, but are dynamic and (within limits) produced through the work that individuals do.

> The important point is that identities are not seen as fixed, essential properties of individuals, but are dynamic and (within limits) produced through the work that individuals do.

McLeod and Yates's research on the way in which young men and women in different school settings and communities do this work is illuminating. They found that 'new times' (that is, working within 'new economies' and the capacity to present the self in new ways) are very unevenly experienced. Their study finds evidence of both change and continuity. Their study emphasises the ways in which middle-class girls have 'a highly honed reflexivity' (2006: 7). These young women are especially alert to how they are seen and heard by others and are able to shape their behaviour in ways that enable them to be seen as proactive, responsive, and flexible. They describe 'Keren' who, in the early interviews, appeared 'bright and happy and as speaking warmly about her teacher' (McLeod & Yates 2006: 80). It transpired that Keren's mother had told her to make sure she smiled a lot in the interview, assuming that the researchers and possibly others would be judging how Keren responded. Her cheerfulness was a reliable mode of self-presentation, which she used for all the interviews for the seven years of the project.

> Her self-conscious presentation as a 'joker', her deliberately 'bouncy' demeanor, her diligence — including in the interviews — and the hard work she put into constructing her future sits against her self-perception as someone who 'takes it as it comes' (McLeod & Yates 2006: 81).

This finely tuned capacity enabled these girls to self-monitor and to be aware of how their actions in the present position them for desired futures and to construct their own biographies. McLeod and Yates found that feminism and wider changes in society (in women's participation in labour markets, for example) appeared to have had a greater and possibly more positive effect on young women's lives than on young men's. This was particularly noticeable in the ways in which young women, and especially those from middle-class backgrounds, had responded to the need to be flexible and adaptive to new conditions. They found that, in general, the young men appeared to be less confident about their futures as they left secondary school. They conclude:

> This is not to suggest that there has been a reversal or inversion of the gender binaries, but rather to point to some emergent themes in the changing forms of masculinity and femininity as we see these young men encounter dilemmas that have been typically aligned with femininity, and these young women work hard towards an autonomous future (McLeod & Yates 2006: 206).

These shifts in gendered patterns and changes in the ways in which masculine and feminine identities are being shaped highlight the challenges faced by young people in different social settings. For some groups of young men, especially those from lower socioeconomic backgrounds, the task of managing to construct reflexive identities and flexible identities represents an enormous burden (Wyn 2007). Class and gender frame the extent of the choices that are open to young people, so that some are positioned more favourably to become what they want to be.

Other researchers have pointed out that the success of some groups of young women may be more fictional than real. Harris, for example, argues that new labour markets open up:

> an exciting and radically different future than could have been imagined by young women even thirty years ago. What is troubling, though, is that these daughters of wealthy families have become postergirls for their generation, implicated in the fiction that all young women can be self-inventing, high-flying, and ideally placed to seize power in the new economy (2004: 48).

'[t]hese daughters of wealthy families have become postergirls for their generation, implicated in the fiction that all young women can be self-inventing, high-flying, and ideally placed to seize power in the new economy' (Harris 2004: 48).

Other studies have also illustrated the importance of undertaking location-based research on gender. Previous work by White (1999) revealed a wide range of experiences and youth cultures that are as much related to whether one grows up in the country, as the child of refugee parents, or as the third generation of inner-suburban dwellers, as they are to gender.

More recently, Kenway et al. have studied the lives of young men in four diverse places 'beyond the metropolis' in Australia through a 'place-based global ethnography of masculinity' (2006: 59). The studies of men in different non-metropolitan places and spaces provides an exploration of how masculinities are constructed in relation to local histories and spaces and to global processes and relations. Their work represents a shift in thinking about gender that moves away from a focus on subjectivities to explore instead the interaction between real lives and representations of masculinities in order to analyse the 'lines between the authentic and the fictional countryside and the authentic and fictional non-urban male' (2006: 3). The research is based on interviews with twenty-four young men and twelve young women aged thirteen to sixteen, but the research involved talking to people of all ages. The book reveals the complexities of masculinity beyond the stereotypes of 'the true blue Aussie bloke in *Crocodile Dundee* (1986), the Southern Man in New Zealand beer advertisements, and the fox hunter in the streets of London' (2006: 3). Globalisation provides a tool for these researchers to analyse the ways in which youth cultural images circulate globally and become a source of young men's 'imagined lives' and the 'mediascapes' that represent out-of-the-way places and people (2006: 59). Interestingly, though, like many other studies (for example, Smyth & Hattam 2004) they find that young men mobilise different knowledge from 'formal school knowledge' in order to advance their own particular agendas and interests, invoking everyday knowledge about life chances and lifestyles (Kenway et al. 2006: 169–70).

But, significantly, this research also goes well beyond the trend to link young people's identities with school (or opposition to school), focusing on the different practices of leisure and pleasure that link young men to the social order. They discuss the kinds of pleasure that young men gain from motor vehicles (cars, trucks, utes, and motorbikes, and even pushbikes and go-karts) that are an everyday part of their lives. They show how the pleasure they take in motor vehicles provides opportunities for intergenerational contact and learning, are often linked with part-time work and career plans, and provide possibilities for dangerous and wild pleasures. Dangerous driving (often on private properties) signifies freedom and masculine prowess. This work is important because it opens up our understanding of the ways in which masculinities are complex and differentiated. Urban-based studies of young people often ignore place: urban landscapes may be interchangeable and hence invisible. The insistence on understanding young men's experiences of their spaces and places, as well as the ways they are represented, opens up understanding of how masculinities beyond the metropolis are different from and like masculinities within the metropolis.

While recent work opens up new questions about masculinities and gender relations, at a policy level we can see how older ways of thinking have retained their relevance. This is illustrated through the continuing significance of debates that focus on disadvantage and gender.

Gender and education: What about the boys?

During the late 1990s and early 2000s, the evidence of shifting patterns of gender and new identity struggles has lead to debate about disadvantage and gender. The feminist reforms of the 1970s and 1980s now formed a backdrop to a political backlash, which received support from conservative governments (for example, in funding men's groups). In some quarters a new gender politics emerged, focused on a politics of opposition between men and women, especially in schooling because it is understood that adult patterns of gender disadvantage are forged through unequal outcomes from formal education. This debate continues to have resonance in discussions of gender.

The debates that have occurred over the question of boys illustrate how contentious an issue gender remains in Australia. The way in which the lines have been drawn, and the responses by the broader community and the education profession, illustrate how old divisions retain their potency. The ongoing debate about gender and schooling also underlines the immense challenge in understanding the effects of gender and how to address disadvantage.

Because the ongoing debate about disadvantage based on gender often involves assumptions about what happened in schools over the last twenty-five years, it is enlightening to briefly consider this history. The issue of schooling and gender was brought into focus in 1975, with the publication of the *Girls, School and Society* report, which coincided with the increasing acceptance by many influential educators that gender is socially constructed; that is, that masculinities and femininities are shaped, contested, and practised through social processes. The importance of *Girls, School and Society* is that it highlighted girls' educational disadvantage relative to boys'. In particular, it emphasised girls' poor school retention rates and their relatively poor performance in the labour market. In this way, the report set some of the parameters that have dominated thinking about the educational effects of gender for decades. It established a tradition for girls' success to be measured against boys' and for equality to be measured by counting participation rates. The report also set in place an approach to gender that treated all boys as a category and all girls as a category.

For twenty-five years, these assumptions have dominated the discourses of education and gender. Much of what we know about the experience of young people in schools is framed by the assumptions inherent in this approach. Hence, Yates suggests that the following story about gender equity in schools would be commonly accepted:

About 20 years ago, governments became aware that girls were being disadvantaged in schooling. They developed policies and funding to improve girls' career aspirations, to make curriculum and pedagogy more 'girl-friendly', and to ensure equal spending on girls and boys. At the same time a huge amount of research and writing (academic and professional) was carried out on girls, their development and their needs. Over this period we have seen a large increase in the proportion of girls completing school as compared with boys and their increasing success in 'non-traditional' subjects such as mathematics. Now it is time for more attention to the boys. Boys' retention rates, learning difficulties, delinquency, suicide rates and general self-esteem are all cause for concern. We don't want to take away from the girls' programs, and more needs to be done in relation to issues such as sexual harassment in schools, but there is a real dearth of good research and professional support for boys, and this is what should now occupy our urgent attention (Yates 1997: 338).

Nearly ten years later, Yates and McLeod comment that debate about girls' and boys' education is simplified in the media to a 'winners and losers account' of schooling, with boys the new losers (2006: 188). This simplistic view is based on the assumption that the disadvantage of girls is now mirrored by boys' disadvantage, an approach that has been called 'the competing victim' approach (Cox 1997), which is especially popular in the media in the form of reports that girls are advantaged to the detriment of boys. The call for more attention to boys is based on arguments that essentialise masculinity; that is, in direct contradiction to the view that masculinities and femininities are socially constructed, the proponents of this argument focus on direct genetic inheritance, chemical theories, the effects of testosterone on behaviour, and differences between men and women in brain structure. Raphael Reed describes the 'crude cognitive psychology' invoked by the claim that, because of their different mental developmental processes, boys' and girls' brains are structured differently by the time they are adult. The consequence of this is that the 'male brain finds it hard to deal with reflective emotional-centered tasks and hence boys have a preference for speculative thinking and action' (Raphael Reed 1999: 99). This approach supports the argument that educational programs need to be re-focused in order to provide a more sympathetic and appropriate response to these inevitable biomedical and physical differences between all males and females. Gilbert and Gilbert conclude that the biomedical, or 'essentialist', arguments for gender differences 'have little regard for evidence or theoretical consistency' and are used to justify rather than explain behaviour (1998: 32).

> Debate about girls' and boys' education are simplified in the media to a 'winners and losers account' of schooling, with boys the new losers (2006: 188)

The evidence shows that in fact the 'boys issue' has been a largely unacknowledged problem in education for many years (Yates 1997; Teese et al. 1995). Studies of school leaving patterns (for example, Lamb 1994) show that boys from low socioeconomic backgrounds have traditionally made up the numbers of early school leavers, while Gilbert and Gilbert (1998) reveal that working-class boys are the least likely to benefit from education. Up to the late 1970s many boys from working-class backgrounds left school in order to take up apprenticeships in trades such as plumbing or carpentry. They aimed to move directly into the workforce in any one of the many industries in which they could start a career on the shop floor and work their way up the career ladder. Even in the early 1980s, a significant proportion of boys planned to leave school once they passed the age of compulsory attendance, to get a good job, and get on with their lives (see Wilson & Wyn 1987). Young women from low socioeconomic backgrounds have a similar pattern. The group that has most increased its participation in education are girls from high socioeconomic backgrounds (Teese et al. 1995). These are the girls who have, in the 1990s, made headlines for their outstanding examination performance in the traditional 'male' areas of mathematics and sciences and precipitated the call for more attention to boys' education.

Apart from the noticeable success by a small group of girls in final year school examinations little else has changed. Yates notes that in the 1970s, as now, it was boys who were falling behind in school and being sent to special education classes, and boys who were more likely to commit suicide than teenage girls (Yates 1997)—knowledge about troubling outcomes for boys that has been around for over twenty-five years. While there have been some gains for girls over that period, the continuities with the past remain significant. Consider the following report that shows that women complete secondary school in 'significantly greater numbers than men':

> The overall gender split in education conceals the marked gender segregation by field of study, a segregation that is closely linked to corresponding patterns in the workforce, and one which maintains historic patterns of female disadvantage. If the position of women in the workforce is better than it was, gender power still works against women (Marginson 1999: 173).

As Yates and McLeod comment, there is a 'massive' amount of evidence documenting the post-school pathways of girls and boys that shows that school success does not readily translate into labour market advantage, nor that failure at school necessarily translates into disadvantage.

Despite improvements in educational participation rates, Australian women do not seem to be able to transform this to their advantage in the workforce. Women receive 85.5 per cent of the wages of men, a difference that has been described as a 'raw gender gap' (Preston 1997), supporting Gilbert and Gilbert's finding that boys' low levels of literacy do not appear to disadvantage them when it comes to earning money (1998: 12).

> Documenting such research explodes the myth that all girls are winners at school and that all boys are losers. It demonstrates how such simplistic renderings of educational disadvantage with regard to boys and its corollary of privilege for girls fail to take into consideration broader social systems and discourses that intersect with gender, such as ethnicity, rurality, class and poverty (Martino 1999: 290).

Instead, it is suggested that the question about boys' education should be re-phrased to ask 'Which boys?' Yates suggests that it is middle-class boys whose interests have been most threatened by the changes in educational participation. She and others argue that an unforeseen consequence of the feminist strategy of improving girls' educational outcomes—so wholeheartedly taken up by middle-class interests—was that middle-class girls would ultimately be placed in competition with middle-class boys.

Our discussion of gender and educational outcomes shows that it is not useful to see gender simply as composed of two oppositional categories: it is too simplistic to see all boys and all girls as belonging to the same two gender groups. The most significant change over the last twenty-five years has been the success of girls from high socioeconomic backgrounds in secondary school and in gaining places in tertiary education. Very little else has changed. Some groups of boys and girls continue to be marginalised from the benefits of education, especially those who do not complete any form of post-compulsory education. These are the groups who would most benefit from attention to their needs.

The boys issue also raises questions about the indicators that we use to measure disadvantage. Exam results on their own can be misleading and so need to be seen in their broader context. Exam results, when looked at together with measures of health and well-being, labour market participation, and wage rates, may begin to present a more realistic picture of the complex relationship between gender, schooling, and society.

Taking a broader approach to gender relations has meant going beyond the category 'boys' to place masculinity itself under scrutiny. This means re-examining some of the gender-based processes in schools that have previously been ignored. The under-representation of boys in the arts and humanities, for example, is seen as a trend that denies a large group of boys access to the important areas of literature, history, philosophy, and studies of society. Teese et al. (1995) argue that many boys are failing school because they are being inappropriately guided into narrow studies in mathematics and the sciences. The focus on mathematics and sciences is at the expense of developing an understanding of the way in which social change affects individuals, or how novels, movies, and other forms of contemporary culture reflect and shape social life. Students who exclusively study the hard sciences do not experience a curriculum that encourages them to reflect on their values, to listen to other perspectives, and to express their views cogently. It is ironic that the competing victim approaches to the issue of the boys reinforces a narrow, singular view of what masculinity is.

This narrow approach has been challenged by a number of researchers. Martino and Palotta-Chiarolli (2001) have produced an anthology of boys' views about life—sex, friends, sport, girls, drugs, music, school, and family. As the authors explain in their Introduction, they 'wanted to give guys the opportunity to tell it as it is for them' (Martino & Pallotta-Chiarolli 2001). Their book celebrates the diversity of young men's lives and challenges simplistic approaches that categorise all young men as if they were a single group, or that all young men are losers in education.

SEXUALITIES, POWER, AND DIFFERENCE

Over the last fifteen years there has been a steady increase in research about young people and sexualities. One such project, conducted in the mid 1990s, was the Australian Centre for Sex Health and Society's unique survey of same-sex-attracted young people, which resulted in the most systematic Australian study of the experiences of same-sex-attracted youth yet (Hillier et al. 1998). The findings provide an interesting and at times chilling account of the experiences of these young people, as they struggle to find a place to belong in Australian society.

The survey marks an important shift in thinking about gender, towards an approach that recognises that there are many ways of being male and many ways of being female. Many of the young people who responded to the survey had never discussed their sexuality with anyone. Half of the young people reported that they had been physically or verbally abused because of their sexuality, an indication that this abuse was systemic and that it happened at school (Hillier et al. 1999). Ensuring that schools are safe, supportive, and secure places for all students to be requires teachers, students, and the wider community to tackle the difficult issue of the hegemony of masculinity.

Half of the young people reported that they had been physically or verbally abused because of their sexuality.

The concept of hegemony is commonly used to discuss the ways in which particular perspectives, understandings, and practices come to dominate (Connell 2002). Connell makes the argument that there are gendered power relations among men, and distinguishes hegemonic from subordinated masculinities. Hegemonic masculinities are those that are narrowly defined and those that are enforced through the use of power (Connell 2002). The significance of the exercise of power (by other students, parents, and institutions) is illustrated by the extent to which research on sexualities inevitably touches on examples of struggle, coercion, and the maintenance of mainstream norms. Gilbert and Gilbert (1998) describe how boys in schools learn to negotiate a cool masculinity that involves a juggling act between being a nerd (good at schoolwork and too like the girls) and an idiot (disruptive). They illustrate the dynamic whereby the ridicule of non-conforming individuals and groups is a key element in maintaining the desirable form of masculinity. In other words, what is happening in the classroom and the playground is, a lot of the time, a process of defining, limiting, challenging, and negotiating masculinity—in relation to girls and femininities, as well as in relation to different masculinities.

The operation of hegemonic masculinity is also described by Walker (1999) in her study of the relationship of working-class young men to 'car culture'. She argues that 'for working-class men, their masculine identity, potency and virility is represented not by the desirability of their woman but by the desirability of their motor vehicle' (Walker 1999: 186). Walker points out that this is a 'doomed' exercise, because these young men do not have the material resources to purchase the most recent models of luxury vehicles. She could also point out that there is plenty of evidence that young men from other classes also affirm their masculine identities through their use of motor cars.

Humour is a common mechanism for controlling what can and what cannot be said in classrooms. Kehily and Nayak (1997) show how boys use humour in classrooms to construct and reinforce gender hierarchies, through put-downs, humiliation, and the celebration of a particular style of masculinity (the 'naughty boy' who is 'centre-stage'). Similarly, in an article titled 'Pete's Tool', Dixon (1997) shows how myths of male sexuality and domination are reinforced through the example of one boy who plays with a workshop tool, rendering a fantasy of masturbation and penetration. These 'playful' interchanges are mechanisms for silencing and denying other identities. Silence and ignorance are powerful forces for constructing boundaries around what can and cannot be spoken, acknowledged, or accepted.

Epstein (1997) argues that, until recently, the extent to which schools are 'sexualised sites' has not been acknowledged. She makes an explicit link between sexism and heterosexism, arguing that homophobia and misogyny are 'so closely intertwined as to be inseparable' (1997: 113). In other words, the joking, fighting, dissing, and mucking-about behaviours that help to keep people in line are directed at boys as much as girls. Non-macho boys, that is.

This dynamic is revealed in the reflections of a gay teacher on the impact of the question a student asked him: 'Are you gay, sir?' (Crowhurst 1999). It was, at the time, a shocking question to ask a teacher. The student who asked the question was transgressing the code of silence about sexuality and, in doing so, was exercising the power that accrues, automatically, to those who conform to the norm. It was not a sympathetic question. Having been asked, the teacher was already positioned as less powerful, no matter how he responded. The laughter from the other students that accompanied the question was an acknowledgment of the double bind the teacher had just been placed in. To say 'yes' would have meant being forced to 'come out'; to say 'no' would reinforce the oppressive silence about sexual identity.

Misson (1999) exposes the oppressive dynamics of heterosexual masculinity in his analysis of classroom talk and students' writing. Analysing young people's discussions of homosexuality, he shows that they operate from discursive positions that have different 'silences'. These are not simply binary divisions between what is said and what is not said, but are both. He shows how ignorance becomes a form of knowledge, and actively creates silence by reducing the options for other kinds of talk. Misson provides the following example:

> Misson shows that young people's discussions of homosexuality operate from discursive positions that have different silences that are not simply binary divisions between what is said and what is not said, but are both, as ignorance becomes a form of knowledge.

I specifically directed a question to one of the boys who had said he didn't like homosexuals:

St M1   I'd run [a homosexual] over if he walked across the road.

RM   OK. You'd run him over if he walked across the road. So you in fact would not want your …

St M1   [They're gutless.]

RM   … a kid of yours to have a homosexual as a teacher?

St M1   No, they'll learn filthy habits.

St F   (Inaudible, but clearly against the statement)

St M1   They will … they will!

(Chorus of comments)

RM   No … No …

St F   (Inaudible, something about 'walking across the road')

RM   Sorry. Can I … can I, I mean, quite seriously ask what kind of habits you think they would learn? I … I …

St M1   What happens if there was something going on in the bedroom and they walk in … and they wanted to know what's going on?

RM   But …

St M1   How are they going to teach children the right thing?

St F1   (overlapping) … at school.

St M1   At school, but when they get home and they see that they've got like two fathers.

(General laughter)

St F1   But we're talking about teachers.

St F2   They don't care (that is, that they've got two fathers).

RM   No, no, no. I … I was actually talking about teachers.

St M1   Yeah? So?

RM   But … but the children do not see the teachers in bed, usually anyway. What …

St M1   (inaudible) … You never know.

RM   What?

St M1   You never know!

RM   Right …

At which point, I decided it was time to change the topic (Misson 1999: 85).

This interchange illustrates the silencing effect of the homophobic discourse that the student doggedly pursues and to which Misson eventually capitulates by giving up the conversation. Through these schoolyard and classroom conversations, normative or mainstream views of heterosexual masculinity and femininity are being imposed—and contested—and the boundaries redefined. A description of the experiences of young people in a British school shows how a group of girls (the New Wave Girls) emphasised their intimacy in order to 'exclude others, promote group unity and to strengthen close relations between pairs of girls' (Blackman 1998). As Blackman points out, the girls' physicality and 'lesbian' displays frighten the boys because they render their masculine sexual bravado pointless.

Misson's example illustrates how attempts to inspire understanding can be used to reinforce prejudice. Eyre (1997) also shows how, despite the intention to be inclusive and supportive, some strategies, which are aimed at increasing tolerance of previously marginalised groups, can in fact further reinforce their marginality. She cites the example of the 'gay speaker' who is invited to present their 'life story' to a class of sexuality education students. While the intended effect is to increase understanding, the actual effect is often to reinforce the 'weirdness' and 'otherness' of the visitor. These strategies tend to heighten the gay person's non-straight identity at the expense of recognising the many other aspects that constitute them, and that would link them to the students.

For this reason, 'difference' has become an important concept in the ongoing project of understanding gender processes and their effects on young people's lives. Young (1990) argues that difference is frequently seen as an oppositional relationship, that categories are seen as opposing each other: negative/positive, inferior/superior or deviant/normal. A non-oppositional understanding of social groups involves valuing the differences and uniqueness of groups rather than seeing them as necessarily locked into a binary, hierarchical relationship. In exploring the two approaches to difference, Young focuses on the relationship between individuals and social groups.

A key element in the production of inequality based on social groupings is the idea of standards or norms, which become a single point of reference against which all are measured. Young (1990) calls this process 'reductionism' because it involves a tendency to reduce all people to a 'unity' (males as a single group or females as a single group, for example) and a tendency to value commonness and sameness over specificity and difference. She argues that valuing sameness produces social injustice, because the capacities, experiences, and full participation of some groups are inevitably ignored or marginalised.

We can see this process in action in the interaction between Misson and the student on the topic of homosexuality that is referred to above. The student's understanding of homosexuality is based on the perception that homosexuality and heterosexuality are oppositional categories, and that all members of the homosexuality group hold basically the same (largely negative) characteristics. As Misson implies, the rationality of this position is not important to the person who holds it.

Gilbert and Gilbert (1998) illustrate the effects of oppositional approaches to gender tendency in their description of computer game playing. They point out that electronic game playing is a place where boys can play at masculinity. They draw attention to the explicit violence and gender politics of many video games that offer boys the opportunity to associate themselves with the world of men rather than the world of women—to be 'megaracers' rather than 'girlie-men' (1998: 77). As Martino comments, at the heart of these practices is a gender politics that is organised around the denigration of the feminine (1998: 292). But at the same time that the feminine is denigrated by these gender politics, so, too, is masculinity. A clear theme in the discussion about the boys is the way in which 'boys themselves are seriously damaged by the expectations and labels of hegemonic masculinity' (Raphael Reed 1999: 106).

Hence, the assumption of sameness, far from ensuring equality, further marginalises and stigmatises individuals who are different. At a personal level, the assumption of sameness generates a split between reason and feeling that cannot be spoken, but which is often felt as a strong emotion. In recognition of the importance of acknowledging difference, especially in the areas of gender and sexuality, some educators have suggested that new, critical methodologies are required that make the oppositional discourses visible and that create spaces where previously silenced discourses can be spoken. Suggestions include:

- listening to boys and acknowledging the multiple interests and lives of different boys, rather than making assumptions about them (Raphael Reed 1999; Martino & Palotta-Chiarolli 2001)

- returning responsibility to boys and girls for the consequences of their actions and making the power of discourse visible to them through drama or writing, which opens up different possibilities (Davies 1997)

- developing a 'pedagogy of the emotions' that builds understanding across the divides of gender, acknowledges the links between private and public selves, and links reason and feeling (Kenway & Fitzclarence 1997).

Summary

Despite the wider forces of change that are affecting young people's lives, statistics reveal the continuing relevance of gender. Our discussion has highlighted the complexity of understanding how gender operates and what it means in young people's lives. New developments over the last twenty-five years challenge older ways of thinking about gender. The increased participation of young women in education and in the workforce has resulted in new patterns and new opportunities for some; however, older patterns of gendered labour market segmentation are still evidence. Research that explores the experiences of girls and boys, and young men and women, in different settings has highlighted the complexity of gender relations and confirmed the importance of understanding how class, ethnicity, and sexuality intersect with gender.

Our discussion has shown how this simplistic, dualistic approach is unhelpful in generating understandings of inequality. We suggest that it is necessary to understand gender as a process in which identities are constantly being affirmed, negotiated, limited, and created. By focusing on Young's (1990) conception of social groups, we have drawn attention to the generation of silences around difference, and the control that some groups have over how others are defined. A critical—and often overlooked—element in gender is sexuality, which demands that researchers, teachers, parents, and young people recognise the multiple ways of being male and being female.

An overwhelming amount of research on young people, gender, and sexualities focuses on how this is played out in school sites. This research is important, because it opens up the possibility of developing 'caring and open-minded' environments in all schools as a goal of educational policy in Australia. A recent education policy document urged schools to develop '… policies and strategies concerning overcoming violence, victimisation and harassment, racism and homophobia to increase a sense of belonging and security for students' (Education Victoria 1998). Still more research needs to be done on the ways in which young people contest, negotiate, and experience gender in other settings and dimensions of their lives, such as in families, in leisure settings, and in friendship groups.

Questions for further exploration

1 Identify the main changes in gendered life patterns for young Australians that have occurred between 1976 and 2001.

2 In what ways have gendered patterns remained the same?

3 What are the main arguments in 'the boys' debate and what are the criticisms of the competing victim approach?

4 Describe some of the ways in which discriminatory gendered practices are perpetuated in school settings.

5 How does the assumption of sameness marginalise and stigmatise individuals who are different?

QUESTIONS

PEOPLES, PLACES, AND ETHNIC IDENTITIES 4

Introduction

This chapter explores the ways in which social structures shape the life experiences of ethnic minority youth. The contexts within which these young people are growing up are often very different, and frequently marked by greater social hurdles than those experienced by non-minority young people. Often this translates into perspectives that are one-dimensional and state interventions that are obtrusive and damaging. One concern of the chapter is to explore the social and historical reasons why certain groups of young people are considered to be outsiders and why they are targeted for coercive forms of social control for being so.

Young people who are members of ethnic minority communities are also active agents in the construction and transformation of the world around them. Another theme of the chapter, therefore, is the way in which these young people are creatively and positively shaping their lives and futures. An important part of this analysis is recognition of the complexities of identity and the crucial part that human agency plays in dealing with social structures that are at times oppressive. The discussions below raise questions about who, precisely, is the outsider, a matter that has communal dimensions and global ramifications. And, ultimately, it hinges upon assertions of young people's own voices and their own place(s) in society.

OUTSIDERS, INSIDERS

Many ethnic minority peoples and Indigenous peoples in many different national contexts are considered to be outsiders in the societies in which they live. In part this is due to the manner in which ethnicity and race are socially constructed and experienced in particular local and regional contexts. Minority status refers to being placed in a subordinate position—economically, socially, and politically—within a social structure, which can occur regardless of whether a group makes up a small number or the majority of a population (as in apartheid South Africa). In most cases, though, minority status is associated numerically with a smaller-sized group living within the context of a dominant cultural, ethnic, or racial group. For present purposes the term 'ethnic minority' refers to non-Anglo Australians who are non-Indigenous (Zelinka 1995).

BOX 4.1

Who is a Tasmanian?

■ *Is it someone who lives in Tasmania?* If so, what about ex-patriot Tasmanians in London, New York, Darwin, or Los Angeles of whom other Tasmanians are proud, and for whom they claim Tasmanian status? Is it possible for the overseas-born son or daughter of Tasmanian parents to become a Tasmanian?

■ *Is it someone who identifies strongly with a sense of place?* If so, does it matter that they have only recently arrived, even though they feel grounded in the landscapes of the beautiful island state? Is it possible for the refugee or the asylum seeker to become a Tasmanian?

■ *Is it only those from Anglo backgrounds?* If so, then where do Indigenous Tasmanians fit in? What about those of us who have been here for generations but who do not fit this mould; say, the Dutch, the Polish, and the Sudanese? Is it possible for them to become Tasmanians?

The status of outsider is assigned in several different ways. It is a deviant status (see Becker 1963) in the sense that the minority group is perceived to be intrinsically different from the mainstream group, and to hold to values, attitudes, and behaviours that are deemed to be outside the norm. Deviance is thus constructed in relation to two key criteria: first, on the basis of action norms that refer to particular sorts of behaviour, and thus achieved characteristics (one can become, say, a Muslim and thereby act in accordance with norms of behaviour appropriate to Islam). Second, deviance is based upon certain perceived attributes, and thus ascribed characteristics (skin colour, for example, is something one is born with). When social difference is used as the basis for differential treatment by people and institutions in ways that privilege dominant groups and disadvantage subordinate groups, this is discrimination. Even though formal or institutional discrimination has become legally prohibited, there remains frequent widespread prejudice against minority groups, as a result of which racism and discrimination, sometimes in more subtle forms, may well flourish.

> When social difference is used as the basis for differential treatment by people and institutions in ways that privilege dominant groups and disadvantage subordinate groups, this is discrimination.

One of the sharpest indicators of deviance in relation to minority groups is the relationship between certain groups and the criminal law. As this chapter demonstrates, the social construction of the Other (the outsider) is often done by reference to the notion of transgression of mainstream norms and expectations. A public representation and crystallisation of this transgression is the over-representation of minority groups in certain types of illegal activities, and in their contact with law enforcement agencies and the criminal justice system. Insofar as over-representation occurs, this can and frequently is said to confirm the reasons for the outsider status in the first place.

This interpretation is flawed empirically and politically skewed to the right. Self-report studies have found that there is a 'striking disparity in delinquency self-reports of ethnic minorities and their overrepresentation in police statistics' (Junger-Tas 1994: 179). This highlights the difference between actual offending behaviour and rates (as represented in self-report studies) and the processes of criminalisation whereby certain select groups of teenagers are arrested, charged, and convicted of offences (as represented in official crime statistics). It also brings to the fore issues of unequal representation of particular groups when it comes to the criminalisation process. In one survey of nine Western countries it was observed that:

> Members of *some* disadvantaged minority groups in every Western country are disproportionately likely to be arrested, convicted, and imprisoned for violent, property, and drug crimes. This is true whether the minority groups are members of different 'racial' groups from the majority population, for example, blacks or Afro-Caribbeans in Canada, England, or the United States, or of different ethnic backgrounds, for example, North African Arabs in France or the Netherlands, or—irrespective of race or ethnicity—are recent migrants from other countries, for example, Yugoslavs or Eastern Europeans in Germany and Finns in Sweden (Tonry 1997: 1).

Comparative research on Indigenous peoples and criminal justice in New Zealand, Canada, Australia, and the USA has also found similar patterns of over-representation (Hazelhurst 1995).

Othering as a social process does not only occur in the context of criminal justice; it can also refer to processes of establishing divisions or boundaries between different groups on other bases as well. As discussed later in this chapter, while many formerly minority status groups and individuals have edged into the mainstream of Australian life (particularly second-and-third-generation migrants of other-than-English-language backgrounds), some have chosen not to identify solely or specifically as Australian. The development of multiple identities that span ethnic, national, and international borders is yet another aspect of how globalisation (of communications, of shared experiences) is providing fertile ground for new ways of being on the part of young people.

> The development of multiple identities that span ethnic, national, and international borders is yet another aspect of how globalisation (of communications, of shared experiences) is providing fertile ground for new ways of being on the part of young people.

Constructing the ethnic Other

Racism features prominently in the lives of many ethnic minority youth in Australia. Australia is a polyethnic society, with a population comprising over 100 different countries of origin and over 150 different languages spoken. While ethnically, religiously, and culturally diverse, it is the case that Australia remains dominated by the majority Anglo-Australian population and that particular non-Anglo groups thereby have 'minority' status (Guerra & White 1995). This is reflected in a number of different ways, in terms of culture, economic patterns, and institutional arrangements (see Jamrozik, Boland & Urquhart 1995).

To appreciate fully the situation of ethnic minority young people, analysis has to be sensitive to the diversity of backgrounds and life circumstances of different young people (see White et al. 1999). In other words, the migrant experience varies considerably and this has a major bearing on youth livelihood and experiences. It depends upon such factors as time period of emigration (for example, job opportunities in the 1950s versus high unemployment in the post-1974 period), place of origin and circumstances of emigration (for example, war refugees or flight from an authoritarian regime), relationship between first and subsequent generations (for example, conflicting values), and availability of appropriate services (for example, English-language courses). Particular groups of ethnic minority young people, such as unattached refugee children, are more likely to experience disadvantage than young people with well-established family and community networks.

The contemporary media images and treatments of ethnic minority young people in Australia are generally very negative. Researchers have commented on how these youth are often presented as being homeless, on drugs, members of gangs, school drop-outs, and basically 'bad' and 'dangerous' (Pe-Pua 1996, 1999). The media are seen by young people as a constant source of biased, sensationalist, and inaccurate information about their lives and their communities (Maher et al. 1999; White et al. 1999). It is frequently the case as well that particular events are seized upon by the media to reinforce the ethnic character of deviance and criminality in ways that stigmatise whole communities (Noble et al. 1999; Poynting 1999; Poynting et al. 2001; Collins et al. 2000; Poynting et al. 2004).

The fusion of class and ethnic dynamics is frequently manifest in the form of class-based policies that have direct and indirect negative consequences for ethnic minorities. This is spelt out in some detail in Wilson's analysis of why African Americans are disproportionately over-represented among the jobless in the USA. A crucial factor is the location of many black Americans in segregated ghettos, a process exacerbated by select government policies and programs (Wilson 1996). Similar concentrations of ethnic minority groups in heavily disadvantaged areas are apparent in Sydney in regards to the Lebanese communities (see Collins et al. 2000), with similar consequences to those described by Wilson. So, too, in Germany, segregation based on class and ethnicity is likewise a major problem, with prevailing policies only making things worse. As observed by Heitmeyer (2002: 106), the usual response is threefold:

> First, market expansion is being encouraged to promote individual competitiveness and allegedly make German society more dynamic. This approach ignores that resulting inequities when mapped on persisting spatial segregation will further expand disadvantages of the weaker social groups, including large shares of youth. Campaigns for a new morality, as a second policy thrust, promote normative compliance regardless of the social conditions and the status pressures youth confront on a daily basis. Preference for new measures of repression accompanied by stronger control and surveillance in urban space constitute a third policy approach to manage social change and growing uncertainty.

Somewhat ominously, but realistically, Heitmeyer (2002: 107) adds that 'not surprisingly, when the traditional forms of social recognition through work and mainstream social institutions become increasingly inaccessible, new forms of recognition are sought. Ethnic encapsulation provides a problematic solution to social recognition because it frequently involves cultures of violence'.

Resurgent interest in street gangs and youth groups in North America, Europe, and Australia (Klein et al. 2001; Gordon 2000; White 2006a) provides some indication of the consequences of such policy answers to the underclass problem.

The fusion of class and ethnic dynamics is frequently manifest in the form of class-based government policies that have direct and indirect negative consequences for ethnic minorities.

The presence of identifiable groups of young people in public places has been publicly associated with images that are negative, dangerous, and threatening. This has certainly been the case with youth gangs, and in recent years the hype and sensationalised treatment of youth gangs have tended increasingly to assume a racialised character (White 1996b; see also Lyons 1995; Poynting et al. 2001): the media have emphasised the racial background of alleged gang members, and thereby fostered the perception that, for instance, 'young Lebanese' or 'young Vietnamese' equals 'gang member'. The extra visibility of ethnic minority youth (relative to the Anglo 'norm') feeds the media moral panic over youth gangs, as well as bolstering a racist stereotyping based upon physical appearance (and including such things as language, clothes, and skin colour). Whole communities of young people can be affected, regardless of the fact that most young people are not systematic law-breakers or particularly violent individuals. The result is an inordinate level of public and police suspicion and hostility being directed towards people from certain ethnic minority backgrounds.

As users of public space, ethnic minority youth are particularly visible due to ethnic markers such as physical appearance and language, and because they often congregate in numbers. Whether these groups of young people constitute gangs as such is a matter of systematic research and careful interpretation. Recent studies have examined so-called ethnic youth gangs in a number of Australian cities (Adelaide, Melbourne, and Sydney) and have demonstrated strong media biases against particular groups (for example, Italian, Vietnamese, and Lebanese), conflicts between and within various ethnically identified groups, and a strongly masculine flavour to group formation and activities (see Foote 1993; White et al. 1999; Collins et al. 2000; White 2006a).

The Adelaide study found that periodically there were fights between Italo-Australian young men and other groups (Foote 1993). Conflicts tended to be based on ethnic identification and involve the Italians, the Greeks, and 'the Australians'. Sometimes the Italians and Greeks would find solidarity with each other in their common difference from the Anglo-Australians. It was the 'wogs' versus the 'skips'. Fights tended to occur as a result of taunts and jeers between groups of young people. For the Italo-Australian young men this often took the form of racist discourse that attacked their legitimacy as Australian citizens and residents. ('They call us Wogs and they say go back to Italy.') Group behaviour and group protection reinforces the cohesion and identity of the group as a whole.

The themes of social connection, identity formation, collective protection, and active resistance to racist provocation have surfaced in other studies as well. A Melbourne study of ethnic youth gangs consisted of interviews with young Vietnamese, Somali, Latin American, Pacific Islander, Turkish, and Anglo-Australian young people (White et al. 1999). The study found that membership of a defined group tended to revolve around similar interests (such as choice of music, sport, and style of dress), similar appearance or ethnic identity (such as language, religion, and culture), and the need for social belonging (such as friendship, support, and protection). Group affiliation was simultaneously perceived as the greatest reason that certain young people were singled out as being members of a gang. This identification process was in turn associated with hassles with authority figures, such as the police and private security guards, and conflicts between different groups of young people on the street or at school.

Another study of ethnic minority youth, particularly in relation to the issue of gang-related behaviour, was undertaken in Sydney's Western suburbs (Collins et al. 2000). The research found that the issue of social exclusion appears to be central to any explanation of youth offending involving particularly disadvantaged groups. Marginalisation was also central to explaining the perception of widespread

> The themes of social connection, identity formation, collective protection, and active resistance to racist provocation are evident across a wide range of studies of youth group formation.

involvement in youth gangs among Lebanese youth. Even so, the main forms of association among Lebanese young people were first and foremost friendship groups. These groups also functioned as a defence against experiences of racism and exclusion from the cultural mainstream.

One of the key findings of this recent research is that ethnic background and identity are often equated with gang membership (see White 2006a). Around Australia, the gangs issue is generally associated, specifically, with ethnicity—so much so that in the public eye 'gangs' equals 'ethnic youth'. In the end, the issue is less one of gangs per se, than one of social identity and the frictions associated with group interactions based on ethnic stereotypes.

Zero tolerance and social identity

The social construction of ethnic minority young people as Other through the lens of criminal justice has significant implications for how these young people see themselves and where they fit into the wider society. Ethnicity may be defined simply as a sense of common identity, but how this is forged varies greatly, depending on the group and the young person in question. For many people, ethnicity as such is not a big issue. It is about how we personally feel, rather than about how others react and respond to us:

> For the majority of us, ethnicity is a mixed bag. The way in which we choose to describe and view our ethnicity is based on how we feel about the different elements of our personal, religious and political histories. For instance, a typical third generation Australian is likely to have a mixed religious background (Catholic, Lutheran, Church of England), a varied linguistic background (German, Gaelic, English) and a different sense of allegiance to the various elements of the family history. The individual may identify as a German-Australian or may regard that ancestry as insignificant in their view of themselves. Such an individual is able to choose their ethnic identification (Guerra 1991: 11).

The element of choice has also been expressed in relation to the concept of hybrid ethnic identities. Research with Arabic-speaking male youth in Sydney, for instance, has explored the dynamic ways in which young people, depending upon immediate social context, identified as being 'Lebanese' (regardless of actual national heritage), as 'Australian' (especially in relation to their experiences relative to their parents), and as 'Lebanese–Australian' (which denotes being in two worlds at the same time). The study demonstrated that identity is used in strategic ways; it is not a static entity but varies considerably in terms of different contexts and relationships, such as home and parents, school and leisure spaces, teachers and other students (Noble et al. 1999; see also Butcher & Thomas 2003).

Identity is used in strategic ways; it is not a static entity but varies considerably in terms of different contexts and relationships, such as home and parents, school and leisure spaces, teachers and other students.

Ethnicity is nevertheless crucial to understanding how and why the othering process takes place. It is not static, but it is not entirely about choice either. The Sydney gang research, as one example, has shown how ethnicity is central to the public portrayal of certain young people. They are popularly described as males of 'Middle Eastern appearance', and members of a 'Lebanese gang', despite the fact that the vast majority of Arabic-speaking youth are Australian-born and have grown up in the context of 'Australian' culture (Collins et al. 2000; Noble et al. 1999). The media, political, and law enforcement portrayals, and targeting, have real and pertinent effects at the level of lived practices. They also influence the construction of social identity by the young people themselves.

Consider, for example, the impact of policing in relation to minority groups. So-called zero tolerance policing (see Grabosky 1999; Marshall 1999) is not particularly new as a model of policing when applied to specific communities. Indeed, the history of colonialism and policing in relation to Indigenous young people and their communities is, in essence, a history of selective intolerance (see, for example, Cunneen 1994, 2001). In a similar vein, the experience of negative contact and harassment has been a feature of police–ethnic minority youth relations long before the advent of zero tolerance policing as a media phenomenon (Lyons 1995; Chan 1994). For Indigenous young people, and many ethnic minority youth, zero tolerance describes the normal and routine, rather than the exceptional and innovative.

It is certainly the case that particular ethnic minority youth seem to be aggressively targeted for zero tolerance types of policing (White 2007a). This, in turn, constitutes a major undermining of community policing and of community relations more generally (Poynting 1999). Furthermore, it is frequently linked to specific types of verbal and physical violence and incidents of police maltreatment of young people. The targeting of ethnic minority youth in this way also reinforces a climate of conflict in which social difference and disreputable status are generated, and combined, in the act of police intervention itself. To put it differently, the more you harass and target specific groups, and the more resentful and uncooperative they become, the more likely they will be perceived as and have bestowed on them 'outsider' status generally. One implication of this is that the negative interventions of the police may well feed into wider race debates by virtue of the tendency for minority groups to be vilified for their alleged lawlessness and antisocial behaviours.

In fact, street violence of various kinds does feature strongly in the lives of young people, especially the young men at the centre of the recent studies undertaken in Adelaide, Melbourne, Sydney, Perth, and nationally (White & Mason 2006; White 2006a). In and of itself, this is fairly unremarkable given the prevalence of certain types of aggressive physicality within marginalised and working-class communities. Being tough and engaging in acts that put one's bodily integrity at risk are generally associated with working-class male culture (in its many varieties and permutations). Typically, matters of physique and the physical have been central to working-class forms of aggressive masculinity that celebrates strength, speed, agility, and general physical prowess (White 1997–98). Under conditions of economic disadvantage, social stress, and group marginalisation, there is even greater recourse to the body as a key site for identity construction and affirmation (see Connell 1995, 2000). Thus, a lack of institutional power and accredited social status appear to leave little alternative to physicality as the main form of self-definition, whether this manifests itself as self-destructive behaviour or as violence directed at the Other.

The material basis for this street violence lies in the disadvantages and injuries of social inequality (see White & Perrone 2001). Recent work has provided sophisticated analysis of the ways in which ethnicity, racism, and masculinity combine to reinforce particular kinds of behaviour and group formation (Collins et al. 2000). In regard to issues surrounding ethnicity specifically, Collins, Noble, Poynting, and Tabar (2000: 143) argue that violence and aggression have more to do with questions of status and masculinity than with inter-ethnic conflict. Nevertheless, such conflicts are important in constructing images of, and social responses to, ethnic minority young men.

As discussed previously, the public images of ethnic minority youth are shaped by racialised media portrayals and by the manner in which police intervene in their lives. They are also influenced by actual incidents of violence, such as fights and bullying, between groups of young people on the street. Institutionalised racism (in the form of restrictive life chances and the dominance of monocultural norms), economic marginalisation (in the form of unemployment and poverty), and reliance upon particular notions of masculinity (in the form of reliance on physical and symbolic markers of toughness) put these young people into a particularly vulnerable and volatile social situation. This, in turn, is associated with a central paradox in the lives of ethnic minority youth; specifically, the assertion of identity and collective social power via membership of street groups and engagement in fighting, while forged in the context of rejecting racism and threats from outsiders, simultaneously reinforces the subordinate or outsider position of, and negative social reaction directed towards, these self-same groups of young people.

> The assertion of identity and collective social power via membership of street groups and engagement in fighting, while forged in the context of rejecting racism and threats from outsiders, simultaneously reinforces the subordinate or outsider position of, and negative social reaction directed towards, these self-same groups of young people.

Throughout the Australian research into ethnic youth group formations clear lines of group demarcation were constantly drawn. While membership of any particular group may have been variable (for example, Laotians and an Anglo-Australian being part of the Vietnamese youth formation), there were broad-brush categorisations used to distinguish Australians, Asians, Turkish, Lebanese, and so on. People know who the 'wogs' are (with considerable internal variations in terms of precision and categorisation) and who the 'Aussies' are (with very few qualifications or recognition of internal categorical differences). These social distinctions have been reinforced at a political level; that is, the history of immigration settlement and the particular ways in which multiculturalism has been propagated at an ideological and policy level have undoubtedly contributed to the maintenance of these commonsense divisions (see, for example, Jakubowicz 1989; Jamrozik, Boland & Urquhart 1995; Vasta & Castles 1996). The institutionalisation of difference in ways that embed social inequalities across and within groups is thus a reflection of broad political and economic processes fostered by the Australian state over time.

In concrete terms, the institutional racism and economic marginalisation experienced by ethnic minority young people is directly linked to group formations that function in particular ways to sustain a sense of identity, community, solidarity, and protection. The assertion of identity, and the 'valorisation of respect in the face of marginalisation' (Collins et al. 2000: 150), manifests itself in the form of group membership and group behaviour that privileges loyalty and being tough (individually and as a member of the identified group) in the face of real and perceived outside threats. It also sometimes takes the form of contempt for Aussies (as the dominant social group) and wariness of other ethnic minority groups that likewise are struggling to garner respect and reputation in a hostile environment.

Fundamentally, then, in a political environment in which race politics is a predominant feature (witness the recent controversies over asylum seekers, the appeal of anti-immigration electoral platforms in many different countries, and the ethnic stereotyping associated with terrorism), the spectre of ethnic criminality is effectively bolstered by the actions of ethnic minority youth themselves, as they struggle to negotiate their masculinities, ethnicities, and class situations; that is, the manifest activities of ethnic minority youth can be distorted and sensationalised in ways that portray them as racist, un-Australian, and socially divisive. The association of street fights with racist attitudes, for example, can be used to assert that the victims of systemic social discrimination are in fact the main perpetrators of hate crimes (defined narrowly as prejudice-based offences). An inversion of real relations and social processes is thus made possible (White & Perrone 2001).

Embodying ethnic difference

Physical appearance, body shape, skin colour, and language all provide publicly available signs of difference and commonality. The norm is generally constructed in relation to the dominant white middle class, and white culture training consists not only of socialisation around particular notions of cultural success and failure, but also of the inculcation of ideas about acceptable body appearance and performance (see Harris 2004). Modification of one's hair, bodily appearance, and style of physical performance to fit the presumed norm is highlighted in the case of pop singer Michael Jackson, whose experiences with plastic surgery (much less other issues) are legendary. Extreme though it may be, this example belies the varying ways in which young people from ethnic minority backgrounds are overtly and subtly influenced by pressures to conform, physically, to dominant bodily norms. From advertising to bans on religious symbols (such as head coverings—hijabs—of young Muslim women), the message is that attaining certain modes of dress and physical being is right and good. Yet for many ethnic minority young people, it is precisely their physical appearance that demarcates them as Other in relation to the ethnic mainstream.

Thus, how you look has a great bearing on how you are positioned in the wider society. The closer one comes to looking 'normal', the less one is treated as different. The ethnic Chinese Australian who speaks with a strong Ocker accent constitutes a hybrid identity that fuses physical difference with language commonality. The interplay of various physical, cultural, and social variables in sports, music, schooling, and other collective activities creates space for expression of shared experiences and identification, as well as assertion of difference based upon ethnic characteristics. The body itself is culturally inscribed in ways that, at a taken-for-granted level, reproduce ethnic difference. A recent study of youth gangs in Sydney illustrates this point.

A crucial difference in gang-related behaviour relates to the physicality of the young people involved—the size and shape of their bodies, the cultural context within which they use their bodies, and the circumstances under which violence occurs. The material and ideological basis of group activity includes important aspects of family and cultural group socialisation processes, and different social constructions of what constitutes fun and the enjoyable.

As part of a national study of youth gangs in Australia, fifty young people in the western suburbs of Sydney were interviewed (White 2006b). The interviewees consisted mainly of young men from Samoan, Vietnamese, and Lebanese backgrounds. Their attitudes towards the nature of violence, and in particular their attitudes towards and actual use of weapons, varied greatly according to distinct ethnic group. For some Vietnamese, the use of weapons was intrinsically tied to body size.

> Maybe 'cause we small people you see and the other ones they're so big. If you fight by hand you can't win. (D—, Vietnamese young man)

But there is more to this than just body size. It also has to do with the specific culture surrounding the body.

Physicality is directly related to ethnicity and takes the material form of different body sizes and shapes. The Samoan young people, for example, are heavier and more thick-set than the Vietnamese, who are of slighter build. The physical body is also the site for cultural construction. Every Samoan young person who was interviewed said that he had played rugby (either rugby union or rugby league). Many of the Lebanese young people likewise had experience in playing rugby, or engaging in contact sports, such as boxing. The Vietnamese, if they played a sport at all, tended to pick basketball or martial arts. It was clear from the interviews that the Samoan young people, in particular, really enjoyed the physicality—the roughness, the aggressiveness, and the body pounding—of their chosen sport.

Consideration of the intersection of ethnicity and class as this relates to the body helps us to understand the quite different perceptions regarding weapons use and masculinity, which vary according to social background. Those young men who are socialised into experiencing and enjoying more brutalising forms of contact sport are more likely to favour violence that tests their physical prowess in some way. Those who do not share these experiences or whose physical size limits their ability to engage in unarmed combat are derided by those who can do so.

They can't do bitches—they can't fight with their fists. (F—, Lebanese young man)

Translated: weapons are for those who can't or won't fight. They are for wimps.

I don't know. I reckon they just don't have the balls to throw fists—use their fists. That's mainly with my group we never—we hated like—hated guns and we hated weapons and, I don't know, we just liked our fist and that. (M—, Samoan young man)

Interestingly, there was some suggestion in the interviews that those young men who adopted this kind of attitude were also those most likely to enjoy fights as a form of recreation and fun. They were also most likely to resort to violence as a normal and first reaction to conflict. Fighting, for these young men, is 'naturally' enjoyable, and a 'natural' part of their everyday life. They don't even think twice about resolving an argument by 'giving 'em a smack'. It is an ingrained reflex into which they have been socialised—at the neighbourhood level, at home, and in sports. Fighting is fun precisely because of its physicality and the adrenaline rush accompanying such violence (see also Jackson-Jacobs 2004).

But are the Samoan young men in this study innately more prone to violence than other young men because of their physical build? As demonstrated above, there are other much more complex ways to explain differences in social behaviour among similarly positioned young men than appeal to biology as such.

Even so, biological reductionism continues to make headlines, most recently in regards to the so-called 'warrior gene' allegedly found among Māori men (Dickinson 2006). The monoamine oxidase (MAO) gene was dubbed the warrior gene by US researchers due to its links to aggressive behaviour. Speaking at the International Congress of Human Genetics in Brisbane in August 2006, genetic epidemiologist Rod Lea, of the Institute of Environmental Science and Research based at

Wellington in New Zealand, went one step further. He observed that his research showed that 60 per cent of Māori men have the MAO gene, compared with only 30 per cent of men of European descent. Thus, in this particular view of genetically determined behaviour, the movie *Once Were Warriors* translates into 'Still Are Warriors'.

Extrapolating from this scenario, some might wonder whether the Samoan young people in the study were somehow likewise biologically predisposed to like fighting. Aggression linked to genetic make-up thus provides fertile ground for explanations that conveniently blame the biology rather than the social environment. In this way racist explanations for youth violence are provided yet another airing—and once again the answer is found, literally, in the body of the Other.

MULTIPLE IDENTITIES

Not all young people from ethnic minority backgrounds are criminalised, nor are they necessarily subject to media attacks and universal racial vilification. The fact is that in such a polyethnic country as Australia there is bound to be a strong element of cohesion, as well as dissension, around ethnicity and race issues, partly due to sheer weight of numbers. It is often said, as part of an ongoing urban myth, that Melbourne is the second-largest Greek city in the world (after Athens). Darwin is unique on the island continent in that the white Anglo population constitutes less than 50 per cent of the total city population, the rest mainly comprising people who originally hail from various parts of Asia and the Pacific, and Indigenous peoples. White racism that paints too wide a target will not succeed in such contexts:

> While some young people very consciously claim their ethnic identity, they also link a more tolerant and open-minded attitude in their association with diverse friendship networks. In this way, culturally diverse groups can give young people the ability to associate less problematically with a wider range of 'others', making cross-cultural connections and affiliations. While many of the young people who took part in our research have a sense of exclusion and rejection from mainstream society, for the most part they are not cynical about a commitment to values of tolerance, equality and diversity (Butcher & Thomas 2003: 32).

For many ethnic minority youth, therefore, the key issues do not reside in criminality, but in social placement. Identity, especially in the context of year after year of multicultural government policy, is easier to negotiate than perhaps otherwise might be the case. Rather than giving up one's identity (based on their parents' culture), analysis now suggests that many young people are taking up multiple identities—it is possible to be comfortable with bicultural identities (see Vasta 1995). As mentioned above, it is possible to use one's identity strategically, to be 'different people' depending upon the situation (Nobel et al. 1999; Butcher & Thomas 2003). This implies a substantial sense of agency or choice in everyday affairs.

Rather than giving up one's identity (based on their parents' culture), analysis now suggests that many young people are taking up multiple identities—it is possible to be comfortable with bicultural and transnational identities.

BOX 4.3

Multiple identities

■ Polyethnic country and the weight of numbers:
- many different settler migrant groups
- significant numbers within discrete communities
- geographical concentrations of population groups.

■ The idea of bicultural identities:
- strategic use of identity
- settler migration societies: here to stay
- inclusion and exclusion
- hyphenated identifications.

■ Transnational identification:
- sports and leisure: virtual identities
- religion, language, ethnicity
- transnational and national identities.

Another important facet of group identity is how long and in what ways a community has settled in the host country. It is important to distinguish between nations that have a long tradition of settler immigration (such as Australia and Canada) and those that have generally relied upon transient migrant schemes (such as Germany and Switzerland). Issues of citizenship rights, access to the full benefits of state support, legitimacy and legal status, and so on have a major bearing on the overall positioning of immigrants in any particular society. Moreover, even within settler immigration societies, differences in the settlement process can have a major impact on the integration of communities into the wider social mosaic. Case studies can shed light on the complexity of the process.

The resettlement process for Turkish migrants in Australia, for example, has gone through several distinct phases (see Elley & Ingliss 1995). The earlier stages of this migratory flow were characterised by the immigrants' clear intention to return to Turkey within two or three years of their arrival in Australia. This view was contrary to the expectations of Australian officials, but was a reflection of the more general Turkish experience of emigration, which did not encompass permanent settlement in another country. The many difficulties faced by Turkish immigrants when they arrived in Australia were thus compounded by the fact that immigration was not seen as a permanent decision. In particular, it was to have a major impact on the experiences of the children and grandchildren of these immigrants.

To understand the unique processes of emigration and resettlement as they relate to the Turkish population it needs to be appreciated that the Turkish immigrant experience was based on the guest worker concept, already initiated in Germany and Holland (Basarin & Basarin 1993), which in turn was based on the idea of short-term immigration. The host country invited workers to emigrate as temporary working residents; when their visa expired, the workers then returned to their country of origin. The rapidly industrialised postwar European countries needed workers and temporary labour to fill factory labour shortages. The host countries had no intention of settling the workers permanently and the workers intended to eventually return to Turkey. In these circumstances, permanent immigration from Turkey was rare.

The Turkish emigration program to Australia, though deemed to be a permanent program by Australian immigration officials, was not necessarily seen this way by the Turkish immigrants themselves. The need to find work and save money was of paramount concern. In the early days of the program the intention to return home was to have a great influence on decisions relating to their children. Learning English and developing stable roots in Australia for their family were generally seen as pointless. Little emphasis was placed on maintaining children in school beyond the compulsory age. Rather, children were encouraged to contribute to the family, find work, or support younger siblings, and undertake family responsibilities. The ultimate aim was to prepare the next generation for their future life in Turkey.

This attitude, coupled with the complication of emigrating to a non-Muslim country, led the community to become somewhat insular. In most families, Turkish was the main language, English was not seen as necessary, marriage took place within the community, and the values and practices of the homeland were emphasised. Maintenance of the Turkish language, Turkish community values, and Turkish religion were thus high priorities. The values of the new country were perceived as undesirable, and as encouraging undisciplined, disrespectful social practices in their children.

By the late 1970s, attitudes to immigration started to change. Many families had made attempts to go back and resettle in Turkey, without much success. The Turkey they had left was not the country they found on their return. It had changed. Many people felt that they did not fit in and that they should reconsider their place in Australia. By the 1990s the process of change associated with longer residence and commitment to staying in Australia had gone further, illustrated concretely in a number of ways. For example, young Turkish-Australians had begun to achieve levels of educational attainment closer to the national norms, a situation very different from the schooling experience of earlier immigrant young people. The school retention rate for young people from Turkish backgrounds and their participation in tertiary education has, since the mid 1980s, been higher proportionately than most other groups in Australia, including Anglo-Australians (Inglis 1993).

A study conducted in Melbourne in 1996, with over 300 Turkish young people between the ages of twelve and twenty-five, provides an interesting profile of the needs and concerns of this group (Fontaine & Kaymakci 1996). The study found that the distinctive cultural, religious, and family background of Turkish-Australians led these young people to consider themselves to be different from the mainstream youth population. They saw their Islamic religion and Turkish background, along with their family, as playing an important part in determining their future in terms of identity, marriage, and place of residence. Interestingly, the study also identified that there were a number of key issues that they shared with their non-Turkish youth counterparts—education, employment, a stable environment, and provision of basic social and recreational services were all highly important.

The social place of Turkish young people of the second and third generation in Australia is complex. It is intrinsically intertwined with questions surrounding their identity and the barriers they face in being accepted by mainstream society. Many Turkish-Australian young people are still growing up in families in which material disadvantage, a family experience of limited English, and often limited formal education are the norm (Inglis et al. 1992). While there have been major changes in educational and occupational mobility and advancement with regard to the young people, many parents and newly arrived immigrants have experienced unemployment and diminished job prospects due to the downturn in the manufacturing industry, and in unskilled and semi-skilled employment generally. Meanwhile, their close ethnic identification and religious affiliation have been associated with various forms of prejudice and racism directed at members of the Turkish community, including the young people.

What this case study illustrates is that becoming part of the mainstream is a complicated process, one that involves participation in important social spheres, such as education and work. It can simultaneously involve possible exclusion or distancing from other groups, including the dominant cultural mainstream, due to strategic choices relating to family, kinship networks, ethnic community associations, religious institutions, and political persuasion. One can have a foot in many different camps, depending on the situation and the particular social context.

In the context of longstanding state policies supportive of multiculturalism (see Vasta & Castles 1996), another aspect of the long-term mainstreaming of ethnicity is the assertion of specific ethnic identities within the presumed mainstream. In some respects, this is evident in the appropriation of hyphenated 'ethnic' identifications among young people (as in, for example, Italian-, Greek-, and Vietnamese-Australians). Ethnic pride wrapped around and fused with specific nationalist discourses and identifications implies strong bonds to one's cultural and inter-generational history as well as one's country of destination or birth.

There is also an element of what can be called transnational identification, which takes several different forms. In Australia, for example, it is obvious in the case of spectator sports, such as football (soccer), in which particular ethnic groups are clearly associated with being supporters of particular football teams in other countries (such as England, Italy, Spain, Argentina, and Brazil). Aside from direct Australian involvement in a contest, ethnic or regional identification surfaces strongly in any international contest between nation states in sports such as soccer, rugby union, and cricket. What is important for the present discussion is that such identifications are seen as 'what you do' as a young member of a particular community, which is generally not seen to violate the sense of being Australian. Global communications, corporatisation of sports and leisure (as is the case with Manchester United Football Club, for example), and relatively inexpensive air travel have all contributed to the ability of youth to engage more expansively in the project of using and identifying with diverse social networks. A virtual identity is thus made possible: a non-European (Australian) identifies with being European through the medium of global telecommunications, yet may never have set foot outside the country.

On the other hand, world events are shaking the foundations of identity in varying, and at times very destructive, ways. Many young women who, for instance, adhere to Muslim beliefs as demonstrated by their wearing of the hijab, are, as a result of the wars in Iraq and Afghanistan, the conflict in Palestine and Israel, the Bali bombings, and the events of 11 September 2001 in New York City and Washington, at risk of being attacked on the street because of their overt religious orientation. Big questions can be asked whether measures taken to ensure a modicum of equal opportunity and safe and secure social environments can be maintained in the face of global upheavals. What will happen, for example, to school programs and approaches that take into account the cultural and religious issues for Muslim youth in the light of recent events (see Hicks & Moh'd 1995)? Research into issues of ethnic identity shows that when pressure is put on young people, whether through racism or in the light of world events, there is some likelihood that they will construct their identity in ways that are more one-dimensional than ought to be the case (see Noble et al. 1999). Nationalism has many different guises and pertains to many different social situations and groups. It is also easily intertwined with religion, sense of ethnicity, race, and other socially constructed categories.

The notion that there are transnational ethnic identities bears close scrutiny. Does talk of the actions and perspectives of 'the Arab world' implicate all Arabic people, regardless of where they live? Is 'Latino' a distinctive ethnic identification, regardless of type of Spanish spoken, very different national contexts, and the diverse movement of people into non-Spanish countries? Does being Islamic, or Christian, or Jewish actually mean sameness in culture, politics, and social mores around the globe? To address these kinds of questions we need sustained analysis of how young people are positioned within certain communities and within their own communities. Globalisation may well lead to supranational identity formation ('I am Muslim first, and Australian second'). But, just as easily, it could be argued that it is racism, exclusive definitions of national citizenship, or social inequality that leads to this kind of transnational identity.

How countries respond to and treat asylum seekers is also an important signal to ethnic minority groups within the social structure. In countries such as Australia, which permit the detention of children of 'illegal immigrants' in poorly resourced detention centres, there is a strong message that 'third-world-looking immigrants' (see Hage 1998) do not belong in this country. This, too, must have a major bearing on how others, already within the Australian community, see themselves and those around them. Problems of transition for some are thus transposed into problems of settlement for others. The challenges of identification and social belonging do not diminish.

This latter point is partly borne out in US research that examined the nature of ethnic identity choices among Asian-Americans. The study found that two-thirds of the respondents preferred to identify themselves in ethnic-specific modes (that is, in relation to particular ethnic identifiers, rather than simply American as such). It was pointed out that although only one in six of the respondents preferred to identify themselves in hyphenated terms — as Asian-American — almost 60 per cent of the respondents indicated acceptance of this pan-ethnic term as part of their identification (Lien et al. 2003). Certainly the Australian experience is that long political traditions of anti-Asian sentiment have had a profound impact on the place and social position of contemporary Asian residents and citizens; it continues to influence mainstream Anglo-Australian attitudes towards their non-Anglo neighbours and is a contributing causal reason for various forms of hate crime directed at the Other, even when the Other has lived in this country for many generations (see White 1997a).

Summary

In tandem with similar processes in many other Western countries (see Males 1996; Muncie 1999; Schissel 1997), marginalised young people in Australia are being systematically criminalised as a distinctive class of youth. The criminalisation of these youth is simultaneously accompanied by high-profile media campaigns of racially based vilification. They are being treated as a problem, and they are being seen as a problem.

Meanwhile, the activities of the young people in banding together to protect themselves from real and potential threats, to valorise their existence through assertion of collective physical power and public presence, reinforces the processes of exclusion—and social containment. In the end, broad contradictions of social structure relating to immigration and racism are made manifest in the practical realities of territoriality and identity formation in the public domains of the street.

In the midst of such turmoil, the sounds and movements of multiculturalism beat strong: the realities of a pluralistic society are demonstrated daily in the passengers on the bus, the tram, the train, the freeway—people of all cultures travel to work and school together. There are, too, strong commercial reasons why 'multicultural capitalism' is to be preserved and fostered (see White 1998a; Castles 1996), even in the face of racist vilification associated with imperialist wars and populist right-wing movements directed against immigrants and ethnic minority people. Within this structural context, young people of ethnic minority background continue to struggle and to assert their identity, as they wish, and, as much as is possible, on their terms.

As this chapter has demonstrated, identity construction takes place at many different levels and has a range of social dimensions. It is, for example, both global and local in nature. We are who we are, depending upon our social location within different spaces (local, regional, national, and international) and different communities (rural, urban, ethnically centred, religious, national, and global)—and we are all of these, simultaneously. To answer the question of, say, who is a Tasmanian, then, requires a sense of ambiguity and complexity.

BOX 4.4

Who are we?

- We are able to be Tasmanian by virtue of where we live (in Glenorchy, Burnie, Geeveston, or Bruny Island), by virtue of those with whom we connect (friends, neighbours, work colleagues, and students), and through the institutions of social connection (school, work, shopping, and leisure).

- We are also not-Tasmanian by virtue of our global links (with the motherland or country of origin in England, Italy, Brazil, Sudan, Canada, or ancient links to this land that pre-date the European presence), and by virtue of our supraregional or supranational community affiliations (as a Christian, Muslim, Latino, Jew, Arab, or Francophone).

- We are also Tasmanian or not-Tasmanian by choice. Insults, hate crimes, and racial vilification create a climate of alienation, distrust, and rejection. Who wants to become Tasmanian when faced with this?

Given that this generation of young people is a globally aware generation—the generation of the Internet—it is essential to acknowledge as well that this awareness opens up the world of possibility for everyone. The immigrant, the refugee, the Outsider brings the world directly into places such as Australia. To not value this is to shunt it aside, the net result of which would be to lose the diversity and resources that these young people bring to our communities. After all, who wants to stay in one-dimensional space, especially when it is apparent to anyone with a computer link that the world is dynamic, complex, colourful, and exhilarating? It is the diversity of peoples and places that make it so.

It is time to realise that young people are themselves living these multiple identities, here and now. They are acting in these multiple worlds and acting on them. A particular personal dilemma for young people, and a social problem generally, is that rarely are these multiple identities made visible. Instead, caricatures—usually based upon food, dance, music, and costume—are dragged out as definers of ethnic affiliation. Separate boundaries are placed upon what is permitted as a public identity and what is to be left as a private identity.

What we ought to be celebrating is the beauty and complexity of our multiple identities, and these, in turn, need to be valued and cherished in the public domain. As research consistently shows, young people want, need, and have a right to a space of their own. Asserting their multiple identities is part of this wider social process of gaining acceptance, legitimacy, and authority. In many cases, as well, it is the outsider who has the most to offer in terms of building bridges between peoples and cultures.

Linked together by place and people, yet cognisant of our multiple identities and social connections, it is in our hands to shape and define our collective identity. And so the process of renewal and reinvigoration continues, over and over again.

Questions for further exploration

1   We are all ethnic. Discuss.

2   A central theme of this chapter is that identity is variable and that young people construct their identity in multiple ways. Is this relevant to how you think about yourself and your ethnic background?

3   What are the objective and subjective elements that go into the social construction of ethnicity?

4   What is racial vilification and how does it affect how young people think about themselves and engage with the wider world around them?

5   In what ways, historically and in contemporary circumstances, can the outsider become an insider?

QUESTIONS

5

INDIGENOUS YOUTH AND SOCIAL IDENTITY

Introduction

This chapter explores the dynamics of the experiences of Indigenous young people, with the main focus on Indigenous youth in the Australian context. The fundamental backdrop to these experiences is colonialism and the terrible legacies of invasion and dispossession. The structural disadvantages generated in and through the colonial process are acknowledged as playing a major part in the lives and prospects of young Indigenous people today. Colonialism has shaped their past and their present. It continues to heavily influence the contours of their future.

Yet, in the midst of devastating histories and oppressive contemporary practices, the story of this chapter is also one of survival and assertion of being. Close scrutiny of the issues reveals ambiguities, paradoxes, and opportunities that make the experiences of Indigenous peoples very difficult to generalise about (for example, everyone within this group experiences the world in the same way) or to pigeonhole (for example, there are essential traits that provide the common link among this specific population group). In other words, the complexities of Indigenous experience demand sensitivity to the exercise of agency among these youth and recognition of very different life experiences, depending upon geographical location and immediate social circumstances.

CONSTRUCTING THE INDIGENOUS OTHER

To understand fully the issues and conflicts pertaining to Indigenous young people, it is essential to acknowledge the continuing legacy and present realities of colonialism in the lives of Indigenous peoples (see Cunneen 2001; Johnston 1991: vol. 2). Since British invasion, the Indigenous peoples of Australia—the Aboriginal peoples and the Torres Strait Islander peoples—have been subjected to myriad interventions, exclusions, and social controls. This is not simply a historical legacy; it is part of the fabric of everyday life for many Indigenous peoples today. The modes of imposed state intervention varied from place to place around the country and took different forms at different times, including, for example, open warfare and resistance through to periods of 'protective' legislation and the struggle for self-determination (Cunneen 1994, 2001).

> To understand fully the issues and conflicts pertaining to Indigenous young people, it is essential to acknowledge the continuing legacy and present realities of colonialism in the lives of Indigenous peoples.

Colonialism has had a severe impact on Indigenous cultures and ways of life, as have the continuing effects of discriminatory policies and practices on Indigenous life chances within mainstream social institutions. The dislocations and social marginalisation associated with colonialism have had particular ramifications for Indigenous young people. It is worth noting that, historically, and in particular, young Indigenous women were prone to policies that were intended to separate them from their families and communities, and that constituted a form of cultural and physical genocide (see Goodall 1990). Today, it has been argued that, rather than breaking up of communities on the basis of a welfare or protectionist rationale, the same thing is occurring through systematic 'criminalisation' of young Indigenous people, although the main target now is young men (*Report of the National Inquiry into the Separation of Aboriginal and Torres Strait Islander Children from Their Families* [*NISATSIC*] 1997; Cunneen 1994).

The negative impact of constant state intervention into the families and communities of Indigenous peoples cannot be underestimated or understated. The Stolen Generations Inquiry estimated that between one in ten and one in three Indigenous children, depending on the period and location, were removed from their families between 1910 and 1970; most Indigenous families have thus been affected by this phenomenon (*NISATSIC* 1997: 37). The earlier policies of forced removals continue to have contemporary effects (Cunneen & Libesman 2007: 146).

> Twice as many Indigenous people who were removed as children reported being arrested; those who were removed reported significantly poorer health (*NISATSIC* 1997: 15). Almost one in ten boys and just over one in ten girls reported that they were sexually abused in children's institutions; one in ten boys and three in ten girls reported they were sexually abused in a foster placement (*NISATSIC* 1997: 163). There has also been a range of complex trauma-related psychological and psychiatric effects that have been intergenerational. These relate to issues such as parenting skills, unresolved grief and trauma, violence, depression, mental illness, and other behavioural problems. A survey by the Aboriginal Legal Service in Western Australia of 483 Aboriginal people who had been forcibly removed found that a third had also had their children removed (*NISATSIC* 1997: 226). Indigenous children are still significantly overrepresented in contact with welfare agencies. Nationally, around 20 per cent of children in care are Indigenous. A significant proportion of such children are placed with non-Indigenous families, which is particularly the case for those in long-term foster care (Cunneen & Libesman 2001).

The nature of state intervention—whether for welfare or criminalisation purposes—has had a profound effect on Indigenous ways of life, their relationship to authority figures such as the police, and to the experiences of young Indigenous people as they grow up in a (post)colonial context.

There is a close relationship between social marginalisation (incorporating racial discrimination and economic and social exclusion) and criminalisation (which constitutes one type of state response to marginalisation). This is demonstrated in a South Australian study (Gale, Bailey-Harris & Wundersitz 1990) that showed that Indigenous juveniles were more likely to have contact with, and intensive interventions into their lives by, the criminal justice system precisely because of their low income and marginalised social status. Extensive research has been undertaken in recent years on the over-representation of Indigenous peoples in the criminal justice system, research that has provided considerable evidence of over-representation in most jurisdictions, and particularly at the most punitive end of the system, in detention centres (Johnston 1991; Beresford & Omaji 1996; Cunneen & White 2007; *NISATSIC* 1997).

> There is a close relationship between social marginalisation (incorporating racial discrimination and economic and social exclusion) and criminalisation (which constitutes one type of state response to marginalisation).

A number of explanations have been put forward to explain these levels of over-representation (see, for example, Lincoln & Wilson 1994b; Smandych, Lincoln & Wilson 1995; Cunneen & McDonald 1996; Snowball & Weatherburn 2006). These generally include such elements as racist bias, cultural factors, discriminatory application of laws, over-policing, offender and offence characteristics, and Indigenous resistance against colonial authorities. The social marginalisation of many Indigenous young people is a major contributing factor to engaging in offensive and criminal behaviour or being perceived as a problem to be dealt with via the criminal justice system (Gale, Bailey-Harris & Wundersitz 1990; Cunneen 1994).

At the same time, a condition of marginalisation should not be universalised in such a way as to suggest that Indigenous peoples as a whole are somehow automatically passive victims of history (as discussed further below). In addition, there is the need to understand social disadvantage within the context of colonialism, dispossession, the destruction of an Indigenous peoples' economic base, and specific colonial policies such as child removal (*NISATSIC* 1997). Aboriginal and Torres Strait Islander peoples are not simply a disadvantaged minority group in Australia; they are the Indigenous peoples of Australia whose current socioeconomic status derives from a specific history of colonisation, and whose political status as Indigenous people gives them a number of rights and entitlements (see Cunneen & White 2007). One also has to take into account the close scrutiny and constant surveillance of Indigenous peoples by government authority figures that has accompanied the colonial project up to and including today.

Some facts about Australian Indigenous peoples

BOX 5.1

- The Aboriginal and Torres Strait Islander population of Australia is estimated to be about 2.4 per cent of the total Australian population

- The Indigenous population is relatively young compared with the non-Indigenous population. In 2001, 39 per cent of Indigenous peoples were under fifteen years of age, compared with 20 per cent of non-Indigenous people.

- In 2002, 74 per cent of Indigenous adults reported the presence of neighbourhood or community problems; for those living in cities and regional centres, the most commonly reported problems were theft and noisy or dangerous driving, whereas those in remote areas reported alcohol, problems involving youth, and illegal drugs.

- In 2002, 18 per cent of Indigenous adults had completed Year 12, compared with 44 per cent of non-Indigenous adults.

- In 2002, Indigenous adults were about two and a half times as likely as non-Indigenous adults to be unemployed.

■ The mean equivalised gross household income of Indigenous adults in 2002 was only 59 per cent of the corresponding income of non-Indigenous adults.

■ Over one in twenty (6 per cent) of all Indigenous males aged 25–29 years were in prison at 30 June 2004 (compared with 0.5 per cent or about one in 200 non-Indigenous males aged 25–29 years).

■ Indigenous peoples suffer greater ill-health, are more likely to experience disability and reduced quality of life, and to die at younger ages than are other Australians

Source: Australian Bureau of Statistics and Australian Institute of Health and Welfare 2005.

BOX 5.1

Perhaps the most crucial factor in terms of the public identity and public life of young Indigenous people is the nature of policing as this pertains to them. Various studies in recent years have highlighted the frequently negative interaction between young Indigenous people and the police (Cunneen 1990a, 2001; Human Rights and Equal Opportunity Commission 1991; White & Alder 1994; Blagg & Wilkie 1995). Many of the confrontations between Indigenous young people and the police take place in the public domains of the streets, parks, malls, and shopping centres. The visibility and minority status of Indigenous peoples, their association in groups, and the historical antagonisms between police and Indigenous communities (it has generally been the police who have taken children away from Indigenous families, for example) contribute to ongoing tension and conflict between the parties.

Indigenous peoples are subject to police intervention at a much higher rate than non-Indigenous people. In many cases, this involves the use of street offence types of legislation to a much higher degree than that associated with non-Indigenous people. A recent New South Wales study (Jochelson 1997) found that local government areas with high percentages of Indigenous peoples tended to have higher rates of court appearances for public order offences such as offensive behaviour and offensive language. There was an over-representation of Indigenous peoples among the alleged offenders for offensive behaviour or offensive language in those local government areas with high Indigenous populations and those with low proportions of Indigenous peoples' in their population (see also White 2002a).

Offensive language: by whom, to whom?

A young Indigenous man in Dubbo, New South Wales (a country town), was riding a bicycle in the vicinity of a petrol station when he was stopped by two police officers. They asked him to approach the police vehicle, which he did. The police enquired about the ownership of the bike. Dissatisfied with the answer, the officers advised that they would be taking the bike to the police station to determine who the owner was. One of the officers placed his hands on the handle bars. In response the young person pulled the bike from the officer's grasp and said, 'Fuck off. You're not taking the bike'. He was arrested for offensive language and later with resisting police and having goods in custody.

BOX 5.2

BOX 5.2

There are several issues that need to be highlighted here. First, the offences are very often precipitated by the intervention of the police in the first place: the police approach Indigenous people for some reason and then become the victim of the offences (Cunneen 2001: 97). Second, except for a notional community, the victim of the offence is almost invariably the police officer (Cunneen 2001: 29). Third, the language in question has variable usages and meanings, and it is questionable whether the police would themselves be genuinely offended by it.

Offensive language is ultimately a matter of meaning, intent, and context. What is particularly galling for many Indigenous peoples, young and old, is the way in which some police speak to them. Young people report being called names such as 'nigger', 'boong', and 'coon' by police (Beresford & Omaji 1996: 81). Cunneen (1991) examined language issues when interviewing young Indigenous detainees and found that police were often racist and sexist in talking with the young people, referring to young Indigenous women as 'black cunts'. Bad language and name-calling were also mentioned in submissions to the Royal Commission into Aboriginal Deaths in Custody: 'What's your fucking name?', 'Where is fucking such and such … ', 'Aboriginal dog', 'Fuck off inside', 'You smell stinking' (Johnston 1991b: 414–15).

The ordinary language of the police, whether directed specifically at Indigenous peoples, and used among themselves, has been found to be replete with words such as 'fuck' and 'cunt'. In one 1996 legal case, a probationary constable made a complaint about the use of offensive language in her workplace. On appeal, the case was dismissed on the basis that 'everyone' used the word 'fuck', and that it was part of 'police culture' (see Brown et al. 2001: 964–5). Yet the use of offensive language charges is on the increase, and this increase continues to disproportionately affect Indigenous peoples.

Source: edited extracts from White 2002a.

Historically, and to a somewhat lesser extent today, state intervention in the lives of young people who are visible in public places such as the street has ostensibly also been premised on a social welfare concern. Goodall (1990) documents how young Indigenous women were subjected to systematic removal from their families, and that they bore the heaviest impact of such policies between 1900 and 1940. Much concern was expressed about the moral danger of Indigenous girls, a phenomenon that has its counterpart in contemporary expressions of unease about young women's public presence as being somehow 'harmful to the local community' (Carrington 1990). The visibility of young women on public streets also makes them targets for police law-and-order campaigns (Payne 1990).

Cunneen and Robb (1987) examined the nature of such law-and-order campaigns in north-west New South Wales in the mid 1980s. They found that the campaigns were largely orchestrated by local power elites in the country towns, and that the key targets of the campaigns were Indigenous people. The calls for more police and increased police powers were equated with clearing the streets of Indigenous people, who were presented as, in essence, the criminal problem. Similar types of research, particularly into the media treatment of Indigenous young people, have likewise found that they are represented almost exclusively in criminal terms (see Sercombe 1995; Hil & Fisher

1994). Attempts to regulate cultural activity and social space by authorities has, for all intents and purposes, become a quest to police specific groups of people precisely because of who they are (that is, Indigenous peoples).

Young Indigenous people are very conscious of the dynamics of racism and policing. Interviews with young Indigenous people in Darwin and Alice Springs made this very clear (see White 1999). When asked about the things that most influence the way other people view them when they were hanging out in public space, the young people most frequently mentioned racism, stereotypes of young people, and the fact that many older people did not seem to like young people hanging around together in groups. It would appear that the feelings of exclusion and undue harassment experienced by many of these young people were the result of negative reactions to them based on a combination of Indigenous status, age, and class position. Typical comments by the young people included:

Being black, people think you are going to commit a crime. (Young man)

Where old people are they stare at us if we're sitting there as if we have no right to sit there, treat us bad and serve us last. We still go but. (Young woman)

Darker skin makes them think we're troublemakers. Some other people just stare at us, some keep walking, some look dirty daggers at us. (Young woman)

I hate going down the shops. They [shop owners] always saying, 'Oh, you been shoplifting'. Everyone gets always accused of shoplifting round here. You can't window shop and browse. You can't even price something. You got to walk in there with the money and buy it there and then. (Young woman)

The position of young Indigenous people in Australian society makes them very vulnerable to over-policing and exclusionary practices. It also makes them angry (White 1999):

The young kids, it's not fair, they being treated like a dog. I mean, they want young kids to get off the street and stop drinking and smoking, but what's the use, it's their choice—we got a right to hang around and do all that, it's just our life, but some people they think that's the wrong way. See, the reason why that mob [particular group of people] smashed the windows and that is because people put 'em off, like people, like, watch 'em, tell 'em to fuck off or something like that, but they just get sick of it and then they just go mad. (Young woman)

This anger has also been captured in a more recent study of street-present young people in Brisbane. The young Indigenous people who were interviewed engaged in paint sniffing (chroming), which attracted pubic attention. In response, they were subjected to intensive forms of policing that was constant and perceived as highly intrusive. As one sixteen-year-old girl commented:

The police are all arseholes. They just harass ya for nothing. They just like … I dunno, they wanna pick on someone … you gotta have the colour skin White … we gotta shed our skins just to walk down the street (quoted in Ogwang, Cox & Saldanha 2006: 420).

As illustrated here, the depth of feeling is in part due to perceptions of racial bias, the sense of injustice when no apparent harm is being perpetrated, and the bad relationship between authority figure and street kid. While chroming ought to be dealt with as a health or welfare problem, it would appear that the young people experience it mainly through the lens of criminalisation (Ogwang et al. 2006).

Until mainstream Australia comes to grips with the continuing legacies of colonialism and the persistent unequal treatment of Indigenous peoples, it is unlikely that present conflicts will be ameliorated. Being made an outsider in one's own land means that just solutions can only be found when visions of restorative social justice are put into concrete practice (see Blagg 1998).

Dynamics of Indigenous identity

As Palmer and Collard (1993) comment, Indigenous young people are active contributors to wider youth culture, are varied in their interests and aspirations, and have made a wide number of achievements in the mainstream of Australian social life.

Indeed, one of the persistent difficulties faced by Indigenous young people is the image they have as offenders and, somewhat ironically, as victims. In forging their own identities and careers, many Indigenous peoples have to confront direct racist representations, as well as a subtle and not so subtle form of reverse, and selective, discrimination. On the one hand, in the public domain of the press and electronic media, aboriginality is closely linked to criminality (see Sercombe 1995). On the other hand, in much academic writing, aboriginality is portrayed in passive, victim terms (see Palmer & Collard 1993). Either way lends itself to stereotypical, rather than more realistic or accurate, views of being Indigenous in a colonial society.

BOX 5.3

Popular misconceptions and problematic premises

- Over-emphasis of the substance abuse and criminal activities of Indigenous young people.
- Denial of contemporary Indigeneity and cultural continuity and assuming Indigenous social disorganisation is at the base of problems for Indigenous young people.
- Focusing most research attention on the activities and lives of Indigenous young people living in rural and remote communities.
- Lacking specificity and assuming homogeneity among youth and young Indigenous people.
- Separating Indigenous young people from their families and communities.
- Adopting an anti-historical or Anglo-historical analysis that relies on non-Indigenous constructions of history, which are often couched in negative, victim-centred, and static aspects of Indigenous peoples' history.
- Viewing Indigenous culture as so distinct and different and regarding Indigenous young people as so marginalised that they only spend time and share cultural experiences with other Indigenous young people.
- Assuming that Indigenous young people experience personal and social problems because of boredom and a lack of meaningful things to do.

Source: Palmer & Collard 1993.

Just as the nature of state intervention emerged differently in different locations around Australia, so, too, the contours of Indigenous life and the response to colonialism have varied considerably within the Indigenous population, which is to say Indigenous peoples are heterogeneous in composition. There are differences within the varying communities and between individuals in terms of political and spiritual beliefs, regional and family ties, traditional and contemporary lifestyles, class and occupational position, and social identity. These differences are crucial to acknowledge in any consideration of specific issues pertaining to Indigenous youth.

> Just as the nature of state intervention emerged differently in different locations around Australia, so, too, the contours of Indigenous life and the response to colonialism have varied considerably within the Indigenous population.

Nevertheless, popular images and representations of Indigenous young people tend to over-emphasise criminal activities and substance abuse while ignoring the significant proportions of young people not implicated or engaged in these activities (Palmer & Collard 1993). Other distorted or one-sided representations are apparent as well. There is, for example, the underlying assumption that all Indigenous young people, regardless of family background, have similar issues and life chances. This assumption leads to little appreciation of social differences within the Indigenous population, apart from social differences that separate the Indigenous and the non-Indigenous. Differences within the Indigenous population are evident in regards to class, gender, and ethnic differences within communities (for example, tribal and family associations, as well as language), which manifest themselves in diverse ways, depending upon immediate social context. A well-paid English-speaking Indigenous woman who is a state official living in an urban centre is very differently placed from an unemployed non-English-speaking Indigenous man who lives in an outback community and is reliant upon state welfare. Yet both share a colonial history of invasion, oppression, and resistance. Both may be subjected to ongoing and persistent racism at a personal and an institutional level.

Some facts about Indigenous peoples

- In 2001, 30 per cent of Indigenous peoples lived in major cities, about 43 per cent in regional areas, and about 27 per cent in remote areas; more than 90 per cent of Indigenous peoples in New South Wales, Victoria, Tasmania, and the Australian Capital Territory lived in major cities of regional areas.
- In 2002, just over half of Indigenous peoples aged fifteen years or over reported that they identified with a clan, tribal, or language group.
- In 2002, 21 per cent of Aboriginal and Torres Strait Islander peoples aged fifteen or over spoke an Indigenous language.
- In 2002, 70 per cent of Indigenous peoples aged fifteen years or over reported that they recognised homelands or traditional country (although they may not necessarily live there) compared with 75 per cent in 1994.
- The proportion of Indigenous adults aged 18 and over who had completed Year 12 increased from 10 per cent in 1994 to 18 per cent in 2002.

BOX 5.4

BOX 5.4

■ Indigenous retention to Year 10 and beyond steadily increased between 1996 and 2004, and was particularly evident at Year 11 level, where the apparent retention rate from Years 7/8 rose from 47 per cent in 1996 to 61 per cent in 2004.

Source: Australian Bureau of Statistics and Australian Institute of Health and Welfare 2005.

The issue of difference and commonality impacts upon Indigenous youth in myriad ways. In simple terms, there are major tensions and contradictions evident within the Indigenous communities themselves; likewise, there are difficulties and opportunities that reside in the relationship between Indigenous peoples and non-Indigenous people. In the case of the former, a key issue is that of identity; in the latter, it is recognition that coexistence is always a two-way street. We have to be aware that the circumstances of Indigenous peoples, collectively and individually, do change over time and that different sections of the Indigenous community have quite different social experiences. A number of contemporary issues can be identified that provide some indication of the dynamics of growing up Indigenous in Australia today.

Identity

A major issue facing many Indigenous young people is who, precisely, are they? This is by no means an easy question to answer. Recent musings on the nature of indigeneity and, indeed, identity generally, have provided striking illustrations of the incredible complexities of defining who we are. Paradies (2006) points out that many Indigenous people are simultaneously non-Indigenous—they have European and Asian ancestry as well as Aboriginal and Torres Strait Islander ancestry. Furthermore, about half of all Indigenous people in committed relationships have a non-Indigenous partner. Yet, as Paradies observes, 'despite this heterogeneity in the Indigenous community, asserting a multi-racial Indigenous identity is neither common nor straightforward because racial loyalty demands that anomalous individuals choose to be either exclusively Indigenous or exclusively non-Indigenous … '(2006: 357).

As Canadian research illustrates, diverse ancestry and the presence of diverse family forms reinforces the fact that Indigenous peoples are heterogeneous, thus undermining the value of portrayals of a 'collective Indian personality' as such. Rather, cultural investigations have identified 'numerous family types including traditional, transitional, bicultural, and pan-traditional'. A distinction is made between the idea of measuring 'Indianness' and describing different transactional styles among Indian families (Webster & Nabigon 1993). To identify as Indigenous is not to impose a rigid definition of how to be Indigenous.

The picture gets even more complicated, especially in the light of the information presented in the facts box in this section (regarding language, identification with others, and so on), and with reference to Paradies's own personal experience:

Due, in large part, to my grandmother being a member of the Stolen Generations, I do not speak an Aboriginal language, I do not have a connection with my ancestral lands or a unique spirituality inherited through my Indigeneity, I have little contact with my extended family, and the majority of my friends are non-Indigenous. Also due to this same history, I am a middle-class, highly educated professional working in the field of Indigenous research. As such I am frequently interpellated as Indigenous and called upon to deploy my Indigeneity in a professional context, while at the same time I am labelled by some as an inauthentic 'nine-to-five black' or a 'coconut', who has stolen the place of a 'real Aborigine' … (Paradies 2006: 358).

As also noted by Cowlishaw (2006), there are struggles between respectable and disreputable Indigenous identities, much of which revolve around varying interpretations of essentialism in defining key traits of indigeneity. The contest is over the real or authentic Aboriginal or Torres Strait Islander, as defined by biological, cultural, and social criteria. One consequence of the tensions arising from this contest is that the search for and assertion of Indigenous identity can be a long, convoluted, and distressing process for some young people.

Deviance

For those who do identify and who are identified as Indigenous, the social world may be filled with complex expectations and, in some cases, violence. A study of street-present young people in urban centres has shown that many felt uncomfortable with their status, especially after seeing how their parents were treated by non-Indigenous people, and so the streets and crime become an alternative measure of who they are and the meaning of success (Johnston 1991). Other research (Ogwang, Cox & Saldanha 2006) has demonstrated that the harder authorities push, and the more vilified they are by members of the general public, the more likely marginalised young Indigenous people are to engage in activities such as chroming.

For young people in remote communities, the response to marginalisation, unemployment, and social devalorisation has included more than self-medication such as petrol sniffing. The small town of Wadeye in a remote area of the Northern Territory, for example, made national headlines in 2004 due to emergence of a new kind of gang culture (Toohey 2004). Hundreds of adults and children were forced to flee the town because of the high levels of violence perpetrated by members of groups with names such as Judas Priest and the Evil Warriors: houses were trashed and elders ignored. The fusion of contemporary music with extreme alienation and group violence shows that identity is diversely and oppositionally constructed within indigeneity as well as in relation to the non-Indigenous.

Disapproval of their dress, manner, speech, and other behaviour by members of the general public can foster continued and renewed antisocial behaviour on the part of some Indigenous young people (Ogwang et al. 2006). But the amplification of this spiral has its starting point in the original marginalisation of these particular young Indigenous people. Infighting of the kind witnessed in Wadeye could be analysed in terms of masculinity, territoriality, and other conventional gang research concepts, but, fundamentally, the deviance is grounded in the material conditions and cultural realities of the specific young people involved. Without addressing these kinds of factors in either case, no amount of coercive intervention will succeed in putting out the fires of frustration, humiliation, and separation.

Work

Employment trends and workplace figures indicate substantial overall improvements in the prospects of young Indigenous people in the last decade (see box statistics above). Improvements in school retention rates have undoubtedly assisted this process. It is important to realise that (measuring) unemployment is not the only way in which to consider the work life and prospects of Indigenous young people. Indeed, the perception of Indigenous peoples as lazy—stereotypes that together with criminality constitute the master frame for Indigenous youth—means that the real story of Indigenous labour is rarely told.

The historical contribution of Indigenous peoples to present-day Australia is regularly ignored in public discussion and academic scholarship. Yet, as various writers emphasise, there are many examples of Indigenous participation as guides, farm workers, cattlemen, carers of children, government advisers, police assistants and trackers, interpreters, and generally as builders of the Australian economy (Haebich 1988; Reynold 1990; Palmer & Collard 1998; Collard & Palmer 2006). The hard work and labour of young Indigenous people is well captured in the following quotation from a Western Australian Indigenous (Nyungar) elder:

> Our mob we cleared and built all that run from Brookton, York, Beverley right through as far as Kondinin. For years young blokes (Nyungars) sheared the majority of the sheep in that area. You talk to the older Nyungar yorgas (women) … when they was younger they brought up and looked after all them kids from the big farming families … we built the fences, milked the cows, repaired the roads, we did everything (quoted in Palmer & Collard 1998: 28).

Having something productive to do is essential to self-esteem and confidence in oneself. Knowledge of how Indigenous peoples have contributed and continue to contribute to the wider political economy is important to this as well.

Education

All young people have to come to grips with who they are, and what they can become, drawing upon the best of the past and the engaging with the opportunities of the future. In regard to education, this has meant consideration of what has been described as two-way schooling, especially in regard to community schools in northern Australia.

Community elders want their kids to move across cultural domains, to experience education in Western schooling and in traditional lore and custom, and be capable of code switching and crossing cultural zones:

> Two-way schooling involves the separation of work into at least two educational and cultural domains, the Yolngu (Indigenous) and the Balanda (Western). This approach demands a commitment to seeing Yolngu custodians of knowledge working with Western-trained Balanda teachers selected for their educational skills in Western content (Collard & Palmer 2006: 29).

This model of learning assumes a two-culture schooling regime, an idea that is useful to explore for Indigenous and non-Indigenous people alike. There is no dispute that education of varying kinds—including via family and elders—is crucial to the development of a sense of self, to better health and well-being, and to brighter economic prospects. Where such education enhances social, cultural, linguistic, and vocational skills, and the capacity to critically think about and interact with the wider world around them, then this is empowering education indeed.

Family ancestry

It has been pointed out that in some (usually regional and remote) communities there may well be a majority of residents with black and white forebears, even if this remains unsaid or is lost in the identification of being one identity or the other. As Cowlishaw (2006: 438–39) describes it, there are instances when some Indigenous peoples get tired of other Indigenous peoples always blaming white people for their troubles, as an excuse for their own unwillingness to accept responsibility. To this phenomenon one Indigenous man's reply was:

'When they say they hate White people they forget their White grandfather.'

Cowlishaw (2006) continues:

As with so many of these discursive moves, this one has an echo from the other side. The words are supplied by a Murri woman who took wicked pleasure in pointing out the Black heritage that White families prefer to forget. 'She's a *Black gin*', she would yell gleefully, ridiculing the complacent claim to superiority of some pillar of the White community.

The politics of personal ancestry, it seems, are closely intertwined with the politics of communal identity, as indicated here and in the words of Paradies quoted earlier. Nevertheless, recognition of family overlap and mixed genealogy does pose interesting questions when it comes to claims of racial purity, superiority, and special knowledge—whether this claim be Indigenous or non-Indigenous.

Acknowledging differences and contributions across the domains of work, education, and family enables us to better appreciate the active ways in which Indigenous peoples engage with the wider non-Indigenous culture and community, and the continuing importance of this interchange. As emphasised by Collard and Palmer (2006), dialogue around these and other issues is important for reconciliation, coexistence, and a mediated future for Indigenous and non-Indigenous Australians.

> Acknowledging differences and contributions across the domains of work, education, and family enables us to better appreciate the active ways in which Indigenous peoples engage with the wider non-Indigenous culture and community, and the continuing importance of this interchange.

It is also important to study the interpenetration of knowledges and cultures for another reason. Quite simply, indigeneity itself is an ongoing and ever-changing cultural project. How one sees oneself, how one dresses, speaks, acts, and relates to the wider social community is contingent upon the range of material and cultural resources open to us. We might consider here the impact of communication technologies as they relate to Indigenous youth in rural and remote communities. Brady (1991: 1–2) has noted that:

Based on my own research observations it is possible to state that many young Aboriginal people in some of the most 'tradition oriented' of the bush townships now sport the trappings and display the 'style' of youth elsewhere: their clothing is determinedly different from that worn by adults; their hairstyles and jewellery, the music they listen to and their comportment—all of these are in deliberate contradistinction to others around them. Television by satellite, local radio and TV stations, videos, cassette recorders, local rock bands and discos, are all features of everyday life in the deserts of Central Australia and the mangroves of the north.

The globalisation of youth culture is accomplished by such means, but this globalisation is always subject to modification, differential appropriation, and contestation at the local level by young people who actively, rather than passively, engage with (Western-dominated) world trends in music and fashion fads.

The appropriation of elements of commercialised hip hop culture provides one example of the process whereby people attempt to redefine their cultural identity in ways that make sense to them. As Lez 'Bex' Beckett, a well-known figure on the Australian hip hop circuit, has commented:

> I write about the positive changes you can make with your life, about everyday living, about the struggle to survive, especially if you are a blackfella … I tell them, 'Keep it Australian', because while it is an American form, we can incorporate our lives into it, we rap our own way (quoted in Notarpietro-Clarke 2007: 41).

Hip hop as a particular type of cultural expression is well suited to appropriation and transmutation into a specifically Indigenous cultural form. Traditional Indigenous languages are oral, rather than written, and hip hop allows for a new, dynamic blend of the traditional and the contemporary. This is evidenced, for example, in the fact that: 'Some skilled artists rap in their local languages, which lend themselves (more so than English) to the lyrical flow of hip-hop' (Notarpietro-Clarke 2007: 42). Both the form (that is, language used, including Australian rather than American accents) and the content (for example, lyrics that express anger about experiences of racism, segregation, and victimisation) of this hip hop allow for the distinctive voices of young Indigenous people to be expressed in a manner that is dynamic, spirited, and meaningful:

> Identities are complex, multifaceted, sociohistorical constructs that are established through public acts of self-representation, private accounting of oneself, or through the experience of being named by others (Jenkins 1994).

The more one considers the kinds of observations presented in this section, the more one ought to realise that the study of Indigenous young people must involve sensitivity to a wide range of issues and complexities. Such analysis can ill afford to essentialise or homogenise the experience of young Indigenous people. Yet, in many youth services and policy situations, this is precisely what happens: the essentialism tends to construct Indigenous youth intrinsically as somehow problem youth. Palmer (1999: 112) describes how one youth service in Perth categorised Indigenous youth throughout its reports and other documents:

> In a section talking about youth issues, Aboriginality featured along with categories such as homeless-ness, unemployment, juvenile justice, low incomes, drug use, domestic abuse and low self-esteem. In this case, Aboriginality was categorised in the same way as social, economic or personal problems facing young people. While it was not articulated explicitly in any of the organisation's material, the implied message was that Aboriginality, in and of itself, was seen as an issue or youth problem to be solved, along with homelessness, unemployment, income support, drug abuse and crime.

In part, the tendency described here has been reinforced in recent years by the emphasis on risk assessment and the efforts of governments to identify and intervene in the lives of those deemed to be at risk (Cunneen & White 2007). How we deal with the tensions that arise when acknowledging social problems without exacerbating them is partly a question of how best to consciously frame strategic action around certain concepts and images, such as Indigenous peoples portrayed in terms of victimhood, and who is doing the framing: the oppressed or the oppressor. As Palmer (1999) points out, there are times when portraying Indigenous youth as the problem does have its positive advantages for Indigenous peoples.

BEYOND YOUTH AT RISK: A MĀORI EXAMPLE

In describing the dynamics that create exclusion of Indigenous young people, we are also aware of the dilemma that all researchers face in highlighting processes that marginalise youth in general. In describing very real problems that young people face, the stereotypes of youth at risk can inadvertently be reinforced, but to avoid discussing the effects of exclusion and marginalisation places the researcher at risk of romanticising young people's lives and ignoring very real effects of social division in young people's lives. Youth researchers in New Zealand are among those who are attempting to move beyond a perspective that sees young people from particular racial groups as victims, to focus on broader issues of social change.

The treatment of young people from particular racial and ethnic backgrounds as trouble-makers and potential criminals is an example of the mapping of implicit racial codes onto particular groups of youth who are seen as at risk. Smith et al., authors of a study of New Zealand youth, note that youth at risk are, for the most part, represented as Māori and Pacific Island youth growing up in poor families who live in poor communities and attend poor schools in urban areas (2002: 170). They point out that these official stereotypes are perpetuated through the failure of experts to invite the views of young people on how they are experiencing life (see also Palmer & Collard 1993; Palmer 1999). As a result of concern that the categorisation of young people from particular backgrounds as 'at risk' had the effect of diminishing the significance of wider social changes on all young people, not just those from particular ethnic backgrounds, the Youth First project was established in New Zealand. One of the most notable contributions of this project was the establishment of tribunals as a research tool to create spaces within which young people could express their views and concerns, and contribute their own analyses of their social circumstances (Smith et al. 2002).

The tribunals provided a youth-friendly space within local communities (many based in *iwi*, traditional Māori territories), with local, trained youth facilitators. The focus was on rural youth, many of whom were Māori. The tribunals provided young people with an opportunity to give status to their own voices as well as to bear witness to their views.

> The treatment of young people from particular racial and ethnic backgrounds as troublemakers and potential criminals is an example of the mapping of implicit racial codes onto particular groups of youth who are seen as at risk.

There were many outcomes of this process. One of the outcomes of interest here is the way that the young people used the tribunals as a means of 'talking back' as the Other. They were very aware of being 'different' because they were rural. One of the youth on a tribunal from a rural

North Island community asked a group of youth, 'Do you guys hate Aucklanders too?' (Smith et al. 2002: 171). As Smith et al. point out, rurality, race, and economic disadvantage are intertwined in a context where the development of one urban region (Auckland) is seen to be at the expense of other urban and rural regions.

Another outcome was the expression of stories of survival and resistance. Smith et al. describe the ways in which many Māori youth 'cut through the crap' to acknowledge the real problems they faced and their hopes for a better future. There were some inspirational survival stories presented with great wisdom by young people as young as ten. These included stories about drugs and alcohol, suicide, family violence, leaving home, and finding a home. There were many testimonies that gave a sense of hopefulness about strategies that young people have developed to support each other through drug abuse and family violence. These strategies may not address the actual problem but demonstrated a capacity for youth to protect others, to show compassion, and to forgive (Smith et al. 2002: 175).

The source of their difference, of being forced to become the Other, is often the source of their strength, as the following quote from a young Māori man illustrates:

> I was shipped away to Invercargill when I turned 12 or 13 yeah and that was a big culture shock. Coming from a place where everything was brown faces to skinheads and all that sort of stuff, yeah that was a real culture shock. I think being down there made me even stronger, all my Maoritanga, you know because it wasn't there.

What is striking is the way in which young people themselves have analysed the impact of absences, silences, and of difference on their own identities.

Summary

A major theme of this chapter has been the ways in which the experiences of Indigenous peoples have been fundamentally shaped by colonialist processes, and yet how variable their experiences are due to the diverse social worlds that they inhabit. As with youth in general, there is great variability in Indigenous communities, and the Indigenous population as a whole is heterogenous across many different dimensions. What unites the many is the shared experiences of injustice, inequality, and oppression at the hands of a colonial state, an experience that continues to the present day (see Morrisey 2006).

The question of Indigenous identity continues to be of crucial importance. How 'Indigenous' is defined has major implications for self-concept and how Indigenous peoples engage with the world around them. In the Australian context, there have been some sixty-seven different definitions of indigeneity in government legislation over the years (McCorquodale, cited in Paradies 2006). We know that there are ongoing disputes among Indigenous peoples themselves regarding who is 'really' Indigenous and who is not. Frequently the debates are framed in either relatively fixed bureaucratic categories (that is, criteria based upon ancestry and social recognition) or moral judgment (for example, acting in certain ways).

As Paradies (2006) argues, it is imperative to adopt an approach that allows for hybrid identities and flexibility in identification with indigeneity. It is also essential to acknowledge differences and arguments within Indigenous circles, as well as the people and matters that cross the Indigenous and non-Indigenous divide, such as environmental activists and social justice issues. Finally, it is crucial that the voices of Indigenous young people be part of the continuing dialogue surrounding identity, resources, and values in the contemporary time period.

Questions for further exploration

1   What do the concepts 'Indigenous' and 'indigeneity' mean?

2   In what ways has the colonial experience shaped the life chances of contemporary young Indigenous people—economically, socially, culturally, and politically?

3   Identities are complex, multifaceted, sociohistorical constructs that are established through public acts of self-representation, private accounting of oneself, or through the experience of being named by others. Discuss this statement in regards to Indigenous identity.

4   The overall position of Indigenous peoples in Australia has improved, even though public policy has reinforced their marginalisation. Discuss.

5   Indigenous peoples are not simply disadvantaged. They are first peoples whose political status provides them with certain rights and entitlements. Discuss from the point of view of social justice and self-determination.

QUESTIONS

6 RURAL GEOGRAPHIES

Introduction

Making a life is a challenging process for all young people. Each chapter of this book describes different areas of life where young people daily face the effects of social change, meeting challenges, and making choices that have come to shape the very nature of their youth. We have described how young people, while negotiating social change, are also shaping their experience of youth. Even though there is enormous diversity, the evidence suggests that new life patterns are emerging. In many respects, young people growing up in rural communities face these issues more sharply than their urban counterparts because structural changes to the rural economy have dramatically affected the very fabric of their communities. Young Indigenous people continue to struggle to come to terms with the effects of the destruction of their traditional ways of life. Non-Indigenous youth in many rural areas are growing up in a time of dramatic changes to traditional rural lifestyles.

Population loss and economic shifts in the rural sector, resulting in a declining contribution of the rural sector to gross domestic product (GDP) and employment, have affected the structure of many rural communities. At the same time, rural education and other services are increasingly unable to provide the necessary ingredients to service the rural populations, which is a direct result of government policies driven by concerns with efficiency and the need to reduce public spending, the consequence of which is the withdrawal of health, social welfare, and educational services from rural communities across Australia.

There is widespread concern that the rapid structural transformation occurring in rural Australian communities is so disruptive to traditional ways of livelihood that young people can see no place for themselves. In some communities, the older generation is actively seeking ways to halt the drift of their young people to cities. Researchers who have begun to chart the effects of social and economic change on different rural communities have identified the emergence of new forms of social and economic inequality. Yet the effects of social change are not uniform. The decline of some rural economies is matched by the emergence of new forms of economic activity in other areas, which offer benefits, opportunities, and growth.

Although young people in rural Australia grow up in very different environments, they share common challenges, such as isolation and the effects of the changing rural economy. For young Indigenous people, in addition to these issues, the historical struggle for land rights continues to play a significant role in their lives. Young people in rural areas also share common challenges, related to the social relationships that characterise rural communities: close social networks and adherence to traditional values, for example, provide a level of security and certainty that is highly valued by some youth. Yet these qualities can be experienced negatively by others, across a range of social relationships, including gender relations, sexuality and sexual identities, class, and race relations.

Australia's rural areas are characterised by a low density of population that makes them very different from rural communities in Europe, North America, or almost any other industrialised country. This feature also differentiates Australia from other, less industrialised but highly populated countries. The uniquely remote nature of Australian rural communities is a significant factor that, historically, has shaped the mythology of the bush and the experiences of people living in rural and remote areas. It has also constituted a challenge to the way in which education, health, and other services are provided to non-urban Australians.

Despite the overall patterns of relative rural disadvantage, there is evidence that new patterns of settlement in some rural areas represent a conscious lifestyle choice. Factors such as clean air, lack of congestion, a sense of community, and appreciation of the environment attract people to rural areas.

Australia's rural communities are shaped by very different economic, regional, social, and geographical conditions across the continent. Life in provincial towns is very different from life in remote or isolated areas; each region has unique characteristics. 'Rural Australia' includes mining towns in the centre of Australia, landlocked and dominated by a single industry; coastal towns based on fishing that service a local farming region; regional centres that were based on a once-viable wool industry and are now struggling to find a sustainable economic base; and Indigenous communities that are engaged in a process of self-determination. Immigration to some rural areas has increased the proportions of the population who were born overseas, thereby increasing the ethnic heterogeneity of rural populations.

> Australia's rural communities are shaped by very different economic, regional, social, and geographical conditions across the continent. Life in provincial towns is very different from life in remote or isolated areas and each region has unique characteristics.

We have tried to keep all of these complexities in mind when writing this chapter about young people's experiences of rural spaces and places. In the following sections we discuss the ways in which 'rural' has been defined and explore its symbolic place in Australian life. We analyse the current trend to assume that Youth + Rural = Problems. Rural youth are often assumed to be disadvantaged, and are seen as victims of change. Instead, youth research reveals a multilayered reality in which the usual dichotomy of rural versus urban is shown to be overly simplistic. While the research on the economic and social–structural conditions of many rural communities presents evidence of disadvantage, it would be a misapprehension to assume that this can be read straight onto young people's lives. Young people's views and perspectives suggest a more complex reality.

DEFINITIONS OF RURAL AND REGIONAL — WHAT IS 'THE BUSH'?

During the first seventy years of the twentieth century, Australia's population became increasingly urbanised, with the proportion of the population living outside the capital cities declining from two-thirds to one-third over that period. Today, the population is overwhelmingly concentrated into its coastal capital cities—Hobart, Sydney, Melbourne, Adelaide, Perth, Darwin, and Brisbane. This pattern of metropolitan concentration has generated a variety of definitions of 'rural' and 'urban'.

Many argue that all Australian residents could be broadly defined as being either rural or non-rural. Those living in urban or metropolitan areas could be categorised as non-rural, while those in other areas of the nation could be described as rural residents. Should categorisation be based on population or on some other variable, such as the predominant industry of employment? Perhaps remoteness should be considered as the basis for defining rurality?

The Australian Bureau of Statistics (ABS) differentiates between rural and urban residents in census data. For statistical purposes, people living in urban centres are classified as urban, while those in other localities are classified as rural where a locality is a cluster of population up to 999 people (ABS 1998a). This definition may suffice for the purpose of analysing national statistics but from the perspective of discussing the lives of young people, regional areas also need to be included in a definition of rural. A more useful definition is to consider rural and regional areas, which are those areas in which people are living outside of the major cities.

Compared with non-Indigenous Australians, high proportions of Indigenous people live in rural areas. In the Northern Territory, Aboriginal and Torres Strait Islander peoples constitute 74.3 per cent of Australians living in centres of less than 2000 people. Overall, 15.7 per cent of Indigenous Australians live in non-urban areas (Bray 2000). This compares with an overall pattern for Australia in which 64.5 per cent of the population live in the capital cities or in major (non-capital) cities and only 8.4 per cent live in non-urban areas (Bray 2000: 3).

But the answer to the question 'What is the bush?' is not simply a technical response involving the categorisation and measurement of populations. The bush has played a significant part in the economic and cultural life of Australians from the earliest days of colonisation. Initially regarded as a hostile environment to be tamed, many rural areas rapidly became the mainstay of the young colony through the wealth generated by sheep and cattle farming; the mining of gold, coal, and later of aluminium, copper, and other minerals; and through sugar, wheat, and many other areas of agricultural farming. The bush has traditionally held a cultural significance for Australians, epitomising a culture that values self-sufficiency and wealth for toil and that sees virtue in the simplicity of a wide sky and fresh air.

In the early decades of the twentieth century, rural youth were portrayed as a representation of the young, developing, and hopeful country, depicting health, optimism, and well-being: 'Boys and girls who live outside of our cities we salute you—[In you] is found the best of home, country, kindred, sunshine and love—every instinct that the heart most deeply enshrines' (*Bulletin*, 13 March 1922).

The mythology of rural life, presented in this way, played an important part in the symbolism of Australia as a nation. It has only been in the last fifty years or so that the economic basis of this sentiment has made the mythology difficult to maintain. The main economic activity of Australia has shifted to the cities, as have employment opportunities. New economies that no longer depend on manufacturing and agricultural production have come to dominate. Meanwhile, the application of new technologies and greater concentration of production in the hands of corporate giants have been associated with an overall decline in the number of rural workers across diverse industries, such as farming and forestry, and the demise of rural communities (Lawrence et al. 1996). As a direct consequence, many rural and some regional areas of Australia are going through dramatic economic and social change.

For Australia's Aboriginal and Torres Strait Islander peoples, the bush is much more than this. The mythology surrounding the bush has failed to recognise the cultural significance that traditional places have always had for Indigenous peoples. For New Zealand's Indigenous people, the Māori, rural areas also often represent traditional *iwi* (tribal) territories, places that are home to institutions such as *marae* (cultural centres) and that hold considerable cultural significance (Smith et al. 2002).

The single most significant theme to emerge from a discussion of the background social, economic, and cultural characteristics of Australia's rural, regional, and remote populations is that of diversity. Broad patterns reveal disadvantage for rural populations in terms of provision of infrastructure, such as health, education, transport, communications, and employment. The fine grain of specific rural locations reveals considerable variability within this broader pattern.

The second theme to emerge is that of change. The rural economic base is shifting away from the traditional reliance on agriculture and mining towards the service sector, creating a demand for a renewed investment in social and human capital in Australia's rural areas.

These observations set the context for understanding young people's experiences of growing up in rural areas and the way in which the lives of young people in rural areas are portrayed by researchers. In the following section, we provide a brief summary of the way in which the research tends to frame young people's lives in rural communities as disadvantaged through the social and economic circumstances under which they are living.

Patterns of disadvantage

In Australia, the rural areas of greatest growth are clustered around the major cities and along the eastern and southwestern coasts. This pattern has meant that in many areas the regional cities and larger towns have grown at the expense of the surrounding district, creating a phenomenon called 'sponge cities' (Productivity Commission 1999: 27).

The age profile of rural communities is also quite distinctive. Increasingly, non-urban populations are characterised by an under-representation of young people in the fifteen- to thirty-five-year-old age group, due to out-migration. In 1996, 1.8 million students attended primary schools across Australia and 1.3 million were in secondary schools (Department of Education, Training and Youth Affairs 1996: 59), of whom, it is estimated, between one-quarter and one-third attended school in rural and remote areas. Out-migration begins at age fifteen, when a proportion of young people leave rural areas to study in cities. At the end of secondary school, around the age of eighteen, it is common for young people to have to leave for larger regional centres or the capital cities to find jobs. The sponge city effect is also created by the trend for older people to move closer to community, health care, and leisure facilities in regional centres.

Older and retired people in cities often move to coastal areas, creating a pattern for the proportion of the population aged over sixty-five to be greater in towns and cities than in rural areas (Productivity Commission 1999).

The pattern for young people living in rural areas is one of lower participation in education at all levels, and of lower overall achievement than their urban counterparts. A national inquiry into rural and remote education found that, on average, the school performance of country students lagged somewhat behind that of urban students. A report on higher education showed that 'university students from rural and isolated backgrounds comprised 19.2 per cent of the total student population in 1997, a participation share dramatically below the equity reference point of 28.8 per cent derived from 1996 equity data' (James et al. 1999: 1).

According to various social indicators, people living in rural areas tend to be less well off than their urban counterparts. People living in rural areas tend to have lower levels of household income and higher levels of unemployment. In most country regions, unemployment levels are higher than in the capital cities; however, there are strong regional differences in unemployment rates. Country unemployment rates are higher in, say, New South Wales than in South Australia and Western Australia (Productivity Commission 1999: 32). In addition, it appears that on average country areas have household incomes below the national average. Once again, there are exceptions to this pattern, but overall the Productivity Commission reports that, between 1981 and 1996, country household income declined (1999: 36).

> According to various social indicators, people living in rural areas tend to be less well off than their urban counterparts. People living in rural areas tend to have lower levels of household income and higher levels of unemployment.

The overall patterns of decline and disadvantage are matched by research on the difficulties faced by young people living in rural communities. In the following section, we summarise recent research on young people living in rural communities in the 1990s and early 2000s.

Young people in rural communities

Young people's sense of well-being is profoundly affected by their social, economic, and physical environments, especially in the context of rapid social change. There is an extensive literature on young people in rural communities that documents the impact of structural, social, and cultural factors on their lives. Not only do these elements provide constraints and contribute to disadvantage, but there are also positives and elements that contribute to well-being.

The things that limit young people's full participation in society are, inevitably, the lack of access to transport, health, education, community services, accommodation, and employment. These elements are often interrelated in young people's experience, so that lack of accommodation, for example, affects access to education, and transport difficulties have an effect on the accessibility of employment opportunities. The following discussion draws on research undertaken by the Australian Youth Research Centre on young people in five rural areas across Victoria and New South Wales. The research involved focus group interviews with young people, as well as interviews with youth workers and the analysis of available literature and relevant documents (Wyn et. al. 1998).

> The things that limit young people's full participation in society are, inevitably, the lack of access to transport, health, education, community services, accommodation, and employment.

Transport

Lack of transport into rural towns and provincial centres is a common problem, especially for young people. The research found that:

within towns there was some public transport, but outside of towns, people relied on cars. Links between towns were maintained by public transport, but bus services operate infrequently, and rail links have been scaled down. People in the north west, including towns like Mildura, were as likely to access services in South Australia as in Victoria, because of the difficulties of transport, and people in towns along the Murray were likely to access services across the river in NSW (Wyn et al. 1998: 10).

This description could apply to a number of rural communities in Australia. Without adequate transport, young people have very limited access to health services, education and employment opportunities, and leisure facilities. Until they are able to drive, young people are reliant on others for transport, which can cause its own problems. Relying on someone else for transport may, for instance, make it difficult to ensure discretion and confidentiality about a visit to the local health centre. Other researchers have suggested a link between the reliance of girls on older boys for transport and the institutionalisation of rape, in which sex is an accepted payment for transport (Hillier et al. 1996; Smith & Borthwick 1991).

The lack of access to alternative leisure has been linked to the dominance of the local footy club as the only source of entertainment. Binge drinking at other local venues is also seen as a form of entertainment. Lack of adequate transportation in this context also ties into problems associated with drinking and driving. Furthermore, the likelihood of car accidents is exacerbated by the physical condition of many country roads, the lack of lighting on such roads, and the distractions and dangers created at times by animals such as kangaroos, echidnas, or wombats on the road.

Health and community services

Lack of access to appropriate health services is a common theme across many rural communities. Hillier et al. (1996) found that young people in rural communities thought health services were very difficult to access. The issue is not simply one of access; the way in which services are offered is also important. Young people place a high priority on services that are confidential and private and on being treated as adults. Having access to bulk billing and being able to enter a health centre discreetly were also seen as crucial, which means that the local health centre is not necessarily seen as an option. Young people in this study said that they would rather travel to a regional centre or to a metropolitan practice than risk embarrassment at the local practice. The focus groups revealed that lack of information might also be a factor. In some cases, young people were not aware of the existence of services that would meet their needs.

The physical, mental, and spiritual health of young Indigenous people is an urgent issue (Commonwealth Department of Human Services and Health 1995). Health for many young Indigenous people involves spiritual dimensions, including the ability to complete their traditional initiation ceremonies, living on traditional land, and hunting. The appropriateness and relevance of services to their needs is a central issue. The annual death rates for young Indigenous people in Western Australia, South Australia, and the Northern Territory are double that of young Australians of the same age for Australia as a whole (Bhatia & Anderson 1994). Wyn et al. (1998: 12) reported:

Primary health care for some Aboriginal communities remains a fundamental issue. Simple public health provisions such as clean water, adequate and appropriate accommodation, and treatment and prevention of gastric, eye, ear and other infections remain a serious concern (Gray & Atkinson 1990).

This state of affairs continues to this day.

Brady's research on the health of young Indigenous people confirmed that young Indigenous people in rural and remote areas face the same issues as other young rural people, but that their health is often more seriously compromised by their circumstances, especially those living in remote communities. Brady reports that one Indigenous health service assessed the major health problems of young Indigenous people as sexually transmitted diseases, alcohol-related problems, poor nutrition, skin disease, and problems associated with pregnancy and domestic violence. (Brady 1991: 8; Brady 1993).

Research on the health of young Indigenous people reaches a consensus that the National Aboriginal Health Strategy and its recommendations should be strongly supported, including the principles of community control of primary health care, with the states retaining responsibility for secondary level, and other, health services (Brady 1991). Based on the available evidence, the Australian Institute of Health and Welfare (2006) reports that Indigenous Australians continue to suffer from lower levels of health than the rest of the population. Indigenous Australians experience lower levels of access to health services than the general population, are more likely than non-Indigenous people to be hospitalised for most diseases and conditions, are more likely to experience disability and reduced quality of life due to ill health, and to die at younger ages than other Australians. Brady also emphasises that both the National Aboriginal Health Strategy and the Royal Commission into Aboriginal Deaths in Custody stressed the special role of Indigenous community-controlled organisations. In the focus groups in several communities, it was suggested that sometimes Indigenous people are unwilling to access any government service through mistrust and fear.

> Research on the health of young Indigenous people confirmed that young Indigenous people in rural and remote areas face the same issues as other young rural people, but that their health is often more seriously compromised by their circumstances, especially those living in remote communities.

Accommodation

Access to affordable accommodation is just as important to young people living in rural areas as it is to young people in the cities. Young people in rural areas often have to move from their parents' home for work or for their education and in many areas there is a scarcity of public housing stock that young people can rent. Quixley's report on young people's housing needs in rural Australia, which remains the most comprehensive study (Quixley 1992), shows how interrelated education, employment, and housing are and how they can combine to have a significant effect on young people's well-being.

Recent research shows that young people in rural areas experience homelessness very differently from their urban counterparts (Australian Housing and Urban Research Institute 2006). The difference is that young people in rural areas have greater difficulty finding employment, rental housing markets are limited and expensive (and often discriminate against youth), and there are more

> Recent research shows that young people in rural areas experience homelessness very differently from their urban counterparts

limited support services in rural areas. The research also highlighted that, despite these disadvantages, many young people who were experiencing difficulties gaining accommodation in rural areas nonetheless valued the friendship and support networks available to them in their local area, and felt more comfortable staying in their known environment than risking seeking support in 'dangerous' metropolitan areas (Australian Housing and Urban Research Institute 2006).

Education

The increased importance of educational credentials in the job market has hit young people in rural communities especially hard, because in order to gain post-compulsory education or training credentials, it is common for rural young people to have to leave home and move to metropolitan or regional centres. There has been some improvement in areas served by university campuses and colleges of Technical and Further Education (TAFEs); however, because of the lack of jobs and the restricted choices for study, students in rural areas tend to be denied the opportunity to develop the kinds of mix of school and work that are now becoming common for urban students (Wyn et al. 1998: 13–14).

Difficulty of access to education for rural youth is well documented and many reports have identified this as a significant source of disadvantage to young people in rural areas (see, for example, Robson 1991; Stevens & Mason 1992; Department of Employment, Education and Training 1990). A study of young Australians living in rural and remote areas and their aspirations for higher education found that rurality and lower socioeconomic status combine to produce the greatest educational disadvantage. The least advantaged students (lower SES students who live long distances from university campuses) have significantly different attitudes from the most advantaged students (urban, higher SES students). At least twice the proportion of the least advantaged students believe that the cost of university fees may stop them attending university (43 per cent compared with 21 per cent) and that a university qualification is not necessary for the jobs they want (31 per cent compared with 15 per cent). Major differences are also found in students' perceptions of their parents' wishes: while 69 per cent of the most advantaged students believe their parents want them to do a university course, only 38 per cent of the least advantaged students believe so (James et al. 1999: xvi).

The costs of higher education are a significant factor in these outcomes (James et al. 1999: xvi). Many rural students and their families face difficult decisions in assessing and weighing up the costs and benefits of higher education. The costs are beyond the reach of lower socioeconomic families. For many of these families, the idea of taking out a student loan to finance higher education is out of the question. A review of the educational decisions of rural youth in Canada and Australia confirmed these observations. It found that a combination of issues served to distinguish rural youth from their urban counterparts:

> Their educational decisions involve different cost, both financial and social. Young people who move away from home often face higher costs for room and board. They also cut themselves off from the social support networks that many rely on to help with the multiple transitions to adulthood (Looker & Dwyer 1998: 14).

The employment and educational options of rural young people are thus constrained by geographical and financial considerations. These, in turn, are bound to affect young people with fewer family or personal economic resources much more than those with more reserves to draw upon.

Despite the lower rates of engagement in higher education, educational provision in rural and remote areas is of high quality. A study of education in rural Australia from 1945–2001 reveals a history of innovation in providing education for rural and remote students (Dwyer & Wyn 2001). Early innovations, such as the School of the Air, which began operation in 1951, and correspondence schools, which began in 1950, ensured that isolated and remote students were not disadvantaged. A preschool correspondence program was established in the mid 1970s, and in the 1960s technical colleges and universities were offering external study programs. The Disadvantaged Country Areas Program, initiated in the late 1970s, also supported disadvantaged country areas by providing the facilities needed to improve educational provision for rural students.

The exception has been educational provision for Aboriginal and Torres Strait Islander students. While there are many innovative educational programs in existence today, the Ministerial Council on Education, Employment, Training and Youth Affairs' report, *Taskforce on Indigenous Education* (2000), and the Human Rights and Equal Opportunity Commission's report, *National Inquiry into Rural and Remote Education* (2000), both identify that the scale of educational inequality for Australia's Aboriginal and Torres Strait Islander peoples continues to be great, despite decades of educational policies that aimed to create greater equality. The reports acknowledge that older prejudices continue to hamper the development and implementation of effective education for Indigenous peoples. There are several key elements that are identified as fundamental to the achievement of educational equality for Australia's Indigenous peoples. These include the right for Aboriginal and Torres Strait Islander peoples to determine their educational policies and programs, the acknowledgment of the history of race relations in Australia, the development of culturally inclusive educational programs, the development of partnerships with communities and across government departments, and the recognition of the links between education, health, and well-being.

Employment

There is a significant proportion of young people who would rather continue to live in their home town, but feel forced to leave by the lack of employment opportunities, including lack of job opportunities in towns, and the difficulty that farm families in some areas have in making a living from the land.

For young people, the lack of job opportunities in their local areas is a particularly serious issue. The focus group interviews revealed that there is a significant proportion of young people who would rather continue to live in their home town, but feel forced to leave by the lack of employment opportunities, including lack of job opportunities in towns and the difficulty that farm families in some areas have in making a living from the land. Unemployment contributes directly to the destruction of rural communities: many of the young make their exodus to towns and cities, and greater strains are placed on the provision of support services for those who remain. Unemployment rates are higher in rural areas, and in some Indigenous communities as high as 95 per cent (Commonwealth Department of Human Services and Health 1994). Although recorded rates of unemployment among Indigenous and non-Indigenous rural youth are high, many are not recorded. In areas where seasonal work is common, the rate of young people's unemployment is masked by the jobs they do for part of the year that tide them over.

Also at stake are young people's health and well-being, which are closely related to how they see themselves and the quality of relationships they have with significant others. The social and cultural issues we are about to discuss are linked to the structural factors outlined above.

Gender relations

Gender issues are increasingly being recognised as among the key social factors that need to be taken into account in developing health promotion strategies for young people. The effects of domestic violence, which young people frequently experience, are compounded by the lack of alternative accommodation, the lack of professional help, and the tendency for local police to be influenced by the community values that turn a blind eye to violence in domestic relationships (Coorey 1990). In some instances, women face the added stress of victimisation from an intolerant community if they leave their husbands (Iley 1993). The issue of family violence is also now being openly discussed in some Indigenous communities, and features prominently in national discussions about Indigenous issues. Moreover, concerted attempts are now being made to develop intervention models that are sensitive to the specific needs and interests of Indigenous rural youth and their communities (see, for example, Blagg 2000). This is an especially sensitive area, given the history of the violent treatment of Indigenous people by whites (Brady 1994). For example, Brady (1994) points out the effect of the institutionalisation of young Indigenous people on missions as a factor affecting the quality of relationships between men and women of this generation.

Narrow conceptions of masculinity and femininity are also of concern for rural youth. Smith and Borthwick (1991) provide examples of the marginalisation of girls and women in rural communities through the perpetuation of double standards and the risk of young women of being negatively labelled unless they are in a relationship with a boy. The focus group interviews revealed that the strong commitment to sports such as football and netball tended to reinforce gender stereotypes. Although sport was a positive aspect of their lives, some young people were less enthusiastic about the expectation that football frequently included a macho drinking culture. Associated with this culture are the practices of bonnet surfing and dirt surfing in some communities, which put young men's health at risk.

But any focus on gender should not imply that rural women are victims within traditionally conservative communities. Women often constitute a formidable, if unacknowledged, political force in rural communities. This was borne out in a study of the experiences of young women enrolled in an agricultural college in Adelaide (O'Brien 1999). The study found that, while college life was culturally and socially dominated by males, the young female students were constantly negotiating and dynamically creating their own social spaces within and outside of the larger student culture. So, although many of the young women 'get sick of the larrikinism of the male students, they are gradually carving out traditions of their own, such as all-female pub crawls and all-female sporting events' (O'Brien 1999: 104). It is argued that these young women are taking organised and collective action to support each other in what is, for them, a fairly hostile social climate. In doing so, they are simultaneously re-shaping the overall social environment.

Suicide

> The very tradition of self-sufficiency may prevent young men in rural communities from seeking help
> when they need it (Graham 1994).

The research literature is divided on the issue of whether suicide rates for young people are higher
in rural than in urban areas. Dudley et al. (1992) show that the rate of suicide in rural areas of New
South Wales has increased, whereas a Queensland study (Cantor & Coorey 1993) found similar
rates of suicide for young men in rural and urban areas, although they found that there were higher
rates of male suicide in all areas of Queensland compared with New South Wales.

The decline of the rural economy and the consequent stress this has placed on the health of
rural people is linked to the high rate of male suicide in rural New South Wales (Lawrence & Williams
1990). The effects of unemployment, poor educational opportunities, and poverty contribute to the
high suicide rate. There is evidence that 'rural youth experience higher levels of domestic violence
and homicides' and 'consume more alcohol and have readier access to firearms than their urban
counterparts' (Graham 1994: 409).

There is also evidence that links suicide with community intolerance of gay people.

BOX 6.1

Nicholas's story

The following extract was originally quoted in a local newspaper. It is about the tragic story of
Nicholas, a young gay man who failed to come to terms with his sexuality in a country town, so
committed suicide at sixteen.

> Nicholas explained that he couldn't live up to the role of a 'typical country Catholic boy'. He knew
> that he would never be accepted for what he really was. 'You're shunned in the Catholic Church if you
> are a homosexual,' a friend said.
> Nicholas felt his place in the church, family, school, and local community would no longer exist
> and therefore his life was not worth living because these things were so important to him.

Source: quoted in Green 1996: 85–86.

The experiences described here are not unique to young country people. Dominant social
practices in Australia generally work against young gay men and lesbians insofar as the stigma
associated with homosexuality denies many of these young people the opportunities that heterosexual young people enjoy. Young lesbians and gay men 'learn that homosexuality is generally not
accepted and often forbidden in everyday life', and that public knowledge of homosexual relations
and emotions may result in, at worst, physical violence, rejection, and expulsion from communities (see Emslie 1999: 161). Unlike metropolitan centres, such as Sydney and Melbourne, where
there are substantial social, economic, and political supports for young lesbians and gay men,
many country areas do not offer appropriate service provision, and the dominance of conserva-
tism and heterosexist culture makes the situation particularly unbearable for some young gay men
and lesbians.

The example of the struggle that same-sex attracted youth may have in rural communities to find recognition is part of a larger picture in relation to suicide in rural communities. A 2004 survey of young Australians in rural and regional areas found that suicide was ranked in the top three issues of concern by 41.3 per cent of respondents aged eleven to nineteen (Mission Australia 2006). Again, this indicates how issues such as poverty, unemployment, sense of hopelessness, and declining opportunities impact on these particular young people.

Youth space and youth culture

Young people in Australia's rural communities have an enormous amount in common with the older people in their communities because they share the same environment. In Indigenous and non-Indigenous communities, young people learn a lot from the older generation, including skills associated with survival in the bush and with the enjoyment of the rural environment. Sport continues to be an important source of solidarity between the generations. Yet, at the same time, young people have different interests and needs from the older people in their communities. Summed up in the inadequate term 'entertainment', the lack of such facilities is raised as a concern by young people over and over again (Wyn et al. 1998: 17).

Young people would like to be able to go to movie theatres (that show current movies), to see live theatre that is relevant to young people, and to participate in dances, discos, or other forms of youth entertainment. The alternatives to these forms of entertainment and sociability are often an early engagement with pub culture and a reliance on the drinking that frequently accompanies sports such as football. Young people in the focus groups were frank about the extent to which binge drinking occurs because of a lack of alternatives.

Without legitimate space of their own, young people are seen as a threat if they gather in public places, such as the main street, the football oval, or other places where, officially, they do not have a reason to gather. The focus group interviews found, for example, that young people in one rural town were gathering in town not to be part of the druggie groups, but because they had nowhere else to be.

The recognition and acceptance of youth cultures in rural communities is important because of the positive part of young people play in the cultural life of rural Australia. It is as important as the creation of jobs for young people and as their educational opportunities. In the context of the changes that have affected many of Australia's rural communities, the creation of stronger youth-oriented communities can contribute significantly to young people's well-being and to their own ability to construct meaningful futures.

The recognition and acceptance of youth cultures in rural communities is important because of the positive part young people play in the cultural life of rural Australia.

White's study of young people in the rural city of Mildura (Victoria) found that most of the young people felt that there was not enough to do in the area. The place where they spent the most time (not all of which is defined as 'hanging out' time) was their home (White 1999a). The second most likely place young people would spend time was at a friend's place. Some forty-two out of forty-seven respondents said that they and their friends get bored. The reasons for this were that there was nothing to do if they were under eighteen, and, because their options were so limited, that they always had to do the same thing. When they were bored, many simply watched television and videos, hung around home, or hung around with similarly bored friends.

When they went out, for the young men it was mainly to meet up with friends: just to 'be with other mates'. Sports, riding bikes, mucking around with cars or motorbikes, and skateboarding featured in discussions of what the young men did with their time. Young women liked to hang around and talk as well, although shopping, rather than sports, was a preferred activity. Unfamiliar places, being alone, feeling unwelcome, and being out at night affected how the young people felt about whether a place was safe or friendly—or not.

Social division

The social divisions that exist in rural communities can seriously limit options for young people. We have already discussed the effects of gender divisions on young people. Race and social class also have a considerable impact on young people's well-being and their options for the future.

People in rural communities belong to the community in different ways. In focus group discussions, young people mentioned divisions between the 'aristocracy' (the traditional land-owning families) and the 'landless' (seasonal workers). It was suggested that 'to belong, be respected and get a job in town, you need to have a surname that matches the street names'. These older divisions are sometimes the source of more contemporary divisions. In recent times, for example, the relocation of people in need of public housing from metropolitan and big regional centres to available public housing stock in rural areas and isolated regional centres has created an added demand on already stretched services. People who move into this situation are often already in distressed social circumstances, with their problems then exacerbated by the lack of public transport and employment in the areas to which they move. In many towns these people form a separate group, whose dependence on income support clashes with local traditions of self-reliance.

For many young people, the best thing about living in the country is 'the security of knowing most (if not all) of the people in your town and the sense of being far removed from the problems of the city' (Hillier et al. 1996: 10–11). Yet this idyllic experience of rural life is not always matched by the reality or by the young people's experience, nor that of their friends. The effect of social class in rural areas is to replace a real sense of belonging with a sense of exclusion.

This is illustrated in research on youth offending in a rural context (Mounsey 1997). An important aspect of this study was an evaluation of how young people's social standing in the local community and the community's perception of the problem impacted on the criminalisation process. The study found that specific families and neighbourhoods were subject to constant stigmatisation. Families of low socioeconomic status were highly susceptible to social exclusion and isolation, which had major consequences for the young people if offending did occur. Thus, 'if such young people did offend, not only was the community's response extremely punitive, but the expectation was also transformed into a reputation which served to reinforce their own social exclusion and isolation within that community' (Mounsey 1997: 31)—after all, everyone knows who the offender is and what they have done. Social and economic marginalisation of young people by way of labelling, stigmatisation, and refusal of employment was a contributing factor in their offending behaviour. Simultaneously, some communities, especially the smaller ones, reinforced this marginalisation once the young person had committed an offence.

Leaving town

While many of the older generation of rural dwellers are concerned at the migration of young people from rural areas to cities, 'leaving here' remains an important priority for many youth. The issues raised above are strongly felt by many young people, for whom the attractions of life in the city (a capital or regional city) are strongly felt. A study of young people from rural areas in the last three years of their secondary schooling revealed that a majority would make choices that enabled them to leave the rural town or area where they were living (James et al. 1999). Rural students were less likely than urban students to see having their family around them as a priority after they left school, reflecting that some rural students were keen to leave home (or reconciled to leaving) for a city lifestyle (James et al. 1999: 31).

Overall, though, it was the young people from higher socioeconomic backgrounds who were the most likely to make the active choice to leave their rural area. These young people often had grown up with the expectation from their families that they would attend university in a city. Among Year 10 students, this was most often expressed as excitement to be in a different social setting and as a time when they would 'grow up'. One student felt that 'the whole idea of going to uni is to socialise'. Others agreed:

> Someone I know who has been to Melbourne says that everyone fits in at Melbourne. If you go to college, you make friends. (Year 10 student from western Victoria)

> I am just looking forward to leaving, and I will be in Melbourne or somewhere. I am just so excited about meeting lots of people. (Year 10 student from northeastern Victoria)

While this was a common view, young people also expressed ambivalence. As one young person said:

> Once you are a country kid, you have to get back to where you are somebody. Because when you are in the city you are a nobody. (Year 10 student from northeastern Victoria)

The pattern for young people to leave rural towns in significant numbers appears set to continue. According to a research by the Australian Council for Educational Research, more than one-third of young Australians from non-metropolitan areas relocate to a major city in the years immediately after leaving school and, although some return, non-metropolitan areas experience a net loss of one-quarter of their young people (ACER 2007).

YOUNG PEOPLE'S POINTS OF VIEW

The research evidence on the areas of life—structural and cultural—that affect young people in rural areas reveal a pattern of relative disadvantage, despite the evident diversity across rural areas. The research evidence presented above has been generated through adult-driven research agendas. Broad patterns of disadvantage have justifiably created concern at local, state, and federal government levels about the provision of adequate health, education, and other social services to young people in rural, remote, and isolated areas. These jurisdictions have a strong interest in finding out what the problems are so that they can do something about them.

For this reason, the research base from which our conclusions about young people in rural areas is drawn tends to be tightly focused on the generation of statistical databases that enable comparisons to be drawn between different groupings. Examples of these statistical groupings are rural and urban, Indigenous and non-Indigenous, low and high socioeconomic status, and male and female. The research base also often describes selected young people's views on topic areas identified by the researchers.

Young people in rural and regional areas are seldom asked to identify what is important to them. Research that does focus on their priorities, experiences, and views challenges many of the stereotypes. In particular, whereas stereotyped views tend to categorise young people as being either rural or urban, recent research explores how young people in rural areas are connected to both local and global communities. Kenway et al. (2006), for example, open up new understandings about the lives of boys and men in rural and regional Australia. Their work challenges the neat dichotomy of rural–urban places and explores how global connections, myth, fantasy, and local identities interact in the lives of these males. Similarly, Thomson and Taylor (2005) show how in the United Kingdom, while mobility is an issue, localities have their own unique 'economy of mobility', involving particular material, cultural, and fantasy dimensions. They show how young people can long for urban culture, be involved in aspects of global culture through digital communication, and yet be confident that where they are is a good place to be. A study of young people in Ireland (O'Connor 2005) also found that young people experienced 'local embeddedness in a globalised world'.

> Whereas stereotyped views tend to categorise young people as being either rural or urban, recent research explores how young people in rural areas are connected to both local and global communities.

In the following section we explore what young people have to say about the priorities in their lives and the issues that have been raised above. There are few studies that have explicitly set out to engage rural young people in research that identifies their views and needs. We discuss two examples of research that is conducted about and with young people: the Youth First project in New Zealand and the Making a Life project in Tasmania, Australia.

Youth First

The Youth First project was conceptualised against the backdrop of research evidence that, like the research described above, positions young people from rural areas as at risk. The researchers noted that within the 'at risk' category, 'there is an implicit racial coding' of youth (Smith et al. 2002). In New Zealand, 'youth "at risk" are for the most part represented as Māori and Pacific Island youth growing up in poor families who live in poor communities and attend poor schools mostly in urban areas' (Smith et al. 2002).

Also noted by the researchers was the 'silence of youth voices' in the policies that were developed to address their needs and that they were dissatisfied with the narrow conceptions of youth drawing on psychologies of adolescence and development that shaped the policies and program interventions. The result was the development of a national study of youth in five provincial towns across the country, which focused on obtaining the diversity of young people's views and experiences of growing up in rural communities. The study was informed by five starting points:

- Economic restructuring, state-sector reform, and, more specifically, educational reforms have had a dramatic impact on young people's lives.
- Discourses of youth at risk have led to an over-emphasis on singular 'issues' that obscure deeper questions about youth as citizens.
- Youth at risk approaches were deeply racialised and links that were being drawn for example between Māori culture and rising suicide rates among Māori youth were dangerously self-fulfilling, under-theorised, and most likely wrong.
- The voices of youth were a missing and silenced component of policies and practices that were being promoted for their 'best interests' and their 'futures'.
- Youth have insightful views and analyses of how society works, have solutions to offer and would be willing to voice those if invited (Smith et al. 2002: 170).

The research approach set out to privilege youth voices through focus group interviews followed by youth tribunals or forums that enabled wider participation by young people, through spaces that were designed for them to speak within (Smith et al. 2002: 171). Having youth-friendly spaces involved different considerations in different areas. In one town, the advice was that if the researchers wanted youth to speak at a forum, they should 'not involve any adult from the local community' on the forum because of young people's need for confidentiality (Smith et al. 2002: 174).

This research found that the young people were able to provide rich testimonies to the significance of place to their identities, and that they were able to express their ambivalence and what they felt were the possibilities about rurality. The outcomes of the research revealed a number of common themes across the different regions, including young people feeling that they were not being listened to, were not permitted to participate as citizens in the public domain, and that they felt anxious about the future (Smith et al. 2002: 174). Each of these areas is important, but the authors of this research focus on a further area that they call 'multiple journeys of identity' because of the insights that it generates about the 'geography of rural childhood' (Smith et al. 2002: 174).

The researchers found that young people had a strong and connected sense of local community identity. Among Māori youth, this involved a sense of *whanau* (extended family) and *iwi* (tribal) identity. The extended discussions elaborating a positive sense of belonging in their community included 'a long list of activities that they do after school, including fishing, catching eels, swimming, mountain biking, helping their *marae* community' (Smith et al. 2002: 175). These animated discussions were in sharp contrast to the previous sessions when presenters had described their community as 'dull and boring'. Many of the stories that the young people shared at the tribunals were stories of hardship, loss, and struggle. Poverty and abuse were elements in some of their stories. The research by Smith et al. does not romanticise the lives of young people growing up in circumstances that are very challenging; however, what they were able to capture was the evidence that:

> In response to the general negative portrayal of youth, young people have been shown to construct their own moral rules and sense of community building, sometimes in a direct effort to educate their elders … Similarly, rural youth who stood out as promoting the rural as a space of possibility are important in that they can be seen to be deliberately constructing, mobilizing and projecting a

conception of community that defies the way they imagine others (for example, Aucklanders) see them (Smith et al. 2002: 177).

Making a Life

The Making a Life project is a longitudinal study of young people in Geeveston, south of Hobart (Wierenga 1999, 2001, 2007). 'Tragic' is how Wierenga describes the history of this small, landlocked town surrounded by a ring of hills. Its original sources of wealth—apple-growing and logging—were devastated by changes to global markets and changed environmental perceptions. The town no longer offers much in the way of employment opportunities, and in the tightly knit community (of 778 people in 1996) 'everyone knows everyone' (Wierenga 1999: 190). The study followed the pathways taken by young people in this small community, through the final years of schooling and beyond. The study revealed important insights into the role of place and geography in the identities of the young people.

Wierenga describes how important an understanding of place was to the young people. She describes how, for some of the young people, their world was circumscribed by the hills surrounding the town. Their lives were focused almost entirely on Geeveston. Others saw themselves as living in Geeveston, but as also 'belonging' to other places. The way that the young people constructed these boundaries in their narratives had a significant impact on their later lives. Over a period of four years, Wierenga was able to map the directions their lives took, the narratives the young people themselves used to describe their lives, and the resources they used to make their lives. She employs a typology that describes their focus in life and their stories of identity. The typology describes four types—'exploring, wandering, settling and retreating'.

A majority of the young women are exploring. They intend to move out, if only to complete their education. They use a more global reference then do young men and have clear stories about identity. A majority of the young men are settling. They are engaged in a localised world and can also tell clear stories about identity. Wanderers want to get out, retreaters intend to stay 'here where it is safe', but no individuals in these two smaller groups could tell a clear story about 'past, present, future and me' (Wierenga 1999: 193).

In this research, as in the study of New Zealand youth in rural settings, one of the most important resources for young people is the capacity to develop their own narratives that locate them in their own environment and that enable them to tell optimistic stories about their futures.

Summary

This chapter has provided an extensive overview of some of the key research and issues relating to young people in rural and remote communities. While emphasising the diversity of rural communities in Australia, we conclude that there are some common circumstances that young people in many such areas experience. The combination of remoteness, lack of transport and other services, and of economic change that is threatening the survival of some towns has led to a tendency to portray rural youth as being at risk or as having problems.

We have presented some of the evidence of challenge and hardship that young people in rural communities face. It is important to acknowledge these realities. At the same time, we have argued that research that simply focuses on problems for rural youth misses something important.

We have drawn attention to research that explicitly attempts to move beyond stereotypical views of rural youth as disadvantaged. These significant research projects offer insights into how young people in rural communities can be participants in research methodologies that generate knowledge about their lives. Without romanticising their lives, these research projects enable an approach that acknowledges the ongoing significance of community and of relationships to youth who have grown up in rural communities, and the way that place is part of their identities. In particular, research involving Indigenous youth is able to show how community-building can be part of their vision for the future.

Questions for further exploration

1 Research tends to identify the differences between rural and urban youth. What are some of the things that they experience in common?

2 In what ways are young people in rural areas disadvantaged compared with their urban counterparts?

3 Describe some of the economic and political issues that are affecting young and older people in many of Australia's declining rural areas.

4 In what ways is the bush important to the idea of what it means to be Australian? Has this changed over time?

5 What do young people in rural areas value about their places?

PART 3

Social Institutions

YOUTH POLICY

Introduction

Young people's experiences are defined through policies that affect many aspects of their lives. While the rules, constraints, and guidelines provided by policy frameworks are relatively invisible—especially to the majority of youth, who live with parents who care for them, who attend school regularly, and who are healthy—most young people benefit from state policies that aim to ensure that they all have access to high standards of education, health care, and protection from harm.

In this chapter we explore the tensions created by the design and enactment of policies that are relevant and beneficial to youth. Our discussion is framed by an awareness of the impact of social change on many aspects of young people's lives. As young people's relationships to education, work, family, and community change, so, too, must policy so that it is not out of step with young people's lives. The state is also changing and this has significant implications for policy frameworks.

We also explore the formal and informal nature of youth policy. We argue that despite the wide range of policies affecting youth, there are common themes. One of these is futurity—the valuing of young people for what they will become. This tendency underlying many youth policies is inevitably in tension with the increasing acknowledgment that young people should participate in policy decision making. Underlying this tension is contestation about the extent to which young people can be regarded as citizens in any sense, or whether they are simply citizens in training.

The links between youth policies and social exclusion are also examined in this chapter. The tendency for policies to address fragments of young people's lives and the lack of coordination across policy jurisdictions have been identified as crucial challenges for the development of relevant youth policy. The chapter concludes with a discussion of the recent interest in new approaches to youth policy, involving joined-up practice and intersectoral collaboration in the interests of developing more holistic approaches to youth policy.

WHAT IS YOUTH POLICY?

The history of state intervention in the lives of young people in Western countries stems from the mid 1800s (see Platt 1977; Harris & Webb 1987; Seymour 1988). It was at this time that governments began to introduce legislation that had a direct impact on children and youth in areas such as education (introduction of compulsory schooling), welfare (including the setting out of parental responsibilities to offspring), justice (especially the provision of a juvenile system), and work (that prohibited children of certain ages from working, for example). Over time, the state has acted as a facilitator of youth development in the form of establishing youth-specific institutions (age-based schooling and children's courts), and as a key agent in the social control of youth activities. In the case of the latter, various categories of youth have been socially constructed as a problem and, as such, requiring concerted attention and intervention, whether this be in regard to youth homelessness or juvenile delinquency.

> Over time, the state has acted as a facilitator of youth development in the form of establishing youth-specific institutions (age-based schooling and children's courts), and as a key agent in the social control of youth activities.

Explicit laws and regulations that permit or prohibit activities on the basis of age have been promulgated across a wide variety of social areas. The boundaries of what is deemed acceptable or unacceptable behaviour have changed over time, and vary depending on specific events and longer-term social trends. So, too, the nature of state intervention shifts according to prevailing economic and political forces (see, for example, Bernard 1992). Today, concern has gone well beyond that of neglected and delinquent children and young people to encompass a wide range of considerations, reflected in, for example, the extensive coverage of issues in the United Nations Convention on the Rights of the Child (CROC). The CROC sets out the rules, principles, and standards with which nation states are meant to comply, in the 'best interests of the child'. How countries respond to such prescriptions is a matter of public policy and institutional practices.

But what do we mean by youth policy? One way of answering this question is to describe existing formal youth policies. In Australia, federal, state, and territory governments all have some form of specific youth policy or youth strategy, located within a government office or department (such as an Office for Youth or a Department of Employment, Education, Training and Youth Affairs), as part of their wider policy framework. At a local level, many local councils and other local government areas have youth policies, some of which are well articulated and detailed. These statements provide frameworks that govern the provision of services to young people and provide the possibilities and limits for young people to participate in local-level decision making. In addition, the frameworks used by the different departments of government, such as those responsible for education and employment, health, juvenile justice, housing, and transport, have strategies, rules, and programs that contribute to youth policy. The Youth Allowance, for example, effectively requires all young people who are not in employment to be attending an educational institution until the age of eighteen. Young people who can prove that they are students are able to obtain concessions on public transport and for some forms of entertainment. The concept of the youth wage enables employers to pay workers under the age of eighteen at a lower rate than workers who are eighteen or older.

At yet another level, policy is formed and enacted in places where young people spend their time, such as schools and workplaces. In schools various forms of policy regarding young people are formalised and enacted that cover a wide range of areas, including the conditions of their participation in the school and discipline policies. School policies generally limit the extent to which young people can have a say in their education. While most schools in Australia have student representative councils that provide an opportunity for student participation, their activities are often limited to organising the school social and limited cultural events.

In workplaces, the treatment of young people as 'flexible' and exploitable workers has come to be formalised in practice. Many workplaces pay young people under the award wage with impunity. Young people are regularly asked to perform 'trial' shifts for which they are not paid and it is rare for young people to be notified when they have been unsuccessful in applying for jobs; these are systemic policies, even though they are not necessarily stated as formal policy. They are practices that affect young people's lives. They are based on the assumption that young people do not need to be taken seriously because they are not yet adults. Even formal policies often contain the assumption that young people are still becoming someone, but they have yet to arrive.

Futurity versus youth participation

Across all areas of formal and informal policy formation and practice, there is a range of practices that affect how young people live their lives. These practices are commonly based on the view that young people are not important as youth, but as future adults. These policies often draw on the language of youth development to assert that young people are important because they represent the future cultural and social capital of our society. There are many critiques of this approach:

> These policies, so commonly expressed now in the reductionist terms of the requirements of international economic competitiveness, are almost exclusively concerned with the production of future workers with particular skills or dispositions. These policies rest on an unexamined premise, on what Prout (1999) refers to as 'futurity'. The present of and for young people, their 'self-realisation' is of little interest or value in these policies (Ball, Maquire & Macrae 2000a: 146–47).

As many commentators have pointed out, policies that locate young people's value in their future as adults also tend to emphasise 'governmentality'(see Kelly 2001); that is, they provide a rationale for monitoring and controlling young people's lives in the interests of protecting the future of young people and of the society.

The Australian federal youth policy that was developed on the eve of the new millennium, for example, was called the National Youth Development Strategy (MCEETYA 2000). Ministers endorsed a youth development approach to young people's needs. The subgroup of the MCEETYA youth taskforce defined youth development as:

> A process which prepares young people to meet the challenges of adolescence and adulthood through a coordinated, progressive series of activities and experiences which help them to become socially, morally, emotionally, physically and cognitively competent. Positive youth development addresses the broader developmental needs of youth in contrast to deficit-based models, which focus solely on youth problems.

It states that young people 'need some guidance as they seek out their place in the world' (MCEETYA 2000: 3). Since that time this strategy has been replaced by an action plan called *Stepping Forward* (MCEETYA 2002), which states that 'young people's opinions and contributions are sought and valued, and they are encouraged and supported to take an active role in their communities and the nation' (MCEETYA 2002: 2). However, the policy provides no explicit strategy for involving young people in ongoing policy formation and it does not indicate that young people were involved in developing the action plan.

There are also state and territory youth policies, which are often located in Offices or Ministries of Youth Affairs. South Australia, for example, has an Office for Youth that offers a youth-specific site for young people to engage directly with government. This includes a Youth Action Plan that sets out a range of strategies for ensuring that young people are engaged with policy development, including forums, round tables, and a minister's youth council. As a key principle for creating better outcomes for young people the policy places an emphasis on youth empowerment. Similarly, the state of Victoria has an Office for Youth that has an explicit youth agenda, Future Directions: An Action Agenda for Victoria (2006), that was developed through a process of youth consultations. Youth engagement is supported through Regional Youth Affairs Networks that include participation by community groups and young people in non-metropolitan areas.

The Northern Territory youth policy provides an example of youth policy making that attempts to bring young people's participation into the policy process. The policy document, called *Building a Better Future for Young Territorians* (2003), was developed by the Office of Youth Affairs through a process of consultation with young people. The resulting policy document is consistent with the government's broader Social Development Strategy, is guided by 'the principles of respect, diversity, access, empowerment, equity and coordination', and aims to 'make sure that young people are able to participate in decisions that affect their lives' (Office of Youth Affairs 2002).

Like the websites for most of the state offices for youth, the Northern Territory site includes the use of an online chat room, in which youth can chat with ministers on topical issues, are provided with expanded opportunities to offer advice and to be consulted, and which has the intention to 'improve opportunities for young people and youth organisations to become involved in regional development planning processes'. It also provides a progress report on details of the programs and initiatives that have been implemented under the policy (Northern Territory Government 2006). In the following sections we will explore the implications these moves towards youth participation have for policy and for youth.

Policy as process

Once policies are posted on the Web they have already been through a process of debate and negotiation. Usually, the elements that make up the policy have been identified as issues by stakeholders and have become a focus of public awareness. It could be said that statements of policy are interim agreements that have been made between the key stakeholders. Even though the power relations may be very uneven—between relatively powerful government and business interests and relatively powerless lobby groups and non-government organisations—nonetheless policies are an outcome of the pressures exerted by each of these groups. Over time, there are clear shifts in position as groups such as the state and federal Youth Affairs Councils, non-government organisations, and lobbyists in state and federal political parties have an effect.

It could be said that statements of policy are interim agreements that have been made between the key stakeholders.

This means that when people talk about policy they are not referring to a static entity but to a dynamic process that can be portrayed as a policy cycle. Policy cycles can be represented as involving the elements portrayed in figure 7.1.

FIGURE 7.1   **The policy process**

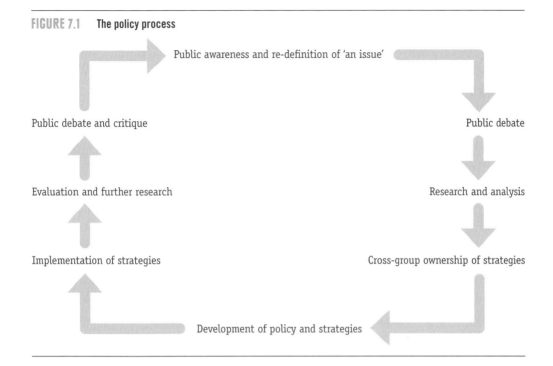

When we look at youth policy as a process, it becomes evident that this policy, especially as it relates to same-sex attracted young people, is messy and complex. For many years advocates of young people's rights have campaigned to have the needs of same-sex attracted youth recognised in policy forums (Crowhurst 1999); however, the public awareness and recognition of same-sex attracted youth did not occur until the HIV virus became a public issue in the 1980s. Concern about the impact of the HIV virus led to the recognition of the social and sexual practices of previously ignored groups.

At the same time, existing policies within the jurisdictions of education and health were able to be appropriated by advocates for same-sex attracted youth. The requirement for schools to provide a duty of care for all young people, for example, has been used to insist that the needs of same-sex attracted youth be fully recognised in schools (Hillier et al. 1999). The 1995 *Equal Opportunity Act* has been used to argue for protection against discrimination on the basis of sexuality; the Victorian framework for student support services (Department of Education 1998) also provides a framework that can be used in the area of sexual diversity. The research of Hillier and others has also played a significant role in publicly identifying the ways in which same-sex attracted youth are marginalised and violated in school and other settings, creating wider public awareness of this issue (see special issue of *Melbourne Studies in Education: Schooling and Sexualities* 1999). In these ways, various existing policy frameworks have been taken up to create safer and more socially just learning environments for same sex-attracted youth, even though there is no explicit policy statement on sexual diversity.

The example of the appropriation of policy frameworks in the interests of same-sex attracted youth highlights one of the most significant tensions within the area of youth policy. Advocates for same-sex attracted youth, as for other groups of young people, such as youth with learning disabilities and challenges or young homeless youth, are primarily focused on the role of young people in the present. Some of these groups also use the language of youth development to support the idea that young people's rights to belong in society as youth should be supported because they are important in the present. The Northern Territory youth policy document (described above), for example, makes important steps in the direction of valuing young people for their contributions to society as youth. It is worth exploring this approach to youth development in more detail, through the idea of young people as citizens.

Young people and citizenship

The relationship of young people to citizenship is a fundamental element in the assumptions underlying youth policy. The extent to which young people can be citizens is a question that is the subject of much debate. As Owen (1996) explains, if citizens are seen primarily as members of the community who have the right to vote and to stand for political office or serve on a jury, then young people under the age of eighteen would understand that being a citizen is something that will happen later:

> This view of citizenship necessarily pushes us towards redundant pedagogies that focus on training people for future roles, rather than equipping them with skills and understandings that can and must be given expression immediately. It reduced young people to either non-citizens or, at best, apprentice-citizens.

Owen further argues that our concept of citizenship should reach beyond the legal definition to encompass the full range of roles that individuals can play in 'forming, maintaining and changing their communities'. From this perspective, young people would be valued and valuable citizens in the present, as well as citizens of the future.

This distinction between a limited, legalistic concept of citizenship and a fuller, more social one has been explored by Evans (1995), using the concepts of minimal and maximal citizenship. She argues that minimal citizenship emphasises civil and legal status, and rights in, and responsibilities to, society. Under a minimal understanding, citizenship is gained when civil and legal status is granted. This is the approach that has traditionally informed most youth policy. With the increasing interest in youth participation evidenced in youth policy, maximal definitions of citizenship are being taken up. Evans defines maximal citizenship as a consciousness of oneself as a member of a shared democratic culture. It emphasises a participatory approach to political involvement and considers ways to overcome the social disadvantages that undermine citizenship by denying people full participation in society.

The concept of maximal citizenship emphasises a participatory approach to political involvement and considers ways to overcome the social disadvantages that undermine citizenship by denying people full participation in society.

Others agree with Evans. Walby (1994), for example, identifies three elements of citizenship, first developed by Marshall in the post-Second World War period: civil, political, and social. The civil element is related to the rights of individuals to individual freedom and liberty of the person and is associated with the courts of justice. The political element is the right to participate in the exercise of political power and is associated with the institutions of parliament, including local government. By the social element, she means 'the whole range from the right to a modicum of economic welfare and security to the right to share to the full in the social heritage and to live the life of a civilised being according to the standards prevailing in the society. The institutions most closely connected with it are the educational system and the social services' (Marshall 1950: 10–11, quoted in Walby 1994: 380).

It is this dimension of citizenship that young people are most frequently denied because of the assumptions about youth that frame education and social services. Education for citizenship in its minimal interpretation requires only induction into basic knowledge of institutionalised rules concerning rights and obligations, an approach that defines citizenship as a form of consumer rights. Limited decision making and power is offered through the exercise of set choices and options that are presented to youth and the provision of advice to decision makers. Citizenship is defined in terms of its formal aspects, such as voting for representatives and decision making that is deferred to adults.

Citizenship is most often addressed within schools as a subject, 'citizenship education', based on the idea that education is preparing young people to have the skills and understandings they will need in the future as citizens. It tends to focus on political and civic elements in citizenship, in which 'the objectives should be to enable Australians to discharge formal obligations of citizenship such as voting and compliance with laws' (Civics Expert Group 1994: 6). To the extent that it remains within this framework, citizenship education offers only a minimal interpretation of citizenship. The effect of this approach can be counterproductive: 'Learning about democracy and citizenship when I was at school was a bit like reading holiday brochures in prison. Unless you were about to be let out or escape, it was quite frustrating and seemed pointless' (Hannam 2000).

Yet this is precisely the approach recommended as the result of a study of fourteen year olds in twenty eight countries. *Citizenship and Democracy* (Mellor et al. 2002) provides an interesting insight into the civic knowledge, attitudes, and levels of engagement of Australian youth. It found that while young people overwhelmingly had positive attitudes towards their country and towards life in general, many were becoming alienated. The report shows that young people see an important role for government but 'do not trust politicians' and do not see themselves as having a great deal of space to debate social and political issues in classrooms. The authors of *Citizenship and Democracy* conclude that measures must be taken to 'help students realise their agency' for the future. In the present, the report simply advocates for citizenship education as a study area in the curriculum, which will prepare young people for a future in which they vote in elections and fulfil their civic responsibilities, but does not discuss active engagement as citizens in the present.

Maximal interpretations of citizenship require education that develops critical and reflective abilities and capacities for self-determination and autonomy. They involve the development of a consciousness of the self as a member of a shared, democratic culture, emphasising participatory approaches to political involvement, and consider ways in which social disadvantage undermines citizenship by denying people full participation in society in any significant sense. As Hannam points out, to be effectively educated for democracy means 'being able to *be* a citizen in a democracy' (2000: 2).

One of the ironies of youth participation is that when young people do mobilise politically, they are seldom taken seriously as participants or as democratic citizens because of the paradox associated with young people's engagement in political activity. On the one hand, young people are encouraged to be active on the social issues affecting their lives, and especially to participate fully in government-sponsored youth forums and the like. On the other hand, as Healy (1999) points out in relation to a series of anti-racist demonstrations by high school students, there is near universal hostility from the political establishment to this kind of political action on the part of young people. A common critique voiced in the media and by mainstream political leaders was that these young participants were being 'duped' by left-wing organisations, who were manipulating the young people for their own ends. Similar types of arguments are frequently heard in relation to young people engaged in anti-capitalist demonstrations or environmental protests. In other words, participation is framed in such a way that legitimacy resides solely in government-defined modes of behaviour and activity for young people. Those who act outside of this framework are deemed not to be bona fide participants, or to not really know their own mind (White, 2007b).

As indicated in Table 7.1, a central theme in many of the debates, commentaries, and portrayals of youth in politics is, indeed, the notion of knowing their own mind. In practice, this manifests itself in varying ways, but the suspicion that young people are not competent to do it for themselves surfaces time and again, whether this be in relation to their role in youth forums or in regards to the age at which people ought to be allowed to vote.

TABLE 7.1 Dimensions of youth political engagement

Activism as Either/Or	Apathy/activism, passive/active, social identity, not being able to make up their mind
Activism outside of approved forums	Disapproval, being duped, not knowing their own mind
Activism inside of approved forums	Someone else's agenda, socialisation, not knowing their own mind
Voting and the Age of Responsibility	Being/becoming, distinct age markers, being competent enough to make up their mind

Source: White, 2007b.

There are, nevertheless, many different degrees and ways in which young people can participate in society. Holdsworth (2000), an advocate of youth participation, has identified nine key areas in the processes of organisations in which young people can participate. He suggests that in each of these areas, organisations can be structured to provide for minimal or maximal citizenship for youth (see Table 7.2).

TABLE 7.2 Indicators for youth participation and citizenship

Organisational	Type of youth participation/citizenship area	
	Minimal	Maximal
Analysing needs and setting objectives	Adults design and execute project and inform young people as a target group Young people are consulted in the early stages but ignored later	Young people define the project with adults or young people plan and execute the project and can choose to involve adults
Information and communication	Young people are not informed or consulted, or information is accessible to them (one-way flow)	Youth and adults collaborate, or young people inform each other and possibly adults
Decision making	Young people are not consulted or are consulted but not taken seriously	Shared decision making between adults and youth, or young people have power over allocation of resources and the direction of the project but can seek the assistance of adults
Administration	No young administrators, or youth are volunteers doing menial tasks	Young people play an integral role in the running of the project
Design and implementation of activities	Youth are consulted in the design, which is by adults	Design and implementation by youth — possibly in cooperation with adults
Advocacy	Youth are present at public campaigns only	Young people have a significant role in public debate
Service, support, and education personnel	Young people are consulted on support-, service-, and education-related issues	Young people are trained to become counsellors with adult counsellors, or are the only counsellors
Employees	Young people are employed in jobs not related to project objectives	Young people are employed as experts and may manage the project
Monitoring and evaluating	Young people are involved	Youth design evaluation tools, and may implement and report on evaluation

Source: United Nations 1999.

Maximal citizenship requires that young people are given real roles in the institutions in which they participate (Holdsworth 2000). It recognises and respects young people's ability to act and contributes to building capacity for young people and their communities. Maximal citizenship is also integrative—it provides a mechanism for building connections between young people and communities. Although this is a challenging task, there has been an increasing interest from the community sector in youth participation and youth involvement in decision making in organisations associated with youth. In 2003 the Foundation for Young Australians, for example, published *Young*

People in Decision-making, a detailed report that challenges all organisations involving young people in decision-making roles to take this seriously (Wierenga 2003). This report identifies a number of reasons for taking youth participation in decision making seriously. Perhaps the most important of these is that young people are a significant group in society and if institutions, communities, and spaces are to be ones where they belong, then youth must be active participants in decision making about what happens in them.

This is especially the case in a time of rapid social change that involves the fragmentation of social life and the erosion of citizenship (Beck & Beck-Gernsheim 2002). In this context, youth participation is not simply a process that lets new members into the decision-makers' club. It is a necessary strategy to ensure that communities and societies can build the capacity of all their members to belong and to develop connections to the new forms of society and social relationships that are emerging. As Dwyer and Wyn (2001) also point out, because young people know no other world than the one in which uncertainty prevails in almost all areas of life, they have developed the sensibilities and perspectives that are required to engage with and live successfully in the 2000s.

Minimal interpretations of citizenship have the effect of perpetuating processes in schools, social services, and youth programs that produce unequal outcomes and marginalise youth. Curricula that have been designed without consulting the young people they are intended to benefit have the effect of reinforcing unequal outcomes from schooling based on social class. The entrenchment of inequality in many educational practices has provoked some educationalists to characterise schooling in the 2000s in Australia as 'undemocratic' (Teese & Polesel 2003). In the provision of youth services, minimal interpretations of youth citizenship have the effect of supporting a fragmented, narrowly targeted approach to youth that often reinforces rather than solves the problems the programs are intended to address. Even when policies are shifting towards the participation of young people in decision making, the practices they envisage remain on the minimal side of the continuum. Figure 7.2 summarises the key elements in youth decision making.

FIGURE 7.2   Continuum of youth involvement

1	2	3	4	5	6
Ad hoc input	Structured consultation	Influence	Delegation	Negotiation	Control

Low involvement ⟵——————————————————————⟶ High involvement

In Australia and in many other countries youth policies increasingly make reference to youth participation (for example, European Commission 2007). Yet, in doing so they face the challenge of a tradition of policies that have been designed to control youth, not to empower them. Most formal youth policies refer to practices of youth participation that reach level 3, which allows young people to have some influence. Most remain at level 2, involving young people in structured consultation. The implications of these constraints are discussed in the following section.

THE EFFECTS OF POLICY ON YOUNG PEOPLE

In this section we explore the impact of government policies on young people. Government policies from almost all jurisdictions have an impact on youth, especially in education, health, and juvenile justice. Over the last ten years or so, researchers have generated convincing evidence that inequalities between groups of young people—based on class, gender, race, and geographical location—have become greater. These inequalities are discussed in other chapters in this book in some detail. In the area of youth policy, this mass of evidence has provoked a rethink about how government policies and the thinking that informs them are part of the problem. Youth researchers have, for example, played an important role in analysing how policies enact governmentality. These analyses show how government policies place the responsibility for managing the uncertainties and inequalities of risk societies onto individual youths and their families. Particular groups of youth bear the brunt of this process. In Chapter 14 we discuss how this operates in the realm of health. In this chapter, where the idea of governmentality is also important, we discuss two other aspects of policy—exclusion and being out of step.

Exclusion

Exclusion, sometimes called social exclusion, is a term that has gained currency in youth studies over the last decade. It refers to the process that results in particular groups of young people becoming marginalised from society (see Chapter 2). An example is the process, described by MacDonald, whereby young people from the economically depressed area of Teesside in the United Kingdom become long-term unemployed. As MacDonald says: 'Research from Teesside and elsewhere indicates that young people who are pushed to the social and economic margins in their late teens may become excluded in the long term, and possibly permanently, from the sorts of lives enjoyed by the comfortable majority' (1998: 169).

MacDonald argues that these young people learn that in order to survive they must work outside the formal economy. A focus on leisure activities as a means of interacting and identity formation comes, for males, to replace the traditional role of employment in the formal economy. As MacDonald and others point out, it is important to recognise this effect of the individualisation of risk (Beck & Beck-Gernsheim 2002). It is also important to explore how policy frameworks and programs contribute to this process of exclusion.

One of the effects of contemporary youth policies has been to increasingly limit the responsibilities of the state for young people's lives. In order to understand and interpret this, it is essential to analyse how youth itself is fundamentally constructed in the interplay between state and age. Mizen (2002) describes the way in which state categorisations of rights and responsibilities establishes the substance of youth as a universal demarcation based on age. There is thus a material foundation to the proposition that age matters, based upon age-related laws, rules, and regulations promulgated by the state. This is illustrated in the link between certain ages and certain activities, in the Australian context, as set out in table 7.3.

One of the effects of contemporary youth policies has been to increasingly limit the responsibilities of the state for young people's lives.

TABLE 7.3 Examples of key transition ages for activities

Under 10	No criminal responsibility; compulsory schooling
10–15	Criminal responsibility (but rebuttable presumption of *doli incapax*), compulsory schooling
15–18	Eligible to leave school, gain a driver's licence, take up a full-time job, engage in sexual activity (although different age provisions may apply for same-sex relationships), qualify for social security payments if various eligibility criteria are satisfied, consent to medical and dental treatment
18–21	Drink and buy alcohol and buy cigarettes, live independently, rent a house, borrow money, open a bank account, marriage, vote, watch R-rated movies
21–25	Adult rather than youth wages, movement towards full adult social security entitlements

But the relationship between state and young people is not only constituted in this process of social categorisation. As noted in Chapter 1, Mizen (2002, 2004) further outlines the nature of the momentous shift in forms of state intervention—from Keynesianism to monetarism—and how this embodied huge changes in the relationship between the state and young people. Political management under Keynesianism included measures such as direct state support for parents, rising youth wages, extending of welfare benefits to young people in their own right, and expanded educational opportunities. By contrast, political management through monetarism has entailed, among other things, moving the cost of child support back onto the family, shifting the costs of education onto young people and their families, depressing youth wages, and making welfare benefits more difficult to claim. While young people share a similar relationship to the state due to their age, how the state carries out its core business in relation to youth and based upon their age has major implications for social divisions within the youth population. This, in turn, also means that certain young people become targets for specific types of state intervention.

In many Western countries, the period of the 1990s was characterised by a particular form of governmentality, in which government departments focused on target groups of young people within their narrow jurisdictions. The emphasis was on individuals at risk. In education, the focus was on finding indicators that would predict failure or early school leaving so that the mainstream could be left alone and only those most in need of intervention could be attended to. Similarly, in other departments and jurisdictions, the knowledge of different groups of professionals was used to identify young people who were at risk of homelessness (housing), abuse (community services), breaking the law (juvenile justice), or mental or physical illness (health). Within each of these areas, distinct and separate professional knowledge and language that defines the problem, the target group, and the solution have been built up. These distinct knowledges create and maintain the professional and service boundaries that limit effective solutions to the problems.

Health professionals, for example, talk of 'interventions'. An intervention from the point of view of a health professional might be a whole-of-school mental health education program that is introduced in schools with the aim of supporting mental health and well-being. But from the point of view of educators, this would be a curriculum innovation. For educators, young people are students whereas for community services personnel they are clients. Even the same terms can have different meanings for different professional groups. For educators, 'acting out' is an interactive drama technique that is used in classrooms; for social workers, 'acting out' is problem behaviour.

Differences in language represent very different ways of thinking about young people, about the identification of problems, and about what to do about them. These differences pose challenges for policy formation. Take the example of a whole-of-school mental health education program. The term 'intervention' is short for 'intervention in a state of affairs that will otherwise be negative'. This approach makes the assumption that there is an identifiable norm or correct state that the program will bring the students back to. The term 'curriculum innovation' is based on very different assumptions about the nature of young people and the role of professionals. The focus is on the embedding of new teaching and learning practices within the organisation of the school that will benefit all students in an ongoing process of improvement. Both understandings are relevant, but they are each only a part of a wider, complex picture of what is happening in young people's lives.

> While the policies and programs have distinct boundaries, the processes that marginalise youth do not.

A further problem is that while the policies and programs have distinct boundaries, the processes that marginalise youth do not. To put it simply, problems are joined up. Homelessness, abuse, failure at school, and mental health problems are examples of a coalition of problems that, while often treated separately by different groups of professionals, can be linked in the lives of individuals.

The problem of professional barriers occurs at all levels of policy and program development. Power's analysis of the British welfare state post-1945 is relevant to many other countries, including Australia, New Zealand, and Canada. Power points out that what has evolved over this period are bureaucratic structures of national or federal and local (state, provincial, borough) boundaries for the implementation of education, health, welfare, and other community sector policies through separate jurisdictions. In most countries there are also boundaries at various local levels, including local councils (Power 2001).

Yet despite this structure, the boundaries themselves have become problematic, as national policies and programs are implemented at the local levels. In Australia, for example, the administrative boundaries of local and regional health areas do not coincide with educational regions. Initiatives such as school focused youth services do not align with other initiatives such as Local Learning and Employment Networks, and these networks in turn are not necessarily the same as school networks. This tendency works against the enactment of more holistic policies that would cross jurisdictional barriers. Power notes that in the United Kingdom the administrative boundaries of welfare provision in boroughs have congruence in some cases; in shires they do not (2001: 14).

The effect of the administrative structures that govern the community and welfare sectors is that over time silos have been established. The term 'silos' refers to the tall, cylindrical structures that stand out on the wide, flat skyline of wheat and grain-growing areas of rural Australia. They are self-contained, impermeable, and unchanging. The metaphor of silos is used to refer to the self-contained nature of government departments, jurisdictions, and their local and regional counterparts.

Under the silo approach, many young people simply do not fit the structures—they fall between silos or are not recognised in the first place, because they do not conform to policy guidelines.

The effect of silo-based policies on young people has been understood as exclusion. The term exclusion has come to be used to refer to the fact that the growing inequalities that affect young people's lives are a social and not a personal problem. It also encompasses the view that social disadvantage is not simply a product of material disadvantage, but also of cultural disadvantage. The focus on exclusion emphasises the 'political–economic and the cultural–valuational dimensions of exclusion' (Power 2002: 17). The experience of the 1980s and 1990s has shown that while poverty is likely to produce social alienation, alleviating material poverty alone will not necessarily reduce alienation from society. Increasingly, it is recognised that the collection of capacities, relationships, and skills that are contained in the term 'social capital' are essential to creating social justice.

Social capital is a concept that has a range of meanings. It is associated with the concept of civic society and with community capacity. As Power (2002) points out, this is because social capital involves 'strengthening the mutuality of communities and enhancing trust' in order to promote greater social and economic well-being.

Many researchers have made the essential link between civil society, strong trust relationships, and social capital. In education, it is clear that young people learn and stay at school because of relationships (ACEE & AYRC 2001). Australian family studies have begun to focus on exchanges and trust as key elements in the construction of civil society (Milward 1998; Winter 1995). Recent longitudinal research with young people in rural Australia has shown how every resource that the research cohort accessed in order to make their lives (for example, goods, infrastructures, understandings, or skills) they accessed only through trust relationships. These relationships could be with other individuals, groups, or institutions, but without a history of trust, the resources on offer actually became completely inaccessible to the young people concerned (Wierenga 2001).

For these reasons, there is increasing interest in exploring how youth policies can support the building of positive links between young people and their communities (real or virtual). First, however, it is important to acknowledge a further dimension to youth policy that contributes to social and material exclusion.

Out-of-step policies

One of the greatest challenges for youth policy is social change. It has been suggested (Dwyer & Wyn 2001) that the post-1970 generation has grown up in a world that is very different from that of their parents, whereas those who have an effect on social change policy are the policy makers and youth researchers who often have grown up before 1970. While these people have experienced youth themselves, it was in a very different world from the one that young people now face. The assumptions that frame youth policies, then, have generally been shaped in a previous era, which means it is easy for youth policies to be operating on assumptions about the world that no longer hold. This is alienating for young people:

> Many young people … find themselves confronting completely changed global situations and problems, on both the large and the small scale, in their own life milieu and in global society. The adults and the institutions they direct have no answer to these because they have never experienced them and do not take them seriously (Beck & Beck-Gernsheim 2002: 160).

In many areas of young people's lives there is, compared with the recent past, an increased diversity of experience. As we point out in Chapters 9 and 11, young people are increasingly workers as well as students, establishing this pattern while they are in secondary school. Yet schools and policies continue to make the assumption that under the age of eighteen young people's primary status is that of student, unless they have formally left school. As MacDonald (1998) and Ball et al. (2000b) point out, despite the fact that leisure is evidently the focus of identity for some groups of youth, youth policies remain fixated on the school–work duo. Youth policies have yet to recognise youth's diversity.

If we look at the policy frameworks that dominate the main areas of young people's lives, it becomes clear that they still reflect the realities of a previous era, in which young people were prepared at schools for structured and defined roles in the workplaces of an industrial economy. As we have discussed earlier, youth policies and strategies continue to be couched in terms of facilitating the transition from school to work. These policies ignore the new reality: for a majority of Australian youth, school and work are simultaneous experiences, not sequential ones (Dwyer & Wyn 2001). The metaphor of pathways has dominated education and employment policies for youth, drawing on the outdated assumption of a linear progression from one life stage to the next. These policy frameworks ignore one of the most significant policy issues for the 2000s—that while young people have high participation in post-compulsory education they are at the same time confronted by greater insecurity and uncertainty with regard to career outcomes and future prospects (Dwyer et al. 2003).

Instead, in Australia and other Western countries, post-compulsory education (schooling for fifteen to eighteen year olds) has become defined as an intervening stage between the two worlds of school and work. In Australia, policy initiatives such as the Youth Allowance ensure that post-compulsory education is almost compulsory. The Youth Allowance provides a means-tested income support allowance for young people under the age of eighteen, provided that they are engaged in full-time education, which places strong pressure on young people to stay in education.

These examples illustrate just some of the ways in which there is a mismatch between young people's lives, filled as they are with complexity, and youth policy. In particular, youth policy overlooks the diversity in the lives of young people in favour of an outmoded notion of a mainstream and linear transitions to adulthood.

In summary, the emerging critique of youth policies and frameworks focuses on the drawbacks of futurity. Focusing on youth as future adults, citizens, and workers has the disadvantage that it ignores the important role that young people play in society—as youth. Futurity in youth policy also has the effect of downplaying the significance of social change on the experience of youth and the implications of their life patterns for the experience and meaning of adulthood for their generation. While it is increasingly clear that being a young person today is different in some fundamental ways from being young in the 1970s, policies have yet to reflect this.

This critique of youth policies also emphasises the need to address the marginalisation and exclusion of youth by developing new approaches that recognise the joined-up nature of problems. In the next section we discuss the directions that these new approaches to youth policy are taking.

Youth policy and intersectoral collaboration

Over the last decade there has been a shift in thinking about the role of policy based on the critiques above. In the United Kingdom and the USA policy makers are reflecting on how to respond more effectively to social problems that are common across different policy jurisdictions, such as health, education, and juvenile justice.

The implication of these ideas for youth policy has recently been explored (Wierenga et al. 2003) and has involved analysing how the delivery of youth services can be supported by government but operated in a form of partnership with communities. A key element in this shift in approach to policy is the recognition that the work of supporting young people occurs in communities (real or virtual). The most important issues—unemployment, drug abuse, poverty, crime, domestic violence, and many others—need to be tackled locally and holistically:

> At a surface level, this task is about finding a language that reconciles some already too familiar social problems (for example, social exclusion) with creative ways of thinking about social solutions and the means to attain them. At a deeper level, we are not just talking about meeting isolated human needs, but the creation of hope (Botsman 2000) and certainty that things can change for the better (Wierenga et al. 2003: 18).

There are already many examples across Australia, in the United Kingdom, and in other countries of programs and networks that involve intersectoral collaboration to provide more effective responses to young people's needs. In Victoria, for example, the Working Together Strategy and Local Learning and Employment Networks have been put in place (Wierenga et al. 2003). Other examples are the work of the Social Entrepreneurs networks (particularly in the United Kingdom and the USA), which are organised around leadership in community action using business methods to deal with social problems (Sanderson 2000: 1). Civic Entrepreneurs, which is also gaining attention, are public servants who understand microcommunity politics and are able to address the links between the macro level of policy and the micro level of community action and leadership by providing 'human bridges' between policy and community (Wierenga et al. 2002: 13).

At a conceptual level, the emergence of interest in youth policies that are oriented towards community capacity building dovetails with attempts to find a way to address problems of social exclusion through community-led solutions. Community development and community capacity building concepts are also relevant, drawing on a wide literature that questions how government and communities can work together. This literature has in common the assumption that the idea of community becomes contested. Many of the examples of best practice draw on the experiences of the most disadvantaged groups, including Indigenous communities and communities with long-term unemployment (Pearson 2001).

> There are already many examples across Australia, in the United Kingdom, and in other countries of programs and networks that involve intersectoral collaboration to provide more effective responses to young people's needs.

As Wierenga et al. (2003) comment, there are many examples of initiatives that focus on young people not as problems, but as resources for the community and as valued members of teams:

> Youth participation, engagement and leadership were a 'hidden' theme, not often explicitly spoken in the interviews, because it had become a fundamental assumption of both interviewer and interviewed.

On reviewing the data, it is clear that it is central to the ways that all of the really effective projects were structured. As staff were being interviewed at Connexions about the 'Artful Dodgers Studio', one of the young program participants was gathering the other participants in another room to write a press release. Around the time Dave was being interviewed at Visy Cares, staff were out in the centre's outreach zones recruiting young Aboriginal and migrant leadership teams … The life-transforming work at the Lighthouse Foundation involves young people having a high degree of scope to choose and negotiate their own and shared directions for growth, based upon their interests, talents and passions (Wierenga et al. 2003: 23).

As different models and approaches are tested in practice, some common issues are emerging. Most initiatives at some point have, for example, to negotiate their relationship with government, which is generally the source of funding. Practitioners often feel that bureaucrats, who control the purse strings, do not have an understanding of how the projects work and what they achieve. Increasingly, relationships with business are also an issue. Some initiatives draw on government and business support for funding and leadership; in other instances, local programs feel that local businesses are not interested in contributing to the building of social capital in their local youth.

The matter of funding and accountability for funding is also an issue. Many programs are labelled 'pilot' programs and provided with only short-term funding. The effect on local youth is that the program is perceived as a stop–start program, relationships with staff are insecure, and cynicism about connecting with youth programs mounts. It is also clear that the measurement of outcomes requires a rethink. Quantifying numbers of 'clients' who have accessed a service does not do justice to the broader aims of maintaining connections with youth. One of the solutions to this problem is to build more effective evidence about what works, so that accountability measures can be related more closely to practice.

There are also major organisational issues and practitioner matters that require much more critical discussion. Conceptually, there often exist difficulties over how certain preferred methods are to be interpreted in practice (see Stokes & Tyler 1997). Multi-agency collaboration, for instance, often begs the question of who is to coordinate the process and what criteria are to be used for evaluating the purposes and performance indicators of such cooperation (Hughes 1996). The issue of accountability looms large here, particularly given the different institutional sectors that may be represented in any such collaborative effort.

It is worth reiterating that the different institutional sectors in a collaborative relationship often have very different core imperatives that can lead to significant differences in outlook and intervention preferences. Intervention that is intended to be multi-agency and multipronged in nature will inevitably be difficult to organise and administer. This type of intervention raises big questions about the precise nature of partnership—who is to do what, and how they are to do it (see White & Coventry 2000). In the United Kingdom, where there has been a tradition of encouraging intersectoral collaboration, there is an emerging critique of this approach. While there is still support for the idea of collaborating across sectors, researchers point out the need to develop a new language to mediate the differences in sectoral and disciplinary understandings (Milbourne et al. 2003; Tett et al. 2003).

Perhaps the largest gap in discussions about intervention strategies, projects, and programs concerns where practitioners fit in to the scenario: 'The forgotten warriors of community change are those who actually have to shoulder the burden of social renovation' (White 2002d: 22). One of the central dilemmas in the social capital literature is that practitioners are told that their job is to intervene to change the lives of children and young people for the better, often by working with young people themselves, when very often their own work (and personal) lives are less than positive. Work-related stress and sheer fatigue are major issues that can affect young and old alike.

A related issue is the acknowledgment of failure or of the shortfall between expectations and outcomes. Building a worthwhile evidence base depends in part on being able to acknowledge mistakes and what has been learnt from them (within and across different countries). It also requires careful appraisal of how appeal to volunteerism can paper over shortfalls in needed government and other assistance.

In the end, the construction of the issues and the allocation of resources (including volunteers) are best judged in relation to questions that ought to be central to the policy process: What constitutes human needs and how are these to be satisfied (see Deacon 1983)? If youth participation is to have meaning, and community-building to be transformative, then there is a need to increase the real choices that people have over how their welfare is to be met. Improving and enhancing collective and individual well-being is, therefore, intrinsically political. For how public policy is determined and implemented always reflects broader struggles over how needs and resources are defined and allocated in society.

Summary

This discussion of youth policy has identified the significance of policy in young people's lives. Our discussion is developed against a backdrop of social change in which young people are shaping new ways of relating to families, new uses of and approaches to education (formal and informal), and distinctive approaches to the world of work. In this context, there is increasing recognition of the need to rethink policies that relate to youth, because older assumptions that identify youth as simply adults in the making are becoming less relevant.

We focus particularly on the challenges to policy formation that are posed by taking up maximal definitions of citizenship. At a theoretical level, this means that even though youth under the age of eighteen are not legally citizens, they can still be considered to be citizens at a civic level. The debate is given impetus because in everyday life the meanings of chronological age are becoming less clear.

The idea of youth participation has currency in many organisations and policy documents. We argue that it is possible to see an increasing engagement with this concept in policy documents, and in the practices of youth-oriented organisations, including schools. Youth participation is especially relevant to the thinking behind new approaches to the state and youth policy. These approaches have developed from a wide range of sources, including the third way, community development, capacity building, and the idea of the enabling state.

Within the spaces that are created when the state decreases its responsibility for youth, these new practices and frameworks for policies offer opportunities to shape relationships within communities and across jurisdictions that draw on young people's insights about what youth need. They also offer opportunities to develop partnerships in decision making and policy and program delivery in which young people are an integral part.

Questions for further exploration

1   What is the state, its institutions, activities, and interventions?

2   Provide concrete examples of minimal and maximal forms of youth participation.

3   Young people engage in civic life in many different ways, some of which are not seen as political, such as riots and graffiti, yet which can be interpreted as part of the politics of everyday life. Discuss.

4   The state in capitalist society is a capitalist state. What implications and consequences does this have for young people in relation to the notion of the marketplace?

5   Is social exclusion an inevitable consequence of state intervention, or can the state once again play a more positive and proactive support role for young people?

8
RELATING AND BELONGING

Introduction

In 1984 the director of the Australian Institute of Family Studies wrote a discussion paper called 'Can the Family Survive?' (McDonald 1984) that described the emerging concern in many industrialised countries about changes to the traditional nuclear family structure that had been dominant during the first half of the twentieth century. McDonald commented that:

> Great concern has been expressed in recent times that the family 'as we know it' is rapidly disappearing. The theme has become a rallying point for the new conservatism in all English-speaking countries, and even prominent feminists such as Germaine Greer and Betty Friedan are among those who want the virtues of the family to receive greater recognition (McDonald 1984: 1).

Over twenty years later, the debate continues. The empirical evidence that sparked McDonald's question continues to fuel debate as some researchers find evidence for the end of the traditional family and others see evidence of successful attempts by people in contemporary society to build new forms of families. With the benefit of hindsight, sociologists are able to discern historical trends and point out that new patterns have emerged. Beck and Beck-Gernsheim (2002: 85) propose that:

> the black-and-white alternative 'end of the family' or 'family as the future' is not appropriate. The focus should instead be on the many grey areas or, better, the many different shades in the niches inside and outside the traditional family network ... these forms signal more than just pluralism and contiguity, more than just a colourful motley thrown together at random. For a basic historical trend can be discerned in all this variety, a trend towards individualization that also increasingly characterizes relations among members of the same family.

This chapter discusses changing family structures and changes to relations among family members, with particular emphasis on their implications for young people. We argue that, whatever its contemporary form(s), the family remains the most important institution for young people's lives, directly and indirectly. The early experiences of children are regarded as increasingly significant to their later health, well-being, and educational outcomes. Family is also recognised as the most significant source of support for older youth (Dwyer et al. 2003). The effects of social and economic inequality across societies are transferred through families to have an indirect but significant effect on young people's lives. Recent research provides evidence of the negative effects of poverty on parents' ability to provide 'warmth, structure and control' (Conger et al. 2000).

We examine the evidence of the changing experience of family life for young people in the late 1990s and early 2000s. Their involvement in increasingly diverse family forms has provided the challenge of understanding how different family structures affect young people's development. We have sought to describe not only how families affect young people, but also the resources that they bring and the ways in which they have contributed to the shape of families in the 2000s.

The chapter begins with a discussion of social change and the family. Drawing on contemporary Australian research from the Australian Institute of Family Studies and other sources, it points out that today, the nuclear family does not constitute the dominant form of household arrangement. Social researchers have highlighted the increasing diversity of family forms, and the trend towards change within individual families through parental separations, divorce, and remarriage. We argue that there is a need to re-evaluate the traditional view that young people have a dependent relationship to the institution of the family and explore the ways in which youth is now associated with new patterns of interdependence between youth and their families of origin. Many young people are responsible for others in their family, through their paid or unpaid labour as child-carers or domestic workers, and through the income many of them contribute to the family's resources.

The rate of marriage break-up in Australian society means that many young people are growing up within complex sets of relationships, some involving one parent and others involving more than two adults in the parenting role, plus increased access to adults in a grandparent role and new forms of sibling relationship. The chapter also describes the increasing significance of the family in youth policy over the last decade. As successive governments have sought to minimise social welfare initiatives, the nuclear family has come to be seen as the agency that should advocate for, protect, resource, and care for young people. We also note that the diversity of family life and certain technologies have opened up opportunities to move beyond the heterosexual family.

FAMILIES, SOCIAL CHANGE, AND DIVERSITY

The evidence of the effects of social change on family life points overwhelmingly to a dramatic change in the meaning and experience of family over the last hundred years and especially in the last thirty years (Gilding 2001). Yet there is very little research evidence about young people's experiences of and views on family life. Here, we consider the key features of these changes and their implications for young people's lives.

Taking a long-range view over the recent history of the family—the last hundred years—it becomes apparent that a diversity of family forms is not new. Gilding notes that in Australia at the time of Federation, working-class households were 'crowded and economically precarious' (2001: 7). He comments that economic insecurity promoted 'flexible household arrangements' in which households included servants, lodgers, extended family, and households headed by women as their husbands sought work in other locations. Other patterns regarded as new are not necessarily so when viewed from a longer time frame. In the nineteenth century, it was common for young people to live at home until they married (Weston et al. 2001). Yet one of the most noted 'changes' to the experience of youth in the 2000s is said to be the pattern for young people to continue living at home until well into their twenties, and even their into their early thirties (Weston et al. 2001). Even after leaving home, many subsequently return for periods of time.

The recurrence of particular elements of family and household relationships over time can give a false impression of continuity. Even though, at a superficial level, there may appear to be similarities between one generation and the next, this does not mean that the causes, experiences, and meanings of these patterns to the participants are exactly the same. It is important, therefore, to understand what particular patterns of family and household formation mean to young people today.

> Taking a long-range view over the recent history of the family — the last hundred years — it becomes apparent that a diversity of family forms is not new.

Underlying the broad statistical patterns of family formation there is a range of causes and circumstances. Milward (1998), for example, notes that it would be wrong to assume that the contemporary pattern of young people to remain in the family home with their parents is simply motivated by financial dependence. She points out that it is important to understand the patterns of reciprocity involved between the generations today: many young people who are living with their parents, she found, are providing care or assistance to their parents. Furthermore, leaving home is not necessarily equated with financial independence. Young people often leave home on the basis of continued financial support from their parents (Holdsworth 2000).

The broad patterns of family formation do not tell the whole story. Weston et al. (2001) point out that the patterns of relationship between generations for Indigenous Australians differ significantly from non-Indigenous Australians. The extensive network of extended family relationships, obligations, and reciprocal relations that make up Indigenous families mean that their relations with kin are complex and often have priority over other spheres of life. Indigenous Australians also have higher rates of fertility than non-Indigenous Australians, meaning that the number of young people in these communities as a proportion of the total population is greater than in non-Indigenous communities. As we have discussed elsewhere, for young Indigenous people, understandings of what it means to grow up challenge the traditional Western models that the process ought to be directed at increasing personal autonomy and independence (Wyn & White 1997).

The statistical profiles of Australian family formation are illustrative of the extent of social change to the institution of the family at particular points in time. For some indicators, such as age at marriage for women, the differences between the generation born in the late 1940s and early 1950s and those born after 1970 are stark.

Figure 8.1 shows that the greatest difference in first marriage rates for women occurred between 1970 and 2000. In 1970, 300 per 1000 women were married for the first time by age twenty to twenty-four; by the year 2000, this rate had fallen to fifty per 1000 women. This pattern has also influenced fertility rates, which have followed the decline in age at first marriage, showing a decline in fertility for twenty to twenty-four year olds and an increase in fertility in older women (Weston et al. 2001: 18). Hence, over the course of one generation one of the most significant changes has occurred for young women: they no longer expect to be married in their early twenties. The trend to later marriage for women is one factor among a number that indicates a change in the lives of young people. The evidence is that they are not forming family relationships in the same way that their parents did. Many of the changes that we discuss in this chapter also relate specifically to this time period.

FIGURE 8.1   **Age at first marriage rates for women**

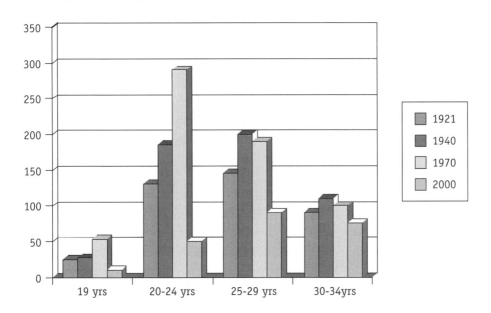

Changes in marriage and fertility reflect the trend for young people to remain single or to defer having children until well beyond their twenties and into their thirties. Young people are entering long-term partnerships later in life than previously (Smart 2002: 28), and the research shows that their rate has fallen overall and that their risk of breaking down in the first few years of formation is 'considerable' (Weston & Parker 2002: 9). What these trends mean for young people's experiences of family is that a more diverse range of relationships is being experienced. Young people are living in a range of household types, including staying in the family home with parents, living with other young people in group households, and living on their own. Young people also expect to experience a range of relationships before forming a partnership (whether by marriage or de facto).

Structural ageing is also likely to have a profound impact on the present and future prospects of young people today. This concept refers to changing demographic patterns based upon the age composition of the population. Populations change in age composition as a result of four inter-related dynamics: births, deaths, immigration, and emigration (Jackson 2001: 203). At the moment the trend in Australia is for the median age to be old — that is, for the population as a whole to be weighted towards the older rather than the younger end of the age spectrum.

Young people are directly implicated in the relationship between structural ageing (the increasing proportion of the population to be found at older ages) and numerical ageing (the absolute growth in the numbers of elderly). As Jackson (2001: 203) observes:

> it is largely numerical ageing that social welfare policy must respond to, and it is structural ageing that is the constraining factor: numerical ageing is adding to the overall numbers receiving income support payments; structural ageing will eventually reduce the size of the labour force (and potential tax base) vis-à-vis the dependent population (although it also has the potential to cause declines in the numbers receiving some payments).

There are several ramifications for young people that follow from this trend. As the number and proportion of older Australians grow, so, too, will the political weight of what is referred to as 'grey power', which will translate into state financial transfers and policy initiatives that are to the benefit of the elderly, some of which, in terms of priority spending areas, will be at the expense of the young. Meanwhile, it is the young who will be expected to pick up the cost of paying for the longer-term care of the old, as well as providing for their own futures.

As the number and proportion of older Australians grow, so, too, will the political weight of 'grey power', which will translate into state financial transfers and policy initiatives that are to the benefit of the elderly, some of which, in terms of priority spending areas, will be at the expense of the young.

Different population cohorts grow older in very different policy and economic contexts, and these have a profound influence on the present situation and future prospects of any particular group. The baby boomers, for example, were relatively privileged compared to present generations of young people in that when they were young, employment rates were high, wages and benefits comparatively generous, housing prices more affordable, government benefits relatively easier to access, and education fees considerably less onerous. By contrast, young people today experience later entry into full-time paid work, youth wages are low, employment is precarious, and many young workers enter the labour market with a substantial debt due to tertiary education contribution schemes, not to mention the high costs of trying to enter into the housing market (Jackson 2002; Hardin, Kelly & Bill 2003). The relationship between age cohorts (that is, the baby boomers and the present youth generation) is an important area of research, not only from the point of view of how younger generations will be expected to support the extended life spans and retirement activities of their grandparents and parents, but also with regard to how cohorts such as the baby boomers, at least within middle-class families, will materially continue to support their children as, now, part of a life-long project (see Pusey 2007).

The other main demographics to have an impact on young people are the high rate of marriage breakdown and the high rates of re-formation of marriages and households, perhaps the most important theme in the literature on young people's experiences of family in the 2000s. It has been estimated that around 10 per cent of Australian children will have experienced parental divorce by the age of ten and that this increases to 18 per cent by the age of eighteen (Weston & Hughes 1999: 14).

The diversity of families in Australia is undisputed. How to characterise these diverse family forms is still under debate. It is common to portray the new diversity as a series of variations on the theme of the traditional nuclear family of two parents and their biological children. Hence, diversity is measured in some studies as an increase in single-parent families, stepfamilies (where one parent is not the natural parent of the child(ren) of the household), blended families (families containing at least one natural child of the couple and one stepchild of one parent), and same-sex parent families. Today, less than half of Australian families (47 per cent) are couples with children (ABS 2002). Of the families with dependent children aged zero to seventeen, 72 per cent were intact-couple families and 21 per cent were single-parent families. The remaining 7 per cent lived in stepfamilies or blended families (ABS 1998b). The figures also show that there has been a marked increase in the proportion of single-parent families in the last thirty years, from 9 per cent in 1974 to 19 per cent in 1996 (AIHW 1997). After parental separation, the vast majority of children live with their mother (88 per cent). Of these, the majority are single-parent families (68 per cent). It has been estimated that by 2021 the proportion of single-parent families will increase by between 30 and 60 per cent (ABS 1999).

Although the proportion of young people growing up in same-sex parent families is small, there is evidence that this proportion is growing (McNair et al. 2002). The available research, conducted across a wide range of measures, on young people who grow up in same-sex parent families suggests that there is no noticeable difference between these young people and those growing up in heterosexual families. There is an increasing body of research on these families that shows that one of the effects of these families is their contribution to a rethinking of the contributions of parents, including biological mothers and fathers, to children's lives. McNair et al. argue that 'lesbian parenthood is reshaping the institution of fatherhood, and the role of men in families, rather than erasing the contribution of men from children's lives' (2002: 48).

> The available research, conducted across a wide range of measures, on the young people who grow up in same-sex parent families suggests that there is no noticeable difference between these young people and those growing up in heterosexual families.

For purposes of statistical analysis, it is convenient to characterise family forms as variations on the traditional nuclear family (or intact family) of biological parents and their children. It also provides an important measure of the extent of change over time. Yet, despite this, there is a sense that this approach is too narrow to take account of the extent of change in and thinking about family life in the last three decades. For this reason, many writers are attempting to find different ways to understand the implications of change on family life.

Young people and family

Despite the extent of change, the family remains the main form of living arrangement for young people to grow up in, so it is important to understand the effects of changes to the family and its implications for young people. One of the most significant and under-researched areas of change is the effects on young people of divorce, repartnering, and serial marriage. Many young people are directly affected by the changes in family structure and arrangements over time, and by the bringing together of complex relationships among family members as marriages break up and re-form.

Research by the Australian Institute of Family Studies shows that children who live in intact families have the highest rates of well-being (Weston & Hughes 1999). The children of sole mothers, they found, were the least happy. These families were the most likely to be poor, but economic circumstances alone did not explain the children's lower sense of well-being. The study found that having a poor relationship with a non-resident stepmother was a significant source of unhappiness for young people. Young people who lived with a stepmother tended to have relatively high levels of well-being and satisfaction. The authors note that the study did not include young people who were sufficiently unhappy with their living arrangements to have left home, and hence it may be biased towards satisfaction.

Comparing the lives of children and young people from different family forms with each other is important, but it may have the unintended consequence of fostering the idea that there is a norm or optimal model for the bringing up children. The very term 'intact' implies that other families are broken, even though the latter term is not used. In an age when many young people now have to engage with the complexities of diverse and changing living arrangements it is important to look beyond these relatively narrow approaches to understand the implications for the kinds of social relations that are being formed more broadly. Even young people in intact families are affected by the understandings and experiences of their peers in families that are different from theirs. Beck and Beck-Gernsheim (2002: 96) argue that the implications of diversity in family forms are indeed significant:

> If children manage to come to terms with changing family forms, this means that they have had to learn to sever close bonds, to cope with loss. They learn early what it means to be abandoned and to part. They see that love does not last for ever, that relationships come to an end, that separation is a normal occurrence in life.

Beck and Beck-Gernsheim suggest that beyond the debates about whether new family forms are good or bad for children, there is the fact that they are learning about family relationships in contexts of change, loss, separation, and re-forming relationships. It is common for children and young people whose parents have divorced to move between the households of their biological parents. They often live with the children of their parents' new partners, forging sibling relationships with their new family and negotiating the different rules about all aspects of life: television hours, pocket money, meals, and bedtimes.

In these situations young people have to make decisions and choices on their own behalf. The realities of these arrangements have led some researchers to move beyond the relatively narrow conception of family forms in terms of their relation to the intact nuclear family (that is, sole-parent, blended, stepfamilies, etc.). New terms have been coined to capture the changing sensitivities and approaches to family life. Beck and Beck-Gernsheim (2002: 96) point out that it is possible to identify 'marriage and divorce chains' and 'conjugal succession'. They also report that some researchers refer to 'multiparent families' and 'patchwork families' in the attempt to make new family forms easier to understand.

For young people, the important point is that these terms acknowledge that it is not easy to know who actually belongs to the family. A single definition of who belongs and who does not belong in families 'has been lost somewhere in the rhythm of separation and new relationships' (Beck & Beck-Gernsheim 2002: 96). The Australian Institute of Family Studies found that members of the same family groups did not necessarily share the same views about levels of satisfaction with their situation. Other researchers have taken this diversity within families further to argue that each member of the family has their own definition of what the family is — of who belongs and who does not.

Sociologists of the family are discovering what many older youth already know: that the maintenance of family ties and links are no longer a matter of course—they are chosen. In situations of divorce, in particular, family relationships are worked out according to the choices made by individuals, including children and young people. Beck and Beck-Gernsheim quote a study of patchwork families: 'From the huge universe of potential kin, people actively create kin by establishing a relationship—by working at becoming kin. And they have wide latitude in choosing which links to activate' (Furstenberg & Cherlin 1991: 93, quoted in Beck & Beck-Gernsheim 2002: 97).

For many young people, this means that they are involved in extensive networks and chains of relationships: they are related to many people but the obligations involved in these bonds are less clear. It is up to individuals to determine what these relationships mean. The negotiation of meaning and of belonging in families has important implications for the way in which resources flow in families.

> Sociologists of the family are discovering what many older youth already know: that the maintenance of family ties and links are no longer a matter of course — they are chosen.

Resources and living arrangements

The flow of resources within families is of particular importance today because, as governments in many Western societies restructure their social policies, increasing pressure is being placed on families to support the individuals within them. This has led in turn to an interest in understanding how families contribute to the social capital of communities. There is concern among some researchers that the decline of the traditional family will herald an era in which civic engagement and community social capital will be eroded (Hughes & Stone 2003). Here, we explore the ways in which family relationships mediate the flow of resources, material and social, for young people.

Family relationships are primarily relationships of interdependency. Each parent and each child derives from the other a range of emotional, physical, spiritual, and other types of human experiences that take place within the context of, and exchange of, a wide range of material and non-material resources. The unique experience of each family is mirrored in the shared experiences of many different families living in similar conditions. The reality of family life is one that is shaped by social forces beyond the family as well as the dynamics of each household.

It has long been acknowledged that different types of capital are produced and reproduced in the family context. The work of Bourdieu (1984, 1990), in particular, is centred on the idea that, throughout their lives, individuals accrue, in varying ways and to different extents, social, cultural, economic, and symbolic capital. In an interesting twist to the discussion of capital, Barry (2006) argues that it is not just the accumulation of capital that preoccupies young people, but also its expenditure.

In a discussion of why young people persist or desist in offending behaviour and activities, Barry (2006) argues that achieving social recognition—an essentially social process—is vital for young people to gain a sense of achievement and social belonging as they move through the childhood and teenage years. The family of origin provides the platform upon which capital accumulation grows and develops. But it is the expenditure of accumulated capital that brings the rewards of individual gratification and social stability.

Some idea of what Barry (2006: 139) means by expenditure of capital is provided in Table 8.1. The dual processes of accumulation and expenditure of capital are largely shaped by the experiences of individuals as they negotiate their home and family life. What one ends up with, at any point in time, and what one expends are influenced by family relationships, networks, and resources.

TABLE 8.1 Expenditure of capital associated with desistance from offending

Capital	
Social	• Having responsibilities to one's family, partner, or children • Becoming a parent • Giving love, friendship, or attention to others • Seeking custody of one's child
Economic	• Buying clothes and other consumables (as opposed to stealing them) • Spending money on one's house or children • Paying taxes and other state contributions
Cultural	• Contributing towards others' development or welfare through employment, teaching, or influence, based on one's own skills and experience • Setting an example by one's actions or words • Encouraging and helping others
Symbolic	• Wanting to give of oneself (as mentor, volunteer, worker, etc.) • Wanting to offer restoration or reparation to the community • Having responsibilities towards one's house or job

Source: Barry 2006: 139.

The physical, emotional, spiritual, and psychological state of children and young people is broadly determined by the social relations and social resources of the family. So, too, are their future prospects, opportunities, and dilemmas. How the family is constituted in public policy, how it is perceived and supported (or undermined) by state intervention, also has a major bearing on how families actually work at the level of lived experiences and material practices.

Flow of material resources

Typically, most government attention on families and children tends to concentrate on the parents' contribution to the welfare of the child. State policies in areas such as financial assistance to ensure young people's participation in education, for instance, take into account parental resources as part of benefit assessment. Furthermore, the rules guiding such provision have shifted significantly in recent years. In other words, the role of the parent in providing financial and other material support for their children has expanded beyond the age of majority (eighteen years of age) upwards to at least twenty-five years. This is acknowledged in government programs and benefit provision, especially through means testing and evaluation of dependent young people living at home.

The combination of poor employment opportunities for teenagers and greater restrictions on the claiming of government assistance for young people up to the age of twenty-five has engendered the phenomena of the stay-at-home young adult and the boomerang young adult. As we have discussed above, recent research has demonstrated that a greater proportion of young people are living at home for longer periods of time than hitherto has been the case in the post-Second World War period (Schneider 2000). This is particularly the trend in relation to eighteen to twenty year olds. Other young people are testing the housing and job markets, but are finding that the financial burdens are too great to handle on their own. As a consequence, they are returning to the parental household, until and unless their economic circumstances change for the better.

> The combination of poor employment opportunities for teenagers and greater restrictions on the claiming of government assistance for young people up to the age of twenty-five has engendered the phenomena of the stay-at-home young adult and the boomerang young adult.

Periods of extended co-residence involving several generations are bound to reshape household relationships in many different ways. Having a young adult in the house is very different from having an under eighteen year old, especially when we consider sensitive issues such as drug and alcohol use, sexual activity, friendship relationships, space for oneself, the allocation and carrying out of household work, the financial costs of clothes, food, and heating, and so on. There are important social dimensions to these issues that warrant brief consideration here.

In some households, family relationships and financial capacities may ensure that any further delay in household leaving is relatively unproblematic, especially in middle-class households in which resources have typically been used to shield young people through the lean years of full-time tertiary education, travel, and leisure pursuits for a much greater length of time than in working-class households (see Graycar & Jamrozik 1989; Jamrozik 2001). More affluent households also provide more physical and monetary space, and greater privacy, for individual household members to do whatever it is they may wish to do. But the relationship of socioeconomic status to patterns of leaving home is not straightforward. Young people living in single-parent households often contribute to the financial security of the household, and to other forms of support for a parent and, where they have them, siblings. Moreover, in cases where parents run family businesses, or where outwork is performed in the family home, children very often undertake unpaid or marginally paid work to assist the household as a whole. In other cases, it may be that a young person may stay at school longer than otherwise intended or warranted, simply in order to claim government benefits that can be utilised by the household.

The total sum of material resources available to any household is determined not only by income generation (number of members of household engaged in what kinds of paid work, for example), but also by housing costs relative to income, family size, inheritance, and sole-parent status. What can change the financial status of a person is transitions associated with the labour market (gaining or losing a job), the state welfare apparatus (gaining or losing a pension or other benefit), marriage (divorce or death of a partner, or marrying into money), and family resources (assets available in relation to number of potential recipients). A change in circumstance for the parent will inevitably affect the family situation of children.

Despite these complexities, there has been a discernible trend in the last three decades for the flow of support between generations to be in the direction of the older generation supporting the younger generations. This is especially evident in the ongoing support of older youth by their parents and in the role of grandparents in supporting their grandchildren, both economically and socially.

There has been a discernible trend in the last three decades for the flow of support between generations to be in the direction of the older generation supporting the younger generations.

In their study of intergenerational transfer, de Vaus and Qu found that 'children were more likely to receive help from older parents than to give help' (1998: 29). This support is given to older youth who are in their twenties and thirties (when the parents are often in their fifties and sixties). De Vaus and Qu found that young people from wealthier and more educated backgrounds did better than others from intergenerational transfers, particularly in terms of financial assistance. They found that young people whose parents rated in the top third of income earners were twice as likely to be receiving income support or financial assistance from their parents, including help with home purchases and home improvements. They also found that the more educated the parents the more likely they were to provide support. Having highly educated parents increased the chances of receiving income support and accommodation by about 50 per cent (de Vaus & Qu 1998: 29). Finally, de Vaus and Qu found that the flows of resources from particular ethnic groups of young people were more likely to go to the parents from the children, particularly from young people from southern Europe, the Middle East, and Asia.

Non-material resources

Changes in state intervention and provision in areas such as family, welfare, employment, and old age policies have a major impact upon families and households. Due to requirements imposed by the state in relation to, for example, sole-parent benefits, many sole parents are now forced to seek work or to enter some kind of training and education if they are to stay eligible for state-provided benefits. Or, to take another example, many households simply cannot survive on one income, so both parents (if there are two) must find outside paid work of some kind, the implication being that less time and energy will be left to undertake domestic duties. One result is greater reliance upon children taking care of themselves and their siblings.

For young women, in particular, these trends can impinge upon their choices in ways generally not seen in relation to young men. In a situation of economic reliance upon the parental household, young women may find themselves trying to prove their value and contribution by engaging in a variety of domestic labour that may include cleaning, cooking, babysitting, organising siblings, and generally taking care of the home front while parents are engaged in income generation. One potential outcome of this process is that young women may work terribly hard, often to the detriment of their own leisure and social relationships, yet the worth of their domestic work can be so difficult to measure (see Game & Pringle 1983). Another consequence of being forced to remain in, or return to, the parental home is the phenomenon of 'infantilisation', a social process in which young adults are treated as if they were still children due to their continued dependence upon parental resources (White 1990; Presdee 1984). With the substantially increased proportion of young people now staying at home for longer periods, it would be interesting to investigate further the ways in which infantilisation may be transforming into new and different forms of 'adultisation', given the weight of numbers. The realities of living at home as a twenty-five year old must at some stage give way to radically different conceptions of what, to the young person and to their parents generally, it is to be adult.

There are important cross-cultural and class differences in parenting practices that ultimately shape family life, regardless of parental presence. Indigenous methods of child rearing in Australia are notably different from the dominant Anglo-Australian norm. Different cultures give different kinds of strategic advice as to how to live one's life, whether to value formal education, how best to generate an income, which religious and moral rules to follow, and so on. It is notable in this regard that analysis of low socioeconomic neighbourhoods in Australia has shown that parents are less likely to be able to support their children's education and less able to link their children into job networks than parents in better-off areas (Hunter 1998). This represents a debilitating form of parental resourcing in an economy that ultimately privileges waged work above any other form of resource allocation.

Other sociological study has indicated the importance of non-material family resources in preparing young people for their projected adult futures. Knowledge about the world and sources of ideas about the world tend to be linked to one's immediate social networks and, in many cases, it is the parents with whom young people have most in common rather than their peers (see Wierenga 1999). Wierenga (1999) describes four different types of cultural orientation towards future trajectories among rural working-class young people in Tasmania, including exploring, wandering, settling, and retreating. Each of these represents a global or local focus, and clear or unclear stories of identity. The essential point of the study is that the more diverse the source of ideas, and the higher degree of trust of social sources about the world around them, the more likely that young people will be explorers: it is the explorers who are most likely to succeed in conventional terms when it comes to finding paid work, establishing their own material resources, and being flexible enough to withstand rapid social change:

> Explorers are the individuals who are availing themselves of the highest number of different future options. By leaving the Valley (even for a time) they will further increase their networks, contacts and ideas, but also their geographical understanding, and their resource base from which they can tell their stories of past and future: in short, expand their cultural universe (Wierenga 1999: 197).

By contrast, young people who are mainly reliant upon a small number of immediate peers and family, who trust their knowledge of the world to a more circumscribed number of people and sources of information, are more likely to be retreaters. As such, they are thereby reacting to the world around them and are subsequently at the mercy of wider social forces. The use of family resources thus may enable young people to expand their horizons or cause them to see their own family as the horizon. Possibilities for education, work, travel, and understanding are to some degree dictated by the vision(s) of those around us, and whether the scope is wide or narrow is reflective of the diversity and intensity of the sources of inspiration. This view is supported by the Life Patterns study of the Youth Research Centre, in which 49.5 per cent of the young people questioned stated that 'family support' was the most positive influence on their lives since leaving school. This was the highest rating, followed by 'self discovery', which was rated as the most positive influence by 38.7 per cent (Dwyer et al. 2003: 14).

As with the case of material resources, the transfer is not unidirectional when it comes to non-material resources. Children also bring to their households a wide variety of influences and contributions. As autonomous but interdependent human beings, young people are exposed to many different outside influences through their peers, their schools, their intimate relationships, their use of information technology, and their sport and leisure pursuits. These experiences constitute vital social resources that, for good and for bad, come back into household and family life. Games, music, dances, sports, fads, fashions, videos, and movies provide opportunities for pleasure, change, and growth for all concerned. In some instances, particular influences may revitalise a household (as with family solidarity fostered by shared interests in music leading to a career in the industry for some). In other cases, it may undermine household integrity (as with family divisions created by disagreements over the deviant effect of certain types of music). The peculiarities of each household are, at least in part, shaped by what young people bring back into the household from their own personal experiences of the social world.

YOUTH, FAMILY, AND DISCOURSES OF BLAME

Dominant family discourses in relation to young people are expressed through policies in education and health, and in relation to delinquency and crime. These discourses essentially link various kinds of behaviour by young people with the nature and quality of parenting that they have received. While it may often be the case that young people's negative behaviour is related to what they have learnt and how they have been treated at home, it is too simplistic to simply blame the parents. Our concern with approaches that blame the parents parallels concern with the way in which the at risk paradox operates (Dwyer & Wyn 2001).

The identification of at-risk youth typically involves three steps: the identification of specific indicators of the problem, the use of indicators to identify a target group, and the implementation of an intervention to bring the target group into line with the mainstream. This popular policy process overlooks the ways in which institutions and policy processes themselves contribute to social problems involving young people, and focuses on changing the child or their parents. The paradoxical element of this process is that the 'at risk' come to be stigmatised, adding to their sense of difference and marginality.

There are many examples of how this discourse operates. It is, for example, common to claim that the blame for disruptive youth lies with their parents. Similarly, in health debates about obesity and diet, it is parents who are targeted and blamed for their children's unhealthy eating practices. We would reiterate that responsibility for many areas of young people's lives does lie with parents, but that it is very one-sided to leave the debate there. To illustrate this, we draw on the area of criminal justice.

The 'parenting theme' (Gelsthorpe 1999) has long been prominent in debates surrounding youth crime and youth justice (see especially Goldson & Jamieson 2002). The usual language alludes to families in crisis, or bad parenting, or parental neglect. A recent study in Finland that examined retrospective reports of parental behaviour from young male inmates, for example, found that the prisoners' childhood family violence and parental problems (linked in turn to the criminality of the inmates) were associated with maternal rejection, paternal rejection, and ineffective parenting (Haapasalo 2001).

The nature of family life certainly does seem to have a major bearing on youth offending, particularly with respect to younger offenders. In a review of relevant literature, McLaren (2000: 62) cites the following as the main characteristics of families of offenders. They:

- have more frequent parental disagreements
- give conflicting directions to children
- show little dominance by parents in family decisions, with sometimes an inverted power hierarchy in which children have more say in decisions than do their parents
- are dominated by negative, rather than positive, emotional expression
- show more communication that is misunderstood or misread by other family members
- indicate less willingness to compromise
- use inconsistent parenting strategies, responding differently to the same behaviour at different times
- show negative parenting patterns; for example, harsh discipline and little shared positive activities with children
- inadequately monitor the behaviour and whereabouts of children
- have difficulties with family cohesion and adaptability.

The listing of these risk factors for youth offending can be matched in many studies that are about the risk factors for young people in relation to education and health. What the identification of these risk factors fails to do is to link young people's lives with broader social processes beyond simply family dynamics, of which they and their families are also a part.

Risk and social division

The concept of childhood varies greatly according to cultural and class norms, which often involve quite different degrees and types of adult supervision and parental control over children. In Australia there are marked differences between some Anglo-Australian forms of parenting (and conceptions of childhood) and those practised by many Indigenous communities (see Johnston 1991). In the latter there is, for instance, frequent encouragement of self-direction and independent action in a manner quite at odds with conventional middle-class notions of child rearing.

Differences in social and economic resources at the household level can also impact on the capacity of some parents to regulate their children's behaviour, even where this is deemed to be desirable or warranted. It has, for example, been observed that for many Indigenous peoples poor educational background and low socioeconomic circumstances contribute to poor self-esteem. One consequence of this is that 'parental authority is undermined as the children observe their parents being placed in an inferior position' (Johnston 1991: 285). The poor material circumstances of some communities, and the particularly disadvantaged position of many sole-parent families, means that enforcement of a universal rule regarding parental responsibility will have unequal and unfair application. In the end, the major socioeconomic problems that generate difficulties for many parents and children are too deep and entrenched to be overcome by ad hoc parent support programs or parent penalty schemes.

These observations raise questions about existing communal support given to parents and children and the appropriateness of designing strategies of intervention that are based on what is, in essence, defined as a 'parenting deficiency'. Family relationships are crucial in the developmental formation of individuals. The task is to nest and nurture positive familial relationships within a web of financial, social, and institutional supports. Where these supports are not available, it is hardly just or socially effective to place the burden of good parenting (in this context referring to parenting that can act as a protective factor in prohibiting criminal involvement) on those least able to respond in conventional ways.

The role of parents, parenting, and families is crucial in the development of young people; however, as indicated above, there is no single model of parenting or family life that can be used as a template for good practice. Rather, personal, family, and community relationships are intertwined in complex ways, and particular circumstances and contexts give rise to a multitude of family forms. The development of appropriate and effective strategies in relation to the family and parents will, therefore, be contingent upon the particular styles, cultures, and resources pertaining to specific groups in the community.

It is apparent that much public policy entrenches social differences based upon social class (among other differences), which occurs in the area of family policy as it does in other areas. Jamrozik (2001) observes that it is mainly working-class families who get caught up with child welfare services that operate largely through identification of problems such as neglected and at-risk children, and that offer coercive or compulsory solutions. By contrast, the issue for middle-class families is childcare, where the problem is constructed more in terms of rights and entitlements and intervention is positive, developmental, and voluntary. It is argued that there is a dichotomy between how rich and poor are treated in family policy, and that this has been increased:

> by the recent policy of shifting the services of the 'welfare' category to the non-government sector, thus changing the nature of services from 'entitlement' to 'charity', bringing to life again the distinction between the 'deserving' and 'undeserving', while the services that are used mainly by the affluent are claimed as 'a right' (Jamrozik 2001: 225).

Regardless of the merits or otherwise of this argument, it is relevant to ask how recipients perceive service provision to which they are exposed. In particular, if some types of service provision or state intervention are seen and experienced as intrusive and/or unfair, then this will have a marked impact on families most vulnerable to these processes.

The identification of family risk characteristics places the conceptual emphasis at the micro level of parent–child relations and individual personality; however, as we have argued, in many cases structural explanations (for example, those that link economic adversity and crime) are very evident (see Goldson & Jamieson 2002). As Goldson and Jamieson (2002: 95) observe in the British context:

> From the 'improper conduct of parents' at the beginning of the nineteenth century, to the 'wilful refusal of parental responsibility' at the end of the twentieth and the outset of the twenty first century, a discourse rooted in individual agency has served to displace any sustained analysis of structural context. This way of 'seeing' is particularly resonant within the contemporary realm of youth justice, and it shows no sign of abating.

By circumventing discussion of social inequality, the focus on bad parents and bad parenting serves to justify increased punitive intervention into the lives of working-class families and youth in ways that simultaneously stigmatise them for their apparent shortcomings. Individualising the problem is achieved through making it appear to be a matter of parental (and, thereby, youth) choice in how people behave and act. Moralising the problem is achieved through stressing its origins as lying in permissiveness or lax discipline. Each allows scope for the imposition of ever more stringent rules to guide those families and children associated with the new perishing classes of the contemporary era.

One consequence of structural changes in state welfare allocations and labour market opportunities is the emergence of a new debate featuring two opposing ideologies. One ideology — children come first — is premised on the principles of the UN Convention of the Rights of the Child that offers the best interests of the child as the key rationale for how we respond to children and youth as a society. At a practical level this translates into policies that, for example, privilege childcare and child rearing as important communal activities and responsibilities. For older children, such as teenagers, this ideology stipulates that the community has an obligation to make sure that adequate educational, employment, and welfare provision is guaranteed as a matter of right.

This ideology also very much sees support of parents as an essential part of supporting children and young people. From this perspective, social differences are important to consider in any analysis of the family, as is social inequality when trying to evaluate potential youth futures. In the end, community strategies are needed to address communal problems.

Conversely, various counterideologies are also apparent in the public domain. The most conspicuous of these is one that ascribes the child's behaviour entirely to the parent. If the youth mucks up, then it is the parent to blame. The family is seen as the cornerstone for many of society's ills. When combined with individualist concerns that place personal destiny squarely in the hands of the individual, we have a recipe for withdrawal of community support. In this view, the state should not put resources into either children or their parents. Its main task is to monitor and regulate, to ensure that moral obligations are met by all, without drawing upon the resources of all.

Summary

Much contemporary concern over the family centres on the demise of the 1950s image of the perfect family formation, an image that Hollywood movies continue to persistently convey, even in the midst of a much more complex reality. High divorce rates, expanding levels of child poverty, media headlines about child abuse, violence within families, and youth delinquency — these are the themes that conventionally present the family as a social problem. Meanwhile, transformations in the world of paid work and in the welfare apparatus of the state are radically altering the nature of household arrangements and family relationships. The stresses and strains associated with paid work (or lack thereof), for example, are exerting pressures on many parents to put less priority on the time, energy, and resources they can devote to child rearing and childcare. Young people are growing up in circumstances where change is normal and where the meanings of family are less defined through tradition. The ways that young people are learning to relate in diverse and impermanent family forms are in turn shaping their own understandings of family life. While the traditional nuclear family of the past is not disappearing, it is now less significant, as families of a wide variety of forms serve the needs of young people and adults.

As this chapter has demonstrated, the family and parents are very often blamed for the problems that are the effects on the young of new social divisions and inequalities. Young people, as part of households and of families, are located within wider social structures (of class, gender, ethnicity, and race) that critically frame their life options, their future trajectories, and their visions for themselves. What happens to family life, and therefore to young people, is thus from first to last a question of the social—a matter of how societies as a whole organise the production, distribution, and exchange of the material and non-material means of life between and across diverse population groups.

QUESTIONS

Questions for further exploration

1 Is the traditional concept of the family useful today?

2 What is structural ageing, and why and how is this concept important to youth studies?

3 How does the family contribute to the formation of various types of social, economic, cultural, and symbolic capital for individuals within the family?

4 Youth are now associated with new patterns of interdependence between themselves and their families of origin. Discuss.

5 The family is perhaps best looked at as a work in progress. In what ways might this statement be interpreted?

SCHOOLING YOUTH 9

Introduction

Getting an education has never been so important in Australia, as is the case in every other Western country. Never before have so many Australian youth been engaged in education through to the final year of secondary education and beyond. Around three-quarters of young Australians complete secondary school, and government policies are pushing for still higher rates of participation. Government policies since the 1980s have aimed to keep up to 95 per cent of young people in secondary school until they complete a school leaving certificate. At the same time, young people have a high rate of participation in part-time work while they are at secondary school. Well over half of seventeen year olds at school hold a paid job. These trends mean that from young people's point of view, school is just one part of their complex lives. Through the senior years of secondary school and beyond, the full-time student is likely to be a part-time worker as well.

Schooling, learning, and education are so integral to understanding young people's lives that these issues appear in most chapters of this book. In this chapter we discuss evidence about the changing role of education in society and the role that young people are playing in developing new understandings of learning and the uses of educational credentials. We suggest that several processes are important to understanding young people's educational experiences. These processes, which are part of broader patterns and forces of social and economic change that affect individual lives, include changes to the role and nature of work and shifts in funding the costs of education. In this chapter we provide an overview of two key aspects of these changes: workplace restructuring and the privatisation of education. We argue that these changes have the effect of creating new forms of older social divisions based on gender and social class. These processes have had a significant impact on how young people experience education.

During the 1970s and 1980s, most schools implemented gender equity policies and programs that were aimed at improving the educational outcomes of girls. Now, debate rages about how to improve boys' educational outcomes, as studies reveal that, as a group, young women have higher rates of school completion than young men do (see Chapter 3). However, despite more than a decade of strong educational outcomes, young women's occupational outcomes still reflect the old gender order. Furthermore, recent research shows that the most economically disadvantaged are also the most at risk of failure. What does this mean about the role of education today? Do educational credentials ensure employment?

The relationship between education and employment is ambiguous. While the big picture presented by statistical data shows that, in general, increased levels of education are associated with increased income and higher-level jobs, the reality is that in the lives of young people, the links between education and work are less definite. In Australia and in other Western countries, the combined evidence about young people's life patterns and the broader social forces mentioned above have provoked heated debate about the kind of knowledge that young people need to establish a life. To provide an understanding of the changing relationship of young people to the social institutions of education, we discuss these complexities in this chapter.

EDUCATION IN A POST-INDUSTRIAL SOCIETY

Western education and training systems are in the process of being transformed from an emphasis on the mass secondary education system that has served an industrial society to meeting the needs of the new post-industrial society. Mass secondary education is, historically speaking, a relatively recent phenomenon. It was introduced in Australia and other Western countries after the Second World War to provide the kind of education that would ensure that young people could contribute to the industrial economies that dominated these countries at that time. In the 1950s, young people needed to be literate, numerate, and punctual in order to take up jobs in manufacturing, sales, and commerce. Studies of educational programs of the 1950s, such as Johnson's *The Modern Girl,* show how education was explicitly programmed to launch the majority of young men, at age fifteen, into apprenticeships and jobs that would become the basis of their lifelong careers (Johnson 1993). Those who stayed at secondary school past the age of fifteen were seen to be destined for further education that would lead to professional occupations. Girls were largely expected to leave school for a lifetime of being a wife and motherhood, skilled in domestic science, and possibly in the feminine occupations of secretary, nurse, or dressmaker. Through to the 1970s, only a minority of young people was expected to stay at school for the post-compulsory years after they reached the age of fifteen.

Today, schooling in Australia is still compulsory to age fifteen, but post-compulsory education is now a majority experience. Post-compulsory education has almost become compulsory because the educational policies of successive governments have placed an increasing emphasis on achieving almost universal participation in education to Year 12. These policies have been driven by the government of the day's agenda to match education to changes in Australia's economic base. Since the 1950s, Australia has shifted from an economy dominated by manufacturing and the processing of raw materials, such as wool and minerals, to a post-industrial economy based on an extensive service sector and information, knowledge, and communications technologies. Australia is now said to be in a post-industrial economy that requires higher levels of skill from its workers in order to be successful and competitive on a global scale. This is the perception, even though a large proportion of GDP continues to be based on mining and export of minerals, wool production, and agriculture.

Some facts about young people and education

BOX 9.1

- Current figures show a decrease in the proportions of low socioeconomic status students (from 63 per cent in 2000 to 59 per cent in 2004) and students from provincial areas (from 65 per cent in 2000 to 63 per cent in 2004) who gained Year 12 certificates (Department of Education, Science and Training 2005).

- Between 2000 and 2004 there was an overall increase in the proportion of twenty to twenty-four year olds who attained Year 12, Certificate I or II, or higher qualifications between 2000 (80.3 per cent) and 2004 (82.8 per cent) (Department of Education, Science and Training 2005).

- Full-time students who worked more than twenty hours are happiest, with satisfaction declining as the number of hours spent in paid employment or study falls (Hillman & Macmillan 2005).

- Those not engaged in work or study were the most unhappy with their lives (Hillman & Macmillan 2005).

- In May 2004, 84.5 per cent of Australian teenagers were in full-time study or full-time work; 15.5 per cent were not in full-time education or employment (Dusseldorp Skills Forum 2004).

For the reasons discussed above, the themes of workplace restructuring, the privatisation of education, and the marketing of education have been the dominant preoccupations of educational policy for the last twenty years. In the following sections we discuss these themes and their implications for young people. In each area, we discuss the evidence of a gap between the policies and the reality of young people's lives.

Workplace restructuring

Workplace restructuring that has occurred in Australia over the last thirty years has involved many complex changes (see also Chapter 11). To summarise this very simply, changes have occurred in:

- the nature of work (from manufacturing and primary production to service jobs)
- the nature of employees (creating a high demand for part-time, school-aged workers)
- the requirements of employers (from on-the-job training to educational credentials)
- the requirements of jobs (the creation of some new high-skill jobs in some industries and many low-skill jobs in others)
- the form of employment (from continuous employment to short-term contracts and from full-time to part-time work).

These changes were interpreted from a policy point of view to require workers that were better trained or multiskilled and flexible in order to support economic growth and greater productivity. Supported by major Organisation for Economic Cooperation and Development (OECD) reports, most education policies have, as a result, placed considerable emphasis on promoting higher levels of education as a key to developing the kind of workforce that will ensure positive economic prospects (see, for example, OECD 2001). For this reason, secondary and post-compulsory education have been defined primarily in terms of the production of the skilled, adaptable, and flexible workforce that will serve the future needs of Australian society.

There are a number of policy documents (for example, OECD 2001; Watson 2003) that refer to the emergence of a knowledge society or the information society. They are reflecting the belief that the future of work will be based around new economies that trade in knowledge and information rather than in wool, cars, or food products. The implication is that in today's society information is a commodity, something to be acquired and traded. The increased use of the Internet and other communications technologies facilitate this trend. Just as with any other commodity, skill is required to know what the latest ideas are, where to access them most efficiently, and how to use and manage knowledge and information. Future workers, it is argued, will need to have skills for the management and control of information and communications.

More recently, the emphasis on education as simply a training ground to produce workers for the new economy is being questioned. While it is clear that the Australian economy of the 2000s requires different and new skills and capacities from those that brought prosperity in earlier times, critics of current educational policy point out that education should not simply be reduced to producing workers. They argue that this approach reduces education and training policy to serving 'the requirements of international economic competitiveness' that is 'almost exclusively concerned with the production of future workers with particular skills or dispositions' (Ball et al. 2000: 146). These requirements, it is argued, are too narrow to meet the real needs of young people and young adults today. It is also argued that society will be better served by having a broadly educated population with high levels of literacy across a wide range of media, which understands historical processes, is knowledgeable about a range of sciences and culture, and has good communication skills. Increasingly, educationalists argue that education should promote mental health and well-being and should be concerned with the cultivation of high levels of interpersonal skills as well as being about the basic three Rs (reading, (w)riting, and 'rithmetic). Education can and should promote social cohesion as well as economic prosperity (Taylor & Henry 2000: 4).

These views and concerns are by no means new. Since the introduction of compulsory mass schooling in the latter part of the nineteenth century in places such as Europe, Britain, and Australia, major arguments and debates have occurred over the role and nature of education in society. Politically, the divide has tended to be between those who promote schooling as a bulwark in defence of the status quo (in terms of curriculum content, institutional processes, and the reproduction of social position) and those who see it as having potential to radically transform existing social structures and relationships (by linking the educational project directly to issues of social justice and egalitarian ideals). Beyond this ongoing tension, traditional divisions arise between those who see schooling primarily, and often exclusively, in instrumental terms (that is, as directly tied to existing and emergent forms of production), and those who see schooling as intrinsically worthwhile for its overall developmental possibilities (that is, as enhancing the human experience by development of a wide range of knowledge, skills, and emotional sensitivities). From a policy point of view, the instrumentalist position presently dominates the educational field.

Since the introduction of compulsory mass schooling in the latter part of the nineteenth century in places such as Europe, Britain, and Australia, major arguments and debates have occurred over the role and nature of education in society.

At a practical level there is evidence that high-skill jobs in the knowledge economy have not emerged to the extent that was predicted a decade ago. Today, the number of jobs in the knowledge, information, and communications sector is small and is contracting. The growth in jobs continues to be in the service sector, which requires workers with relatively low levels of skill. Indeed, much of the expansion of jobs has been in the part-time labour market, and students (secondary school students and post-secondary) overwhelmingly hold these jobs.

A difficulty for those who argue that education is primarily instrumental is the fact that increases in educational participation do not necessarily improve young people's employment outcomes. In many OECD nations youth unemployment rates remain high (in some nations the rate is three times that for adult workers) and, while those with qualifications are less at risk than those without, the assumed relationship between qualifications and career no longer holds. With few exceptions, policy makers have paid little attention to how their education and training policies would achieve the goal of delivering careers in the restructured labour market, which means that the real outcomes of educational policies that encourage young people to complete post-compulsory education do not match up well with the policy directions.

The reality of young people's lives calls into question the link between participation at the post-compulsory level and policy assumption of improved employment prospects for all. In the USA, for example, the high-skilled jobs that are currently in demand represent only a small proportion of actual employment growth. As Levine has shown:

> The five most highly-skilled occupations will only employ 6.1 percent of workers by the turn of
> the century. Meanwhile, such occupations as cooks, waiters, custodians, security guards, and other
> relatively low skill occupations will experience the greatest numerical growth between 1984 and 2000,
> at which time these jobs will employ 16.8 percent of the workforce (1994: 36).

Even the highly qualified are entering into a radically restructured labour market in which greater flexibility and contingency are at play, and for whom dilemmas arise because the meaning of career has changed. The images (and advice) young people are offered with regard to transitions between study and work still promise a world of predictability of outcomes, permanence of career, and security in future prospects. Yet we know for a fact that 'employment is becoming increasingly fluid, occupational boundaries are changing or dissolving and more jobs are temporary' (Stern, Bailey & Merritt 1997).

The effects of workplace restructuring

Workplace restructuring has a number of related implications for education. Education has become more important to individuals because of credentialism: as education participation rates have risen, employers have come to demand seemingly ever-increasing levels of educational credentials for the jobs they offer, even if the jobs do not, strictly speaking, require the skills that the credentials represent. This may account for the fact that many graduates are disappointed with the nature of the work that they are offered (Dwyer & Wyn 2001: 121). Marginson found that it took up to five years of entry level type employment for Australian graduates to reach a job that was commensurate with their qualification and skill level (Dusseldorp Skills Forum 1998: 19).

Other researchers have found that young Australians are more likely today than in the past to hold low-skill positions (Wooden & Van den Heuvel 1999: 35). This is not simply isolated to the Australian experience—the labour market outcomes of education are also being questioned in other Western countries. In the United Kingdom:

> Many graduates, for example, enter jobs for which they are 'overqualified'. They therefore feel dissatisfied, do a bad job and leave at the first better opportunity. So, while educational investment may sometimes be an enabling factor for productivity growth, the assertion that economic development necessarily follows from educational investment is a statement of pure faith (Ainley 1998: 562).

This means that the link between education and employment is far less certain than education policies imply. Although educational policies have pushed schools to become narrowly focused on education for work by emphasising the link between education levels and employment success, this relationship is difficult to demonstrate except at the most general level. Overall, the higher the level of qualifications, the better the employment outcomes. As Marginson comments:

> As a group, higher education students are advantaged, both in terms of where they have come from and where they are going. On average they come from families with higher than median incomes, and are significantly more likely to have attended one of the independent private schools, which in Australia is perhaps the key indicator of social status and economic influence. Similarly, all else being equal, these young adults are more likely to take part in the labour market, more likely to secure full-time work, more likely to enter professional careers and more likely to earn higher than average incomes and purchase significant assets during their lifetimes (1999: 169).

Hence, we have the paradox that while education is seen as increasingly important for economic growth of the nation, it is increasingly difficult to demonstrate clear labour market outcomes for individuals. This paradox has, in turn, implications for the other main trend in education—privatisation.

The privatisation of education

The trend to withdraw public funding for education in Australia has led to the privatisation of education, which has resulted in the costs of education gradually being shifted onto individuals and families. Recently, this shift has been most evident in the higher education sector. Between 1995 and 1999 Australia reduced public spending on higher education by 12 per cent, and achieved a 43 per cent increase in private funding (OECD 2002). By far the greatest proportion of this private funding comes from the contributions of students and their families for university and other post-secondary courses and programs.

The trend towards private funding of secondary education has also been strongly encouraged by Australian governments through two mechanisms:

1 increased levels of subsidisation of private schools with public funding
2 withdrawing public funding for state schools.

This contrasts with principles that underpinned the establishment of universal secondary education to the age of fifteen in Australia on the basis that education was a public good and should be made freely available (free, universal, and secular). Education at that time was seen to be important in the production of the type of human capital that would support Australia's industrially based economy. In the 1980s this position began to be eroded and the costs of education were increasingly passed from the state to individual families, evidenced in the 1990s reform movements in education in Australia and most Western countries that were driven by the rhetoric of the 'new human capital' approach. This approach draws on the idea that education produces value because it is an investment in human capital, but with a new twist: the idea that education is a private good because individuals supposedly reap the major benefit of the investment through enhanced career prospects and outcomes.

> The trend to withdraw public funding for education in Australia has led to the privatisation of education, which has resulted in the costs of education gradually being shifted onto individuals and families.

Marketing education

The reduction of public funding for education at all levels has created the need for educational institutions to market themselves. In Australia, New Zealand, and to a certain extent in the United Kingdom and parts of Canada, new policies have established an environment in which all schools are in a position to compete with each other in the educational marketplace. In the USA, schools have been deregulated to allow the proliferation of special purpose schools that cater to various educational markets. Schools are in competition to get the 'best' students so as to position them in this educational market and parents shop around to find the best school for their children.

In Australia and New Zealand, many secondary schools attract international fee-paying students in order to generate revenue. In Australia this shopping around has brought about significant changes in the balance between private (also independently funded but subsidised by government funding) and government schools. Currently, around 70 per cent of Australian students are educated in government schools, but in some states and territories, such as Victoria, there is a slight but discernible shift towards enrolments in independent schools. Elite government schools increasingly mimic the private schools, and both market themselves through their students' results in final year examinations, which are the main marketing tool of these schools. They are used to offering the promise of success—in gaining entry to prestigious university courses and in getting the best jobs.

Yet, in marketing themselves, schools face a problem. The nexus between education and employment is fragile. Schools cannot provide hard evidence that they prepare young people for jobs or that they enable young people to secure the careers they want. Increasingly, schools are not even able to guarantee that young people will gain entry into the courses they want. Despite the fact that the rationale for education is the generation of human capital for personal gain, it is the very link between education and personal, individual economic benefits that is problematic.

While statistics on outcomes show that 'those with the least amount of education fare least well in the labour market' (Collins, Kenway & McLeod 2000), the detail at the individual level is far more complex, as we shall see. In place of demonstrating how education and learning are directly related to improvements in student outcomes or to reducing inequalities in society, educational institutions have turned inwards to individual-based, standardised testing as a measure of

> The nexus between education and employment is fragile. Schools cannot provide hard evidence that they prepare young people for jobs or that they enable young people to secure the careers they want.

the worth and success of educational programs. Educational management approaches, such as the school effectiveness movement, advocate the evaluation of educational programs through internal reference points, such as the teacher, the classroom climate, or the leadership approach of the school principal. While it is difficult to argue that schools should not be effective and teachers should not all excel in their profession, these issues become less relevant if they are not linked to wider questions about how schools serve communities, and the disadvantaged and advantaged alike. The provision of league tables (in the United Kingdom, for example) based on exam results produces the appearance of highly competitive and effective schooling systems in which parents can have confidence. Yet this is a narrow and possibly unrealistic way of showing how education counts.

It seems ironic that as life for young people has become increasingly complex, requiring high levels of initiative, flexibility, and personal skills, education systems limit their role by focusing on highly abstracted measures of educational achievement. Most place an overwhelming emphasis on measuring literacy and numeracy. While these capacities are in themselves useful, the focus on limited, standardised measurements of these capacities does not demonstrably advance young people's learning. There is, however, plenty of evidence that this approach frequently alienates those most in need of education (Connell 1994). Researchers have shown that these tests not only alienate individuals, but also have the effect of punishing the poorest schools and rewarding those that are the most wealthy by masking the cultural, social, and economic dimensions of educational inequality:

> Poor achievement on a large scale is a recurring fact of life, never officially acknowledged — except backhandedly to justify cutting funds to government schools, to impose punitive testing programmes and to demand ever greater contestability and transparency from schools already exposed to failure (Teese 2000: 2).

For these reasons, schools are at risk of marketing the production of false certainty for young people and their parents through ritualised educational mechanisms that appear increasingly out of touch with the uses that young people make of education — and the ways in which they learn. Education systems risk alienating the very children and youth who should benefit from learning. The hierarchical, entrenched, age-based organisation of school and inwardly focused testing procedures only serve to underline the differences between schools and real life for the young.

Commodification of education

The privatisation and marketing of education go hand in hand with the notion of education as a commodity. Education is increasingly portrayed in terms of its exchange value on the market, rather than its use value, as something good in its own right and for its own sake. One consequence of public policy changes in educational funding is that public education is no longer 'free'. State schools can, for instance, only manage financially by transferring particular costs (such as school excursions) directly to parents, some of whom find it extremely difficult when it comes to ensuring their children's full participation in what the school has to offer.

The costs of education are, in turn, linked to the phenomenon of the commercialisation of schooling: education is being increasingly seen in commercial terms and specifically as a site of business investment. Thus, advertising campaigns and corporate sponsorships are now infiltrating primary and secondary schools from a wide range of business quarters. Some schools receive equipment from particular suppliers, such as computer companies; in this case these companies will benefit from brand name promotion. Such processes basically serve to privilege particular products and product names among a captive and impressionable population. The financial benefits from such sponsorship are felt at a practical level by principals trying to manage tight budgets and parents who otherwise would have to fund raise or pay out of their own pocket for certain school expenses. The role of transnational corporations in influencing and shaping school curriculum, as well as direct corporate production of educational resources, is worthy of systematic study and critique.

Increasingly, students are conceived of as consumers or clients, with particular needs befitting this specific consumer–consuming population. From a human capital perspective, the school is a place that augments the labour market value of the student. Individual students will do better or worse in the competition for jobs, depending on the particular type of education and schooling they receive. The idea of market competition between schools and sale of education as a product is premised upon what the school has to sell to parents and their children. In essence, the message is that the school's task is to provide their client or consumer with those particular skills or attributes that will enhance their prospects when they are in the labour market (or future educational markets, as with university education). Schooling, in these terms, is thus constructed around instrumental purposes and goals, yet again further reinforcing the individual benefit (rather than collective rationale) of education.

Unequal outcomes

The educational policies of the 1970s were firmly located within a framework that placed education as one of the key mechanisms for ensuring that all young people, regardless of their social background, had an equal chance to succeed. Social justice was a central theme in policy documents and government reports. The 1975 Schools Commission report, *Girls, School and Society*, was instrumental in demonstrating that socioeconomic background and gender were the factors that most strongly influenced young people's outcomes from education. Then, as now, girls from the lowest socioeconomic groups were most likely to fail in school, to leave school early, and to be in the most disadvantaged sector of the labour market (Collins, Kenway & McLeod 2000; see also Chapter 3). The important point for this chapter is that the assumption made by the 1975 Schools Commission report was that education had a central role in ensuring that social inequalities did not simply translate into educational disadvantage.

One of the most notable outcomes of this approach in Australia was the Disadvantaged Schools Program; other important programs were in Aboriginal Education, the Country Areas, and English as a Second Language Programs. Each of these programs was based on the assumption that the educational disadvantage experienced by individual students would be most effectively addressed if there was a focus on:

> whole-school change and improved school–community relations rather than on fixing up individual deficit students … Instead of individual pathology and 'blaming the victim' assumptions, there was a focus on how school structures, curricula and pedagogies contributed to the reproduction of educational disadvantage across generations (Lingard 1998: 2).

Unfortunately, the shifts in policy and in educational practices over the last twenty-five years referred to above have had the effect of marginalising discussion, research, and policy on equality and social justice. Educational critics argue that by the 1990s social justice had been omitted from federal education policy altogether (Blackmore et al. 2000). Responsibility for educational outcomes has come to be seen instead as an individual responsibility of parents to ensure the best 'deal' for their own children, rather than a public responsibility to provide high-quality, relevant education for all children, which is based on an understanding of social justice.

> Responsibility for educational outcomes has come to be seen instead as an individual responsibility of parents to ensure the best 'deal' for their own children, rather than a public responsibility to provide high quality, relevant education for all children, which is based on an understanding of social justice.

Given the evidence on inequality and education this policy omission is surprising. Over time, the privatisation of education has meant that schools in the poorest neighbourhoods are unable to draw on the level of resources that schools in wealthier suburbs can. Schools are faced with the problem of dealing with the unspoken and unacknowledged effects on young people of social and economic inequality. These effects are clearly written in exam results: 'In the urban regions where working-class and migrant families are highly concentrated, every third girl can expect to receive fail grades in the least demanding mathematics subject in the curriculum. Among boys—whose attraction to mathematics is even more fatal—failure strikes more than 40 per cent' (Teese 2000: 2).

Teese contrasts this with the wealthier suburbs such as the 'up-market inner east', where 'only 12 per cent of boys and 8 per cent of girls fail in preparatory mathematics ... It is the same with chemistry—the more democratic of the physical sciences. In this subject, four out of ten girls from the most depressed urban environments receive the fail grades of E+, E or UG (zero grade), as do more than three out of ten boys' (Teese 2000: 2).

In other words, in the 2000s social class is as much a significant force for structuring young people's life chances as it has been in the past. The effects of the polarisation of wealth in Australia are clearly evident in the patterns of outcomes from schooling. Research by Teese (2000) and Yates and McLeod (2000) shows how Australian education systems actively contribute to class-based inequalities. They draw on the work of Pierre Bourdieu to provide a theoretical framework for understanding how education systems reproduce the class structure of societies through culture (see Bourdieu & Passeron 1977). Teese has analysed the enrolment patterns and examination results for students across different schools in Melbourne since 1947 to show how the mass secondary education system perpetuates class- and gender-based inequalities. Yates and McLeod's longitudinal study of young people's experiences of four different schools from the age of twelve to the age of eighteen shows how schools contribute to young people's identities. Their study of one elite school, one from a disadvantaged area, and two from the middle class has generated important knowledge about the kinds of orientations different schools develop in young people around social justice issues.

Teese's study shows how class-based inequalities are perpetuated and controlled through a curriculum that serves the interests of upper-class families. Yates and McLeod show how some schools actively contribute to the generation of elitist understandings of life while others provide their students with understandings that are oriented towards the achievement of social justice. Teese explores in detail how control over the curriculum is exercised in his study of Melbourne schools.

A central element to this process is the way in which school subjects are 'codified, authoritative systems of cognitive and cultural demands' (Teese 2000: 3). Put more simply, and simplistically, this means that the curriculum and other aspects of the school are cultural expressions. The way in which these cultural expressions are structured and presented advantages some groups (middle- and upper-class families) and disadvantages others (working-class families). Yates and McLeod argue that the cultural impact of school education goes far beyond the effects that are measured through success and failure, and the proportions of students who are represented in these groups. Commenting on students from one of the middle-class schools, they say:

> Their future sense of themselves as capable and as responsible for their own outcomes is enabling, both individually and in terms of social patterns, but it also feeds how these young people see and relate to others, including some lack of sympathy for those who are disadvantaged or targets of bullying and racism (Yates & McLeod 2000: 73–74).

The students from the other middle-class school have experienced a different curriculum, one that has sensitised them to social justice issues but which, according to Yates and McLeod, has not placed them in a competitive situation in the labour market:

> At Suburban High, students are more successfully schooled in a broad range of 'social justice' concerns, and, in our most recent interviews, are carrying their sensitivities and willingness to speak out about racism and sexism into their post-school social relations. But, at least in the immediate post-school phase, they appear to be placed in a more uncertain relationship to the labour market (Yates & McLeod 2000: 74).

These research findings contribute to a much wider literature on education that challenges current policy directions and offers suggestions about new directions for the formation of a more just and equitable education system that will serve the needs of all young people in the future. While educationalists continue to debate these issues, young people are themselves making changes to education through the ways in which they engage with and use education. In the next section, we consider education from the perspective of those who are most involved and who have the most at stake: young people.

YOUNG PEOPLE'S EXPERIENCES

This section draws particularly on the findings of the Australian Youth Research Centre's Life Patterns longitudinal research program. This program provides evidence for the argument that that young people born after 1970, the post-1970 generation (Wyn & Woodman 2006) are the first generation in the industrialised countries to enter a world in which post-education employment is not taken for granted (Dwyer & Wyn 2001). They have had to forge their identities within a new social order. For the majority of the post-1970 generation, formal education is a continuous process, employment is precarious, and individuals are less and less able to rely on established pathways and structures to establish their livelihood. By engaging with new workplace practices that involve flexible practices, short-term and insecure employment, and balancing work, leisure, and study, young people are embracing an adulthood that differs in significant ways from that which was experienced by the previous generation. These changes and their significance for identity formation and life patterns have been noted by many social theorists, including Beck (1992) and Giddens (1991), and by other youth researchers in other Western countries, such as Walkerdine (1996), Lesko (1996), Furlong and Cartmel (2007), Rattansi and Phoenix (1997), Andres (1999), and Ball, Maquire and Macrae (2000a).

This body of research provides evidence of the emergence of new patterns of life in which education, work, and leisure are significant elements, sometimes competing and sometimes interwoven, in young people's lives from an early age. Their experiences provide some important insights into the ways in which the meanings and uses of education are being actively shaped by young people as they themselves grapple with a changing world.

> There is evidence of the emergence of new patterns of life in which education, work, and leisure are significant elements, sometimes competing and sometimes interwoven, in young people's lives from an early age.

Young people's experiences of study and work provide a striking illustration. Increasingly, young people are combining study and work, a trend that appears from a relatively early age in Australia and other Western countries. Mizen et al. (1999) suggest that the phenomenon of 'child workers' in the United Kingdom is becoming the norm and Chisholm (1997) reports that the study–work combination among school students is a 'significant activity pattern' in a number of European countries. Over 60 per cent of the sample in Rudd and Evans's (1998: 54) study of young people in the United Kingdom had a part-time job at the time of the study and in the Netherlands it was found that 'blending' areas of life, especially work and study, had become common (du Bois-Reymond 1998: 67).

A recent study of young people in New South Wales confirms that it is normative for Australian youth to be involved in the workforce while they are students. Focusing on the work experience of 11 000 children from Year 7 to Year 10 across twenty-two schools in New South Wales (NSW Commission for Children and Young People 2005), the report exposes the often unacknowledged extent of formal and informal work in which young people are engaged. It found that 56 per cent of children between the ages of twelve to sixteen had worked in the previous twelve months, that work participation increases with age, and that girls are 1.2 times more likely to work than boys, reflecting girls' role in the care of other children and relatives. Those in rural and regional areas are twice as likely to work as those in metropolitan areas, a reflection of the use of children's labour on farms. Children's work is not related to economic necessity, though. Children in the least disadvantaged areas are more than twice as likely to work as children in disadvantaged areas. Children's work is most commonly babysitting, food and drink sales, leaflet and newspaper delivery, and cleaning and general farmhand work; most work less than six hours a week.

The extent to which young people of school age across many Western countries are engaged in paid work suggests that they are actively choosing to mix school and work. Chisholm (1997: 14) notes that one-third of the fifteen to twenty-nine year olds in the European *Labour Force Survey* are positively choosing part-time employment while they study. This evidence is supported by the findings from the Life-Patterns project in Australia and in the matching data from the Canadian surveys. Only one-third of the Australian sample indicated that they would 'prefer to study without work' (Dwyer & Wyn 1998).

Recent research from the United Kingdom (Ball, Maquire & Macrae 2000a) provides further evidence that there are significant shifts in the meanings and uses of education for young people. Ball et al. suggest that 'our focus upon education, training and work marginalises or obscures other points of focus that may be "really" much more important in the lives of young people' (2000a: 146). Their analysis insists on the significance of 'leisure and social life' as one of three 'primary arenas of action' that young people negotiate and balance (2000a: 147). The other two arenas that they identify are 'work, education and training' and 'family, home and domesticity'. While there will be ongoing debate about the definition of these arenas, Ball et al.'s analysis helps to illuminate the extent of interplay between education, work, and other life concerns. For young people, this means the negotiation of complex choices and uncertain pathways.

Raffo and Reeves (1999), for example, found that young people in their United Kingdom study were making their own decisions about their levels of participation in the classroom and which lessons they would attend. These young people were exercising active choices about when they would leave school, whether they would take time out from education, and which qualifications to study for. This research provides evidence that young people are developing a perspective on schooling in which education is only one of a number of options that they are managing. Young people's pragmatic choices, involving mixes of school and work through secondary school and during their post-secondary education and training, have significant implications for the provision of secondary education in the future. Many of these young people are, effectively, part-time adults, making adult choices and decisions about many aspects of their lives.

> Young people's pragmatic choices, involving mixes of school and work through secondary school and during their post-secondary education and training, have significant implications for the provision of secondary education in the future. Many of these young people are, effectively, part-time adults, making adult choices and decisions about many aspects of their lives.

What these studies reveal is an emerging disparity between the stated goals of education and youth policy and the changing priorities and choices of young people. In particular, the linear notion of transitions appears to be increasingly at odds with the complex patterns of life experienced by young people in the United Kingdom, the Netherlands, Canada, the USA, and Australia. For this reason, researchers suggest that there is a need to adopt a more holistic view of education in relation to young people's lives. The multidimensionality of young people's lives has challenged the assumption of the centrality of education and training in young people's lives that informs contemporary post-compulsory education and training policy. The complexity of a young person's world, a world in which schooling and work are often simultaneous, contrasts with the policy assumption that education is the prior experience to which work is subsequent. Researchers have pointed out that young people are developing complex life and transition patterns that are interconnected, often fragmented or broken, circular and unpredictable. These patterns contrast sharply with the simple, linear patterns that educational policies and programs are based on.

Even before they leave school, young people's experience of the labour market has taught them that employment—the obtaining and retaining of it—is precarious. The image of permanent careers and predictable outcomes from programs of study that emanates from the career counsellor's room contrasts sharply with the reality of young people's transition processes through the years of secondary schooling and beyond. Wyn and Dwyer (2000: 151) point to five key elements to these new patterns of transition:

- overlaps between study and work
- the decline of opportunity for the uncredentialled
- the increasing deferment of career outcomes
- an increase in part-time employment outcomes for graduates
- a growing mismatch between actual credentials and employment outcomes.

Commenting on the situation of young people in the United Kingdom, Furlong and Cartmel (2007: 34–35) describe new patterns of transition from school to work in the following way: they are more protracted, increasingly fragmented, and less predictable. These elements contribute to patterns of transition in which the emphasis is on contingency and in which the responsibilities and costs of uncertainty are borne by individuals. In this context, education takes on a new significance. Education is central and yet marginal to young people's lives. It is central because in the risk society the project of reinventing selves places a strong emphasis on the role of education as a lifelong process; it is more marginal because of the competing role of work and other life concerns alongside education. Young people can no longer assume that the achievement of a career will provide them with a job for life; indeed, they do not necessarily want a job that will last their entire working life. Gaining credentials does not provide job certainty either, but it does provide young people with options. Yet, while they are studying, young people cannot afford to postpone engaging with other areas of life. The result is a generation of young people who have learnt to develop flexible approaches to study and work and to manage multiple and complex responsibilities.

Transitions and educational ideals

Analysis of the experiences of young people allows us to better understand the basic tensions within education today. It also provides an opportunity to reiterate fundamental propositions concerning key elements of an ideal education. There is an emerging divide between the promise of education (that is made to all) and the reality of education (that particularly privileges the interests of some). As illustrated above, unequal outcomes, and the complex experiences of education, demonstrate that contemporary forms of schooling are frequently not best suited to current societal needs. Research and discussion of schooling and youth alienation provide substantive evidence of great unease and dissatisfaction on the part of many young people with their school experiences (see White 1996c). In part, the problems of schooling are attributable to the narrow transitional brief demanded of education vis-à-vis the workforce, combined with the negative responses students may have to aspects of the school content, authority figures, methods of teaching, competitive school processes, and unrealistic expectations.

One answer to present school dilemmas is to assert the importance of providing broad, liberal education, an education that is creative and comprehensive. The United Nations Convention on the Rights of the Child sets out one contour of an ideal education. Article 28 of the Convention says that each child should have the right to education on the basis of equal opportunity, and that this education be of a broad holistic nature. When the Convention talks about education, it is talking about developing human potential to the fullest. Education here is not narrowly defined in terms of competency, skills, training, or instrumental knowledge. Rather, it is a developmental concept of education. In this kind of framework, all students have the right to know, and they have the right in an abstract sense to develop their capacities to the fullest extent. The ideal education is one that is oriented towards developing one's physical, psychological, mental, spiritual, and creative well-being.

By contrast, certain forms of urban pedagogy further entrench disadvantage by denying students the benefits of a well-rounded and challenging education. American research, for example, has examined how some urban public schools appear to do little more than prepare their African American and ethnic minority students for inferior employment and mediocre social opportunities. This is because the urban pedagogy on offer (defined as the dissemination of information and images to minority urban youth) creates a less than demanding intellectual education. This approach to education, in turn, also creates and reinforces an employer prejudice against young minorities (Duncan 2000). Canadian research demonstrates the importance of having active encouragement and sound expertise on the part of teachers in supporting student learning. Attitudes towards school are shaped by a sense of engagement (social and intellectual), which is best fostered by active student involvement in the learning process within a disciplined atmosphere of mutual respect (Superstein 1994). In other words, taking into account lessons from each of these case studies, both the content and process of education are crucial to the overall learning environment.

A holistic and developmental conception of education implies that education can never be other than a lifelong experience. To live is to continually develop one's capacities. Learning occurs in many different forums, including work and family life. The ideal educational system, therefore, is one that allows for intermittent attendance—the dipping in and dipping out of education at different points in one's life. As life changes, so, too, do our interests and capacities. Conceptually, the challenge is to entrench the notion of educability as the centrepiece of the educational project. This concept refers to the idea that everyone has the capacity to learn, that we learn at different rates at different times, and that learning never stops throughout the course of one's life (White 1996c). Greater practical emphasis needs to be placed on holistic forms of education that encompass varying curriculum contents and focuses, and on flexible systems that acknowledge the ebbs and flows and real processes of learning. These are familiar (some would say old-fashioned) standards; it is somewhat ironic, therefore, that they appear to fit nicely with the pattern of youth experiences in contemporary society.

> A holistic and developmental conception of education implies that education can never be other than a lifelong experience.

Summary

Despite the evidence of significant social change over the last twenty years, the design of education systems in Australia still reflects the thinking about the relationship between education and society that was current in the immediate postwar era. Two elements in particular now seem to be at odds with the ways in which young people are shaping their lives in the first decade of the twenty-first century. First, age-based categorisation remains a fundamental organising principle in almost all schools. This feature of schools is based on the assumptions and frameworks of developmental psychology, which has provided normative models for educational practice. Second, schooling is premised on the assumption of a linear relationship between school and work. Young people's life patterns increasingly challenge these linear and categorical assumptions as they make pragmatic choices in balancing and negotiating a range of personal, occupational, and educational commitments in their lives.

The impact of social change on young people's lives offers a challenge to some of the most basic assumptions underlying education, including:

- the use of age categories as the main basis for the organisation of teaching and learning
- the assumption that 'student' is the primary identification of school-age students
- the notion that growing up involves a linear progression from school to work
- the construction of certainty through technologies of assessment that is unrelated to student outcomes.

In meeting the challenge to reshape education in the post-industrial era, young people's participation will be fundamental. Young people are actively engaging with new life patterns. They have developed perspectives and understandings about education, work, and life that should be placed at the centre of educational provision. The shift towards individual responsibility and choice means that young people will be less prepared to be passive recipients of education, which means that their participation in all aspects of schooling, including decision making, will become an expectation.

Finally, the research illustrates that youth is not simply a stage on the way to the more important life stage of adulthood. Indeed, as the employment stability that once characterised the idea of adulthood is being eroded, the point of transition from youth to adulthood is being challenged. Youth is an important part of society in the present, and the blurring of the markers between youth and adult will serve to reinforce the status of young people in our society.

Questions for further exploration

1 In what ways is the relationship between education and employment ambiguous?

2 Workplace restructuring and the privatisation of education have further entrenched social division and social inequality. Discuss.

3 Should education been seen simply as a private good, since individuals supposedly reap the major benefit of the investment through enhanced career prospects and outcomes?

4 What does the concept of 'educability' refer to?

5 Many students, including high school students, are effectively part-time adults, making adult choices and decisions about many aspects of their lives. Why and how is this the case?

DOING BAD: JUVENILE JUSTICE

10

Introduction

This chapter provides an overview of youth involvement in the criminal justice system. It discusses the nature and dynamics of different kinds of youth offending, and describes the key characteristics of those young people deemed to be young offenders. The main targets for analysis—and state action—tend to be the same: working-class young people in particularly marginalised social positions. The chapter discusses how the young offender is socially created, and the role and place of the police in young people's lives. Analysis of the material conditions that give rise to serious and persistent youth offending is provided in our discussion of the community context for crime. To some extent these conditions are also acknowledged in the contemporary interest in restorative justice as a means to respond to youth offending.

The history of juvenile justice is the history of state intervention in the lives of working-class young people, ethnic minorities, and Indigenous peoples. It is a history premised on attempts to deal with neglected children and delinquent youth; to control and manage sections of the population that do not fit notions of respectability, or that do not directly contribute to the economy via paid employment. To understand contemporary juvenile offending and juvenile justice requires some appreciation of the fact that it is the poor, the vulnerable, the dispossessed, and the marginalised who are most likely to be the subject of intervention. Why and how this is the case is one of the concerns of this chapter. As will be seen, there are strong links between the criminal justice system as a form of social control and processes of social exclusion associated with changes in community and class resources (see Chapters 1 and 2). Just as the young offender is socially constructed by the interventions of the criminal justice system, so too offending behaviour of a serious and persistent nature is forged in the context of specific kinds of social relationships and communal processes.

CREATING THE YOUNG OFFENDER

Most young people engage in rule-breaking behaviour at some time; that is, most people have at some stage broken the law or taken part in some type of antisocial behaviour. The kinds of things young people might do include drinking under age, crossing the street against the red light, riding a train or tram without a ticket, trying marijuana, making noise late at night, not going to class, and so on. Most of these activities are relatively harmless and trivial and most young people are not criminals, nor will they continue to engage in unlawful activities—and certainly not serious ones—once they move into their post-teenage years.

So what makes a young offender? Basically, a young offender is a person who has been officially designated as such by the criminal justice system. In a very real sense, regardless of what a young person has or has not actually done, their status in society will be determined by the nature of their contact with law enforcement officers and the juvenile court system. How the system processes young people who have committed a crime or who have engaged in certain types of offensive behaviour largely determines who will be labelled a young offender.

How different young people are dealt with at all stages of the juvenile justice system largely shapes who, in the end, is officially considered a young offender. Becoming a young offender, then, is not only about what a young person has done, but it is also very much influenced by how the system responds to the young person and what they have done.

> How different young people are dealt with at all stages of the juvenile justice system largely shapes who, in the end, is officially considered a young offender.

Offender profiles

In practice, who is actually criminalised (that is, labelled a criminal) tends to follow a distinctive social pattern. Regardless of the fact that most young people do something illegal or wrong, some young people tend to be over-represented in the juvenile justice system.

Indigenous young people tend to receive fewer formal cautions than non-Indigenous young people, and they tend to be proceeded against in the juvenile courts in larger numbers. They are also over-represented in detention centres and various custody orders (Cunneen 2001). Why this is the case is the subject of much debate. But issues of racism, bias, and discrimination, as well as the impact of poor social conditions on behaviour, are clearly related to the extent of Aboriginal and Torres Strait Islanders' contact with the criminal justice system.

In effect, the criminal justice system has a series of filters that screen young people on the basis of offence categories (serious/non-serious, first time/repeat offending) and social characteristics (family background, income, employment, education). It is the most disadvantaged and vulnerable young people who tend to receive the most attention from justice officials at all levels of the system, from police through to detention centre staff (Cunneen & White 2007), a trend that tells us as much about the operation of the juvenile justice system as it does about the young offender. It also has implications for how we explain why some young people appear to commit certain types of offences more than others.

The crux of the developmental approach to understanding juvenile behaviour is that crime is a consequence of cumulative risks and combinations of factors, and that these vary over the life course (see Developmental Crime Prevention Consortium 1999). The analysis of multiple causal factors, combined with an acknowledgment of the need for multiple forms of service delivery, is also important with regard to the profile of young offenders: complexity of explanation and complexity of response mirror the complexity of offending itself.

Social factors in offending

The data consistently show that young people who become criminalised and enter farthest into the criminal justice system tend to exhibit certain social characteristics (see Cunneen & White 2007). A typical young offender profile would include the following elements:

- the peak age for theft is sixteen, for robbery seventeen, and for homicide nineteen
- young men are far more likely to be charged with a criminal offence than young women, and are more likely to re-offend than young women
- increasingly, young offender populations now include greater proportions of ethnic minority youth from specific groups, although the bulk of young offenders are from Anglo-Australian backgrounds
- Indigenous young people, male and female, are over-represented within the juvenile justice system nationally
- juveniles officially processed through the criminal justice system tend to come from low socio-economic backgrounds, with unemployment and poverty being prominent characteristics
- many young people who appear before children's courts do not live in nuclear families
- those young people most entrenched in the juvenile justice system are likely to have a history of drug and alcohol abuse
- a disproportionate number of young offenders have intellectual disabilities or mental illness.

These social characteristics must be taken into account in causal explanations of offenders (and discussions of risk and protective factors). They must also be accounted for when it comes to the development of general and youth-specific services and interventions.

The general pattern of offending can be also be broken down in terms of extent and seriousness of offending. Typically, it is the case that a large proportion of juvenile offenders stop offending as they get older, and that a relatively small group of re-offenders account for a large number of court appearances (Coumarelos 1994; Cain 1996). Children and young people who offend can be categorised into three main groupings (McLaren 2000; New Zealand Ministry of Justice and Ministry of Social Development 2002; see also Loeber & Farrington 1998), ranging from low-risk to high-risk offenders.

Types of offenders

- Low-risk or minor offenders, who do not commit many offences and who generally grow out of offending behaviour as part of the normal maturation process.
- Medium-risk offenders, who commit a number of offences, some serious, mainly due to factors such as substance abuse and antisocial peers.
- High-risk offenders, who begin offending early (between ten and fourteen), offend at high rates, often very seriously, and are likely to keep offending into adulthood.

BOX 10.1

The age at which offending first occurs, or at which criminalisation of the young person happens, has a major bearing on subsequent contact with the criminal justice system (see, for example, Harding & Maller 1997). The younger the person, the more likely future re-offending. Again, different ages and different types of offending demand different kinds of responses.

Responding to youth

Comparative analysis of juvenile justice systems and processes indicate a number of global commonalities, as well as important national and regional differences in the perception and treatment of young people (Muncie 2004, 2005; Muncie & Goldson 2006). General trends include a winding back of welfare provision and greater focus on deeds rather than needs, adulteration in some jurisdictions where young people are increasingly formally being treated as adults, and repenalisation of many aspects of juvenile justice—including use of youth curfews, mandatory sentencing, zero tolerance policing, and the like as well as detention—greater attention given to concepts and practices of restorative justice, and at least some acknowledgment of the importance of the UN Convention on the Rights of the Children in deliberations about juvenile justice. As Muncie (2005) emphasises, global processes of neoliberalism are translated into a multiplicity of social forms with great variation, depending upon specific local contexts. How international trends are played out at the national and regional level is contingent upon a range of factors, not the least of which is local history and local sensibilities.

Having said this, there are two broad trends that are worthy of close attention, especially since these are of direct relevance to understanding and interpreting contemporary juvenile justice developments within Australia. In simple terms, these can be described as the emphasis on risk and risk aversion, the emphasis on responsibilisation, and:

Risk

Prediction of risk has emerged as one of the most far-reaching changes in theory and practice in relation to juvenile justice in Australia. Indeed, the concepts of risk (risk factors, risk assessment, risk prediction, risk management) permeate juvenile justice systems. There are at least four different ways that the concept and measurement of risk is used in juvenile justice (Cunneen & White 2006: 102–03):

- in the context of risk and protective factors associated with offending behaviour
- as an assessment tool for access to programmes for young people under supervision or serving a custodial sentence
- as a classification tool for young people in custody to determine their security ratings
- as a generic measure for activating legal intervention (for example, 'three-strikes' mandatory imprisonment).

When combined with government attempts to get tough on crime, especially when it relates to juvenile offenders, the emphasis on risk can open the door to highly punitive and highly intrusive measures. Closely linked to the concern with risk is the employment of actuarial methods of assessment, in which potential problems and problematic youth become the focus of government attention through a priori categorisation of young people based upon standardised risk assessment. Young people are deemed to be at risk not necessarily because of their actual behaviour, but because they fit a particular risk profile. It is who they are and who they associate with that counts, rather than how they live their lives. Not surprisingly, risk tends to be constructed through the use of categories that actively construct low income, unemployed, ethnic minority, and Indigenous young people most liable to state intervention. Priday (2006: 347) notes that the tools used for risk assessment often require subjective assessments—about family relationships, parenting practices, lifestyle, and living conditions—in ways that precisely weigh against more vulnerable and disadvantaged youth. Such measures also distort their actual circumstances and relationships, since the assessment criteria are based upon white, middle-class norms, assumptions, and values.

From the point of view of definition and classification there are major difficulties with the notion of risk. There are, for instance, social biases built into how state intervention is informed by notions of risk. Moreover, the apparently objective and scientific methods of risk assessment belie the subjective and partial values that underpin them (Priday 2006). Beyond this, a key problem with the risk approach is that it is premised on the notion of prediction. Specifically, much of the risk and protective factor type of analysis implies that with enough empirical data about a person, gathered by using standardised assessment tools, then the more likely one can predict individual futures.

> Young people are deemed to be at risk not necessarily because of their actual behaviour, but because they fit a particular risk profile. It is who they are and who they associate with that counts, rather than how they live their lives.

While to some extent social characteristics and social background provide insight into probabilities of opportunity and life chances (based on historical experience and previous patterns), it is much more problematic to generalise from general trends down to individual experience. We know, for example, that there is a strong correlation between poverty and crime, yet all poor people do not become engaged in criminal activity; nor are all criminals necessarily from a poor background. Poverty may be conceptualised as the field of resources and relationships that may predispose some young people to be delinquent compared with others, but it cannot predict which young people will deviate and for what reasons.

Conversely, crime and delinquency are socially patterned: certain categories of young people tend to be criminalised more than others (low income, Indigenous). This fact alone demonstrates the influence of social background on life opportunities and the manner in which the state intervenes in young people's lives. But this is less a matter of the factors that predict delinquency than the factors that predict state intervention (Cunneen & White 2007). There are, then, limitations of any approach or perspective that tries to use risk assessment in order to predict behaviour, and thereby intervene in a preemptive fashion in the lives of young people.

Critical reflections on risk and criminal career

- Be wary about presuming a tight, causal fit between particular risk indicators and later, or concurrent, behaviour (association but not determinism).
- It is difficult to identify any earlier, individual or family level factors that would predict unquestionably those who would follow delinquent transitions (one-third of non-offenders also shared the same type and number of risk factors as the frequent offenders).

BOX 10.2

BOX 10.2

■ Which of the multitudinous risks experienced by young people might be claimed to be most significant, which risks propel some people towards crime, and which do not (the same factor can have different consequences for different people at different times; the same risk factor can have different consequences for the same individual at different points in the life course)?

■ There are issues surrounding reliance on large-scale quantitative studies of criminal careers insofar as it is qualitative biographical interviews that help us to elucidate the subjective experiences of transition (significance of contingent, unpredictable events and experiences in the creation of youth transitions of different sorts—stuff happens).

■ Tendency in much criminal career research to overplay individual-level risks (rooted in concepts of pathological, antisocial personality types) at the expense of those that are presented by the historical and spatial contexts in which youth transitions are made (rapid and widespread de-industrialisation and concomitant rise of economic marginality and poverty for working-class youth, unprecedented influx of cheap heroin—new imported risks).

Source: drawing upon the work of MacDonald 2006.

It is somewhat ironic that while risk is constructed in relation to the notion of determinism (one's social background, for example, determines the likelihood of engaging in juvenile crime), the other leading concept underpinning juvenile justice today puts the emphasis on voluntarism (the element of free will in human behaviour).

Responsibilisation

The notion of responsibilisation has several interrelated components. These include (Muncie 2004):

■ communities should take primary responsibility for crime prevention
■ individuals should be held responsible for their own actions
■ families, in particular parents, have a responsibility to ensure that their children do not develop antisocial tendencies.

A fundamental premise of responsibilisation is that responsibility for safety and well-being is no longer in the hands of the (welfare) state, but rather has been transferred back to communities, families, and individuals. It is yet another aspect of individuation, the notion that it is up to the individual to make a life for themselves, to negotiate their own pathways through the economic and social structure, and to accept that life is basically a do-it-yourself kind of project.

In regards to juvenile justice, responsibilisation in the Australian context tends to be implicated in how punitive justice and restorative justice approaches to punishment have been institutionalised in practice (Cunneen & White 2007). In general, there has been a significant shift in recent years away from a welfare or treatment perspective and towards a justice or retributive view of juvenile justice. Young offenders are seen to be responsible for their own actions, and so must suffer their just deserts for any transgressions they have committed. With restorative justice, the emphasis is less on punishment per se than with repairing the harm. But even here, the emphasis tends to be on holding the young person accountable. The burden of responsibility basically falls on the individual to atone for or change their behaviour (Muncie 2004). In each case, the focus is the young offender.

The dual focus of the juvenile justice system is coherent and consistent from the point of view of risk analysis and responsibilisation. In other words, the point of intervention is less about the welfare and/or rehabilitation of the young person than with making them accountable and ensuring a modicum of community safety. A hybrid system that combines punitive features with reparation philosophies makes sense only insofar as it reflects the profile of young offenders mentioned earlier. The serious and persistent offender is liable to be punished up to and including the use of detention. The low-risk offender is made to make amends for their wrongdoing by repairing the harm and perhaps making an apology. Meanwhile, the potential offender is dealt with through deployment of risk assessment technologies and ongoing surveillance in order to prevent future deviation.

While the instruments and personnel of criminal justice are extensive and varied, especially once a young person has been targeted for state intervention, one thing remains the same over time — the central role of the police in bringing young people into the system.

POLICING YOUTH

The police are the gatekeepers to the criminal justice system. Unfortunately, very often the relationship between police and young people is mixed at best, and fraught with conflict at the worst.

The ways in which young people and the police relate to each other is partly a reflection of how they perceive one another (see Cunneen & White 2007). These often negative perceptions are grounded in real experiences and situations. One significant aspect of police–youth relations is that much of the contact takes place in public venues such as the street, shopping centres, malls, and beaches. The difficulty here is that many of the places where young people congregate and hang out are basically commercial spaces. As such, the primary objective and use of such places is dictated by consumption and commercial trading activity (White 1994).

In this kind of setting, young people often become the prime targets for intervention by police and private security guards because they usually travel and hang out in groups, which may be perceived as disturbing to customers or other users of the space. Or, they are perceived as non-consumers, or at best marginal consumers, and hence as not suitable patrons within the commercial venue. The visibility, perceived lack of financial power, and behaviour (hanging around in groups, making noise) often make young people unwelcome visitors, regardless of whether they actually break the law or engage in offensive activity.

For many young people, the conflicts associated with their presence in the public domain are linked to their lack of youth-specific public space (spaces designed with their particular interests in mind) and lack of youth-friendly space (spaces designed with their particular activity needs in mind). The fight for a space of their own manifests itself in resentment at the intervention of authority figures in their activities, especially when no law has actually been broken (see Chapter 15).

> In public spaces, young people often become the prime targets for intervention by police and private security guards. This is because they usually travel and hang out in groups, which may be perceived as disturbing to customers or other users of the space. Or, they are perceived as non-consumers and hence as not suitable patrons within the commercial venue.

Meanwhile, there is considerable pressure on the police to use strong measures to clean up the streets and to make people feel safe in public places. Retail traders, older customers, and commercial interests often call on the police to move groups of young people away from the commercial districts. From the police perspective, such pressures are difficult to ignore or to avoid (White 1994; Loader 1996).

As a result, a big issue for young people is that they are constantly made to feel that they are outsiders, feelings confirmed daily in the form of exclusionary policies, and coercive security and policing measures that are designed precisely to remove them from the public domain. For young people, this is often seen as unfair (given that they have nowhere else to go) and unwarranted (given that they have not done anything wrong). Then, if they resist efforts to move them on or if they clash with authority figures over the use of public space, they can sometimes be drawn directly into the juvenile justice system, with charges being laid for offensive behaviour, resisting arrest, and the like.

For their part, the police in some jurisdictions are attempting to redefine their public order tasks. If, say, conflict is occurring in a particular shopping centre, the police may play a bridging role between the relevant parties (retail traders and young people, for example), and get them to agree to some kind of accommodation of interests. Sometimes this can involve a commercial centre setting up some kind of youth service, or possibly hiring a youth worker (for examples, see White 1998c).

But more often than not, the way in which police intervene in the lives of young people is driven by political considerations and legislative initiative. While the legislative basis for action varies from one state or territory to another, the general trend around Australia has been for police services to be granted extensive new powers vis-à-vis young people (see, for example, Sandor & White 1993; Blagg & Wilkie 1995; Mukherjee, Carcach & Higgins 1997). These range from casual use of name checks (asking young people their names and addresses), to move-on powers (the right to ask young people to move away from certain areas), the right to search for prohibited implements, and an enhanced ability to take fingerprints and bodily samples of alleged young offenders. If granted powers, police generally use them.

The removal of young people from public spaces has also been accomplished through specific legislative measures. In 1994 the *Children (Parental Responsibility) Act* (NSW) was passed, increasing parental responsibility for the behaviour of their children and police powers to remove young people from public places, without charge. In 1997, this legislation was replaced with the *Children (Protection and Parental Responsibility) Act*. Among other things, the Act allows the police to remove young people under sixteen years of age from public places without charge, if the police believe that the young people are at risk of committing an offence or of being affected by a crime, are not under the supervision or control of a responsible adult, or if it is believed the young person is in danger of being physically harmed, injured, or abused. The Act does not specify the sort of offences that might be committed, but, under this Act, if an offence were actually committed, the police would not be picking the young person up.

In the first six months of 1999, 145 young people were removed from public places in the four local government areas where the legislation was operational. Of these, 90 per cent were Indigenous children (Chan & Cunneen 2000: 53). The apparent discriminatory use of the law by police has led to a complaint under the *Racial Discrimination Act*. Evaluations of similar types of zero tolerance policing in places such as the USA have likewise highlighted the discriminatory effects of such policing and the implication of such strategies in the violation of civil and political rights (see Cunneen 1999; Dixon 1998).

There is now a quite extensive literature on the relationship between police and ethnic minority young people in Australia (see, for example, Guerra & White 1995; Moss 1993; Pe-Pua 1996; Maher, Dixon, Swift & Nguyen 1997). The tension between the two groups is fostered by a range of stereotypical images pertaining to young people (for example, ethnic youth gangs) and the police (for example, repressive figures associated with authoritarian regimes). Several studies and reports have highlighted the lack of adequate police training, especially cross-cultural training, in dealing with people from non-English-speaking backgrounds, particularly refugees and recent migrants (Chan 1994, 1997; New South Wales Office of the Ombudsman 1994). At any rate, the relationship between the police and young people with South-East Asian, Middle Eastern, and Pacific Islander backgrounds has been particularly negative in recent years (see Lyons 1995; Maher et al. 1997; Collins, Noble, Poynting & Tabar 2000). Members of these communities have complained that they are unfairly targeted by the police, that they have been subjected to racist policing, and that they are regularly harassed by authority figures such as police and security guards (White et al. 1999). These issues, and those relating to the police and Indigenous young people, are dealt with further in the chapters on Indigenous youth (Chapter 5) and ethnic minority youth (Chapter 4).

In many Western jurisdictions attempts to restrict the street presence of young people have taken the form of youth curfews or anti-loitering statutes, and, in the case of the United Kingdom, legislation that is designed to ban and penalise antisocial behaviour. Curfews are used extensively in the USA, although the specific features of each curfew vary considerably in terms of times, activities, target populations, and enforcement. Evaluation of curfews has indicated that their success is best guaranteed when coercive measures are accompanied by opportunity enhancement measures, such as leisure and recreation, educational activities, musical forums, and so on (Bilchik 1996). With regard to the overall effectiveness and purposes of curfews, and whether they may inadvertently criminalise youth behaviour that is in and of itself not illegal or criminal, big issues remain (White 1996d).

Street-clearing legislation has long been linked to efforts of the establishment to deal with the most destitute sections of the population. In particular, the history of vagrancy laws in the United Kingdom, Australia, and the USA is a history of social control over selected population groups—the poor, the unemployed, the ethnic minority, the Indigenous, and the transient (see Brown et al. 2001; Santos 2001; Walsh 2004). In the context of anti-gang strategies, a number of attempts have been made in the USA to strengthen anti-loitering legislation to specifically target street gangs. In many cases, these laws have been struck down by the Supreme Court as being unconstitutional. It has been observed, though, that where governing bodies enact ordinances or laws that are directed at specific kinds of loitering (for example, that which blocks city footpaths) or specific kinds of behaviour (for example, particular gang-related activities), then anti-loitering legislation may pass constitutional scrutiny (see Santos 2001).

> In many Western jurisdictions attempts to restrict the street presence of young people have taken the form of youth curfews, anti-loitering statutes, or legislation that is designed to ban and penalise antisocial behaviour.

How young people are viewed and treated through legislation and police intervention can create major tensions on the street. What young people think about their circumstances, how they think about themselves, and how others view them all have major repercussions for the ways in which they relate to issues of crime and society. Invariably, as well, the social position of young people also brings them into regular contact with agents of the criminal justice system.

The nature of youth offending

How we view crime committed by young people is very much influenced by media portrayals of the issues and the young people themselves. It is certainly the case that juvenile crime is big news (see Schissel 1997; Males 1996; Bessant & Hil 1997). Hardly a day goes by without some reference to young offenders in newspapers, on radio talkback shows, and in television news coverage. The persistence and pervasiveness of such reporting and commentary means that it is hard not to be fearful of crime and not to be suspicious of young people. The media are saturated with stories about 'young thugs', 'hooligans', 'ethnic youth gangs', 'school vandals', and 'lazy teenagers' (see Sercombe 1999). Much media coverage of youth crime hinges upon the idea that there is some kind of youth crime wave. A crime wave implies that there is an actual increase in a certain kind of crime—drug-dealing, robbery, or mugging—and that more and more young people are engaging in a particular kind of criminal activity.

Contrary to most media reports, youth crime tends to be relatively minor in nature. Most young people do not offend seriously and, in fact, very few become serious and persistent offenders (Cunneen & White 1995, 2007; Mukherjee 1997a). The crimes most frequently committed by young people, for which they are arrested or charged, are those relating to property crime (usually of items of relatively low value) and public order (use of bad language or making noise in a public place).

> Contrary to most media reports, youth crime tends to be relatively minor in nature. Most young people do not offend seriously and, in fact, very few become serious and persistent offenders.

There are myriad reasons why any particular young person may engage in crime, although broad social patterns in offending behaviour are apparent. Theories and studies of juvenile offending point to a wide range of causal factors (Cunneen & White 2007), including individual factors (ranging from personal choice and psychological damage arising from an abusive childhood, through to mental illness), situational factors (such factors as poor school performance, homelessness, and deviant peer cultures), and social structural factors (relating, for instance, to inadequate moral education and socialisation, racism, and social inequality). There are, then, a multiplicity of specific factors that help to explain crime.

It is the combination of these factors, and their association with certain categories of young people, that explains variations in the propensity for criminal behaviour and/or criminalisation among young people. The profiles of young offenders tend to look basically the same: young men with low income, low educational achievement, no employment, and a weak attachment to parents who move frequently, are the most likely to wind up in juvenile detention centres.

The last three decades in Australia have seen a significant rise in the number of girls (under eighteen) being arrested for major offences compared with the arrest rate for boys or for women. Research on New South Wales court appearances during the first half of the 1990s indicates that the rates for assaults, robbery, and drug offences all show greater increases for young women than for young men, although the absolute rates are much lower for females (Gliksman & Chen 2001). Queensland research noted that although young men commit a far greater number of serious assaults, serious assaults comprise about three times the proportion of finalised court matters for girls compared to boys—6 per cent compared to 2 per cent (Ogilvie et al. 2000: 4). Changes in the offending behaviour of young women require sustained research that needs to be sensitive to a number of factors, including the relationship between offending and drug and alcohol use, changes in welfare regulation and social security, and responses of criminal justice agencies to young women, among other things (see Gliksman & Chen 2001; Cunneen & White 2007).

While times are difficult for many young people, available evidence does not suggest a major crime upsurge. While most youth crime is relatively trivial in nature, much of this activity takes place in public, and therefore highly visible, city spaces.

Community contexts and restorative justice

Generally speaking, police interventions and attempts at legislative panaceas do little to address the core issues of why some young people appear to 'go bad'. This is readily acknowledged in youth crime prevention literature. As reflected in Canadian (Canada, National Crime Prevention Council 1996), US (Catalano & Hawkins 1996), British (Utting 1996), Australian (Developmental Crime Prevention Consortium 1999), and New Zealand (New Zealand Department of Corrections 2001) research and commentary, among others, what young people do is a complex issue. The key ideas are that there are many different causal dimensions to youth behaviour, that there are many different transition points and progressions for different types of behaviour, and there are many different approaches that can be drawn upon to channel youth behaviour in positive pro-social directions.

In practice, why certain young people commit certain crimes is only answerable by consideration of their personal life history, their immediate life circumstances, and their position in the wider social structure. The decision to commit vandalism, say, may incorporate elements of an abusive childhood, difficulties at school, unemployment, and bad experiences with authority figures. It may also simply be fun. All too often, though, the problems experienced by a growing proportion of young people—to make ends meet, to find secure full-time employment, to cope with stress and educational competition, to forge a meaningful social identity—are construed in such a way as to make young people themselves the problem.

> In practice, why certain young people commit certain crimes is only answerable by consideration of their personal life history, their immediate life circumstances, and their position in the wider social structure.

The economic, social, and political marginalisation of people is uneven and, in Western societies, is based upon wider social divisions linked to class position, ethnicity, Indigenous background, and gender relationships. The social costs of marginality are inevitably translated into the economic costs of crime. But the social costs of marginality are also transformed into behaviour that is officially defined as antisocial and dangerous. All of this is bound to have an impact on the self-image of marginalised young people and their efforts at self-defence in a hostile environment. The pooling of social resources and the construction of identities that are valued by others (if only one's peers) finds expression in a range of cultural forms, including various youth groups and gang formations (see, for example, Collins et al. 2000; White 2002c).

According to a growing body of academic research, the social and economic character of a region has an influence on the activities and opportunities of disadvantaged individuals. Thus, local community context is an integral part of why some people have a greater propensity than others to commit crime. But the circumstance of economic adversity, in and of itself, is insufficient to explain fully the relationship between disadvantaged people and crime (see Weatherburn & Lind 1998, 2001). In addition to a correlation between reported parental neglect and poverty, there are higher rates of crime in those neighbourhoods in which the level of economic stress is sufficient to push the number of juveniles susceptible to crime past a certain limit. Thus, according to Weatherburn and Lind (1998: 4), 'Low socioeconomic status neighbourhoods will generally have larger populations of delinquents and will therefore produce higher rates of interaction between juveniles susceptible to involvement in crime and juveniles already involved in crime'.

The precise nature of peer group interaction is influenced by other local neighbourhood factors. It is not simply a case of there being a critical mass of young people who together collectively contribute to the creation of a crime-prone neighbourhood. The social dynamics of specific areas also shape the nature and extent of juvenile offending. Research carried out in the USA (Sampson 1991, 1993) and the United Kingdom (Hirschfield & Bowers 1997) has pointed to the importance of social cohesion in understanding the relationship between crime and disadvantage. Here it is argued that areas of disadvantage with high levels of social cohesion will tend to have lower levels of crime than similarly disadvantaged areas with low levels of social cohesion.

Neighbourhoods that have strong social cohesion (that tend to be fairly stable in terms of residential tenure and home ownership) are able to exert greater degrees of informal social control by the area's residents. This takes the form of the monitoring of play by local children, intervention to prevent acts of truancy or vandalism by local youth, ostracising troublemakers, and confrontation of people who are exploiting or disturbing public spaces (Foster 1995; Sampson et al. 1997). These types of analyses suggest on the one hand that: 'The more that an area that is at a disadvantage economically pulls together as a community, the greater its capacity to combat crime' (Hirschfield & Bowers 1997: 1296). On the other hand, it is argued that concentrated disadvantage will decrease collective efficacy, and thus informal controls will be undermined (Sampson et al. 1997).

The nature and dynamics of poverty, unemployment, and marginalisation have a lot to do with which young people commit which sorts of crime or antisocial acts, to what extent they do so, and for what purposes. Selected groups of young people, often living in the same suburb or housing estate, tend to receive disproportionate attention from authority figures such as the police, and as such are more likely, and at a younger age, to come into contact with the criminal justice system. In a nutshell, the residues of social injustice are cleaned up by the institutions of criminal justice. How it does so is changing in several important respects, particularly with regard to the widespread adoption of restorative justice as the leading strategy with which to tackle youth offending.

The idea of restorative justice has been embraced in many jurisdictions around the world today, particularly in relation to juvenile justice (Braithwaite 1999; Bazemore & Walgrave 1999a). Restorative justice refers to an emphasis on dealing with offenders by focusing on repairing harm, and in so doing involving victims and communities as well as offenders in the reparation process. Restorative justice emphasises re-integrative and developmental principles and offers the hope that opportunities will be enhanced for victims, offenders, and their immediate communities, with the direct participation of all concerned in this process. The benefits of restorative justice are seen in terms of its emphasis on active agency (young people doing things for themselves), cost-effectiveness (compared with detention or imprisonment), victim recognition and engagement (often through face-to-face meetings with offenders), and community benefit (participation and through community service).

Compared with previous theoretical approaches to offending, restorative justice does appear to offer a practically effective, philosophically attractive, and financially prudent method of doing justice: it is peacemaking in orientation rather than punishment-based, and socially inclusive rather than reliant upon experts and officials. It attempts to provide a symbolic and practical solution to actual harms rather than a response to violation of laws (that represent, in abstract, acts against the state). Victims and community, as well as offenders, are central to resolving issues of harm, rather than being peripheral to the processes of criminal justice.

For present purposes, it is important to note that within restorative justice frameworks the idea of social harm is generally conceptualised in immediate, direct, and individualistic terms (and as such ignores the broader social processes underpinning, and patterns of, offending and victimisation). One consequence of this is that the emphasis on repairing harm tends to be restricted to the immediate violations and immediate victim concerns, thereby ignoring communal objectives and collective needs in framing reparation processes (see White 2000, 2003). Thus, the heart of the matter remains that of changing the offender, albeit with their involvement, rather than transforming communities and building progressive social alliances that might change the conditions under which offending takes place. To put it differently, community empowerment, which connotes a concern to intervene in and perhaps to transform community relations, does not feature strongly in some of the more popular restorative justice models, such as family group or juvenile conferencing (see Bazemore 1997).

Theoretically, and in selective practical circumstances, restorative justice may be effective in providing offenders with greater developmental possibilities, and ensuring greater victim and community satisfaction and engagement in criminal justice matters (see Chan 2006). At an experiential level, it offers constructive and positive outcomes and possibilities for individuals brought into contact with the criminal justice system—especially compared with retributive and treatment approaches. But, at the same time, such interventions tend to deal predominantly with offenders from working-class backgrounds—Indigenous and ethnic minority people in particular—without generally changing the circumstances under which they live.

Nevertheless, there is a sense in which the basic principles and practices of restorative justice can be thought of as prefiguring the changes required to create a just and equal society (see Bazemore & Walgrave 1999b). The restorative justice approach does contain the seeds for creatively and constructively responding to the injustices of life suffered by most, usually working-class, offenders. At the least, it implies a recognition that families and communities have an important role to play in trying to grapple with the causal reasons for personal offending. In some, still exceptional, cases, restorative justice also offers young people themselves a pivotal role in the justice process as decision makers as well as offenders.

BOX 10.3

Youth doing restorative justice for themselves

In Edmonton, Canada, the Youth Restorative Action Project (YRAP) has emerged in counterpoint to the usual adult-dominated, highly controlled, and ultimately conservative operationalisation of juvenile conferencing. Starting from the premise that community also includes young people, the YRAP has challenged the participatory elements of standard restorative justice forums (by engaging youth in the decision-making processes directly) and the purposive elements of standard restorative justice forums (by mobilising discussions and resources around social justice issues).

In their first case, the YRAP dealt with an incident involving a racially provoked knife attack by an Asian youth. The case was sent to the YRAP for sentencing recommendations, a process that involved participation by a committee of racially diverse young people, some of whom had experienced racism. This particular conference was held in a creative space for young people (a place of art and music activities). While understanding the sense of victimhood felt by the offender, the YRAP group made it clear that violence was not justified. They then probed the young offender about how he could have more positively handled the situation.

In the end, the sanction agreed upon was that the offender, through use of an audio or visual project using the local recording facilities, produce a statement on the negative elements of racism. The result was a hip hop song penned, produced, and performed by the young offender. Such creativity in dealing with offending behaviour, and explicit acknowledgment of the social context within which offences are committed, stemmed from the experiences of the young members of YRAP as young people. Furthermore, a commitment to social justice—arising from firsthand experience of marginalisation and social inequality—ensures that they are emboldened to act without the cultural and bureaucratic baggage of conventional justice systems.

Source: summarised from Hogeveen 2006.

In one sense, while the state is the instigator of the action taken against an offender, under the restorative justice model it is the community that is given greater scope to deal with the concrete issues surrounding victim needs, offender circumstance, and particular social contexts. Responsibility can thereby be shifted from the state (in its more formal and coercive forms) to friends, families, and community members for managing conflict and resolving immediate social problems. This can only occur insofar as offenders tend to confront the process as individuals, and as individuals who lack high degrees of social and economic power. Personal and communal change is thus possible to the extent that clear social objectives are part and parcel of the restorative justice process. Therein lies its hope and potential.

Summary

The vast bulk of youth crime is fairly trivial in nature. Most of it is directed at property or is against good order; only a very small proportion of youth crime involves violence against the person. The vast majority of formally processed young offenders come from particularly vulnerable and disadvantaged social backgrounds.

In responding to youth crime and the images of youth deviance, many nation states employ a combination of coercive measures, such as youth curfews, aggressive street policing, and anti-gang interventions, and developmental measures, such as sports programs, parent classes, and educational retention programs. This carrot-and-stick approach reflects the hybrid nature of youth crime prevention and juvenile justice responses to criminal activity. The latter is characterised by the interplay of retributive (for example, use of detention), welfare (for example, drug treatment), and restorative justice (for example, juvenile conferencing) measures.

While the specific approach to juvenile justice varies considerably from jurisdiction to jurisdiction, a common element is the target groups and essential construction of the problem. Most justice systems deal predominantly with offenders from working-class backgrounds, including Indigenous and ethnic minority people, and thereby reflect the class biases in definitions of social harm and crime, as well as basing their responses on these biases. In so doing, they reinforce the ideological role of law-and-order discourse in forging a conservative cross-class consensus about the nature of social problems. The reinforcement of this discourse also unwittingly enhances the legitimacy of coercive state intervention in the lives of working-class people, even if under the rationale of repairing harm, as in the case of restorative justice.

At a social structural level, such processes confirm the role of crime as the central problem (rather than poverty, unemployment, and racism), thereby neglecting or avoiding entirely the roles of class division and social inequality.

Given the nature of juvenile offending and the characteristics of the typical young offender, it is important to deal with issues of youth crime in a holistic way. Generally speaking, the best remedies to juvenile offending rest upon income security, meaningful paid work, participation in community life, community solidarity, and public accountability. Youth experience is a continual process of connection and reconnection with significant others and mainstream institutions. The challenge in relating to young people is to empower them, individually and collectively, so that they feel as if they have—and that they actually do have— a real stake in the wider society. This is the real politics underpinning law and order today.

Questions for further exploration

1   Who tends to get criminalised as a young offender? Why?

2   The privileging of individualisation and responsibilisation in juvenile justice essentially disregards social–structural analyses and reformulates the problem as basically one of individual failings. Discuss.

QUESTIONS

QUESTIONS

3 How has risk assessment and risk analysis contributed to the further entrenchment of social inequality within the juvenile justice system as a whole?

4 How does where you live affect the propensity to engage or not engage in criminal or antisocial behaviour?

5 What is, or ought to be, the relationship between restorative justice and social justice?

PART 4

Social
Identities

WORKING THE
MULTIPLE ECONOMIES

11

Introduction

Key aspects of the relationship between young people and the world of work are discussed in this chapter. For young people, paid work is very often a necessity—in terms of supplementing incomes, of vocational and workplace experiences, and with regard to maintaining group friendships and peer networks. The chapter discusses the general nature of work and broad trends of youth engagement in paid work across different economic spheres. The types and dynamics of work are explored from the point of view of overall labour market opportunities, the position of young people within the labour market, and the payment and experiences of young people as workers.

Work for young people has become ever more central to their lives—by its presence (in relation, for example, to the increasing prevalence of the school–work combination) and by its absence (given that those not in school find it especially difficult to make ends meet without some kind of employment). At an experiential level, work is desirable to young people because they want to have buying power. It is also desirable because they get access to the adult world and practices.

The structural context of work involves dynamics that affect diverse groups of young people in different ways: it closes off opportunities for some, while simultaneously offering greater flexibility for others. Yet all young people are in some way implicated in the changes in the nature of work, particularly in respect to the constant shifting of jobs and employers. How young people respond to these challenges is of considerable interest. Similarly, while access to waged work varies within the youth population, there are still broad similarities in the way in which waged work involving young people is constructed; namely, through the artifice of a teenage labour market. These types of issues are also explored in this chapter.

THE NATURE OF WORK

The starting point for an examination of young people in the world of work is not young people but the world of work itself. To understand the position of young people as workers, it is essential to consider what is happening generally in the world of work and to ask what, specifically, is the nature of work in the kind of society in which we live (see Chapters 1 and 9).

The wage is the primary means by which most people gain the means of subsistence. As we have discussed in previous chapters, one of the changes that has affected young people of this generation is the simultaneous process of increasing young people's reliance on obtaining a wage and reducing their options for social security benefits (see our discussion of monetarist policies in Chapter 7). At the same time, employment has become increasingly uncertain, so much so that researchers now refer to the labour market for young people as 'precarious' (Furlong & Kelly 2005).

Production processes and precarious employment

From a financial point of view getting a job is of utmost importance. It is also important from a social point of view (social status, self-esteem, personal development, and existential security). But finding paid work is only one part of a complex process of negotiation in the sphere of production. Work is not only a question of remuneration—how much we get paid for what we do—but also a question of the quality of the work experience, which has a big bearing on people's lives. And here there is a range of questions one might ask regarding the conditions of work, who makes the key decisions at work, divisions of labour within workplaces, and the connection between workers and what they produce. Workplaces vary greatly in terms of structure, practices, and cultures. Major determinants of workplace dynamics include the size of the firm or shop, the location of the workplace, the nature of the service or good that is being produced, and how labour is allocated within the workplace setting.

> Work is not only a question of remuneration—how much we get paid for what we do—but also a question of the quality of the work experience, which has a big bearing on people's lives.

Some of the more interesting and important research being done in the sociology of work is that which focuses on the phenomenon of precarious employment (see, for example, Campbell 1997). This type of analysis makes a direct link between social marginalisation and certain patterns of employment and unemployment. As a concept, precarious employment refers to a combination of low pay, employment insecurity, and working-time insecurity. Given the relevance of this to the work situation of many young people now and into the future, the concept is worth exploring in greater detail.

A feature of precarious employment is that individual workers get locked into a situation where they have access solely to low levels of pay, which may be due to a range of factors. The occupational wages may be officially low, as is the case of junior or youth wages (see below). Wages may be low due to the low number of hours worked, which, in turn, may be linked to flexible work schedules that demand workers come in only at certain peak times. Low pay may be justified by reference to the productivity of the work and skill requirements of the workers, regardless of profits generated in the workplace. Wages may also be kept low due to formal and informal wage agreements that link job security to the low wage. The net result of these types of processes, arrangements, and accepted practices is that workers employed in such jobs rarely have much more than subsistence wages. In many cases individual workers may have to rely upon more than one job, or depend upon parents or spouses, in order to maintain their households or spending patterns.

A second feature of precarious employment is the insecurity that attaches to the job. This takes a number of different forms. Employment insecurity simply refers to instances where employers can dismiss or lay off workers without great difficulty or costs. Job insecurity is where the employer shifts workers from one job to another at will or where the content of the job can be altered (including reduced). The work environment may be risky in some way (unsafe or polluted) and this, too, can produce work insecurity over time. Or employers may impose fragmented, shortened, and irregular hours, so that workers feel working-time insecurity because they do not really have much control over how many hours they work and when they will work them. This list of possible insecurities goes on (see Campbell 1997).

A third feature of precarious employment is the volatility in the labour market itself, which produces great variation in the rhythm and routines of work. Most new job creation has been of a part-time nature, and much of this is comprised of casualised part-time work; that is, the growth in new jobs has tended to be in service and retail industries, in positions that offer low pay and little skill development or requirements, and that make workers easily interchangeable. Under these circumstances, it is easier to structure workforces around people who work intermittent and irregular hours and who do not cost as much to hire as those in continuing part-time positions. Those caught up in precarious forms of employment also include people engaged in marginal self-employment, as outworkers or leafleters, and those involved in either government-sponsored employment schemes or community projects that have a fixed term of employment. Even workers who are in permanent employment may be threatened by insecurity based on large-scale retrenchments in public-and private-sector workplaces, and by continual pressures on working-time security (demands to change shifts, annual leave dates, lunch, and other breaks, or to expand the spread of ordinary hours beyond the norm, for example).

The workplace policy context in Australia has fostered and reinforced the precariousness of the labour market generally as a result of the federal government's introduction of comprehensive changes to industrial relations in Australia with the passage of the *Workplace Relations Act 1996 as amended by the Workplace Relations Amendment (Workchoices) Act 2005* (Clth). This Act radically altered the conditions under which employees would undertake their work.

Key features of the Workchoices legislation

■ The formation of a single national industrial system to replace the separate state, territory, and federal systems for constitutional corporations.

■ The establishment of the Australian Fair Pay Commission to replace the National Wage Cases at the Australian Industrial Relations Commission.

■ The streamlining of Certified Agreements and Australian Workplace Agreements, including increasing the maximum agreement life from three to five years.

■ A reduction in allowable award matters.

■ The creation of legislation for five minimum workplace conditions.

■ The exemption of companies with fewer than 101 employees from unfair dismissal laws.

■ The exemption of all companies from unfair dismissal laws where a dismissal is for a bona fide operational reason.

■ Increased restrictions on allowable industrial action.

BOX 11.1

BOX 11.1

■ Mandating secret ballots for industrial action.

■ Discouraging pattern bargaining and industry-wide industrial action.

While ostensibly justified on the basis that the new legislation provides both employees and employers more choice and flexibility in workplace arrangements, the Act has been heavily criticised by the Australian Council of Trade Unions (ACTU) and others who argue that it actively disadvantages workers. For young people, the main concerns are that this Act makes union protection more difficult to obtain than previously (which itself has always been very uneven in regards to the rights of young workers), makes it easier for small businesses to sack young workers (an issue that is especially problematic for young workers, given that many work for small businesses), and it is associated with a marked deterioration in young workers' pay and work conditions (which tended to be poor to begin with).

It is notable, for example, that the legislation scrapped the No Disadvantage Test for the individual Australian Workplace Agreements (AWAs). This test had compared a proposed agreement to an underpinning and relevant industrial award that had or should have covered employees up until the proposal for an agreement. The No Disadvantage Test weighed the benefits of the award against the proposed agreement to ensure that, overall, employees were no worse off. Instead of this, the Workchoices legislation requires simply that employers provide five minimum entitlements, which cover:

■ maximum ordinary working hours
■ annual leave
■ parental leave
■ personal or carer's leave
■ minimum pay scales.

For young people, who already are among the lowest-paid workers in the country (in part due to their position in the youth labour market, as outlined below), the consequences of the new legislation have been especially negative. Recent research about the impact of the new industrial relations laws has shown that the majority of workers are suffering wage cuts under the new minimum wage setting process, that many workers are losing award coverage, and that those people on AWAs are being affected by reduced or abolished overtime pay and penalty rates, axing of annual leave loading, reduction in rest breaks, reduction or abolition of public holiday payments, and reduced work loading (ACTU 2007). Between July 2005 and May 2006, government figures showed that 598 individual AWA contracts were signed by young people under the age of fifteen, 7779 individual contracts were signed by young people aged between fifteen and eighteen, and 13 269 individual contracts were signed by young workers aged eighteen to twenty-one (ACTU 2006). In the majority of cases the signing of the AWA involved substantial changes to pay and conditions. The net result of the legislation is that the lowest-paid workers, among whom younger workers are disproportionately represented, are the ones most likely to experience pressure to accept lower pay in poorer working conditions where there is little or no job security.

The advent and rise in precarious employment as a phenomenon in the West means that there is an intrinsic link between marginalisation and employment:

> We are increasingly seeing in many countries the consolidation of patterns of intermittent employment, in which persons fluctuate between periods of unemployment, short-term and low-paid employment, participation in government sponsored training or employment schemes and periods of withdrawal from the labour force (Campbell 1997: 9).

To put it differently, the nature of intermittent employment involving low-pay, low-quality jobs translates into a form of ongoing social deprivation that spans both unemployment and employment. Temporary jobs at low rates of pay and with little opportunity for skill development are hardly new to many young people.

But while these experiences are not new, they are also not tied to previous workplace eras and cultures. Precariousness is no longer a feature of specific labour markets, usually associated with some working-class occupations and industries. Rather, most workplaces today have seen the expansion of highly elastic employment regimes. The effects of recent social changes mean that there are paradoxes in contemporary young people's engagement with work. Their engagement with the student labour market means that work becomes a part of their lives early (before they leave school) but it is relatively precarious work and continues to be so across all groups, not just the working class. The contingency and precariousness of work for all groups is one of the most important changes.

This has meant that while the conditions of work for young people across all class groups have come to incorporate these elements, it is important to see how those who are privileged use the resources at their disposal to make their lives work within these conditions. Many researchers have noted that cultural capital has become significant in the successful management of the difficult conditions of the labour market today (Dwyer & Wyn 2001; Willis 1998). One ingredient for success is an orientation towards long-term planning. Recent research has demonstrated that life chances are closely linked to the abilities of young people to be proactive in the planning of their futures; abilities, that have, in turn, 'structural foundations in social class' in that it is those young people at the upper end of the class structure who are more likely to have such abilities than those lower down on the socioeconomic scale (Evans 2002: 259).

> Precariousness is no longer a feature of specific labour markets, usually associated with some working-class occupations and industries. Rather, most workplaces today have seen the expansion of highly elastic employment regimes.

Young people are very aware of precarious work, but they are adjusting to it by placing a priority on horizontal mobility (see 'Young People's Responses', below) and placing great emphasis on developing 'multi-dimensional lives' that reflect and constitute a response to labour market uncertainty (Dwyer & Wyn 2001). Young people are thus not simply victims of circumstance (related to changing workplace structures), but are active agents who are engaging with the world as they find it. After all, they do not have any other memory of work to draw upon. They are a generation that is fixed on the moment, since this is all they have known. Precariousness is thus not perceived as a problem; it is that which all young people have to negotiate as a natural part of their particular generation's immediate experience. The following section sets out the wider structural context within which young people are engaging with the world of work.

Youth employment trends

The collapse in the availability of full-time work has had most dramatic impact on the young. Whereas just over twenty-five years ago, two-thirds of all sixteen to nineteen year olds in Australia were in full-time work, this had dropped to well under 20 per cent by the 1990s, and by the turn of the century there were very few full-time jobs for teenagers in Australia at all (Spierings 1995). As Jamrozik (1998: 76) further points out: 'In 1966, young people accounted for 13.6 per cent of all employed persons, but by 1995 they accounted for only 6.9 per cent. They lost their share of employment in all sectors of industry, including those industries which over this period achieved a very high rate of employment growth'. In a similar vein, it is notable that between 1986 and 1991 the proportion of young people (fifteen to twenty-five years) in full-time employment decreased by 11 per cent (ABS & NYARS 1993). This decrease was most significant for those aged fifteen to seventeen years, of whom 57 per cent were full-time employed in 1986 but only 30 per cent full-time employed in 1991. It has been estimated that 300 000 full-time jobs for young people were permanently lost over the twenty-five year period to 1991 (State Youth Affairs Councils and Networks 1992).

While the onset of this trend may have been more rapid in Australia, the same general facts hold for all of the developed countries (Furlong & Cartmel 2007). There are, simply, virtually no full-time opportunities for teenagers who want to work but who lack qualifications, skills, and experience. This shift has come about as a result of a number of structural features of the Australian economy, polity, and labour market. The instability and dilemmas associated with new patterns of work organisation are apparent in the above discussion of precarious employment. It is significant that industries that lend themselves to such precarious employment patterns include those that young people might be expected to be most involved in; namely, wholesale and retail trade, and recreation and personal industries. As Jamrozik (1998: 76) points out, while youth employment increased only in these two sectors (while decreasing in all others), that increase was still lower than the increase of total employment in these sectors between 1966 and 1995.

Precarious employment and uncertain job futures as applied to young people have to be set in the context of a combination of simultaneous social processes. These can be summarised as follows.

The rise in youth unemployment

First and foremost, there has been a persistent problem of high levels of youth unemployment throughout the developed world, which, averaging around two to three times the level of adult unemployment, ranges anywhere from 15 per cent upwards, depending upon the country, the specific group of young people being examined, the way unemployment is defined (one common ploy to reduce the official figures is to remove 'discouraged' workers from the figures, since such individuals are no longer in the labour force—they may not have jobs, but they are not officially unemployed), and the minor cycles of upward and downward movement of unemployment.

In Canada, for example, youth unemployment rates since 1976 have tended to average between 15 and 20 per cent for the fifteen to nineteen year olds, with the rate in 1993 being 19.7 per cent (Glenday 1996: 159). In Australia, the figures are similar with peaks and troughs across the years since the worldwide jump in unemployment in the mid 1970s, the low point being in the 12 per cent range in 1982 and the highest peak at over 25 per cent in 1991, but with the long-term underlying trend being distinctly upward—'ratchetting upwards', in the words of Wooden, during each recession peak 'and never quite returning to pre-recession levels' (Wooden 1996: 151).

The rise in school retention

Second, and related to these developments, there has been a dramatic and steep increase in school retention. In Victoria, for example, in the years between 1983 and 1992, the percentage of students undertaking studies at Year 12 level (the last year of high school) more than doubled, moving up from 36 per cent to 78 per cent (Dwyer 1996). Unfortunately, neither in Australia nor in other developed countries can it be said that the school curriculum has been modified to meet the needs imposed by this new group of students. Thus, for those students who wish to flow into the traditional university entry curriculum (the old 'college track' in American terms; see Polk & Schafer 1972), the ploy of educational retention may have some payoff. For those without this interest, the curriculum is a virtual wasteland. Students find themselves stranded in an educational holding operation without purpose or direction.

It is hardly surprising, then, that a common finding in Australia is that retention rates are actually now reversing direction, as discouraged students choose the streets over the situation they face in schools (Smyth & Hattam 2004). Since the 1992 high point in Victoria, the levels of Year 12 have steadily declined, to a level of 71 per cent in 1995 (Dwyer 1996). Moreover, the public schooling funding crisis, coupled with issues of how best to manage unwilling school participants, has generated the problem of what to do about school exclusions. A recent UK study (Smyth & Hattam 2004) points out that young people who have been formally excluded from school (for, say, misbehaviour) are more likely to be involved in criminal and nuisance activities than their non-excluded counterparts (Hayden & Martin 1998). Leaving school early, by choice or decree, has major implications for what young people do with their time and where they will do it.

The increase in part-time, casual employment

Third, insecure part-time and casual positions have increased dramatically, with the number of fourteen to twenty year old part-time workers more than doubling between 1980 and 1996 (Spoehr 1997: 2). While the number of full-time jobs available for those twenty-five and older increased by 12.1 per cent between 1995 and 2003, the number for teenagers declined by 6.9 per cent, and young adults by 15.1 per cent (Senate Community Affairs References Committee 2004: 278). Systematic study of labour market trends indicates the dramatic nature of the shifts in youth participation from full-time to part-time work, from paid work to educational participation, and from educational and work participation to unemployment, and what work there is tends to go to students rather than unemployed young people.

While technically keeping some young people off the rolls of the unemployed, most such work will not provide avenues into full-time, long-term, and career-oriented jobs. The work tends to be a temporary measure associated with the educational and recreational financial needs of students, or simply a stepping stone into yet more work of the same nature. For employers it represents a source of cheap, malleable labour.

The closing off of income opportunities

Fourth, it is important to acknowledge how each of these developments has impacted on the income opportunities of young people. The income of young people has been severely affected by broader economic restructuring: directly in terms of potential paid work by the young person, and indirectly through the financial pressures placed on families to support their children. Many young people have no income at all and are dependent upon their parents.

Paid work that is available for teenagers tends to be reserved for students and is located primarily in the retail and services sectors (White, Aumair, Harris & McDonnell 1997). It is comprised of low-skilled work in the formal and informal (that is, cash in hand) waged economic spheres, and youth wages continue to be pegged at a level below that of other workers, regardless of the productivity of young workers (White 1997b). Figures show that real earnings from full-time work among fifteen to nineteen year olds fell by 6 per cent between the early 1980s and the mid 1990s; earnings from part-time work fell by 29 per cent (Sweet 1998: 9). More generally, for those receiving outside income from a variety of sources, the average income of fifteen to nineteen year olds has fallen significantly in real terms since 1982. This includes incomes for full-time workers, part-time workers, and those receiving government benefits (Landt & Scott 1998). Research has shown that women, workers with no post-secondary educational qualifications, and younger workers under the age of thirty are over-represented among low-paid workers (Senate Community Affairs References Committee 2004: 74). It is notable as well that minimum full-time wages have fallen well behind average wages over the last two decades to just 50 per cent of average earnings, a reduction of 15 per cent since 1983 (Senate Community Affairs References Committee 2004: 80). The struggle to make ends meet is, then, a major concern for young people and their parents, particularly those in low-income residential areas.

Changes in labour market skills

The issue of low-skilled work is not only relevant to discussion of income opportunities, but also goes to the heart of the changes that have occurred—and continue to occur—in workplaces generally. Much of the government rhetoric of the 1980s and 1990s concerned the relationship between educational attainment and employment outcomes. The adoption of a metaphor of 'pathways' in national planning strategies was evident, for example, in Norway (Heggen & Dwyer 1998), the USA (Commission on the Skills of the American Workforce 1990), the United Kingdom (Department of Employment/Department of Education and Science 1991), Canada (Canadian Labour Force Development Board 1994), and Australia (Commonwealth of Australia 1994). The key presumption of much policy development was that Western countries generally were to be increasingly based upon a knowledge economy, one that required not only adaptable workers but also highly trained and skilled workers.

The promise of the knowledge economy for highly paid, highly skilled work, and for the employment of many more workers in these areas, was not fulfilled. The kinds of skilled jobs that were proposed were not delivered, fewer full-time jobs were created, and those few that were created required lower skills levels than anticipated in the knowledge economy projections (see Dwyer & Wyn 2001). Finding a job that was permanent, full-time, and somewhat related to the person's field of expertise or study has become increasingly more difficult to realise, not less.

YOUNG PEOPLE'S RESPONSES

The labour market conditions that we have identified have had a particular impact on young people because, of necessity, they have had to cope with these features. The increasing precariousness of employment, the increasing use of credentialism by employers, and the climate of uncertainty over jobs are elements of employment that this generation takes for granted.

Recently, the Life-Patterns study carried out by the Youth Research Centre at the University of Melbourne argued that young people who were born after 1970 constitute a distinct 'social generation' that distinguishes them in significant ways from the previous social generation—the baby boomers (Wyn & Woodman 2006). Terms such as 'Gen X' and 'Gen Y' are often used within the popular media to describe distinctive qualities and characteristics of new generations of young people. We have argued that shifts in subjectivity and in identities have accompanied the changes in society that this generation has had to respond to. These changes include the increased uncertainty associated with the transition into work, the requirement to have more educational credentials, and increased pre-cariousness of employment. Rather than seeing young people's life patterns as a failure to live up to the patterns of the previous generation, we have emphasised the distinctive nature of their identities.

This study found that young people were fairly pragmatic about work. At age twenty-two to twenty-three they rated financial independence as the most important characteristic of adult life. Two years later, at the ages of twenty-four to twenty-five, they stated that 'having a steady job' was the highest priority in their lives; involvement in work as a career and earning a lot of money were among the lowest priorities (Dwyer & Wyn 2001: 27). Dwyer and Wyn suggest that the labour market conditions that this generation have encountered may have shaped their attitudes to work. The uncertainty of the labour market has meant that the acquisition of new skills on their part is requisite if they are to make a go of things. The emphasis on 'horizontal mobility' by American youth (Willis 1998) is one example of how skill acquisition in precarious work circumstances translates into particular attitudes towards work. Willis found that young people placed a high value on the relative independence that they gained by being in a position to move jobs when it suited them. The instability and 'flexibility' of the labour market has been transferred to young people themselves, so that 'independence is having a pointless job that I can quit any day' (Willis 1998: 351).

The Life-Patterns study found that this attitude was relevant to young people across different socioeconomic groups. In fact, it tended to be the better-educated young people, those from higher socioeconomic groups, who articulated the positive value of horizontal mobility against their parents' goals for upward social mobility:

The overall high level of recognition of the help and support given by their families indicates an appreciation of the benefits they have derived from that parental priority. At the same time, their insistence on balancing a range of commitments in their lives points to a tendency towards *horizontal* mobility which at times their parents (and other researchers) find difficult to accept (Dwyer et al. 2003: 26).

While employment has emerged as the highest priority in terms of gaining security, the young people in the Life-Patterns study clearly expressed the view that flexibility, not predictability, is the best way that they can ensure their financial independence.

At the age of twenty-three, some of the respondents had observed at first hand the effects of a stratified society on them and their peers. Some pointed out that class relations are relatively visible ('Environment plays a role', 'Poor people keep getting poorer'); others were aware that it is difficult to get a good start in life when you are poor, stating, for example, that 'Formal training should be made more available at an economic rate for the people who have to start off economically disadvantaged' (Dwyer & Wyn 2001: 29). Despite this awareness of structural inequality, the attitudes have proven to be remarkably common across the group. There was an overwhelming emphasis on achieving a balance in life, involving space for the development of personal relationships, and a downplaying of the centrality of work as a source of identity.

> There was an overwhelming emphasis on achieving a balance in life, involving space for the development of personal relationships, and a downplaying of the centrality of work as a source of identity.

Similar types of concerns about the fluidity of work and life have been expressed by young people from traditional working-class backgrounds, although the terms of this expression reflect very different class realities. McDonald (1999) describes a series of tensions in the lives of marginalised young people in a disadvantaged neighbourhood. For many, the world of work is experienced as exclusion. The notion of a job for life in the local factory is long gone, and many youths feel like outsiders when it comes to the labour market. These young people are likewise aware of the restructuring of work. They have developed a range of personal rationalisations to explain why, as individuals, they cannot fit into the new work structures. These rationalisations, such as, for example, those based on the idea that it is hard to adapt to a job after being out of the workforce, are important to maintaining a sense of identity. This is especially so given that work has been so central to working-class consciousness, and now, for many working-class youth, it is no longer there.

On the other hand, as they negotiate the labour market, young working-class people also respond to the world of work through the lens of class consciousness. As McDonald (1999: 44) points out, the experience of being unemployed is not totally imposed. In talking about participants in his study, he observes that:

> There is an element of choice, of affirmation—all have quit jobs that they find humiliating. Their experience of work is described in terms of power relationships, where the worker is confronted with a boss who represents a form of power that doesn't necessarily reflect any logic of productivity. In a culture where individuals are disengaging from social roles, and where social norms or shared expectations are decreasingly important in shaping relationships, a boss's power is increasingly perceived as arbitrary. Once relationships of authority no longer reflect rationality in terms of productivity, they are viewed as a personal affront, a violation of dignity.

The meanings of work for the young men in McDonald's study are thus tied up with notions of creativity and autonomy in the workplace itself. Where this is not possible, then the result is exclusion.

Work opportunities and economic activity

Research has indicated a process of ghettoisation in a number of localities around Australia (Gregory & Hunter 1995; Vinson 2004), which is to say that particular neighbourhoods are filled with poor, unemployed people who, because of low skill levels, few educational opportunities, and longer physical distances from potential job sites, are mired in ghetto-like conditions. The spatial entrenchment of poverty is manifest in analyses of the impact of economic upturn as well. As Gregory and Hunter (1995: 33) comment, it is 'people who live in poor neighbourhoods who are increasingly not at work, that part-time jobs are going to young people and women who live in high SES [socioeconomic status] neighbourhoods and that income is rising in the best SES neighbourhoods but falling in poor neighbourhoods'. In other words, when job growth does occur, it tends to go to people living in the better-off socioeconomic areas rather than incorporate the poorer neighbourhoods.

The level of resources and facilities at a local level, the income sources available to young people and their families, and the public perceptions of young people all influence what young people do to get money and what they do with their time. The income-generating activity of low income young people is diverse, and involves a range of legal, illegal, and criminal activities (White et al. 1997). We shall return to some facets of these activities shortly.

Many young people today are struggling to come to grips with two essential facets of their lives—what to do with their time, and where to get enough money to do what they wish to do. The issue of income looms large for many young people. For in a capitalist consumer society, one in which most services, amenities, and activities require cash payment in return for participation, the importance of a regular, adequate income becomes highly significant. How young people interact with and choose their peers, and how they deal with mainstream institutions of family, leisure, sport, education, and criminal justice, is very much influenced by financial, as well as social, resources.

Analysis of the employment and work-related activity of young people has indicated that, for most, there are five broad spheres of economic activity within which they are able to be active, ranging from formal paid employment through to the criminal economy (see White et al. 1997; Cunneen & White 1995). The most prevalent ways of gaining money are through paid work in the formal and informal waged spheres. But even here the issues of low wages, part-time work opportunities, and poor working conditions affect the amount of income available to teenagers (White 1997b).

Spheres of economic activity

■ The *formal waged* sphere, which includes paid employment and which is taxed and state regulated.

BOX 11.2

BOX 11.2

- The *informal waged* sphere, which includes paid employment on a cash-in-hand basis, which means it is off the books in terms of formal state regulation of work and taxes.
- The *informal non-waged* sphere, which includes goods and services being exchanged without monetary payment, as in the case of domestic labour within the parental home.
- The *welfare* sphere, which includes income benefits received from the state to assist young people in education, training, and while unemployed.
- The *criminal* sphere, which includes activities that cannot be undertaken legally in any economic sectors, on or off the books.

Research on youth unemployment demonstrates a clear regional and neighbourhood level bias in youth unemployment rates (Wilson 1996; Hunter 1998; Vinson 2004); that is, employment is often unevenly distributed geographically, and is particularly devastating for specific groups of young people, such as Indigenous Australians, rural young people, and young immigrant refugees (Johnston 1991; Moss 1993). The concentration of large numbers of unemployed young people and rural young people in particular geographical locations and/or among certain population groups increases the difficulties of gaining paid work for specific individuals. It simultaneously fosters the shared identification and physical segregation of unemployed young people with each other. It thus can act to preclude these young people from attaining jobs and to make them more visible in the public domain as an identifiable outsider group.

Youth wages and the teenage labour market

The struggle to make ends meet is, then, a major problem for young people and their parents, particularly in low-income areas. The low wages paid to young people are not due simply to market fluctuations or recent labour market changes. Low wages are related to entrenched social judgments about the value of youth labour and to the ways specific youth labour markets have been historically constructed. The social construction of youth in the last century and a half in industrialised countries has been premised upon the removal of children, and later teenagers, from the full-time labour market (see Greenberg 1993), so the history of 'youth' as a distinct category is in essence a history of the exclusion of young people from full-time paid work. This has had major economic and cultural consequences on how young people are perceived in society (in relation to dependency, responsibility, and material needs), and continues to play a major role in how young workers are subsumed ideologically into age-specific rather than production-specific categories. Dominant notions of young people as, say, adolescents in the process of becoming adults (that is, as somehow deficient), often obscures their status as people who are already doing (that is, performing competently in the here and now) (see Wyn & White 1997). The overall message is that if, socially, young people are less than adults, then as workers they are likewise worth less than their adult counterparts.

The social representation, institutional location, and income and employment insecurity of young people feed a system in which exploitation and marginalisation of the young is the norm. In the case of young workers, it has been pointed out that whereas the principles of comparative wage justice (equal pay for equal work) had been applied in most areas of wage fixation, young people are the only ones who are paid on the basis of personal characteristics—that of age (Short 1988). Thus, young people are not only exploited via systemic processes of surplus value extraction, but they are also subject to specific situational forms of exploitation that serve to further undermine the value of their labour power (White, 1997b).

To assess the nature of youth labour in the contemporary era, we need to consider the productivity of young workers, the nature and basis of their hours worked, and their rates of pay.

Productivity of labour

In the industries in which most young workers are concentrated (retail, services, and manufacturing) their productivity is, by and large, the same as that of other workers in the industry: the quantity of goods and services being produced is not age-divided, but is set by external factors such as training, skills development, and adherence to global standards of productivity. Whether it be fast-food outlets; retail such as chemists, clothing and video shops; babysitting or nannying; door-to-door sales and mowing lawns; petrol stations; restaurants; cafés; supermarkets; cleaning; delivery services; building labour, or factory work; age is rarely directly relevant to the actual work carried out. This is not to say that structural opportunities and workplace demands for young people do not vary according to age. Teenage workers, for instance, tend to be concentrated in areas of casualised work in industry areas such as services and retail, which do not require high-level skills. The emphasis is on presentation of self rather than specific technical knowledge and skill. Thus, the productivity of young workers does not rely upon an advanced, let alone sophisticated, skill base but on general physical competence and basic social skills. For older workers, those over the age of eighteen, the structure of opportunity changes and becomes more complex. Greater societal and personal emphasis is placed on gaining full-time work in a wider variety of industry, where workplaces often demand people with greater skill levels and work experience.

Nature of hours at work

Very few teenagers are employed full time in the formal waged sphere of the economy. Employers prefer to hire secondary and tertiary students over unemployed young people (Boss, Edwards & Pitman 1995). Most of those young people engaged in paid work are concurrently students, a fact that has significant implications for their experiences of work. The casual and part-time nature of the work available and as required by students, and the fact that it predominantly takes place in the service and retail industries, is reflected in work times and hours of work. Times of work vary (weekends, weekdays, nights, days), as do the number of hours per week. The general advantage to the employer here is the flexibility provided by young student labour. Productivity is maximised by having student workers available only when it suits the business—peak trading times, weekends, and special sales events. Some employers also put pressure on young workers to put in extra time for which they are not paid. Thus, above-average exploitation is achieved through ensuring that the work is at the most productive times of the day or week, when workers are forced to work at maximum output, and by not paying the young person for all the hours they might actually work.

Value of labour power

In the absence of evidence of age-divided productivity (are older workers any more productive than younger workers in a fast-food outlet?), the idea of a youth wage disguises the fundamental fact that ultimately it is the employer who benefits the most from such arrangements by being able to pay a wage that is less than the socially defined value of labour power for most adults. Ideologically, the exploitation of young workers is defended through appeal to notions of specific and lesser youth needs (relative to those of adults), the presumed economic role of parents in supporting young people, and the idea that teenagers, possessing relatively low skills and having little formal training, are worth less than other workers, regardless of actual labour output or the actual value created by their labour that is appropriated by the employer. Institutionally, this treatment of young workers has been entrenched through formalised distinctions drawn between 'adult wages' and 'youth wages', which, in turn, has been shaped by the origins and the development of apprenticeships, which offered training, job security, and future advancement, and by the concept in Australia of a 'family wage', which established a policy framework within which women and children were paid lower wages due to presumptions regarding dependency and the status of the adult male as the household breadwinner.

Experiences of work

Much of the focus so far in this chapter has been on the structure of opportunities available to young people in relation to entry into particular workforces and in relation to specific types of socially constructed labour markets. Employment and wages are also important considerations. So too, are the actual experiences and dynamics of workplace activities.

Children and work

In Western countries the exclusion of young children and under-fifteen year olds from paid work is usually marked by clear legislative and educational boundaries. Institutions such as the International Labor Organization (ILO) mirror many of the legislative frameworks of advanced industrialised countries by setting fifteen as an appropriate minimum age for entering the labour force (Hobbs & McKechnie 1997). Simultaneously, most countries also set minimum school-leaving ages, again often set at fifteen. Compulsory education and exclusionary labour laws thus shape the age at which children in general may legitimately engage in paid work.

Employment and wages are also important considerations when it com. So, too, are the actual experiences and dynamics of workplace activities.

But, at ages younger than fifteen, work they do. It has been estimated that worldwide the number of working children between the ages of ten and fourteen varies between 73 million and 500 million (McKechnie and Hobbs 2002). The huge discrepancy in these numbers reflects a problem with statistical measurement (unreliable government figures) and definitional issues (for example, the figure rises when we include children who combine work and other activities, such as attending school). There can be no doubt though that a sizeable proportion of the world's children is engaged in work of some kind. As pointed out in Chapter 9, a recent study of the work experience of 11 000 children from Year 7 to Year 10 across twenty-two schools in New South Wales found that 56 per cent of children between the ages of twelve and sixteen had worked in the previous twelve months (NSW

Commission for Children and Young People 2005). The study found that work participation varied depending on age, gender, geographical location, and social disadvantage.

The stereotypical view is that child labour is a problem, mostly pertaining to the developing countries. Against this view, systematic research in Britain has demonstrated that millions of children will have had paid employment outside the family before they reach the age of sixteen (a finding similar to that of New South Wales). The work is highly varied and includes such work as jobs in shops, hotels, and restaurants; employment as cleaners, telephonists, newspaper and milk deliveries; office work; home working (for example, sewing garments); factory work; farming; and the sex industry (for example, prostitution) (McKechnie & Hobbs 2002), and the New South Wales Commission for Children and Young People's study (2005) found that most work by children was experienced by the children as positive (aside from sex work and related industries). But it is also the case that, more often than not, legislation regulating working age, the times within which work is allowed, and payment levels is ignored. Fundamentally, much of this work takes place in the informal sectors of the economy that, as mentioned above, make young people even more vulnerable to exploitation, workplace abuse, exposure to unhealthy and unsafe environments, and lack of union protection.

Is work by children necessarily a bad thing? Discussions of child work and child labour are now reframing the issues in terms of the potential costs and potential benefits of employment for children. Much of this research is informed by what children and young people themselves have to say about their work experiences. McKechnie and Hobbs (2002) conceptualise the costs and benefits of employment in terms of a balance between the following factors (see also Hobbs & McKechnie 1997):

Cost Bad—health and safety, limit free time, negative effect on education, instrumentalism, less parent/peer contact.

Benefits Good—autonomy, self-reliance, economics/business, knowledge, work experience.

They argue that: 'Although everyone will condemn exploitative and harmful work practices, some employment has the potential to provide youth benefits, both socially and financially' (McKechnie & Hobbs 2002: 240). They further point out that there is a need to reconceptualise the work–education relationship, and to not restrict ourselves to a view that says that childhood is somehow naturally and exclusively a time for school, and which thereby omits the contributions of work to skills and knowledge development.

Teenagers at work

Even though children and teenagers are frequently aware of their weak position in the workplace, they continue to turn up to the job. Competition for paid work is fierce, and many are forced into difficult work environments for low pay, which, combined with the limited job opportunities available to them, means that many young people are reluctant to contest the terms of their employment or to fight for improvements: young people are less likely than adults to take industrial action on issues relating to wages and conditions, or to join or actively participate in unions, which in turn makes them cheap to employ.

Structurally, teenagers constitute a very fluid component of the workforce. The flexibility afforded by this age grouping is seen in the variable and changing nature of youth employment over time (number of young people in education and/or employment), the specific character and form of youth employment (part-time or full-time), the distinctive patterns of youth employment in terms of industry participation (retail, service, manufacturing, public service), and variations in wage structures (youth wages, allowances, training allowances).

The fact that the majority of workers under eighteen are students (Boss, Edwards & Pitman 1995; Wooden 1996) contributes to the acceptability of their situational exploitation. Students, almost by definition, are transient workers—very few students remain with the fast-food outlet, retail shops, or the clerical service with which they may find temporary work while they are studying. The high turnover of the workforce means that employers have considerably more power than usual to set the terms of employment. Such terms include low wages, unsafe or unhealthy work environments, termination of employment at will, the hiring of people for trial periods during which they are not paid, and so on (see White et al. 1997). Given that there are many students and non-students who may be willing to suffer such constraints and burdens for a short time, the 'choice', when it comes to employment, is considerably narrowed for job applicants.

Many work in the informal sectors of the economy—cafés, restaurants, supermarkets, milk bars, fast-food outlets—while others work in retail shops such as chemist's, clothing shops, petrol stations, and video shops. Other types of work, usually cash in hand jobs done to supplement an existing income, or possibly a government benefit that tends to be well below the poverty line to begin with, include piecework done at home, work in family businesses, baby sitting, nannying, and hairdressing (see White et al. 1997). In this way, an apparent win–win situation is created, one that appears to cater to the needs of both employer and employee.

> A combination of few employment options and inadequate income sources means that many young people are willing to work for cash in hand as a means to supplement existing income.

For many teenagers, finding a paid job is the central task; the status of the work as formal or informal is of less importance. In any case the actual work tends not to differ greatly from sector to sector, and their status as employees—their pay and conditions—are virtually the same, and thus same problems run parallel: poor or unpaid wages, uneven or irregular hours of work, harassment, and lack of job security. Young people, already vulnerable due to high levels of youth unemployment and the feeling that they are at the mercy of employers, are socialised into the idea that the teenage labour market is distinctive, that it always has been and always will be exploitative based upon age-based distinctions. Many young people take this for granted as part of the overall work experience. The key criteria for assessing their experiences tend to revolve around whether they are treated fairly by the employer; often this simply means being treated with respect or in a friendly manner (White et al. 1997).

The post-teenage years

By the age of twenty-three to twenty-five, young people have clearly established a tendency to place a priority on gaining the mix of work experiences and qualifications that would enable them to be flexible, and, even under conditions of employment uncertainty, to exercise a certain amount of control over their lives. In the 2002 Life-Patterns survey, when the participants were aged twenty-seven to twenty-eight, this study found that these views had become more definite.

By this time, a majority had achieved full-time jobs (75 per cent), although, even after gaining tertiary qualifications, many had periods of unemployment or were unable to gain full-time work. Since 1996, as many as 82 per cent of the sample had changed jobs and one-fifth had changed jobs at least five times (Dwyer et al. 2003: 18). It is worth noting that as many as 55 per cent changed jobs because they felt they were able to achieve a better option in doing so.

The attitudes of the Life-Patterns cohort suggest that they have begun to come to terms with uncertainty and are redefining the meaning of career and work. As one respondent commented:

> I feel that I studied hard to receive a degree in my chosen field, however, I feel that there was no guarantee of job security. I worked in the field for 7 years, and changed jobs several times. In my last position I was retrenched from my job and have since changed career paths (Dwyer et al. 2003: 18).

Other respondents found that the work they were offered did not use their qualifications or was disappointing after their expectations for employment in a high-skill or knowledge economy were raised:

> I am in a job that I enjoy at the moment. It is only a job and not something I can make a career of. I just feel that I have had all this build up with my tertiary education and initially finding work in a related field only to end up doing a job that is not related and that really wouldn't require the amount of study that I have completed.

> My work is a day to day existence that doesn't contribute to society as I had hoped for.

The Life-Patterns study also highlighted the costs of study and work for this generation. Participants expressed the common theme of finding it difficult, if not impossible, to achieve a balanced life. They have been the first generation to achieve such uniformly high levels of education and have managed to gain a foothold in a precarious labour market, but what many have found is that the benefits are not there. As one respondent expresses it: 'I sacrificed relationships, etc., to study and get a career established — which I have not achieved and what I really desire more than a successful career is a happy family life, etc.: marriage and children.'

> They have been the first generation to achieve such uniformly high levels of education and have managed to gain a foothold in a precarious labour market, but what many have found is that the benefits are not there.

One-quarter of the participants expressed concern about their health and fitness and one-fifth expressed regret and concern about their personal relationships. At the same time, their focus on personal development and autonomy is reflected in a shift in the way that they define career. The emphasis has moved from the definition of career in terms of the structure of a job or their contribution to an occupation to a notion that is more aligned with personal development.

Over 80 per cent of the cohort define a career job in terms of a 'state of mind': as a job that offers 'scope for advancement', 'commitment', and 'personal fulfilment' (Dwyer et al. 2003). They also overwhelmingly state that a career is not necessarily your job, and that a career for life is a thing of the past. Dwyer et al. argue that there is a correspondence between the outlook and actions of the Life-Patterns participants and 'choice biographies' (Beck & Beck-Gernsheim 2002). By their late twenties, these young people have experienced the reality of precarious employment, retrenchment, and the difficulty of finding work that really draws on their qualifications. They have learnt through experience that the only option is for them to make meaning out of life themselves, which, for them, involves a heightened awareness of their personal development and developing the skills of making the right decisions for themselves. As one participant commented: 'It's up to you to organise your life. To work out what you want — no one else'. The idea of a permanent job no longer holds much relevance for these people. Instead, they place a high priority on achieving a balance of commitments and on developing a flexible set of skills so that they can be autonomous and make their own decisions about employment and the other facets of their life.

Summary

Young people are confronted with the difficulties of negotiating a labour market that is precarious and exploitative. There are major difficulties of entry, especially into full-time work in the formal and informal waged economic spheres. Aside from these issues, young people are faced with the prospect of trying to juggle study and paid work, and making enough money for their basic subsistence and consumer activity, often taking on more than one job at a time in order to make ends meet.

Work has its costs. The construction of certain types of work as teenage work serves more often than not to open the door to greater than normal wage exploitation. Many young workers experience work as an activity in which they are compelled by circumstance to learn how to deal with harassment, discrimination, poor working environments, irregular hours and income, and bullying. The work can be frustrating and boring.

But as well as these costs, work also holds the prospect of significant benefits. It is a source of income and social connection. It is a place where learning skills knowledge can be developed, and personal growth can occur. It can be fun, invigorating, and challenging.

Work is, by nature, about adult concerns, even where youth as an age category is used to distinguish who does what and for how much. Work is also the crucible within which many young people grow up as they experience the realities of global capitalism as the dominant organising force in contemporary industrial societies. Work (or the lack thereof) is and will continue to be vitally important to young people throughout the course of their lives.

Questions for further exploration

1 What are the main sources of income for young people in Australia?

2 What are the major differences between the world of work for young people today and young people of thirty years ago?

3 The teenage labour market is a fiction that perpetuates the continued exploitation of young people as workers. Critically discuss this idea and, where appropriate, provide examples.

4 What is a trade union? Is unionism relevant to young people in the workforce today?

5 Choice is a concept that is highlighted in debates about and defences of contemporary industrial relations policy. It is also central to the decisions that young people make about work. Are we talking about the same thing?

YOUTH IDENTITIES AND CULTURE

12

Introduction

This chapter discusses the complex issues surrounding youth identity. It reveals how youth identity is a complex and integral aspect of the lives of different groups of young people and argues that the task of social scientists and analysts is to see the expressions of global youth culture and the role of local circumstances in shaping different youth identities. There is also a need to capture the interplay between social context and group and individual activity in the social construction of identity and culture.

Much of the chapter is devoted to a discussion of the way in which young people are required to make choices about their lives, choices for which in many cases the previous generation is unable to provide a template. Decisions are made in relation to drug use, income sources, school and work, types of music, engagement in subcultures, and consumption patterns. As this chapter demonstrates, there is no uniform or straightforward relationship between individual biography and cultural formation. Rather, identity is always contingent upon immediate social circumstances, the weight of historical factors, and the agency of young people themselves.

Today, the construction of identity has become an individualised project. For some, this opens up opportunities, with themselves at the centre of choices about where and when to work, what kind of leisure activities to pursue, and with whom to associate. Employment occupies a less central place in the construction of identities. For groups of young people for whom choices about employment are not available, identity is also shaped around other factors, including their relationship to state welfare apparatuses. The chapter concludes by suggesting that in exploring youth identity construction we are, perhaps, also glimpsing a new way of being adult.

YOUNG PEOPLE, SOCIETY, AND IDENTITY

The idea of identity is critical to most writing about youth. It is almost impossible to understand the decisions made by young people and the actions they take without understanding how they see themselves in their world. This is especially so at this point in time, as young people must engage with a world that is different in so many ways from that of the previous generation. As we have explored in other chapters, there is evidence that the key relationships and institutions that frame young people's ideas and experiences of their self, such as family, school, workplaces, and the media, have changed over the last thirty years. As a consequence the relationship between young people and society has shifted. To put this differently, the answer to the question 'Who am I?' is changing, as individuals' relationship to their social world changes.

> The idea of identity is critical to most writing about youth. It is almost impossible to understand the decisions made by young people and the actions they take without understanding how they see themselves in their world.

In exploring young people's identity, we take a social view of identity. From this perspective, identity is tied to social context. Social context is a broad term that is used to describe the sets of relationships (through family, friends, and school), economic conditions (jobs, wealth), and cultural influences that impact on individuals. These and many other elements of social context are the circumstances that shape identities. They provide the possibilities for identities and the opportunities for different identities to be shaped. This means that, as social conditions and circumstances change on a wide scale, new patterns of youth identities are formed on a systematic basis.

Even though the meaning of the concept and the way in which it is used has gone through changes over time, and despite its importance, few researchers define what they mean by youth identity. As Connell points out in his discussion of identity in relation to gender, in the sixteenth century, the term 'identity':

> was a philosophical term that meant exact agreement, sameness. It was used when a writer wanted to refer to a thing or person remaining the same over time, or despite different circumstances … By the nineteenth century the term 'identity' had become thoroughly naturalized in English and was used in literature as well as philosophy and mathematics. It was still generally used with the meaning of 'sameness' though sometimes in the sense of personal existence or to emphasise who I am as against who I am not (2002: 85–86).

Connell describes how, progressively, as society changed, 'who I am' became a problem for individuals to resolve. In the 1950s, German psychoanalyst Erik Erikson (1950) developed the concept of personal identity 'based on the Freudian insight that adult personality is formed by a long, conflict-ridden process of growth' (Connell 2002: 87). This understanding of identity has provided a powerful and enduring framework for theories of youth and adolescence because Erikson proposed that most of the important work of 'searching for' and establishing an adult identity is carried out during adolescence. While many contemporary youth researchers would not necessarily agree with the deterministic elements in Erikson's model of development, there is widespread, if implicit, agreement that youth is the most important period of identity construction. Subsequently, psychiatrist Robert Stoller (1968) added additional elements to the idea of identity as a unitary, integrated whole by focusing specifically on gender. Stoller argued that a 'core gender identity' is formed in the first few years of life (not in adolescence) and saw identity as being 'plural' or constituted through different 'identities', such as gender, race, or class (Connell 2002: 87).

Connell concludes that with the shift from identity to different identities, such as sexual or gender identities, the term has lost some of its meaning. He points out that what have been called 'sexual identities' may be 'configurations of sexual and social practice' that have emerged in response to historically transitory social conditions. The term 'identity', he argues, has been massively over-used and 'often serves merely as a pretentious synonym for self, reputation, or social standing' (2002: 90).

Today, the term 'identity' appears to cover a wide range of meanings, including identity politics. Yet sociologists of youth cannot dismiss the idea of identity too readily because, located as they are at the junction of generational change and social change, young people have to do the work of making meaning of life and in particular of answering the question 'Who am I?' in this life. The concept of identity, along with that of self, provides a broad, very loose framework within which sociologists of youth interpret and describe the relationship between youth and society.

> Today, the term 'identity' appears to cover a wide range of meanings, including identity politics. Yet sociologists of youth cannot dismiss the idea of identity too readily because, located as they are at the junction of generational change and social change, young people have to do the work of making meaning of life and in particular of answering the question 'Who am I?' in this life.

The focus in the 1990s and early 2000s on identity builds on the earlier work of youth researchers who linked social conditions and particular dispositions among youth. Cohen (1997), for example, noted how young people in working-class neighbourhoods responded to changing economic conditions by managing their appearance and emotions to make themselves employable in the emerging service industries. White (1990) has also discussed how one of the specific goals of education policies in the 1980s was to create employable youth with the right attitudes to work.

Others sought to understand the effects of social change on individual lives—and on society. Wexler focused on the role of schools in the formation of young people's identities. He saw schools as one of the few public spaces where people could engage with each other to make meaning. In the context of the Reagan government's cutbacks in funding public institutions and the reassertion of 'traditional values' in the USA, Wexler was conscious of the decline of the public sphere and the 'decomposition of social relations'. His point was that by the early 1990s, there was a change in the idea of society, which he describes as 'the end of the social' (1992: 111). He saw the political changes occurring in schools in the USA as involving sets of 'practical deconstructions of the social' (1992: 111) that indicated a crisis in American public life.

Against this backdrop, Wexler explored the impact on young people of these institutional and political changes to schools. He argued that schools are important because in school, students 'establish at least the image of an identity' that serves to organise the course of their lives (1992: 10) and that schools are places 'for making the CORE meaning, of self or identity among young people' (1992: 155). In Wexler's words: 'The primary tracking in school is of the self, and students are not victims but symbolic workers in the identity production process' (Wexler 1992: 10).

Wexler argued that this process is profoundly 'classed' and that in the absence of a broader sense of civil society, the effects of schooling are to create identities around schooling's fundamentally classed nature, in which there are 'winners' and 'losers'. But, he argues, without a strong sense of society, in the end all are losers, because 'success without society' is empty and because the 'failures' become disconnected and alienated from society. He suggests that one of the effects of the failure of institutions (such as schools) to support the construction of a deeply socially based sense of self and identity for individuals is that identity has to be constantly asserted and performed. Under these conditions, connecting to networks provides 'more predictable sources of status recognition for visible displays of proven self value' (1992: 144). Wexler's focus on the identity-constructing work that young people do in school is an important reminder of the social role of education, which is often overlooked.

A more recent study of the way that school creates identities is McLeod and Yates's (2006) study of young people in four different school sites (we described some of their findings in Chapter 3). The focus on four different sites and social locations enabled McLeod and Yates to demonstrate how the identity-constructing work that young people do is strongly framed by their families, their peers, and the school culture. They show how 'becoming someone' involves an active engagement by young people; making the self has become a project, one for which some groups are more adequately resources than others. They also show how identity construction is a process that limits the efforts of individuals to make themselves from particular subject positions that are possible within particular social conditions. Another important Australian study, by Smyth and Hattam (2004), shows how young people do identity work despite and against rather than with school. Their study provides important insights into the resources that apparently disadvantaged young people draw on to make something of themselves within environments that they consider to be hostile.

Wexler and McLeod and Yates's descriptions of the enactment of identity and self overlaps with some elements of Beck's descriptions of 'risk and danger biographies' (Beck & Beck-Gernsheim 2002). The decline of the public sphere that Wexler identifies in the USA is also described by Beck and Beck-Gernsheim as the growth of 'individualisation' in Germany. While acknowledging clear differences between classes (or 'better educated' and 'poorer' youth) in the way in which this is taken up, Beck argues that there has been a shift in priorities or values. He contrasts traditional values, which involved unambiguous priorities linked to local communities and shared goals in life, with new values. These new values have a focus on 'self-enlightenment and self-liberation as an active process to be accomplished in their [young people's] own lives, including the search for new ties in family, workplace and politics' (Beck & Beck-Gernsheim 2002: 38).

The shift in values, which he characterises as 'reflexive modernity', is seen by Beck as one of the unintended consequences of social and economic change. He argues that previously institutionalised functions, such as the nation state, the hierarchical family firm, and the centralised union movement, have been displaced, either onto global entities that are difficult to connect with or onto individuals (Lash 2002). Beck notes that under these circumstances of complexity and fragmentation, power and inequality operate more through exclusion than exploitation. Rather than having rules to follow, individuals must find rules and have the capacity to reflect and respond, constantly and quickly, to their circumstances. In fact, he uses the term 'reflexion', which is not the same as reflection. 'Reflexion' is the term Beck uses to describe reactions that cope with a world of speed and quick decision making (Lash 2002).

> Beck notes that under these circumstances of complexity and fragmentation, power and inequality operate more through exclusion than exploitation. Rather than having rules to follow, individuals must find rules and have the capacity to reflect and respond, constantly and quickly, to their circumstances.

The evidence of rising rates of suicide in the Western world (especially among males) has led to speculation about the relationship between suicide, identity, and the nature of contemporary Western societies (Eckersley & Dear 2002). Eckersley seeks to make a link between the individualisation processes that Beck and Beck-Gernsheim (2002) refer to and the rise in suicide for young people, as well as for older people. At the heart of this argument is the idea that society is failing young people. While some researchers have emphasised the opportunities that risk society offers young people, Eckersley points out that 'young people can feel cast adrift once they leave home and school and make their own way in the world'. He argues that it is important to acknowledge that the demise of traditional belief systems and narratives of meaning has made the journey harder and may inevitably leave some individuals without a sense of social connection at all.

New identities

Contemporary work on the relationship between youth, social change, and social institutions also makes identity a central focus, exploring the effects of local conditions and global processes on young people's sense of self. In the United Kingdom, Ball et al. (2000a) have argued that in 'new urban economies' they see the emergence of 'new identities'. They emphasise the 'reflexive individualism' of young people who have no choice but to create identities that are contingent on specific, local circumstances. Ball et al. argue that young people from very different class backgrounds actively build and rebuild identities around leisure, work, and location. Describing the lives of three young people who live in London, they conclude that:

> Despite living in the same locality, each of the three young people works within different and stratified horizons and time-spans … Their accounts of their 'choices' and decisions in the London education and labour markets, point up the different 'opportunity structures' which frame these 'choices' and the different 'futures' and identities towards which they are struggling (2000a: 298).

Comparing youth in various parts of Europe, Evans, too, focuses on identity. She asserts that young people's identities are an important focus now because young people are at the forefront of changes in labour market structures: 'Research into the position of young people finding their way into the social landscapes of late modernity promises unique insights into the operation of new forces at work' (Evans 2002: 245).

Evans specifically highlights the importance of understanding more about 'learner identities' because increasingly insecure and flexible labour market systems place emphasis on young people to be proactive and optimistic. In other words, supporting young people's identity work could be seen as part of the role of educators, placing a greater emphasis on brokerage and advocacy. Hence, the idea of identity has become an important tool for analysing the implications of social change on the relationship between youth and key social institutions.

The Youth Research Centre's Life-Patterns research program has focused on the issue of youth identities in a context of social change. The study produced evidence that new identities are being shaped as this generation engages with the contemporary world. In other work (Wyn 2004, 2005) we challenged the tendency for youth researchers and policy makers to characterise young people's transitions as faulty or failed, using the experiences of the baby boomer generation as a standard against which the subsequent generation is judged. Drawing on data generated through the Life-Patterns study we argue that the lives of the generation born after 1970 need to be seen within the specific social and economic context of their time. Indeed, we have suggested that their circumstances are sufficiently distinctive to claim that they constitute a new 'social generation' (Wyn & Woodman 2006).

As they have constructed their lives in relation to the conditions that they have encountered, young people have created distinctive generational subjectivities. We have found that young people need strong personal resources to make difficult individual choices and to survive the disruptions and uncertainty that result, and that they have placed an emphasis on resourcing themselves for their futures. As many as 80 per cent of the participants who originally did not continue their studies after completing secondary school returned to study in the following five years. Of the entire cohort, as many as 57 per cent gained more than one post-school qualification. In their attitudes and goals for life in the present, we identified a shift in the weighting given to old and new priorities. While a negative interpretation can be placed on the high priority given by our participants to notions of personal autonomy and flexibility, this does not mean that they are not interested in political action (Fyfe & Wyn 2007). It does mean though that we need to look in different directions to see evidence of political engagement. Given the sense of alienation that many young people feel with formal politics, we would need to keep an open mind about the mix of new and old forms of political engagement that young people take up (see Chapter 7).

While there is evidence that a shift is taking place, we are cautious about making the assumption that there has been a dramatic break in the fundamental social structures of our society. What there has been is evidence of shifting priorities as the young people take up the old and the new in making sense of their world. Dwyer et al. conclude that the post-1970 generation is generally positive. In 2002:

> as many as 91% express real satisfaction with their own personal development. By and large, they feel that they have made the right choices. They are learning how to shape life for themselves, even though many of them also admit that maintaining the right balance remains a real challenge for them (2003: 26).

Their overwhelming emphasis on flexibility of lifestyle and employment and personal autonomy needs to be seen as an orientation that will endure into their thirties and forties, rather than dismissed as a stage of life. The Life-Patterns study provides evidence of a broader shift in identity formation, in which young people are engaging earlier, incrementally, in adult practices. In doing so, they are shaping approaches to life that will endure beyond youth. The increasing significance of leisure and recreation in the formation of identities cannot be dismissed as just a youth phase; rather, it could be said that a new adulthood is being foreshadowed by young people, which will involve a different mix of priorities and different possibilities for identities from the previous generation.

Social practices and social identity

Identity is forged in the context of specific social practices, which may be collective in nature, as with youth subcultures and the youth music scene (see below). They may also be institutionally driven, as in the case of the relationship between young people and the social welfare system or the state. In either case, individuals negotiate who they are and who they wish to be in relation to external objective factors and internal subjective experiences. Identity formation is never fixed; it is always a work in progress. Similarly, the notion of social identities is useful in capturing the idea that identity is constructed in complex and multilayered ways. Some examples of social practices that are linked to specific kinds of identity formation are outlined below.

Drugs and social identity

Drug taking is socially patterned, and these patterns are intricately linked to social identity and social background. Drug use is also associated with varying notions of and responses to risk. Some types of drugs are seen as riskier than others; some types of drug users are seen as more at risk than others. How particular groups of young people are identified with particular drugs is an integral part of the history of drug law enforcement and to their social identity generally.

This history of the war on drugs has its origins in the racialisation of certain activities and their subsequent criminalisation by the state, which occurred in different places at different times, but the end result was the same: racially based moral panics in the USA, the United Kingdom, and Australia, based around cannabis and opium, were used not only to ban certain types of drug use but also, simultaneously, to exclude certain racial and ethnic minorities from mainstream social life (Cody 2006; Blackman 2004). The human targets of the anti-drug campaigns included minority groups such as Chinese, Mexicans, African Americans, Aborigines, and West Indians in predominantly white nation states such as the USA. Existing patterns of drug use were utilised to provide a cover for state intervention that actively constructed the ethnic minority and Indigenous person as the Other. Echoes of this historical process are still evident in portrayals and responses to the 'drug problem' today.

The high profile given to illegal drugs in the mass media has been accompanied by moral panics over drug use among teenagers. Headlines about deaths linked to the taking of ecstasy and lurid details about deaths due to heroin overdoses have further reinforced public concern over how best to tackle the presumed war on drugs. While there is some evidence that drug use, and drug-dealing, among teenagers is widespread (White et al. 1997; Lennings 1996; Tressider et al. 1997), the patterns of use vary considerably and appear to be mainly related to socioeconomic circumstances. A national survey of illegal drug use among young people in the fourteen- to nineteen-year-old age group found that 38 per cent of the people in this group had used an illegal drug in 1998 (New South Wales Law Reform Commission 2001: 29). A South Australian study found that young offenders have significantly greater use of all drug categories except alcohol, which was only slightly higher, when compared with drug use by male sixteen-year-old secondary school students (Putnins 2001: 7). Drug use, especially heroin use, among some sections of youth from higher socioeconomic backgrounds has occasionally made headlines, indicating the problematic nature of drug use for this population as well as for their less advantaged peers. Drug use connected to youth dance cultures continues to generate controversy.

Many portrayals of drug use are framed in terms of the deviant status of the activity and/or the user. But how specific groups of young people are identified vis-à-vis drug use varies depending upon the social class and ethnic background of the people involved. Sercombe (1999) points out that in cases involving young, white, middle-class people there is great likelihood that they will be presented as 'victims' of the drug and vulnerable to bad influences outside of their own control. They are pawns in the drug game, and have little or no choice in the trap within which they have found themselves. By way of contrast, working-class drug users are portrayed as inherently bad, as intrinsically untrustworthy, and as choosing to engage in drug use and drug dealing.

How young people are represented in the media has an influence on how they identify as a user of drugs and to their relationship to drugs generally. It also influences how authority figures such as the police view particular categories of young people, especially when it comes to stereotypes that link particular drug offences (for example, heroin) with particular ethnic minority groups (for example, Vietnamese Australians). Social identity in this instance is forged in the context of preexisting, historically given prejudices that influence how people outside a community view and interact with members of that community (see Maher, Dixon, Swift & Nguyen 1997; Maher, Nguyen & Le 1999). A reputation based upon drug use (and distribution) thus becomes a hurdle to negotiate in developing a non-deviant social identity.

> How young people are represented in the media has an influence on how they identify as a user of drugs and to their relationship to drugs generally. It also influences how authority figures such as the police view particular categories of young people, especially when it comes to stereotypes that link particular drug offences (for example, heroin) with particular ethnic minority groups (for example, Vietnamese Australians).

The prevalence of and distinctive ways in which drugs are actually (rather than stereotypically) used by young people also shapes how they view the activity and their involvement in it. Recent discussions about the nature of teenage drug use are pointing to the normalisation of young people's drug use. Specifically, in the light of documented significant increases in the prevalence and frequency of teenage drug use in recent decades in Western Europe and other places, including Australia, it is suggested that young people are viewing and using drugs very differently today than previously (see Parker et al. 1998; Gatto 1999; Duff 2003; Hunt, Evans & Kares 2007). Whereas drug use has typically been associated with deviance and law-breaking behaviour, among contemporary youth it is now regarded as normal and an uncontroversial aspect of the young person's life experience.

As discussed by Duff (2003), it may well be the case that many drug users are 'well-adjusted, responsible and outgoing' (rather than pathological, mentally ill, or irresponsible), and that they use drugs recreationally in very deliberate and strategic ways. Rave dance parties and ecstasy use, for example, represent a conscious connection between particular pleasure pursuits and the drug that best suits the occasion. The consumption of different substances is used strategically to express one's allegiances to particular youth cultures and scenes, and thus to reinforce a particular social identity (see Duff 2003). Sophisticated analysis of youth drug use further refines this conclusion. Shildrick (2002: 36) argues that 'a concept of "differentiated normalization", which allows for the ways in which different types of drugs and different types of drug use may be normalized for different groups of young people, may be a more appropriate tool for understanding contemporary youthful drug use' than perspectives that see normalisation in more generalist terms. Hunt et al. (2007) uses the narratives of young people themselves to account for how they view risk and pleasure around drug use, and how these perceptions influence their decisions to use or not use drugs.

The relationship between drug use and identities has been explored in detail in the work of McLean (2005), whose study focused on chromers. Chroming involves inhaling the fumes from spray paint or glue to gain a high. Chromers are a relatively small group of drug users; they are generally young (twelve to eighteen) and often move on to use 'better' drugs (for example, heroin) when they can afford it. The significance of McLean's study is that she shows how these young people use drugs to create spaces where they can do amazing things. Her interviews with young people show how they enter other worlds (some of which are actually videogames such as Powerball) where they experience a sense of power and agency. As McLean argues, it is important to recognise the pleasures that young people gain from drug use, because policy messages that recognise this instead of simply casting drugs in a negative light are more likely to be effective.

Drug use, whether of licit or illicit substances, is an inevitable part of growing up in contemporary Western society. As with other types of activities in which they engage, young people make choices and selections in regards to drug use. As with other activities, the choices they make have major consequences in terms of their personal social identity, their ability to make informed decisions about use in the future, and the network of peers with whom they hang around. Rather than passively responding to anti-drug messages and propaganda, young people determine for themselves whether to use drugs, how they will do so, and the cultural and social contexts within which particular drug use is appropriate—or not. In other words, drug use and social identity are constructed through specific and defined material ways of doing things.

Respect and humiliation

Social identity is not only associated with leisure and recreational activities, but is also very much influenced by how the state intervenes in the lives of young people. Many of the contemporary methods of state intervention tend to treat young people in general, and working class and underclass young people in particular, with suspicion and mistrust. This is apparent with regards to street policing and constant cries to impose youth curfews and the like on young people. It is also built into public policy and the welfare apparatus of the state.

> Social identity is not only associated with leisure and recreational activities, but is also very much influenced by how the state intervenes in the lives of young people. Many of the contemporary methods of state intervention tend to treat young people in general, and working class and underclass young people in particular, with suspicion and mistrust.

At the same time that, say, industrial relations laws are rhetorically justified on the basis of work choices, welfare provision is increasingly doled out on the basis of obligation and responsibility to engage in self-improvement and job finding. An entrenched blame-the-victim mentality permeates government. When young people refuse to work in exploitive environments or are excluded from local labour markets that simply do not have places for them, they become targets for coercive state measures. The responsibility for 'failure' is the young person's. Nowhere is this more apparent than in regards to welfare payments.

The importance of developing young people's sense of worth and self, fostering positive social relationships within the community, and broadening their sense of citizenship is undisputed; however, much institutional policy and practice undermine these very ideals. Australian young people receiving the Youth Allowance, for example, are now obliged to engage in Mutual Obligations/ Activity Test Requirements to, as the Centrelink information pamphlet states, 'actively seek work, constantly strive to improve their competitiveness in the labour market and give something back to the community that supports them'. It is up to recipients to earn their benefits.

The introduction of such mutual obligation requirements has been detrimental to many young people who are already struggling to make ends meet. It is notable, for example, that young people under the age of twenty-five are disproportionately likely to be penalised by governments for breaching social security rules. In February 2001, while jobseekers under twenty-five represented only 30.6 per cent of those people receiving Newstart Allowance and Youth Allowance, they made up 50.6 per cent of all Activity Test breaches (such as not accepting a 'suitable' job) and 57.6 per cent of all administrative breaches (such as failure to attend an interview). The financial consequences for young people are particularly severe, given their already low level of payment (Australian Council of Social Services 2001).

Our concern here is not with the financial aspects of these processes. Rather, a key issue here is the ways in which the operation of government agencies impact upon the self-identity of young welfare recipients, in particular, the withdrawal of state support, especially in the context of alleged wrongdoing, and how this withdrawal propels young people into a deviant identity and reinforces their deviant status. Thus, systems that are meant to compensate for disadvantage (such as the Youth Allowance) may, through their particular delivery mechanism, actually exacerbate social alienation and disadvantage. Breaching may constitute a form of deprivation of needed resources and a form of institutional humiliation. Institutional processes may thereby generate varying types of antisocial behaviour, and angry young men and women.

The deprivation of income is often associated with particular types of criminal activity, such as shoplifting, which, in turn, can be interpreted as a form of survival crime, given the community context in which the offending occurs. This also involves a cost transfer from social security (a federal matter) to criminal justice (a state concern). As well, it shifts the identity of the young people from one of disadvantage to criminality. For young people caught up in these circumstances, there are incredible constraints on the decisions they can make about what to do and how to survive that directly impact on their self-image and how they are viewed by others around them.

The street presence of particularly disadvantaged young people has, in recent years, been tied to concerted campaigns to reduce so called antisocial behaviour. It would appear that the incivility of young people on the streets mirrors the incivility of the state in meeting their needs and treating them with respect. Gaining respect on the part of young people—among peers and on the streets—may be achieved through active resistance to authority figures, be they welfare officials or police. Insofar as the helping hand is wrapped around the iron fist, the resentment, fear, loss of faith, and alienation that young people feel may translate into other forms of social valorisation, as evidenced in the social importance of gangs as a youth group formation (Collins et al. 2000; White 2006a). The outlaw identity is forged in the context of a curtailment in attaining legitimacy within the existing systems of welfare provision and social control.

The importance of positive social recognition to personal identity and well-being has been emphasised in recent work by Barry (2006). Being responsible and having opportunities to contribute positively to those around them is denied some young people because of structural constraints, such as unemployment, addiction, and interaction with the criminal justice system. An important element that also constrains some young people is reputation, which goes to the heart of identity in that the perception of oneself by others and the experience of stigmatisation have profound effects on how people feel about themselves and their life chances. The young people in Barry's (2006: 155) study 'spoke either of not being trusted or not being able (through, for example, ill-health resulting from addiction) to take on responsibility, or of being unable to overcome discriminatory attitudes and practices of potential employers, the police or the local community more generally'. This led many of the young people to feel despondent about themselves and to lose motivation to change or engage with the wider world around them.

Youth culture

The idea of youth culture is an enduring theme in youth studies. We have previously argued that the idea of youth cultures and subcultures is 'neither simple nor uncontested' (Wyn & White 1997: 72). This continues to be the case, and is reflected in the broad movement from the idea of youth sub-cultures as such towards identity, a shift that reflects an interest in understanding the subjective interpretations of individuals and has resulted in less emphasis on the existence of definable groups, social structures, and organisations with which young people are affiliated, although these, too, are still relevant to investigate. It is a shift that is part of a wider move among researchers and analysts towards understanding individual subjectivities and to understand their relationship to collective affiliations.

This perceived change in analytical focus is confirmed by Bennett (2000) in his discussion of young people and popular music. He describes how the previously influential paradigm of youth subcultures had, by the 1970s and 1980s, come to have a narrow focus and was under criticism for its tendency to see youth as representations of cultural forms, rather than exploring their diverse realities. Bennett argues that the subcultural approach to youth was significant because, through the early sociological work of the Chicago School, this approach enabled sociologists to describe how young people themselves were capable of generating norms and values of their own that differed from those of the wider society. In the 1920s and 1930s, these studies (for example, Whyte 1943) provided evidence that local groups of young men were generating social understandings and systems of meanings in their own right—subcultures—generally involving 'deviant' behaviour. This important insight has provided the framework for much of the youth research that followed.

In the United Kingdom, the tradition of studying local youth 'delinquent subcultures' was continued in the 1950s through to the 1970s through research on local gangs in Liverpool and Glasgow (Bennett 2000: 17). The shift to studying style—the expression of one's identification with particular cultural frames of reference and sensibilities—as a subcultural phenomenon was headed by the Birmingham Centre for Contemporary Cultural Studies (Willis 1977; Hebdige 1979). The work of this group drew attention to the fact that, following the end of the Second World War, when incomes rose for young workers, for the first time consumer markets began to cater to different styles. This gave prominence to the style-based subcultures of young people in the United Kingdom, subcultures that were seen to be based on young people's own norms and values. The difference between these and the earlier Chicago-school studies was that in the British studies, Marxist perspectives were added. From this relatively new perspective, the youth cultures were seen to be expressions of resistance by working-class youth in relation to 'structural changes taking place in British post-war society' (Bennett 2000: 18). These changes included the disintegration of traditional working-class residential communities and the broader economic changes that resulted in the shift from trade-based occupations and manufacturing to a service economy.

Many researchers now question the correspondence framework of these earlier perspectives. Chatterton and Hollands, for example, question the value of subcultural perspectives that continue to position working-class youth leisure as paralleling elements of their parent culture, emphasising tough masculinity, territoriality, and solidarity (skinhead culture, for example) (2003: 72), an emphasis that meant that issues of gender were not developed enough to acknowledge young women's lives (Wyn & White 1997) or to explore the ways in which gender relations are played out within different subcultural groups. In particular, the links between the structural conditions of class society in the United Kingdom and young women's lives have not been widely addressed. There are exceptions: work by McRobbie (1991), Walkerdine (1996), and Lucey (1996) has specifically looked at the ways in which class location offers opportunities as well as constrain middle- and working-class girls in different ways. Others have explored constructions of femininity in relation to feminism (Harris 1999; Hopkins 1999; O'Brien 1999). Rather than employing subcultural theories, their work has focused on changing modes of femininity, subjectivity, and identity.

In more recent times, the concept of youth cultures has gained currency in analysing young people's consumption patterns (Muggleton 2000). At a popular level, style as subculture has been manifested through the use of terms such as 'Gen X' and 'Gen Y' to attempt to describe distinctive lifestyle characteristics of successive generations. Closer investigation of these terms reveals that they are too broad to provide a useful analysis of generational change. They are superficial in the sense that they do not provide any analysis of the social, economic, and political conditions that generate change or of the people who constitute them. Yet the fact that these terms, and others like them, persist in the popular media and the popular imagination suggests that there is widespread awareness of changes in the ways that young people are living their lives.

Subcultures and social identity

Youth identities have been linked to all aspects of young people's lives. Researchers have associated identities with particular pastimes, with the way young people are treated by institutions, and with the choices that young people make at different points in time. The history of research on youth subcultures illustrates the multilayered and fluid nature of youth identities.

One of the more popular and enduring youth subcultures is that of hip hop. In the Australian context, hip hop is particularly, but not exclusively, linked to the expression of self-identification for many people of Indigenous and ethnic minority backgrounds. Hip hop incorporates four interrelated elements. The terminology varies, but these elements include MC (rapper), DJ (turntablist), breaker (breakdancer), and writer (graffiti or aerosol artist). Referring to the work of Frith, Mitchell (2003) emphasises how hip hop does not simply reflect identity, but that musical practices themselves also function as important processes through which identity is actively imaged, created, and constructed. In other words (given the masculine nature of the activity), the music makes the man in the same moment that the man makes the music, although this, too, is shifting as more young women engage in hip hop activity. Identity is manifest in the self-definition of individuals as being part of the hip hop scene—a scene that has all the hallmarks of being a distinct subculture.

Hip hop as a global youth subculture

BOX 13.1

■ It often locates itself in and is located by mainstream media as underground in relation to the music industry, the mass media, and mainstream society.

■ It has a strong do-it-yourself (DIY) aspect in producing recordings, concerts, media, and public events.

■ It has been subject to sporadic bursts of commodification and incorporation as a musical genre (rap) that serve to further entrench and consolidate notions of authenticity.

■ Graffiti remains a largely illegal, clandestine, and surveillance-defying subcultural activity.

■ It remains largely a male-dominated, music-based activity with strong organic links between its four elements of MCing, DJing, break dancing, and graffiti-ing.

■ Its practices tend to follow, with local variations, internationally recognised, US-derived dress codes, musical idioms, dance movements, and visual styles.

■ It is based on strong ethical, stylistic, and largely universal notions of authenticity delineating true hip hop from commodified versions.

■ There is a strong attachment by its advocates to the four elements of hip hop as alternative ways of knowing the world, and as important identifiers of places of origin, neighbourhood, family, community, and ethnic-group identity.

■ There is a strong pedagogical dimension in that there is an emphasis on self-education, training, and development of young hip hop practitioners.

■ There is widespread use of different forms of stylistic bricolage (incorporation of many diverse cultural materials and influences) in hip hop practices of sampling, MCing, breaking and graffiti-ing.

■ Most of hip hop's activities follow implicit career paths, complete with skill-based hierarchies, values, and rules.

Source: drawn from Mitchell 2003.

Specific youth subcultural forms can be identified in and are generally recognised by terms such as 'punks', 'goths', 'bogans', 'ravers', 'hippies', and 'bikers'. The boundaries between certain distinctive practices and group identifications are fluid, and the content of each subculture can and does change over time. Youth subcultures are frequently identified with a specific music genre and specific groups may be formed around particular sounds (ravers, metalheads, homeboys, goths, technos, rastas, punks). In addition to shared interests in the same music, they may also form on the basis of shared interest in particular kinds of activities (skaters, bladers, surfies, bikers, dancers). Youth subcultures may originate in and be identified with particular national contexts (such as teddy boys in England, and bodgies and widgies in Australia in the 1950s). They may disappear in one form (for example, mods and rockers) only to reappear in another at a later date or in a different social environment (for example, sharpies in Australia). Whatever their specific features and

Whatever their specific features and characteristics, youth subcultures offer young people an opportunity to display their uniqueness, their distinctiveness, a way of asserting identity in relation to presumed adult norms as well as in relation to each other.

characteristics, youth subcultures offer young people an opportunity to display their uniqueness, their distinctiveness, a way of asserting identity in relation to presumed adult norms as well as in relation to each other (see White 1993, 1999).

Membership in or association with any particular subculture is highly variable. While most young people identify with particular peer groups, the sole identification with one particular group or style in a manner that is rigidly fixed over time is relatively unusual. Young people move around a lot. They mix with a wide variety of peer groups (sports, studies, families, neighbourhoods), and may engage in a wide variety of subcultural activities and styles in a relatively short period of time. The fluctuating nature of youth identification and engagement with subcultures is well captured by Hebdige (1979: 122):

> different youths bring different degrees of commitment to a subculture. It can represent a major dimension in people's lives—an axis erected in the face of the family around which a secret and immaculate identity can be made to cohere—or it can be a slight distraction, a bit of light relief from the monotonous but none the less paramount realities of school, home and work. It can be used as a means of escape, of total detachment from the surrounding terrain, or as a way of fitting back in to it and settling down after a week-end or evening spent letting off steam.

To some extent, then, young people choose who they want to be in terms of subcultural affiliations, including how far they want to engage with a subcultural form and which elements of any particular subculture they wish to appropriate.

But social identity that is constructed around subculture is not detached from the wider social structure. As we have argued elsewhere, there is a tendency in some subcultural analyses to separate out youth from their immediate community positions as members of particular class, gender, ethnic, and racial communities:

> What gets emphasised is their unique characteristics as members of a particular category of youth (for example, punk, Rasta, hiphop, graffiti, street dancers, surfies, skegs, wogs, druggies). What gets under-emphasised or unacknowledged are the *continuities in culture* (for example, language, world view, dress, relationship to 'outside' institutions such as school, police and work) which transcend the generations (Wyn & White 1997: 79).

Some examples of these continuities include the links between African American to hip hop, West Indian to Rasta, and Anglo-Celtic to punk or skinhead. The masculine nature of some subcultures compared with others (skinhead versus gothic, for example) is likewise indicative of the gendering of subcultural practices, a process that can be analysed in relation to wider sociostructural arrangements and ideologies. As discussed below, it is important not to overstate the structural contexts and continuities of cultural life, nor to underestimate the great variability in how young people experience, consume, and produce their own specific ways of being.

Music, consumption, and youth subculture

As noted above, contemporary music has provided a medium for the development and expression of distinct sets of sensibilities, meanings, symbols, and practices. Music, produced by and for young people, has provided successive generations of youth with cultural forms that have marked their age group and distinguished them from their parents since the 1950s. Music features in young people's lives in various ways, often as an omnipresent feature of their daily lives. Different strands of music have been seen as constituting youth subcultures.

Straightedge music, for example, is described by Wood (2003) as a 'cultural collectivity' that is defined against mainstream forms of music. The central feature of straightedge is its committed opposition to the use of licit and illicit drugs, alcohol, and casual sex; its members are also known for their vegetarian or vegan lifestyles and their opposition to animal exploitation (Wood 2003). Music is the focal point for this subculture. As Wood explains:

> Gigs enable straightedgers to visit with one another, to form new network ties, to hear straightedge music, to slam dance or mosh, and to purchase straightedge merchandise such as compact disks, records and T-shirts ... National and international straightedge culture is united by a number of crucial 'culture transmitters', such as commercially available straightedge music recordings, fanzines/magazines, and straightedge Internet websites and message forums (2003: 35).

Wood's description of the way in which several straightedgers see their involvement in this subculture invites the interpretation that these young people see straightedge as a form of consumption through which they express their individuality. As Wood comments, although straightedge appears to exist as a relatively stable subculture, its members take a highly individualised and 'variable' approach to their involvement. It would seem to involve identity in the most general sense—more an affiliation than an identity as such, which validates their current lifestyle choices.

There is debate about whether it is useful to see the distinct, often locally based musical expressions that emerge as core elements of youth subcultures. Bennett points out that while music is the focus around which young people organise the use of abandoned warehouses and factories to become dance music venues, this collective use of space and experience of music does not necessarily constitute a subculture. Although the local nature of much music does provide young people with narratives through which they make meaning of their lives, they do not 'involve the formation of a separate subcultural identity' (Bennett 2000: 67). This is disputed by Mitchell (2003) who, as indicated earlier, argues that hip hop is an identifiable global youth subculture with a number of distinct social features.

Bennett shows how contemporary music is many things. Music is often 'deliberately fashioned in such a way as to enable a clear articulation of collective attitudes or statements that respond directly to everyday situations experienced in specific locations' by young people (Bennett 2000: 68). It can also, like straightedge or urban dance forms such as house, techno, and jungle, offer select involvement in 'private' events in which participants share particular sensibilities (resistance to mainstream club music or to perceived mainstream practices and relationships).

Bennett's studies of youth provide a strong argument for an understanding of music in the lives of young people that, at the very least, extends the notion of subculture. His studies of

Music, produced by and for young people, has provided successive generations of youth with cultural forms that have marked their age group and distinguished them from their parents since the 1950s. Music features in young people's lives in various ways, often as an omnipresent feature of their daily lives.

performance and participation in local music events (hip hop in Newcastle [UK] and Frankfurt, for example) document how young people create their own space—they appropriate and make habitable their local environment in their own way. Hip hop is an example of a global cultural form that is reproduced in specific local contexts by young people in many countries.

In their study of hip hop cultures in Sydney, d'Souza and Iveson (1999) argue that there are many variations in the way in which this cultural form is taken up. Their study focuses on the ways in which hip hop musical forms have been appropriated by different groups of young people in Sydney's suburbs to create a genuine form of localised cultural expression (see also Mitchell 2003). They argue that through this process of appropriation of global hip hop, different groups of young people actively produce a range of practices associated with hip hop music as part of their own cultural production. D'Souza and Iveson emphasise that hip hop is most usefully seen as a form of cultural practice, not simply as the consumption of particular products. They illustrate this by describing the ways in which the cultural tools of hip hop provide a credible alternative to white youth cultures practised by 'skips' (white Australian youth) for 'wogs' (migrant youth). As Andrew Wiradilaga, MC-ing under the name Tekniks, and with what he calls a 'half Indonesian–half Australian' background, puts it, 'We as people are realising we can do this in our own format. We realise what the culture's about and we can do it in our own environment' (d'Souza & Iveson 1999: 61).

These examples provide valuable illustrations of the ways in which music in particular becomes part of the cultural identity of young people. But these descriptions can give a false impression of separate, discrete groupings of young people. Muggleton's research on youth subcultures suggests that a more complex process is at work. He argues that young people 'engage in a radical stylistic pluralism, embracing and celebrating the fluidity and ephemerality of different subcultural identities on offer' (2000: 79), and concludes that his research on different youth subcultures in the United Kingdom provides evidence that young people identify with particular musical and stylistic approaches in a fragmented and heterogeneous way. The term that he uses to describe this kind of identification is that they have a 'liminal' sensibility, in that they resist the labels of particular styles. Muggleton found that it was not possible to classify many of the individuals in his study into subcultural types, and that to a certain extent the expression of particular styles crossed class boundaries.

Chatterton and Hollands also argue that 'hybrid forms of consumption are central for understanding contemporary youth cultures' (2003: 73). They point out that as young people are excluded from the more traditional sources of identity through work, other sources, such as fashion, music, leisure, and recreation, have become more central to identity formation. They point out that 'club cultures' have created the possibility of 'cultural mixing' of styles of dress and music (Redhead 1993). Yet Chatterton and Hollands strike a note of caution about the extent to which concerns about hybridity of youthful identities ignore the role of locality and social division in young people's lives. They argue that while young people's lifestyles and cultural forms are fragmented, they are also segmented. Chatterton and Hollands illustrate the ongoing importance of locality and social division through their study of young people's experiences of night life. They find:

a continuing polarisation between highly mobile, 'cash-rich, time-poor' groups of young people who can access a variety of entertainment choices, a large mainstream middle ground, and those experiencing unemployment, unstable employment, low wages, high debt and restricted leisure opportunities (2003: 84).

Young people may believe that they choose how they relate to various subcultures, to music, and to the consumption process generally, but they do so under the influence of a range of historically given conditions and external environmental factors. One of these factors is the renewed and fierce emphasis on physical appearance in the construction of oneself.

Consumption, the body, and appearance

Social identity in the present time period is made complicated by how consumption is shaping self-concept and presentations of self. Girls' performativity, for example, not only relates to school performance but also extends to their bodies (Wyn 2000). Appearance and consumption are significant aspects of the project of the self that 'successful' girls must manage. More generally, the effects of consumer capitalism on young women, through the creation of pressures towards physical self-perfection and self-image, have been noted (Bartky 1990; Bordo 1993). Other researchers have drawn attention to the implications of body performance on boys. In a study of young men in the United Kingdom, Frost (2003) has explored the implications of 'appearance-based identity construction' on boys' lives. Avoiding the positioning of men as the new victims of society, Frost argues that appearance has become just as important for young men as it is for young women. For both, 'doing looks', having the right clothes and the right bodies, are very important. Frost points out that in contemporary society (which she describes as late capitalism) many academics have argued that the visual display of identity has become especially significant.

The new significance of the visual display of identity has been linked to the rise of consumption and the association of material goods with selfhood. Researchers argue that not only do young people choose identities, but they also shop for them, purchasing styles, brands, and products that create the desired visual image. From this perspective, the market offers the means to create multiple styles of being (Frost 2003). Displaying the right image extends beyond clothes and accessories to include the body itself. Having the perfect body can be as important as having the right clothes.

Research in the United Kingdom by Miles and colleagues (Miles 1998; Miles et al. 1998) has demonstrated that purchasing consumer goods is central to the formation of young people's identities. Clothes are important as a source of individuality, but also to fit in with their peer group. As Muggleton (2000) points out, the seeming contradiction between apparent conformity and being different can be understood if a distinction is made between within-group and across-group conformity. In relation to the 'mass conformity of the conventional majority' (Muggleton 2000: 67), young people can express their individuality through their affiliation to a particular group.

In turn, these insights into the ways in which young people experience consumerism have led to concerns about their impact on youthful identities. Specifically, the patterns of consumption have been linked to the production of problem identities.

The first area of concern is that the idea of choice—of choosing, even of being able to purchase, an identity—has created the possibility of a different relationship to the body. The body has become somehow separated from the person, and, in the process, become a project, something to be actively shaped and constructed to fit in with particular ideals. As Frost points out, exercising control and self-discipline over the body offers a sense of mastery in an uncertain and unpredictable world. The body becomes an imperfect object over which the young person struggles to maintain control:

> The visual body image offered by the market place is of perfection, the desire of consumers attached to notions of perfection, and the identificatory process incorporating this version of self may then open up dissonance if the young person is not able to emulate physical perfection (Frost 2003).

It has also been suggested that the element of choice in this may be over-emphasised. From young people's point of view, taking up particular styles of body shape and dress may be experienced as pressure, and often is. Failing to conform usually leads to anxiety, guilt, and a sense of exclusion. Frost's study of young men in the United Kingdom describes the damage that is done through the creation of standards of appearance and style that few can attain. She points out that while markets create the impression of choice, this is far from the reality. Her interviews with young people found that they saw 'doing appearance' as 'highly competitive, judgmental and [involving] potential rejection' (Frost 2003).

The structural inequalities of class and poverty connect to the emotionally quite brutal lived realities of young people—the power of the pecking order, popularity or unpopularity, and ingroup membership or exclusion—via the conspicuous display of expensive consumer goods. The impression gained from what little interview material is available would suggest that although middle-class affluence may give some young people a position outside this 'hierarchy of cool … some middle-class boys from affluent back-grounds … looked down on working-class boys for buying designer clothes' (Frost et al. 2002: 94): for most young people there is no space outside this competitive system (Frost 2003: 61).

Frost's study also found that race 'cross-cut' the hierarchies of 'cool'. In particular, racial stereotyping that linked to colonial relations in the United Kingdom meant that some young people would always be excluded, regardless of their efforts. Her study highlights the damaging effects of the relationship between youth identities and consumption.

Summary

The concepts of identity and culture continue to be central to research into and thinking about young people. This chapter has identified how the ways in which these concepts have been used is changing. It describes how youth identities and subjectivities have become a central focus as researchers, theorists, and policy makers analyse the effects of social change on young people's lives. The role that young people themselves play in shaping the meanings of youth in contemporary society has become increasingly acknowledged.

While there are broad patterns in the new identities that are identified across different developed countries, the research also highlights the diversity that exists across and within nations. The divisions of social class, gender, and race continue to shape identities, but researchers are cautious about how far traditional sociological concepts can assist with our understanding of these social relationships in the lives of contemporary youth.

Questions for further exploration

1   What is meant by the term 'social identity'?

2   Drug use is socially patterned. So, too, is the response of the state to the 'problem of drugs'. Discuss.

3   Young people are made by music, even if they are the ones making the music. Discuss.

4   Youth subcultures continue to be relevant to how young people see themselves and their peer groups. What subcultures can be identified in contemporary Australian society?

5   The phenomenon of 'doing appearance' is sometimes associated with the idea of problem identities. Why is this the case?

QUESTIONS

13 YOUTH IN A DIGITAL AGE

Introduction

Over the last ten years, digital technologies have transformed our lives in ways that, until recently, we would never have dreamt of, but that we now take for granted. Digital information and communication technologies, which have had a profound effect on social relations, are seen by many social theorists as a defining feature of modernity. Within the youth research debates on the nature of social generations, there is also general agreement that immersion in digital communication technologies is one of the defining features of Generation Y, for whom traditional communication boundaries of time and space, of producer and consumer, have been crossed or blurred, as digital communication technologies, released from limits of physical space, bring a new way of visualising and experiencing communities and offer new possibilities for constructing identities.

While digital information technologies may have had a significant effect on older people's lives, their impact on young people is even more profound because the world of communication technologies is the only world they know: they are digital natives. As Gere has observed, 'the ubiquity of digital technology, and its increasing invisibility make it appear almost natural' (2002: 198). To put this another way, while older people make reference to 'new' communication technologies, younger people do not regard digital technologies as new. They take for granted the use of digital technology for communication in their personal, leisure, and commercial life. It is routine for Australian children and young people to use computers as an educational tool, in and out of school. Young people use the Internet for personal communication (email, blogging), as a medium for seeking information, and for shopping, banking, and organising travel. Young people expect to use a wide range of digitally produced and mediated leisure and communication, including mobile phones, iPods, MP3s, and CDs, and enjoy television programs and films that are increasingly produced and distributed digitally. Indeed, young people increasingly produce as well as consume these media. Personal publishing and blogging are now commonplace, gradually shifting the balance from using the Internet as a source of information to using it as a tool for communication. A recent poll conducted in the United Kingdom shows that one-third of fourteen to twenty-one year olds have their own online content (Gibson 2005).

Digital communication use by young Australians

BOX 13.1

- In 1998, only 16 per cent of Australian households had access to the Internet; by 2002, 46 per cent of households had access (Australian Bureau of Statistics 2003a).

- Households' possession of a mobile phone increased from 44 per cent in 1998 to 72 per cent in 2002 (Australian Bureau of Statistics 2003b).

- In Queensland in 2003, nearly 27 per cent of young people aged eighteen to nineteen and 46 per cent of people aged thirty to thirty-nine owned a mobile phone. In both age groups males were slightly more likely to own a mobile phone than young women (Australian Bureau of Statistics 2003c).

- People under the age of twenty-five are by far the greatest users of the Internet (40 per cent) (Lloyd & Bill 2004).

- Those aged from ten to nineteen have the highest rate of Internet use (60 per cent). Of these, young people in the fifteen to nineteen group are slightly more likely to use the Internet, with use declining from the age of twenty (Lloyd & Bill 2004; Australian Bureau of Statistics 2003d).

- Young people drive the booming market of mobile phones in Australia. Of fifteen to seventeen year olds, 80 per cent own or have access to a mobile phone (Tjong et al. 2003), while the age for first ownership of a mobile phone is estimated at fourteen years old (Australian Psychological Society 2004).

While there is widespread agreement that digital technologies have had a profound impact on young people's lives and that they have the potential to create even further, far-reaching changes to social relations, there is a divergence of opinion on the nature and impact of these changes. Do digital information technologies affect fundamental aspects of social relations, such as identity formation? Do these technologies influence the nature of young people's social relations? If so, how far-reaching are these changes and what drives the direction of change? Do digital information technologies offer liberating, emancipating opportunities for the creation of new communities and spaces where young people can belong, or are they inherently constraining and oppressive? In this chapter we draw on the available research to discuss these issues.

Opinion on these questions ranges across a very broad spectrum of writing on youth, including youth culture and subcultures, literacies, citizenship and participation, media production and formation, marketing, and commerce. This writing is informed by research from a range of academic fields, including cultural studies, youth studies, literacy and semiotics, educational sociology, political science, media studies, and business studies. Within this broad field, we find common conceptual themes as writers pursue the question of how digital information technologies affect social relations. In the following discussion, we draw on this broad literature through two of these recurring (and related) themes: identity and citizenship.

> Do digital information technologies affect fundamental aspects of social relations, such as identity formation? Do these technologies influence the nature of young people's social relations? If so, how far-reaching are these changes and what drives the direction of change? Do digital information technologies offer liberating, emancipating opportunities for the creation of new communities and spaces where young people can belong, or are they inherently constraining and oppressive?

Interpreting social relations through identity tends to place the emphasis on the ways in which digital technologies influence how individuals make and communicate meaning about themselves and their lives. Shifting the focus to citizenship places the emphasis on the ways in which these technologies contribute to and shape community, belonging, and engagement with society. These dimensions are interrelated and both support the argument that digital information technologies have blurred the distinction between producers and consumers (of culture, of text, and of meaning). More recently, the term 'prosumer' has been coined to describe the phenomenon of simultaneous consumption and production within virtual space. The way in which these concepts and positions are taken up through different perspectives is discussed in more detail below.

DIGITAL COMMUNICATION AND SOCIAL IDENTITIES

The concept of social identity is central to understanding the impact that digital information technologies have on social relations. In this section we extend our discussion of identities provided in Chapter 12 to build on the concept of identity as a product of discourses—sets of practices that are part of the fabric of life. As they are increasingly integrated into everyday life, digital communication technologies have become a significant medium through which children and young people learn about themselves and their relationship to others and the world. Young people's relationships with friends, family, and institutions are conducted in part through the use of mobile phones and the Internet. These technologies have become a medium through which meaning and social identities are constructed.

There are two key ways in which information technologies do this. First, digital technologies open up the available positions that individuals can take up because they create new social spaces (that are often referred to as 'virtual'). Second, because identity is formed (and performed) through and within the shifting patterns of our connections with others, digital technologies offer a wider and different range of possibilities for connecting and communicating with others compared with face-to-face relationships, and hence increase the possibilities for performing identities.

There are two key ways in which information technologies contribute to the making of identities. First, digital technologies open up the available positions that individuals can take up, because they create new social spaces (that are often referred to as 'virtual'). Second, because identity is formed (and performed) through and within the shifting patterns of our connections with others, digital technologies offer a wider and different range of possibilities for connecting and communicating with others compared with face-to-face relationships, and hence increase the possibilities for performing identities.

Producing identities

Digital information technologies offer new opportunities for young people to produce identities through the development and performance of identity in virtual space. They provide new spaces from which individuals can speak and a medium for performing the self. Merchant (2005) argues that identity is not about identification but about 'action and performance', for 'wearing and showing, not storing and keeping' (Merchant 2005: 304). He echoes the approach taken by Beck and Beck-Gernsheim (2002), who argue that one of the hallmarks of social change over the last thirty years is that identity must be constantly performed and enacted anew and that individuals are required to 'stage manage' their own biographies. Because they are part of the process through which we do this, digital technologies are intimately implicated in who we are and how we relate (Merchant 2005).

Digital information technologies provide powerful media through which stories of identity can be narrated: mobile phones, email, chat rooms, and spaces such as YouTube, minihompy, and MySpace. Although these spaces are virtual, they nonetheless become part of the everyday practices that are used by significant numbers of young people to construct identities. Some researchers (Burbules 2004, for example) have challenged the use of the term 'virtual' with regard to digital communication because it implies a lesser status (not real) than traditional media or face-to-face communication. For many young people the distinction between virtual and real is blurred through the interweaving of face-to-face and real relationships with digital spaces, activities, and communication. As these critics point out, if the distinction between virtual and real is helpful, it should also be applied to older communication technologies. Pen and paper have traditionally been used for the construction of narratives of identity through letter and diary writing. The virtual dimension of these older communication technologies and their role in providing ambiguous spaces for identity construction and performance is illustrated through the contemporary use of surviving letters to construct new interpretations and narratives about people's lives (for example, Kulyk Keefer's novel *Thieves* about Katherine Mansfield, and Peter Carey's *True History of the Kelly Gang*). The point is that the performance of identities always occurs through communication with others, regardless of the medium available; they do not exist totally apart from everyday life (reality).

Digital identity resources

Today, as in the past, the construction and performance of identity draws on available cultural, symbolic, and material resources. Identity is seen as a dynamic process and is told, performed, and retold in a variety of settings through various forms of storying or narrative. This has been well documented within youth studies, focusing on the material and cultural resources used by young people to story their lives (Wicrenga 2008, for example). Digital technologies have facilitated new forms of communication—for speaking, storying, and narrative communications between people—new possibilities that are especially influential for young people.

The creation of person-to-person and online communities generates new possibilities for individuals to access and perform narratives and to create meaning. In their different ways, these elements provide resources for the construction and performance of identity because they enable individuals to control and experiment with their portrayal of self and to draw on a rich and ever-expanding palate of images, phrases, references, and words. Digital technologies also enable us to transcend the limits imposed by face-to-face interaction on how we construct the place from which we speak.

It is also important to acknowledge that digital communication often simply represents an extension of older forms of communication. Digital technologies allow an extension of the possibilities for the repositioning of time and space that was pioneered through the use of landline telephones. The Internet enables people to connect with each other, just as face-to-face communication, landline phones, or letter writing does.

> Identity is seen as a dynamic process, and is told, performed, and retold in a variety of settings, through various forms of storying or narrative ... Digital technologies have facilitated new forms of communication—for speaking, storying, and narrative communications between people—new possibilities that are especially influential for young people.

The idea that digital communication enables young people to express and experiment with aspects of identity has become a focus of interest for educationalists. Beavis and Charles (2005) have argued that computer-aided writing and computer games are a resource for children and young people, enabling them to play with different identities and to challenge expectations. Their study describes how children use computer games to challenge traditional gender assumptions. Merchant (2005) describes how children, drawing from their own lives and from popular culture, use digital writing to write and perform their identity to create their personal narratives when communicating with each other.

Digital communication involves communication between people and websites. While this is never entirely interactive, it does provide a powerful medium for communication as people access sites such as ninemsm, YouTube, minihompy, and MySpace that connect the cyber traveller with sites that construct children and young people in particular ways by providing spaces within which young people can practice narratives. Some of these sites, ninemsm for one, offer young people access to pleasures associated with consumption and games, features that also offer opportunities for identity performances within the confines of commercially produced content. Others, such as miniHompy, which is especially popular among Korean youth, invite young people to inhabit their own cyber room, which they can augment and decorate with a wide range of items purchased through the site, where they can invite others to visit, and where young people can buy gifts to present to others who are participants in the site. The use of a personal avatar (a representation of a figure such as, say, a cute cartoon figure or an animal) within these spaces enables young people to play with representations of selves.

More recent research by Kenway et al. (2006) has found that some young men use cyberspace to 'radically reconfigure' their social behaviours and to engage in 'pernicious, aggressive and often malicious' (virtual) behaviour. They argue that cyberspace allows these young men (who might be shy and not usually argumentative) to develop short-tempered egos online (2006: 196).

Digital communication has also become a tool for furthering what Harris (2004) calls 'the culture of celebrity' (promoted by many television shows). Some young women (and young men, though considerably fewer) have used the available and relatively inexpensive technology of the Internet and web cameras to promote themselves as celebrities on a world scale, using a filmed segments of their everyday lives and turning a private space (a bedroom or kitchen) into a very public space that is accessible to viewers on a world scale. Harris (2004) comments that this use of the webcam has turned the electronic surveillance now used in schools, streets, malls, and shops into a tool for their own use and gratification.

Marketing to youth

The commercial use of digital spaces raises questions about the uses of digital communications and the implications of this use for their identity construction. As Atkinson and Nixon (2005) point out in their discussion of the Australia-based ninemsm website, the web is a 'commercially saturated' context for 'communication practices, meaning-making, identity and community formation' (Atkinson & Nixon 2005: 389).

Through extensive market research involving large-scale surveys and ethnographic research, media organisations aim to understand the identities, affinities, and aspirations of young people, who are valuable as consumers to be delivered to advertisers. Atkinson and Nixon describe how ninemsm does this through the construction of personas: imagined individuals whose identities are constructed from extensive research on young people. Personas provide a form of identification for users of the site and a means for selling advertising. The persona created by ninemsm is the persona of consumption—the individual who is driven by the imperative to consume. While academics and policy makers are just beginning to understand the role of information and communications technologies (ICTs) in constructing young people's identities, commercial interests are leading the generation of knowledge and its application in this field.

Drawing on this research, new commercial opportunities are being opened up that are blurring the distinction between different digital technologies (for example, mobile phones, television, the Internet) and between reality and fiction. Young people can download to their mobile phone or MP3 player free episodes of youth-oriented soap operas. An example is a program called *Girl Friday*. Each episode is 3½ minutes long, and if viewers register they can receive 'personal' emails and text messages from Girl Friday, which replicate friend-like messages (for example, 'I know that you like folk music, there is a gig on at the Espy'), or can find out more about her life. Through these short episodes, and augmented by text messages and emails, the story of Girl Friday evolves and young people are encouraged to feel a personal identification with the program. The soap operas open up new possibilities for delivering a target audience to advertisers and at the same time, because of the interactive element, provide advertisers with detailed information about their audience.

The investment by commercial interests in digital communication that impacts on young people's identity formation raises questions about the extent and implications of commercially produced and mediated digital sites. This is an area for further research, but it is important not to fall into sentimentalising young people as 'innocent and vulnerable' and 'requiring protection from the predations of the media and the markets that drive it' (Atkinson & Nixon 2005: 400). Neither is it appropriate to take up simplistic positions that romanticise young people as savvy, media-wise, and entrepreneurial: recent research on young Australians' use of and contribution to online information found that they were reluctant to reveal personal views and provide personal information online. Mirroring the pattern of face-to-face interaction, young people were more inclined to participate in an online activity if the online community was related to a real-life community, was built around a particular topic or activity of specific interest to them, and where the online community included others whom the young person knew and trusted (Chang & Lee 2006).

While use of digital communications may change, there is evidence that for many young people it simply augments existing personal relationships. A study of text messaging by young people found that they use it is because it is quicker than a telephone call, cheaper than making phone calls from their mobiles, and more convenient than other communication methods (Eldridge & Grinter 2001). The

It is important not to fall into sentimentalising young people as innocent and vulnerable and requiring protection from the predations of the media and the markets that drive it. Neither is it appropriate to take up simplistic positions which romanticise young people as savvy, media-wise, and entrepreneurial.

study found that text messages are used primarily to arrange social events or a time to call; it was common for young people to send a goodnight message to their closest friend almost every night.

With regard to media influences on young people, recent reviews conclude that there is no proven direct line between the encoded messages of popular culture and the messages that individuals receive or decode (Dolby 2003: 265). Others (for example, Boase & Wellman 2004) point out that digital communication technologies are significant but they do not 'determine' social relations.

In summary, various forms of digital technologies are an integral part of the lives of many young people today, and in the future are likely to be even more so. Theorists argue that these technologies are implicated in fundamental ways in the formation of young people's identities because digital technologies are a medium through which social relations are conducted as well as a force that shapes the nature of these social relations. In the following section we discuss this in more detail through a consideration of the role of digital information technologies and citizenship.

CITIZENSHIP AND CYBERSPACE

In addition to providing new landscapes within which identities are shaped and performed, digital communication technologies influence with whom we connect and how we belong. The concept of citizenship (discussed in Chapter 7) extends our understanding of the role of digital communication technologies in young people's lives to encompass community, participation in society, and belonging.

Research on citizenship and young people's use of digital communication has mostly focused maximal citizenship—the extent to which young people have a consciousness of their involvement in a shared democratic culture—and explores how digital communication technologies may foster new forms of democratic and social participation.

Cultural formation

The longstanding interest in the links between popular culture, citizenship, and belonging (Willis 1977; Giroux 1994) has generated some interesting insights into digital technologies and increased participation in society. Popular culture, including the cultural forms produced through ICTs, is seen as a powerful pedagogy through which young people learn about their social world and express their understandings of their world. Youth studies has tended to focus on the ways in which young people actively and creatively take up the objects and symbols provided through media and use them for their own purposes, creating new symbolic meanings and new spaces for communication and meaning-making that go beyond the personal to create new social movements and cultural forms.

The research highlights the blurring of lines between production and consumption. Willis (2003: 402), for example, suggests that 'active consumption' by young people is a kind of production. He argues that there is a seemingly endless stream of cultural symbols and forms that young people appropriate, and that it is important to separate the 'predatory' from the 'creative' elements within consumer culture in order to understand the ways in which young people 'acculturate commodities into their everyday lives'.

Echoing the work of a number of the educationalists cited above, Willis (2003: 392) points out that, far from being passive consumers, young people creatively respond to electronically produced cultural products in ways that surprise their makers, 'finding meanings and identities never meant to be there'. He is interested in the ways in which these cultural forms are used in everyday life in the places where young people meet in shared physical space—schools, malls, and nightclubs. Harris (2001) provides an example of this. She argues that young women have used zine culture within cyberspace to create discourses about girlhood that disrupt and challenge conventional media stereotypes of femininity, drawing on and transforming commercially available popular culture. Young same-sex attracted people have made effective use of digital communication to find a safe space within which to connect with others and with information (Hillier, Kuldas & Horsley 2001).

Digital communications enable young people, through digital sites, to use popular culture as a resource for political struggle. There are many examples of the use of digital communication by young people to foster political organisation and action. One example is the online communities that were formed to support particular groups, such as same sex-attracted youth. The use of digital communication has made it possible for geographically isolated individuals to connect and for these groups to have social and political visibility and hence to actively assert their rights as a group (Yang 2000).

Cultural citizenship

Dolby, too, sees political possibilities in the blurring of citizen and consumer through the use of digital communications, involving the mobilisation of citizenship within a framework of consumption. Like Willis, she believes that popular culture can become a 'prominent political space for the negotiation and enactment of a new dimension of citizenship: cultural citizenship' (Dolby 2003: 270).

The idea of cultural citizenship brings together the conceptual fields of identity and citizenship and focuses on the more political aspects of identity, as suggested by Willis, Dolby and Harris above. Digital communications technologies provide a medium through which dispossessed or marginalised young people, who are not necessarily connected in physical space, can create a sense of belonging and identity by drawing on and appropriating cultural representations from texts, images, and music. This use of digital communication is an extension of the use that marginalised groups of young people have traditionally made of popular culture to construct political identities and a sense of belonging. A classic work by Dimitriadis (2001) examines how African American youth at a community centre used rap texts in their daily lives, opening up possibilities for understanding their world and shaping identities and politics that were effective in their world. In a more recent example, Hollands (2005) suggests that Mohawk youth in Southern Ontario use a variety of cultural symbols available in the conventional media (movies, rap music) to overcome the dichotomy between 'authentic' aboriginal and 'white Canadian' culture, and construct what Hollands calls a 'hybrid' identity that enables

> Digital communications technologies provide a medium through which dispossessed or marginalised young people, who are not necessarily connected in physical space, can create a sense of belonging and identity, drawing on and appropriating cultural representations from texts, images, and music.

them to 'reinvent themselves as modern indigenous people' (2005: 6.9). Holland's work emphasises the importance of working, selectively and critically, with the communication media that young people relate to, because the alternative is to condemn them to a world in which the only 'authentic' Indigenous culture is rooted in the past (see also Chapter 5 in regards to Australian Indigenous peoples). A similar point is made by Dolby (2003) with regard to the use of popular culture by black students in a South African school, and the use of rave culture to differentiate racial groups and resist white culture.

While the approaches taken to hybrid identities and consumer citizens may seem a little optimistic, their explorations set out a possible framework for harnessing the potential of digital technologies to enable young people to participate in their communities in a more maximal way. Furthermore, the conceptual work by Hollands (2005), Dolby (2003), and Willis (2003), for example, provides a basis for moving beyond the merely commercial, limiting elements of digital communication technologies to working constructively and positively with media that young people know in order to enhance their well-being.

In Australia, new forms of cultural engagement have been made possible through digital filmmaking, an obvious but often overlooked site through which young people can engage in digital communication. The 2003 movie *The Finished People*, for example, using new digital processes, allowed new youthful voices to be heard. The director, producer, and co-writer (with the actors) was a young person named Khoa Do. In 2002 Khoa started teaching filmmaking skills to a group of young, mostly homeless people in Cabramatta who had been deemed at risk. The film was made on a micro budget, using the young people in his course as actors and writers, and in other production roles. The film, which tells a story of three young people who are homeless in Cabramatta, blurs the line between fiction and reality and explores from the protagonists' point of view how they came to be where they are. The script draws heavily on the life experience of the young people involved in the film.

Digital divides

The use of digital communication technologies reflects patterns of inequality within and between countries. Effective digital infrastructure and capacity to purchase digital technology is limited to countries and individuals that are relatively wealthy. Since the 1990s, South Korea, for example, has invested significantly in digital communication, fostering important educational and commercial opportunities. In 2005, Korea had 33 million Internet users (72.8 per cent of the population), while in many countries digital communication is still limited to urban areas.

Age-based divisions are also emerging. Vromen (2005: 3) points out that there is a significant digital divide among eighteen to thirty-four year old Australians. While young people under the age of twenty-five are the most frequent users of the Internet, the strongest correlations are between socioeconomic status and Internet use. The main characteristics of regular Internet users are high weekly family income and employment, especially in professional occupations, high level of education, and living in cities rather than regional or rural Australia. Vromen argues that this means that Australian young people, especially when they are no longer studying, cannot all be categorised as active Internet users.

Lack of access to digital communication in a digital age tends to reinforce inequalities. A recent study of young people and their work (Stokes, Wierenga & Wyn 2004) found that young people without access to mobile phones were not able to access and respond to casual employment opportunities in a way that was expected by the employer. They were also limited in terms of availing themselves of opportunities to find social support through new online and offline communities.

The pattern of use of digital information technologies by Indigenous peoples in Australia provides a graphic illustration of the digital divide (Norris 2001). While information technologies have the potential to enhance connectedness and access to vital information for Indigenous Australians, the reality is that existing material and economic inequalities tend to determine who has access to information technologies and who does not. In 2002, 56 per cent of Indigenous peoples reported that they had used a computer in the last twelve months and 41 per cent reported that they had accessed the Internet in the last 12 months. Use of any form of information technology was much higher in non-remote areas, where computer usage and Internet access rates are roughly double those for people living in remote areas. Those living in non-remote areas were also much more likely to have a working telephone in the home (82 per cent compared with 43 per cent). When the effects of age differences between the Indigenous and non-Indigenous populations have been removed, Indigenous peoples had lower levels of digital information technology use than the non-Indigenous population. Indigenous peoples aged eighteen years and over were two-thirds less likely to have used a computer and around half as likely as non-Indigenous people to have accessed the Internet in the last 12 months (Australian Bureau of Statistics 2002).

There is also emerging evidence to show that traditional gender divisions are being represented in the uses of digital communications. Drotner (2003) found that boys and young men found it easier to talk about sexual issues with the opposite sex through the mobile phone rather than in person, while girls and young women used it to keep in contact with their best girlfriends. Interestingly, females stressed that the being in contact was more significant than what was being communicated. Other research has found that young women were more likely than males to share personal information with their friends and family through telephone and email communications, making it easier for women to expand their social networks (Boneva et al. 2001). For males, telephone and email are seen more as an instrumental tool, while females see it as another way of sharing feelings, but overall this research did not find significant differences in the amount of time spent on the Internet between men and women.

Vromen (2005: 3) points out that there is a significant digital divide among eighteen to thirty-four year old Australians. While young people under the age of twenty-five are the most frequent users of the Internet, the strongest correlations are between socioeconomic status and Internet use. The main characteristics of regular Internet users are high weekly family income and employment, especially in professional occupations, high level of education, and living in cities rather than regional or rural Australia.

New forms of political engagement

Because young people are at the forefront of using digital communications, there have been widespread predictions that this would result in a corresponding surge in new forms of political engagement. Peer run sites, such as www.vibewire.net, provide access to information and debates about the things that concern young people; these sites also offer an alternative to the commercially saturated sites referred to above.

Vibewire was launched in 2002 with the aim of providing a space for youth culture and for young Australians' political expression. Vibewire provides a site for the exploration of political and public issues, and promotes cultural commentary in the areas of film, theatre, art, and music. During the 2004 federal election, Vibewire ran *electionTracker*, a political commentary by four young online journalists who wrote daily entries from John Howard and Mark Latham's campaign trails. Vromen (2005) notes that pieces by these online journalists were regularly picked up by the mainstream media.

While in general there has been little evaluation of youth Internet sites, an evaluation of Reach Out! an interactive website which provides advice and information on young people's mental health, found that 80 per cent of its users were women with an average age of eighteen and who were overwhelmingly metropolitan based (mainly from Sydney). An evaluation of Vibewire found that 70 per cent of its users were women aged between twenty and twenty-five years, and the vast majority were also urban-based (81 per cent). Two-thirds of the Vibewire users who were surveyed had participated in an online forum and 40 per cent had written an article for the site (Vromen 2005).

The emergence of these kinds of sites and many others has resulted in speculation about new ways in which young people might engage with political processes. The evidence on the actual use of digital communications technologies to foster maximal citizenship is less optimistic. Based on an indepth study of 287 eighteen to thirty-four year old Australians, Vromen (2005) concludes that people who are politically active and engaged use the Internet to supplement this, but found no evidence that the Internet or the use of other digital communication technologies were the primary focus of political engagement. Her conclusions are supported by Atkinson and Nixon (2005) who claim that, even for those who are interacting through digital communications, this does not live up to the 'democratizing, emancipatory potential that is sometimes claimed for it'.

As Fyfe and Wyn (2007) conclude, the portrayal of young people as using new technologies to engage in new and innovative forms of political engagement is based on a romantic view. Digital communications are most likely to be used by young people to support critical discussion and action alongside more traditional forms of political engagement.

Despite this caution, there is a substantial body of work that explores the impact of digital communications on young people's citizenship and engagement in society. The overwhelming weight of this literature points to the need for the institutions that have responsibility for young people's learning, engagement, health, and well-being to recognise how much of young people's lives are shaped, influenced, and constructed through communication technologies—and to recognise the possibilities for positive action within this domain.

> The evidence suggests that while new media such as the Internet undoubtedly have the potential to affect the direction and outcomes of political activism at all levels, in itself it does not necessarily ensure political action or civic engagement. The overwhelming weight of this literature points to the need for the institutions that have responsibility for young people's learning, engagement, health, and well-being to recognise how much of young people's lives are shaped, influenced, and constructed through communication technologies—and to recognise the possibilities for positive action within this domain.

Harmful use of digital technologies

The uncensored nature of digital communications is at once a strength and a weakness. While there is considerable scope for the positive use of cyberspace for the promotion of new learning and new civic and personal engagement, it can, at the same time, be used to cause harm. It is important to recognise that these media can be used for negative purposes. A quick tour through the millions of available websites and blogs reveals that some are designed to foster harm or social exclusion. In one study, conducted by Wyn and Cuervo (2006), sites were revealed that are aimed at people who have eating disorders (bulimia, anorexia), and that offer hints on how to hide their condition and how to lose more weight.

Wyn and Cuervo (2006) also note that the Internet is used by hate groups to promote racism, discrimination, and violence, to divulge their views, and recruit new members. While in the past hate groups would recruit members, especially young people, through fliers, newsletters, and small rallies, now the Internet provides an easily accessible and direct way to gain recruits. Lee and Leets (2002) found that young people who spent more effort analysing and processing these messages were able to resist the narratives and found them racist and distasteful, while those who put less effort into analysing the messages received them more favourably. The research concluded that controlling the development of web pages by hate groups attracting young people to discrimination and violence is a major difficulty faced by government, parents, and school authorities.

For some young people, the digital world offers a more attractive alternative space to their non-digital world, and they spend as much time as they can there. Some researchers have labelled this 'digital addiction' and it can take the form of excessive video game playing, accessing particular websites (pornographic sites and gambling sites, for example), or becoming obsessed with chat rooms (Young 2004).

ICTs have also opened up new opportunities for bullying and harassment. Ybarra and Mitchell (2004) ague that Internet harassment is a significant public health issue for the harasser and the harassed alike. They comment that aggressors tend to be associated with poor parent–child relationships, substance use, and delinquency. The traditional offline bully tends to be male, while online bullies are just as likely to be female as male, and are more likely to be high-school aged than middle-school aged (Ybarra & Mitchell 2004). More recently, attention has been drawn to the increased use of mobile phones to marginalise, bully, and harass. An Australian study found that at least 30 per cent of the young people in Years 7–9 surveyed have experienced some kind of bullying or threats through their mobile phone (Australian Psychological Society 2004).

Summary

Even as this book goes to press, digital communication technologies and their uses by young people are evolving in new ways. This chapter has provided a framework for considering the complex and changing interrelationship between digital communications and young people's lives, through the lenses of identity formation and of citizenship. These concepts provide a framework through which we can analyse the uses and impacts of digital communications on social life as new generations take up opportunities—and experience the consequences—of these technologies.

The chapter has emphasised the taken for grantedness of communications for many young people. While digital communication in the form of mobile phones, interactive websites, and blogs are seen as new to older people, they are simply part of everyday life for many young people. We have also emphasised the need to neither romanticise young people's engagement with digital communications nor to portray them as victims of it. The evidence shows that many young people have a critical and active engagement with different forms of digital communication, blurring the traditional boundaries between consumption and production. Digital communications are used by young people to enhance and extend political and civic engagement.

There is also evidence that digital communications can provide spaces for the construction and performance of identity, can act as a means of connection for isolated or marginalised young people, and can act as a forum for political and civic engagement. Even so, a digital divide exists, a divide that reflects broader patterns of physical isolation and socioeconomic inequality. Some young people do not own a mobile phone and many do not have personal access to the Internet.

Another form of digital divide exists, that between the formal world created by institutions that serve young people (schools, health care) and their informal worlds. Learning within schools bears increasingly little resemblance to the increasingly multimodal and multimedia out-of-school practices. Institutions such as schools and health centres have been slow to respond to the opportunities offered by digital communication for expanding the ways in which learning and well-being are promoted.

Questions for further exploration

1 Digital information technologies offer liberating, emancipating opportunities for the creation of new communities and spaces where young people can belong, yet they can be constraining and oppressive as well. Discuss.

2 What is the difference between 'virtual' and 'real' communication? Is this a useful distinction to make?

3 In what ways have digital technologies expanded opportunities for the construction and performance of identities, and what are the limitations of this?

4 What are the implications of the digital divide for young people?

5 Is there an emerging divide between the use of digital communication by young people in informal settings such as the home and their uptake in formal settings such as schools and universities?

QUESTIONS

DEFINING WELL-BEING AND HEALTH

14

Introduction

In this chapter we explore a number of issues related to young people's health and well-being. As we demonstrate, this is a surprisingly complex area. Young people in Australia and other Western nations are participating in education at higher levels than ever before in history, yet their health remains a matter of public concern. Young people are also concerned about their health, placing an emphasis on well-being that challenges some of the taken-for-granted approaches to youth health.

In discussing young people's health, one of the key issues is the way in which discourses of health have come to shape understandings of youth and youth transitions to adulthood. This chapter looks at the significance of concepts of at risk and protective factors as well as other elements in the taken-for-granted understandings of youth preparation for adult life. These concepts have also been integral to the definitions of normal or mainstream behaviour and patterns of life.

The literature on youth health reveals an emerging focus on well-being. There is a widespread interest in the ways in which young people themselves manage to be well and in the role of institutions such as health, education, family, and juvenile justice in promoting young people's well-being. This emerging focus operates within a tradition of quantifying and measuring ill health, but we suggest that it is important to distinguish morbidity and ill health outcomes from well-being, and to focus on the social relations that are associated with well-being. This approach is highlighted by the way in which young people themselves define their own health and well-being.

HEALTH, WELL-BEING, AND THE RISK SOCIETY

CASE STUDY: Sue

Sue, a participant in the Youth Research Centre's Life-Patterns research program (Dwyer & Wyn 2001), describes herself as a 'very studious' student at school. She was captain of the school in her last year, which involved 'a lot of duties' that took up a great deal of her time. In addition, she studied very hard because she wanted to get into a really good course, get a good degree, and find a good job. Sue excelled in her results and gained access to a difficult-to-get-into course

BOX 14.1

BOX 14.1

in manufacturing management, a scholarship course that involved a practicum in the USA. She graduated from this course in three years and, at the age of twenty-one, was immediately employed in a role that involved IT management. She took the job on because 'her degree led her to it' and because her parents had pushed her to succeed.

Sue was very motivated to succeed in her job, to save hard, and establish a good life for herself. She was earning very good money. However, this involved: 'Long hours; the responsibility fell back on me as the consultant. You work in a team with their people but they are used to only working 9–5, so you'd have to pick up things and work till 9.00 every night ... Stressful expectations are put on you. *This* document by *this* time. Continual deadlines, non-stop.'

Despite this, Sue continued to work hard. In her third year with the company she was given a substantial promotion; in that same year she began a 'serious relationship'. She said, 'I've grown up in the last few years and I've realised that you can do what you want in life, but don't get too stressed—life's too short.'

To her parents' horror and her partner's disbelief, Sue took the decision to throw her work in and to use her financial reserves to travel, a decision she saw as one of the things that she was most proud of to date. At the age of twenty-four she was now working for $8.00 an hour in retail at a snow resort in Canada: 'I am here to ski, to improve my skiing and to relax and have fun. I am much more relaxed than I was a few months ago.'

This change gave Sue the opportunity to reflect on her life and to consider other options that would enable her to develop other capacities and skills. At the time of her last interview, she was trying to balance the pros and cons of using her remaining funds to travel further or to undertake further education in an entirely different field. Sue felt that at the moment her priority was to relax. Looking to the future, heritage management was something that she could imagine doing in her thirties; she aimed to get some experience in the field through voluntary work before undertaking a Masters program in heritage management.

Managing choice

By the standards of our day Sue is a highly successful young woman. Her school success foreshadowed a brilliant career of her choice. Like many of her counterparts, she demonstrated that she could excel at examinations and at the same time hold positions of responsibility within the school, but pressures to succeed across so many dimensions of their lives also created pressures and stress (Wyn 2000). We found that many school students, like Sue, are eager to have the opportunity to develop the skills of managing multiple responsibilities and demands. A key element is the management of achieving a balance between the competing demands on them so that they can have a space in which they can pursue personal development and in which they can escape from the constant pressure to ensure their futures. Woodman (2004) calls this process 'balancing temporalities'. He is referring to the need to balance the future-oriented world of work and study that operates in social time with 'inner time', a space and time zone that is bracketed from social time that is present-centred and embodied. Young people do this in various ways. In his research on young school-aged people, Woodman found that they often used leisure (including playing computer games) and sport to create a space where they can simply enjoy the present.

Indeed, having the capacity to manage choices so that they achieve a balance in life is emerging as a defining characteristic of contemporary youth (Wyn & Woodman 2006).

Sue made a good impression in her workplace and was soon promoted to more senior roles involving the use of her skills and capacities to the full. Yet her description of this situation focuses on the increasing risk to her well-being. She uses the word 'stress' many times and feared that she would, in time, shift beyond being stressed to slip into a worse situation. Ultimately, Sue made the decision to remove herself from her work situation and from the broader social relations that had propelled her into it. It was not an easy decision and it was clearly a shock to her parents. Although they eventually supported her decision, it was obviously a difficult time. Sue said that sticking to her plan to resign from her job against her parents' advice was one of the things in her life to date that she was most proud of.

At the time of the interview at the snow resort she was relieved to be just enjoying herself. Like the young people in Woodman's research, Sue found it necessary to focus on being in the present. The story she tells in the interview is one of success and power, but not the conventional story that she would have told a year earlier. Having felt that her well-being was at risk, and finding no support for remedying the situation, she made her own pathway through the problem. Sue feels very successful now, but in a different way.

The risk society, individualism, and health

Variations on Sue's story are repeated many times in the Life-Patterns research program (Dwyer & Wyn 2001). In 2002, when the majority of the cohort was aged twenty-seven to twenty-eight, only 56 per cent were prepared to claim that they were physically healthy or very healthy; only 58 per cent were prepared to claim that they were mentally healthy or very healthy.

Young people's concern about their physical and mental well-being has motivated decisions about their lives: 'My health has taken a back seat to my career and now my health is suffering.' This assessment by one participant in the Life-Patterns study sums up the feelings of many participants. Table 14.1 below shows that health and fitness was the area of greatest concern in their lives.

TABLE 14.1 Areas you wish were better (2002)

Areas you wish were better	%
Health and fitness	26.3
Personal relationships	21.5
Work/career	19.2
Educational attainments	19.2
Personal development	7.3
Social life	7.1
Family life	7.0
Total	100.0

For some, achieving better health has involved travelling in order to get outside the straitjacket of social expectations about work, life, and success. For others the journey has been more spiritual or focused on changing daily practices to include meditation and reflection or more physical activity. The participants were exploring a range of self-prescribed remedies for their feelings of stress and lack of fitness, including going to the gym, taking up bike riding, visiting a naturopath, or taking yoga classes.

> For some, achieving better health has involved travelling in order to get outside the straitjacket of social expectations about work, life, and success. For others the journey has been more spiritual or focused on changing daily practices to include meditation and reflection or more physical activity.

It would be easy to dismiss these patterns as the preoccupations of a self-absorbed generation. Indeed, their focus is very individualised. The Life-Patterns study found that while the focus on health and well-being was pronounced, during their mid twenties these young people spent relatively little time involved in organised social or political movements, community work, or action to improve the environment, even when they expressed a strong interest in these activities. Some researchers (Beck & Beck-Gernsheim 2002, for example) argue that the lack of collective action among young people can be directly related to the kind of society in which they live.

More recently, Furlong and Cartmel (2007) have argued that new patterns of life have lead to new forms of risk and vulnerability that are disproportionately borne by young people from lower socioeconomic backgrounds. Furlong and Cartmel also acknowledge that 'the processes of individualization, coupled with the stress that develops out of uncertain outcomes' have contributed to the emergence of new risks, such as mental health problems. The exposure to risk and vulnerability leads to a greater focus on managing their own biographies and life patterns, leaving less time to focus on the bigger picture.

Young people's focus on their own health and well-being is a natural response to a society that is characterised by processes of individualisation. Beck and Beck-Gernsheim's recent work, which explores the way in which people are becoming individualised, provides a useful insight into the experiences and orientations of Sue and her contemporaries.

The process of individualisation, they argue, is a direct result of the collapse of traditional social structures and the failure of those that continue to provide security and predictability. Education, for example, continues to be a significant social institution, as it was for the preceding generation, but the outcomes of education are less predictable for individuals today than they were in the 1960s (Dwyer & Wyn 2001). The family is still an important institution for a majority of people, but sociologists now disagree about how to define it and, with a 50 per cent likelihood of marriage breakdown, traditional families do not necessarily provide stability or security for individuals.

Beck argues that in response to this social situation, individuals have to make choices about employment, study, and relationships based on their own judgments, often before they have time to fully understand the situation. Information technology and globalisation offer access to endless information, but even experts have difficulty in making sense of things. In order to make their decisions, individuals have had to develop the capacity to be reflexive; that is, to see themselves in a wider context to try to understand what the impact of their decisions will be.

Reflexivity also involves monitoring oneself and trying to see oneself as others might. Much of the activity of individuals consists of reshaping and renegotiating their mutual engagements and relationships in everyday life, which means that people take on the responsibility of making and performing their identities, as Wexler (1992) explores in *Becoming Somebody*.

Health has moved to centre stage in this process of individualisation because health is one of the key elements of personal life that has to be managed by the individual. As Beck and Beck-Gernsheim comment, maintaining health has become one of the most central 'projects of the self' in today's society and it has to be constantly reproduced by individuals. The project of the self (Beck & Beck-Gernsheim 2002: 140) involves an orientation towards self-management within various 'codes of success'. From the standpoint of the rational and responsible individual in today's society, the body itself is an outcome of choices and actions. This means that responsibility for good health is seen not only as a good thing, but also a necessary thing and a moral obligation. Failure to reach the standards of health, fitness, well-being, and optimisation that are the individual's responsibility is accompanied by guilt.

A number of researchers have linked the aspect of individualisation with the high rates of anxiety among young women (Donald et al. 2000; Wyn 2000; Harris 2002) and with youth suicide. Paradoxically, the individualisation process leads to conditions under which health is a focus of life, and yet under which increasing numbers of young people choose to take their lives.

> Health has moved to centre stage in this process of individualisation because health is one of the key elements of personal life that has to be managed by the individual.

YOUNG PEOPLE'S (ILL) HEALTH AND WELL-BEING

Knowledge about young people's positive health and well-being is still emerging, but the most recent available data show that overall young people enjoy good health compared with other age groups. In 2001, 76 per cent of young Australians aged between fifteen and nineteen and 59 percent of those aged eighteen to twenty-four rated their health as 'excellent' or 'very good' (AIHW 2003, p. ix). The powerful exception to this trend is the health and well-being of young Aboriginal and Torres Strait Islander youth, which remains poor (AIHW 2003, p. v). Young people living in rural and remote areas also tend to have poorer health than young people living in metropolitan areas, and have high rates of regular cigarette smoking, drinking at hazardous levels, and using illicit substances, often higher than young people in metropolitan areas (AIHW 2003).

> Most young Australians enjoy good health compared with other age groups. The powerful exception to this trend is the health and well-being of young Aboriginal and Torres Strait Islander youth, which remains poor.

Young people's health is overwhelmingly conceived of and measured as an absence of ill-health, pathology, and mortality. A quick survey of the literature on young people's health reveals a rich source of up-to-date information on young people's ill-health. Overwhelmingly, this literature shows that in some key areas young Australians are actually becoming less healthy (Stanley 2001). Since the 1980s, the inequalities in health outcomes among Australian children, based on socioeconomic status, have widened (Turrell & Mathers 2000). The following discussion summarises some of the key areas of behaviour that place young people's health at risk.

Areas of concern

Concerns about young people's health focus on just a few areas: substance use and abuse, including licit and illicit substances (alcohol, cigarettes, and drugs such as marijuana, heroin and other substances), mental health, including anxiety and eating disorders, and obesity.

Illicit and licit drugs

There is no evidence that rates of use are increasing, but substance use, licit and illicit, is part of life for many members of this generation; they are likely to use alcohol on a fairly regular basis. In 2001, in the age group of eighteen to twenty-four, 57 per cent of males and 42 per cent of females were 'regular drinkers' of alcohol, and nearly one in five drank at a level of high risk (AIHW 2003: 202). In the fourteen to seventeen age group, 20 per cent of males and 17 per cent of females were regular alcohol users, half of this age group were occasional drinkers, and 7 per cent were high-risk drinkers (AIHW 2003: 202). Compared with other groups, young people were more likely to have had alcohol-induced memory lapse weekly (4 per cent) or monthly (11 per cent) in the past 12 months (AIHW 2003: 197), which means that a small but a significant proportion of young people is abusing alcohol. A study of young people in Queensland found that a total of 33 per cent of the young people reported binge drinking in the week prior to the survey (Donald et al. 2000). Fourteen per cent of the sample reported driving while under the influence of alcohol at some time in the previous year. A study of Australian university students found that 70 per cent of students drink to 'hazardous levels' (Davey et al. 2002).

Of the illicit drugs, young people regard cannabis as acceptable (and as less harmful than tobacco). A study reported by the AIHW (2003) found that in 2001, 40 per cent of males and 26 per cent of females aged twelve to seventeen had used cannabis in the past twelve months. The same study found that 13 per cent of young people had used amphetamines and 12 per cent had used ecstasy (AIHW 2003: 207). The research indicates that the mean age of initiation into illicit drug use is marginally lowering. For cannabis use, the mean age was 15 years, and for ecstasy it is 18 years (AIHW 2003: 205). Marijuana use is now common among young people, with half of the 15–24 year olds in a Queensland study reporting that they had used marijuana and one in five reporting use in the previous week (Donald et al. 2000). Cigarette smoking is also of concern. A study conducted by Women's Health Australia found that one third of young women were smokers, and that 41 per cent did little or no exercise (Brown et al. 1998). With regard to cigarette smoking, in 2001, 16 per cent percent of 12 to 17 year olds identify themselves as smokers, and of 18 to 24 year olds, 27 per cent of females and 36 per cent of males were smokers (AIHW 2003: 199).

Obesity

There has been a lot of press about young people and obesity over the last five years. Based on self-reported height and weight, 8 per cent of males and 11 per cent of females aged fifteen to seventeen were classified as overweight or obese in 2001. Of those aged eighteen to twenty-four, 16 per cent of males and 25 per cent of females were classified as overweight or obese. In an assessment of their own weight, 28 per cent of males and 9 per cent of females whose self-reported height and weight placed them in the overweight category thought their weight was acceptable; 13 per cent of females and 1 per cent of males whose height and weight placed them in the underweight category reported that their weight was acceptable (AIHW 2004: 188). Some researchers argue that this focus on obesity takes a particularly unhealthy approach, individualising the responsibility for managing health and making health into a performance (Wright & Burrows 2004).

Infectious diseases

Young people are also prone to infectious diseases, including those that are spread through intravenous drug use and sex; 54 per cent of the sexually active young people in the Queensland study said that they had not used a condom during their most recent sexual encounter.

Mental health

One of the areas of greatest concern is young people's mental health. A recent Australian national survey of mental health found high levels of childhood mental health problems compared with a limited number of children and youth who receive professional help (Sawyer et al. 2000). This study found that 14 per cent of four to seventeen year olds experience mental health problems. In Queensland, one in four females and one in eight males had symptoms that indicated high-level depression. The report also found that as many as one in three young people had had suicidal thoughts at some time in their lives (Donald et al. 2000). In Western Australia, one in five teenagers has a mental health problem (Stanley 2002).

One of the areas of greatest concern is young people's mental health.

The many reports on young people's mental health reveal very similar outcomes, but one of the difficulties of making direct comparisons across these different studies is that each uses slightly different measures of mental health and depression. The term 'depression' may be used to refer to a wide range of behaviours and feelings. There are many different groups of disorders that can be identified under the broad umbrella of 'mental health', including anxiety disorders, depressive disorders, and substance abuse disorders.

Despite these complexities, there is strong evidence that mental health problems are emerging as one of the most significant health concerns about Australian youth. Three per cent of males and 6 per cent of females (eighteen to twenty-four) were found to have very high levels of psychological distress that were associated with being unemployed or not completing school beyond Year 9 (AIHW 2003, p. ix).

Young people aged eighteen to twenty-four have the highest rates of mental disorder, but generally these rates decrease with age (Australian Bureau of Statistics 1998c). For females aged eighteen to twenty-four, the rates of disorder were 14 per cent for anxiety disorders, 11 per cent for depressive disorders, and 11 per cent for substance use disorders. The figures for males reveal a different pattern: 9 per cent for anxiety disorders, 3 per cent for depressive disorders, and 22 per cent for substance use disorders. The different reports also confirm that young people have high rates of thinking about suicide. Across several measures of suicide, suicidal ideation, deliberate self-harm, and depression, the Queensland study concluded that fifteen- to seventeen-year-old females had the highest levels of problems of all groups (Donald et al. 2000: 27).

Even though it is focusing on ill health rather than well-being, the research on young people's mental ill health is informative. The Queensland study found that there are identifiable adverse life events that contribute to unhappiness or distress. They differ for young men and young women, particularly in the fifteen- to seventeen-year-old age group, although in general the patterns are the same. For fifteen- to seventeen-year-old males and females the three most common adverse life events were problems with friends, problems with parents, and anxiety about school or university; boys and girls placed equal emphasis on the adverse effects of being bullied. Girls were three times more likely to say that failure at school was a source of distress than were boys. Boys placed an equal emphasis on concern about failure at school and problems at work, whereas girls' concerns about problems at work were almost non-existent. For boys, a relationship break-up was seven times more likely to cause distress than for girls.

By the ages of eighteen to twenty-four, patterns have changed. Significantly, problems at work now feature prominently, with 26.3 per cent of young women and 22.1 per cent of young men reporting this as a source of adverse experiences in their lives. Ironically, for young women, work is a greater source of negativity than unemployment. In this age group, young women report higher levels of overall negative life experiences than the boys do, although both report that financial hardship, relationship break-up, anxiety about university performance, and problems with friends and family are the greatest sources of negativity.

Achieving a balance

It is interesting to consider the match between the official figures on young people's health and their own perceptions. There is a range of sources of information about what young people think that draw on a number of sources. Some examples are presented in Box 14.1.

BOX 14.1

Young people's concerns about their health

- The most important current issues for male and female respondents (fifteen to eighteen years old) were keeping fit, getting more education, and having lots of friends, although females, unlike males, considered getting more education to be more important than keeping fit (Australian Institute of Family Studies 2006).

- In 2003–05, 22 per cent of school-aged young people in New South Wales were concerned about the amount of pressure on them, 15 per cent were concerned about their body image, and 11 per cent were concerned about drugs (NSW Peer Support Foundation 2006).

- In 2004 young people aged eleven to twenty-four stated that the issues of most concern to them were alcohol and other drug issues (43.5 per cent), bullying and emotional abuse (36 per cent), coping with stress (35 per cent), suicide and self-harm (33.7 per cent), and family conflict (32 per cent) (Mission Australia 2004).

Young people's concerns are fairly consistent with the issues that concern professionals and members of the community. It is important to note the high profile that issues related to mental health, such as pressure and stress, are given. In this sense, young people's emphasis on having a balanced life that involves the importance of friendships and leisure, including sport, as a way of ensuring their well-being, is backed up by the research. It has been found that leisure and social relationships are the most important protective factors against depression. For males, participation in outdoor activities, more frequent attendance at movies, concerts, and plays, having close friends and socialising with them frequently, and more frequent reading were all identified as protective against depression (Donald et al. 2000: 65). For young women, the same activities were protective, as well as participation in dance and more frequent watching of television.

Research into the perspectives of school-age young people on health matters has revealed that, for these young people, health is something to be achieved—by eating the right foods, by exercising, and by avoiding bad habits such as smoking, drug taking, and binge drinking (Easthope & White 2006). Well-being, on the other hand, is more a matter of who you hang around with and how close you are to your friends. While responsibility for health might be individualised, the context within which this responsibility is exercised is nevertheless social in nature. This is shown in the way in which well-being tends to predominate over health concerns in the actual behaviours of young people. Feeling good and feeling healthy, for example, seem to stem largely from being happy and comfortable in one's sense of well-being. This, in turn, is generated in and through one's social networks, which may also involve health-risking behaviours such as smoking or binge drinking. In other words, behaviours are more influenced by friends (who might smoke, say) than knowledge (of harmful effects of smoking, for example). Achieving health and well-being in this context is contingent upon having a circle of friends and a supportive family, and the behaviours associated with each of these.

Research on the health behaviour of young people (under the age of sixteen) reveals that they are generally very conscious of the need to achieve a balance in life in order to be healthy. Woodman (2004) argues that school-aged young people consciously struggle to balance the 'temporalities' of the future-oriented and pressured nature of school (becoming) with the need to experience the present (being). He shows how this often involves active choices about how to create a space for themselves through sport, music, drug use, and friendships.

For those older groups of young people who are beyond school age, issues of health and well-being tend to become a bit more complicated. The struggle to achieve a balance in life activities has been one theme in the Life-Patterns research, which found that: 'In addition to employment and education, other priorities regarding locality, living arrangements, lifestyle, experimentation, leisure and multiple personal commitments are also seen by them as part of their "human capital" and are already being taken into account in decisions about study and career outcomes' (Dwyer & Wyn 2001: 34).

Researchers in other countries have also noted the emphasis that young people place on having a balanced life. In the United Kingdom researchers have drawn attention to 'leisure-led identities'. Ball, Maquire, and Macrae (2000) quote a Coopers Lybrand survey that found that for many young people 'a rewarding life outside work was more important than pay and promotion' (Ball, Maquire & Macrae 2000: 65). They suggest that this response may be led by middle-class youth, who have greater access to leisure activities because of their privileged resource base.

Nonetheless, working-class youths' responses to the world they are living in are worth noting. Ball et al. comment that for the working-class young people in their study 'their social lives are not just sub-cultural practices, they are pivotal elements of their identities and are equal to, if not more important than, their educational selves' (Ball et al. 2000: 59).

These researchers conclude that there are three intersecting 'arenas of action and centres of choice' that are pivotal for young people: family, home, and domesticity; work, education, and training; and leisure and social life. The challenge, they suggest, is to include all three arenas in our thinking about young people and point out that young people's involvement and engagement in leisure is a 'silence' in the two most important areas of knowledge about young people — education and health.

But, following the ideas of Beck (1992), it may be more likely that the emphasis on leisure and balance is the expression of a generation (that Beck calls 'freedom's children') in which:

> the old and apparently eternal pattern of 'more income, more consumption, more career, more conspicuous consumption' is breaking up and being replaced by a new weighting of priorities, which may often be difficult to decipher, but in which immaterial factors of the quality of life play an outstanding part (Beck & Beck-Gernsheim 2002: 161).

Beck and Beck-Gernsheim (2002: 161) suggest that this new pattern means that control over a person's time is valued more highly than more income and more career success. This is because 'time is the key that opens the door to the treasures promised by the age of self-determined life: dialogue, friendship, being on one's own, compassion, fun and so on'.

Young people are themselves defining health and well-being in ways that move well beyond the traditional understandings and that challenge the organisations and jurisdictions that are charged with treating and preventing their ill-health. Young people are actively shaping new ways of living that set out patterns for living healthy lives because they have no other choice. Their concerns about how to live responsibly in a complex and diverse society are not answerable from the standpoint of current social and political institutions.

To return to the Life-Patterns study, it is not surprising that it found an emerging gap between the amount of time that young people were spending on their health and fitness and the amount of time they wanted to. Only 5 per cent of participants estimated that they spent most of their time on health and fitness, compared with 21 per cent who said they would prefer to spend most of their time on this area of their lives. Many of the participants took the opportunity to write about their feelings of frustration, regret, and perhaps guilt about their health:

> My health has taken a back seat to my career and now my health is suffering.

> After ten years of university education and nearing completion of a veterinary medicine residency to sit for specialist exams in three months I am exhausted. I watch no TV; have minimal social life no family life. I work at the hospital >100 hours a week and all other time is spent studying. I have achieved great things academically, but have studied continuously to the detriment of my life, family, health, fitness, and pleasure for the last fourteen years. I am tired!

> My concentration on work, partner and family/friends has left my fitness level and personal well-being less than where I would have hoped it would be. However, I'm currently changing this and allowing myself to be no. 1 priority so that my fitness improves.

More importantly, what these young people do not identify from their individual perspectives is that one of the effects of individualisation is constant, changing, and shifting pressure on people as they make choices and bear the responsibilities for them. The statistics on mental health problems suggest that the risk society may also be characterised as the anxiety society. For those who are able, and who have the good fortune to have a strong constitution or very good social supports, there are many opportunities among the wide variety of choices to be taken. But for those who are not so fortunate, the burden of individual choice and responsibility weighs heavily.

The next section explores the issues of young people's well-being and health by examining the assumptions that dominate health policy and programs.

DISCOURSES ON YOUTH HEALTH

Understandings of young people are framed in significant ways through ill-health discourses. This may seem ironic, given that, in general, young people are the healthiest group in our society. The focus on ill-health has contributed to policy approaches to young people that rely heavily on assumptions about youth as a group who are at risk and who require protection. Health policy approaches are also strongly influenced by economic rationalist thinking about targeting the health dollar to achieve efficient and effective outcomes. These assumptions are, in turn, based on the premise of futurity: the assumption that children and young people are of importance because of their future status as adults.

Youth health discourses are also connected to the processes of governmentality. In this section we provide an overview of these discourses and how they affect our thinking about young people and their health. The discourses tend to overlap, but for purposes of discussion it is useful to identify the following.

Economic assumptions

The discourses of health tend to be framed by economic-based assumptions about the 'burden' of ill health and the 'waste' of productive lives. The assumption is that young people are primarily of value because they represent economically productive adults in the future. In presenting the Australian government's vision for policies in health, Mallise, for example, comments that the failure of children to reach 'their full potential' has 'a significant burden of future cost, both economically and socially—to individuals, their families, and communities as well as to governments' (2001: 103). Concern about young people's health has led to a focus on investing in children and young people, as language draws on an approach that sees people largely in economic terms and seeks to quantify the optimal investment in children to ensure productive adults. From this perspective, researchers ask:

- How much parental time is necessary for the good health and well-being of children, both as children and as an investment in their adult outcomes?
- Does inequality in resources in childhood produce substantial avoidable inequality in adult outcomes?
- If some types of resources matter more in these respects than do others, and if so, which are they? (Richardson 2002)

The discourses of health tend to be framed by economic-based assumptions about the 'burden' of ill health and the 'waste' of productive lives.

While it may be possible to answer some of these questions, it is interesting to reflect on how useful the answers would be. To take the first question, how would one know the necessary time to invest for good health and well-being across the diversity of families in Australia? Would this lead to core and non-core functions of parenthood? Would the necessary amount of time for one generation be the same for the next? Information about these things would be difficult to interpret because health researchers and policy analysts have invested very little in understanding just what good health and well-being means.

Health and morality

Achieving and maintaining good health comes to carry moralistic overtones. In a society in which good health is seen as an individual responsibility, ill health is a form of failure on the part of the individual. Good health is achieved through making the right choices; eating unhealthy foods, failing to exercise enough, or becoming overweight are seen as evidence of failure to appropriately monitor the self. Catching a cold, for example, is evidence of failure to keep one's resistance at an appropriate level.

As well as being free of disease or ill-health, the individuals can demonstrate health through their appearance. Looking healthy is one way of demonstrating one's ability to manage a healthy identity. The evidence of good health can be displayed by being thin (for women), well muscled (for men), and through a range of interventions to the body, including tanning, plastic surgery, liposuction, and the use of botox. Young people are increasingly implicated in this process in which health becomes a commodity and are particularly the target of public concern about low levels of physical activity and increased levels of obesity (AIHW 2002).

Closely linked with morality is the issue of shame and health. If mental health is one's individual responsibility then to be unable to cope is to be positioned as abnormal and, worse, shameful. Young people who are simply not able to demonstrate that they can manage to project a coherent and healthy identity can be overcome by a shame that overshadows all else.

To make this link is not to say that young people are necessarily at risk. Indeed, recognising the social origins of health and well-being involves making a critique of the way in which the idea of risk in health has traditionally been linked to individuals. As Kelly (2001: 23) comments: 'The discourses of youth at risk seek to individualise the risks to the self that are generated in the institutionally structured risk environments of the risk society' (Beck 1992).

Health as an individual property

Defining health as a result of individual decisions and behaviours is a dominant theme in the literature on young people's health. In many reports and studies, ill-health is recorded in the minute details about hundreds of indicators, relating to all aspects of young people's individual behaviours and their bodies, behaviours such as drug use or binge drinking, and as individual properties such as chlamydia, depression, and cystic fibrosis. The standard approach is to collect information about individuals and then aggregate these variables across individuals and contexts. These aggregated ill-health statistics provide a broad profile across populations that can be used to identify trends.

At the same time, they tend to obscure patterns over time and across different contexts. The outcome is a lot of statistics and figures that do not necessarily tell us very much about how individuals and groups define, manage, and achieve well-being. Nor do they provide a basis for understanding why and how specific groups of young people experience problems.

Some researchers are beginning to use different ways of assessing health and well-being. Eckersley (2001), for example, has begun to identify the questions that need to be asked in order to explore the possible link between individualisation as a social process (as identified by Beck and others) and the levels of youth suicide that are causing concern. This line of questioning has led Eckersley and others to seek political rather than medical(ised) answers to the questions about various aspects of young people's ill-health, especially suicide. This means that rather than seeking linear, direct, causal relationships between life events of individuals and suicide behaviour, the focus is on the complex way in which shifts in the general qualities and meaning of life in a society influence individual behaviour. Taken from this perspective, health becomes a property not just of individuals, but also of social groups and whole societies.

Even when young people's struggles to establish a life and to belong are recognised, they are often reduced to the adolescent developmental issues. Hence, rather than recognising the full complexity of life, including the interrelationship between emotional, spiritual, mental, and physical well-being, young people's mental health is often reduced to the developmental journey towards becoming a self-managing, rational adult. The very distinction between mind and body, between mental, physical, and social elements of life for young people may be part of the problem, because they mask the real and complex struggles that young people have in making a life.

The tradition of defining health as an individual property leads to the use of measures of health outcomes as if they were a measurement of health. The focus on outcomes obscures the fact that health is a social process and that the measure of outcomes is not measuring the process; it is usually measuring the ill-health product of social processes that are not working well. As emphasised in a recent study of school-aged young people, even in the context of the ideological and material emphasis on individualisation and responsibilisation, what most counts in the development of positive mental and physical well-being are the social supports of family, work, schools, clubs, and services (Easthope & White 2006). When these are available, accessible, and youth-friendly, better health and well-being are more likely.

> The very distinction between mind and body, between mental, physical, and social elements of life for young people may be part of the problem, because they mask the real and complex struggles that young people have in making a life.

Risk and protective factors

The challenge of achieving a balance between individualised accounts of young people's health and social accounts is illustrated in the literature that focuses on risk and protective factors. Indeed, young people's health is almost universally discussed within a discourse of risk and protection. While there have been many critiques and analyses of the use of these concepts within education and youth studies (Kelly 2001; Wyn & White 1997), there is very little literature that problematises the concepts of risk and protection from a health perspective.

One of the effects of the measurement of individual ill-health is that researchers can identify patterns of behaviour and circumstances that are linked with negative health outcomes. These patterns come to be known as risk factors and are important because of their potential to provide a basis for predicting what conditions will compromise the health of individuals and groups. They offer an opportunity for health professionals to identify these associations as risks and to develop programs that will have the effect of intervening in the slide towards ill-health and negative outcomes and bringing the jeopardised youth back into the mainstream. As Kelly comments, all at-risk discourses are basically premised on 'probabilistic thinking about certain preferred or ideal adult futures' and the untested links between these futures and 'present behaviours and dispositions' of young people (Kelly 2001).

Even though this approach is commonly used in policy development in young people's health, it is very limited. It is one thing to identify factors that are associated with outcomes such as homelessness or mental illness; it is another to establish that they are causal. As Donald et al. point out in relation to young people's mental health: 'The approach of identifying risk and protective factors is inherently reductionist by nature, whereas in truth, mental health is complex, multifaceted and associated with a range of individual, familiar, social, community and cultural factors' (2000: 5).

The note of caution that these authors strike is relevant to all areas of youth health. The identification of risk and protective factors is useful for the development of prevention and early intervention strategies, and yet 'it is difficult to balance the utility of reductionism with the complex reality' (Donald et al. 2000: 5).

But complex reality is the basis for understanding how protective factors work. Well-being is associated with being able to express oneself, to feel connected with others, and to participate in a range of experiences not necessarily governed by standards of success and failure. Even the term 'protective' appears too limited to encompass the broader concept of developing an ethics of living in which a diversity of identifications is possible.

Governmentality

The threads of each of the above areas connect at some point with the concept of governmentality, a concept derived from French philosopher and historian Michel Foucault (1991) that refers to the sets of practices and techniques that make government possible, which include the ideas that provide the rationale for professionals to operate in the interests of young people in various settings: health, juvenile justice, and education. In each of these areas there is a body of knowledge and evidence base that enables professionals to operate with certainty about the dispositions, skills, and knowledge that young people will need in order to be normal adults and that enable them to intervene in young people's lives when necessary. One of the inevitable outcomes of this process is that youth are problematised and regulated. Illustrating this process, Roman (1996) discusses how a demonstration by young people in Canada is constructed by the government to create clear boundaries between normal and abnormal behaviour and to define the at-risk as not only risking their own futures but also the future of the nation.

From this perspective, the definition of at risk is one of the ways in which professionals associated with young people contribute to governmentality in that they create truths about young people's lives: about what is normal and deviant, healthy and unhealthy. In the area of health, such professionals are backed up by powerful technologies for measurement, identification, assessment, categorisation, and quantification. These constructed truths can have a powerful effect, positive and negative, on young people's lives. The identification of at-risk youth is intended to bring them into the mainstream but it can have the effect of stigmatising them as outsiders (Dwyer & Wyn 2001).

While the concept of governmentality provides a useful frame for understanding how discourses are shaped, it is also important to recognise that many young people do experience real problems. The critique of discourses on youth health raises the double-bind effect identified in Dwyer and Wyn (2001). Those who take young people's health problems seriously can be charged with fanning a public scare campaign; those who point out the element of moral panic can be accused of trivialising the real problems of youth.

Perhaps it is best to consider actual youth experiences of health problems and health services in determining the dynamics of youth health issues. Research into the health issue of young homeless people, for instance, has found that this population suffers from a range of illnesses common to teenagers (acne, respiratory complaints, headaches) but some of these were being left untreated or being inadequately treated. This group was also disproportionately over-represented in alcohol and other drug use, and had very poor quality and insufficient diets; not surprisingly, depressive ideas and fatigue are very prevalent among this group (Lovett 1994). There are clearly some major health issues here that do require some type of interventionist measures.

From the point of view of health services, young homeless people frequently see these as part of the problem (see White 1998b). This is especially the case when health professionals lack awareness of and training in health issues likely to be encountered in homeless young people. Institutional issues include those of gaining informed consent in cases of under-age young people when there is lack of access to parents and guardians. Importantly, there are frequently feelings of distrust, hostility, or anger on the part of homeless young people towards health service providers because of status, authority, and differences in social position. Moreover, many young people cannot cope with, or are angry about, rejecting attitudes on the part of health or medical workers on the basis of language, hygiene, dress, behaviour, literacy, drug use, and tattoos (National Health and Medical Research Council 1992).

Alternative ways of delivering health services to young people are needed that would take into account youth experiences of health services. A few suggestions in this area include such things as: listen—to be useful, the first thing a health-care professional needs to do is to listen to what the young people have to say; let young people know that you are able to provide advice and information about other health matters (or to refer them to someone who is appropriate); bring medical staff up to date on current popular youth cultures; and buy and read magazines directed at young people and leave them in the waiting area (Tressider 1996).

Health, as defined by the World Health Organization, refers to the complete physical, mental, and social well-being of people. Health services need to understand these dimensions, as lived out at a practical level, in order to assist those young people who require their assistance.

Summary

This chapter began with the case study of Sue whose story emphasises the seriousness with which many young people are taking their own well-being. Our discussion links this consciousness with a social climate in which individuals must make difficult decisions and choices about all areas of their lives. Health has not traditionally been seen as one of the key elements in decision making; it is education and employment that have tended to dominate thinking about young people's transitions to adulthood. But now there is emerging evidence from Australian and overseas literature that for older youth a constellation of health and personal development concerns has joined the education–work duo.

There is an overwhelming mass of evidence to show that, despite being the educated generation, there are some areas in which young people's health is of concern. The chapter identifies a number of these areas and focuses on mental health as one of the areas in which young people's health is worsening. Mental health is also one of the areas that young people themselves define as an area of concern.

Yet, as the discussion demonstrates, the ways in which health is discussed and identified may itself be part of the problem. The chapter identifies how discourses of health can be bad for young people's health. A focus on ill-health outcomes and on health as an individual property distracts attention from the fact that well-being is produced through social processes. The social processes become trivialised and marginalised by approaches that focus exclusively on the effects of these processes—the outcomes.

Health discourses provide a dominant framework through which youth is defined in our society. This chapter identifies some of the ways that this occurs: through the association of health with individual moral responsibility; the discourses on at-risk and protective factors; and the use of economic approaches to health. In each of these areas, youth health can be understood as part of a process of governmentality that positions youth as future adults and provides the boundaries of normal and abnormal youth behaviour that frame the work of many youth professionals. Finally, it is acknowledged that young people's experiences and narratives provide an important touchstone in understanding youth health.

Questions for further exploration

1   What is the difference between health and well-being?

2   Individuals are responsible for their health, but health is always a social process. Discuss.

3   Most young people have excellent health. Why?

4   What are the key problem areas in regards to young people's health and well-being? Are these specific only to young people?

5   Why are the perspectives of the lay person so important to research on issues associated with health, illness, and well-being?

QUESTIONS

CONSTRUCTING A PUBLIC PRESENCE

15

Introduction

Much of the cultural life of cities and towns today takes place in inner-city and suburban shopping centres. As well as being major sites of commercial consumption, these centres attract flows of people from many different social backgrounds; they are exciting places to hang out, with entertainment centres and fast-food outlets, and are easily accessible by public transport services. For many young people the construction of social identity is intertwined with being in a public place and exhibiting a noticeable presence among their peers. To be seen, and to watch others, is part of a ritual process of identity formation and affirmation.

The growing importance of the city as a site of social identity is due to a range of factors, including the need for community connection in an increasingly globalised social environment. In his study of youth patterns of going out in Newcastle, England, Hollands (1995: 1) observes that economic restructuring has had major effects on work, education, and domestic identities, and that the city has an increasing role in shaping young people's experiences. He argues that: 'The shift from these more traditional sites of identities to increased identification with the city through consumption, and their participation in extended socialising rituals, represents a broader response and re-adjustment by young people to "modernity" and post-industrialism'. Hollands (1995: 18–19) points to several factors that affect the relationship of Newcastle young people with city life:

> First, it is a 'public space' in the sense that going out is a visible display of identity. Second, urban regeneration, in terms of leisure, public entertainment and the redevelopment of clubs and pubs, occurred in the same time frame as the region experienced its most rapid economic decline. And finally, this new consumption space did not readily discriminate against either students or the local population on the basis of age, class or gender criteria, and many young adults responded by appropriating sections of the city by claiming them as their own.

While city space has its attractions and compelling qualities for many young people, economic status has an impact on how they experience the city and how others view them.

From the point of view of commercial consumption, say, many young people today are considered to be worthless. They are unable or unwilling to purchase the goods and services on offer in the commercial spaces. Yet they use the consumer spaces as public spaces for their own purposes. Often this involves the production of noise, literally and figuratively.

The position of young people as consumers—or as non-consumers—is a major factor in how they are treated institutionally within commercial settings, and in how young people themselves relate to shopping centre environments.

It means being who they are through adoption of particular kinds of dress and language, demonstrating certain kinds of style by acting in particular ways, of establishing themselves as beings with social worth in a wider societal context than that which emphasises financial value.

The position of young people as consumers—or as non-consumers—is a major factor in how they are treated institutionally within commercial settings and in how young people themselves relate to shopping centre environments. For those without adequate economic resources to buy consumer goods, there are strong pressures to engage in alternative consumption activity, which, in dealing with their lack of consumer purchasing power, takes the form of taking the possessions of others (Adamson 1998). The exclusion from the legitimate spheres of production (that is, paid work) and thus exclusion from other forms of legitimate identity formation (as workers), also forces attention to alternative sites where social identity can be forged. In particular, if social identity and social belonging have been made problematic due to institutional exclusion from paid work and commodity consumption, then the appeal of street culture and the street scene becomes clear.

YOUTH SPACES IN THE PUBLIC DOMAIN

The public presence of young people is intertwined with the rise of consumerism, the mass privatisation of public space, and the intensification of the regulation of that space (Davis 1990; Chatterton & Hollands 2003; White 2007c). The use of public space by low-income, marginal groups of young people has been accompanied by concerted efforts to make them invisible in the urban landscape. The response of state police and private security firms to their presence in the commercial spaces of shopping centres, for example, has been to move them on, to exclude them from community life and participation (see White & Alder 1994; Chatterton & Hollands 2003). Thus the use of space itself has increasingly been constructed around the notion of space as a commodity—those with the resources have access, those without do not. This process of social exclusion is not neutral. It is primarily directed at the most marginalised sections of the youth population. There is also much resistance on the part of young people to these pressures, as they strive to carve out a space of their own, symbolically and territorially.

A further aspect of social identity formation is the unavoidable fact that many young people in contemporary society are alienated from mainstream institutions. Why be respectful of others when others do not respect you, just because you are unemployed, or poor, or different? Why make an effort to conform, when the collapse of opportunity has meant that conformity no longer guarantees social rewards (if it ever did)? And why allow yourself to be pushed out of public areas when, through no fault of your own, you do not have enough money and there are no other places to go?

The mass privatisation of public space and the transformation of community space into commercial space (Sandercock 1997) has meant a considerable narrowing of places where young people can comfortably hang out freely. Simultaneously, the public visibility of young people has been heightened by the concentrations of people into more select gathering places (malls, train stations, shopping centres), by the fact that young people tend to hang around in groups, and by the diversity of social and economic circumstances in which young people find themselves. Concern has also been expressed over unpoliced or unwatched places (such as beaches or parks after dark) that have not been privatised, but that are associated with the activities of young people.

Accompanying the visibility of young people have been rising public perceptions that young people, especially those in disadvantaged social positions, are engaging in more antisocial behaviour and criminal activity. The fear of crime in recent years has largely stemmed from a fear of young people (see Bessant & Hil 1997). Simultaneously, state responses to perceived criminality have also been based on concerns to protect and care for young people. This is particularly so in cases where young people are seen to be vulnerable to victimisation by others, or to being drawn into criminal activity by virtue of their disadvantaged situation.

Public space, including the street as broadly defined, is one of the few havens for young people who want to please themselves about what they do, when they do it, and with whom (even though they are subject to numerous restrictions). The street is 'free in both commercial terms and in terms of close control' (Corrigan 1979: 123) and offers young people a degree of power and freedom not found in many other institutional contexts (White 1990). As a place to hang out, public space refers to a wide range of specific locations, places where young people have a degree of room to move, as well as to watch and interact with their peers and others. Public space as a concept can also include cyberspace as another zone in which young people can likewise find freedom and test boundaries (see Chapter 13). Conversely, it is not uncommon for young people to complain about issues such as lack of adequate seating, no sheltered areas, inadequate skating facilities, a feeling that they had to purchase something in order to be there, bad lighting, inadequate transport, legal restrictions such as being too young to go to nightclubs, and harassment from authority figures as factors affecting youth satisfaction with public places and venues (White 1999a).

In addition to highlighting the common issues and problems many young people experience in their uses of public space, it is important to acknowledge the specific character of different kinds of space. One way to do this is to distinguish between youth-specific and youth-friendly amenities and why each dimension plays an important part in how young people experience and use public space. Youth-specific amenities refer to those venues and amenities that young people themselves feel are most interesting, accessible, and suitable for them, and that reflect their particular needs and desires for entertainment and recreation. Youth-friendly amenities refer to venues or amenities of all types, where the general atmosphere is one in which young people are treated with respect and dignity, and where they feel safe, secure, and welcome.

Youth-specific amenities

Where public amenities are located is a significant factor in how and where young people spend their time. A Brisbane study highlighted the importance of appreciating the localised nature of access to public amenities and spaces. Young people were asked whether or not there were enough things to do in their local area for people of their age. The venues and amenities referred to included:

- swimming pool
- library
- shopping malls
- video store

- movies
- fast-food outlets
- video/games arcade
- parks/sports ground (Lynch & Ogilvie 1999).

It was found that ease of access to amenities was consistently related by young people to a sense of having enough or not enough to do. Importantly, very few respondents experienced a general lack of amenities, although some specific amenities may be hard to access, and others are easier to access. In general, the Brisbane study seemed to indicate that access to amenities could have an indirect effect on potential offending behaviour insofar as it affected the level of satisfaction young people had of things to do. This is important, in that the Brisbane study also found that young people who felt there was not enough to do in their neighbourhood were more likely to offend than those who were satisfied with their neighbourhood.

In a Melbourne study, young people were asked where they spent most of their time (White et al. 1997). It is notable that the most frequent responses were 'home' and 'at a friend's place'. Here it can be emphasised that, while the public debates over young people tend to centre on their activities in public spaces, the primary place of social interaction is in fact the private space of the home. Further to this, when young people do venture out into the public domain it becomes even more important that they have youth-specific places to congregate in. Likewise, the content of their activities in the public sphere has to represent something of a break from a usually more controlled and regulated home environment—that is, there has to be something of excitement or interest beyond the mundane routines and regimes of family life.

It ought to be acknowledged as well that the home is also a key site for Internet connection, which includes various forms of telecommunication and web browsing, and is thus a major portal to the world outside (see Chapter 13). In cyberspace the social boundaries are fluid, and personal experiences as initiator and receiver are varied. But physical activities outside of this space and outside of close parental control demand that, eventually and at some stage, young people find alternative venues outside of their home.

Consistent with other contemporary studies (see, for example, Crane 2000), the Melbourne research found that shopping centres were by far the most likely places where young people hang out with their friends when they do venture out into public places. A distinction can be made here between access to a general amenity, such as a shopping centre, and access to youth-specific amenities, such as a games arcade. It is an important distinction because while young people in the Melbourne study indicated ready access to shopping centres, they simultaneously indicated that they get bored there. Indeed, almost 80 per cent of the respondents said they get bored.

> While the public debates over young people tend to centre on their activities in public spaces, the primary place of social interaction is in fact the private space of the home.

As well as in shopping centres, the Melbourne study found that when they go out, young people also tend to hang around in groups in other public spaces such as commercial venues and the street. Where they go and how they spend their time is intimately related to neighbourhood level provision of amenities. The availability of public transport, leisure services, recreational facilities, parks, open-air plazas, gardens, and so on has major implications for a young person's 'pride of place', their attachment to neighbourhood institutions such as schools, and their preferred social activities (White et al. 1997).

The first question of access is whether certain amenities are available at a local level. A related issue is whether amenities, wherever they are located, are designed specifically with youth interests or needs in mind or if they incorporate within them youth-specific activities. Ideally, provision of youth-specific amenities would include activity-based venues or programs and, more simply, social spaces in which young people can do nothing in comfort and safety.

Youth-friendly amenities

Access to amenities is not simply about the physical presence or otherwise of certain types of facilities and spaces. It also has a social dimension. A crucial issue here is the conditions under which young people can actually use certain amenities and the conditions under which they actually view an amenity—whether it is youth-friendly, which revolves around questions of money and social status.

In a survey of young people in Melton (Victoria), the following places were identified as being favourite places to go to or hang out:

- friends and their homes/family
- parks and reserves
- cinema
- sport-related activity
- pub
- fast-food outlets
- bowling
- places to skate and rollerblade
- waves facility
- shops
- arcade/snooker hall (Wooden 1997).

The young people participating in the survey were asked to identify key criteria for what makes a place youth-friendly or youth-unfriendly. Youth-friendly criteria include such things as type of people, acceptance, friendly people, environment, good entertainment, no violence or threats to safety, and cheap food and drinks. An unfriendly place was characterised by bad service and location, being treated badly by staff, fights and feeling unsafe, drugs and alcohol, police present, and being alone as a teenager in such a place.

It is important, as well, to consider how the functions or basic institutional rationale of a space often has a lot to do with how the place is used by young people and how proprietors respond to them.

The primary purpose of shopping centres, for example, is commercial business. As such, the public space of these institutions is more aptly defined as 'commercial space', even if access is open to the public at large. The legitimate use of such space is constructed around the buyer–seller cash nexus. Those who have the money are allowed to purchase the goods and services on offer. It is well known that those without are often the target for concerted campaigns to exclude them from the shopping centre precincts, which is a constant theme throughout research into youth and public space (see White 1994). It highlights the dearth of non-commercial activities available for many young people, and indicates the potential difficulties they face when congregating in venues that are based upon money transactions. This can be a very frustrating experience, one that is exacerbated by the heavy-handed interventions of authority figures who attempt to move young people on, regardless of whether there are viable alternative places to go.

Part of the issue of access has to do with whether young people are made to feel that they are a bona fide part of a community or whether they are perceived as threats to it. Part of the Brisbane research cited earlier (Lynch & Ogilvie 1999) involved examination of the uses of the only local pool in an economically disadvantaged neighbourhood. Pool management had instituted a policy that T-shirts could not be worn in the pool. Many of those wishing to use the facility were Indigenous young people, for whom wearing a T-shirt constituted a culturally appropriate expression of personal modesty. But apart from any cultural considerations, there are also practical aspects to wearing a T-shirt: wearing a baggy T-shirt constitutes a reasonably effective sun protection strategy, particularly for those who do not buy sun screen (which has important health and financial implications). In addition, in the middle of summer, walking home from the pool in a wet T-shirt is an eminently practical way of staying cool just that little bit longer. By forbidding T-shirts, the pool authorities immediately disenfranchised a significant proportion of the local young people.

> Those who have the money are allowed to purchase the goods and services on offer … those without are often the target for concerted campaigns to exclude them from the shopping centre precincts.

Rightly or wrongly, this policy was interpreted as a deliberate tactic of exclusion, consistent with the day-to-day racism many of these young people continually experience. Whether there were sound reasons for the pool management's decision was irrelevant to the young people: the policy was interpreted by them as meaning the pool was not theirs.

A consistent theme in much of the literature dealing with young people's use of public space is that young people rarely gain a sense of ownership when it comes to the use of amenities (Lynch & Ogilvie 1999). At one level, the availability of amenities such as swimming pools, rollerblading rinks, and non-commercial public spaces enables young people to familiarise themselves with the feeling of being autonomous. In other words, such venues and facilities provide an opportunity for young people to interact with their peers without close family or state control. These interactions form an important part of the process of identity formation, separate from those constrained and determined by their family situation.

At another level, the opportunities to further develop themselves and their own relationship with the wider social world are often restricted by the actions of the institutional providers of amenities and public spaces, which takes the form of unnecessarily restrictive rules in the use of some amenities, the presence of security apparatus and personnel, the active intervention of state police and private security guards in their affairs (regardless of whether a criminal act has occurred), and general media treatment that suggests that young people have no real value or place in the larger scheme of things. All these elements can transform general community amenities, even youth-specific amenities, into youth-unfriendly spaces.

CULTURAL SPACE AND SOCIAL TRANSGRESSION

Young people in Western countries spend a lot of time in the public domain of the street. The street is significant in the lives of most young people, regardless of social background (White 1990). Different groups of young people use public space for very different reasons. For some young people their presence on the street and engagement with street cultures is of a passing and transient nature. For many others the street becomes an important and often central feature of their daily routines and living. Any categorisation or classification of young people using public spaces is always going to be problematic, given the diverse and overlapping nature of youth peer groups, activities, and personal situations. A rough indication of how young people use the street is useful in explaining why and how moral panics over the public presence of young people periodically emerge. The groups that have received the most media and police attention in Australia, Canada, the USA, and other Western countries are the street kids and youth gangs (Sercombe 1999; Hermer & Mosher 2002; Venkatesh & Kassimir 2007).

> Any categorisation or classification of young people using public spaces is always going to be problematic, given the diverse and overlapping nature of youth peer groups, activities, and personal situations.

Street kids

There are major ambiguities and conceptual issues associated with the term 'street kid' (Wilson & Arnold 1986; White 1990; Tait 1993; McDonald 1999). Nevertheless, the label does give some indication that the children so labelled are in some way on the margins of society. For some young people the street is a temporary site used for recreation or adventure-seeking, but not as the sole or permanent living space. These users of public space have been described by Pe-Pua as 'street-frequenting youth' (1996). For others, the street may represent an escape from authority and abuses of the parental home or welfare institutions, an escape that may eventually separate them from support networks and secure, safe home environments. These young people may be labelled as 'homeless youth'.

Definitions of the young homeless generally refer to teenage children who have no safe, secure accommodation. There are several formal definitions referred to in the literature (see Prime Ministerial Youth Homeless Taskforce 1996; House of Representatives Standing Committee on Community Affairs 1995), with the following as probably the best synthesis of the main ideas (House of Representatives Standing Committee on Community Affairs 1995: 26):

Young people are homeless if they are living without any family assistance in the following circumstances:

(a) no accommodation at all (for example, streets, squat, car, tent etc.);

(b) only temporary accommodation (with friends, relatives or moving around between various forms of temporary shelter);

(c) emergency accommodation (refuge or crisis accommodation etc.); and

(d) other long term supported accommodation for homeless people (for example, hostels, youth housing programs, transitional accommodation).

Homelessness is a social process that involves degrees of separation from family and progressive self-identification with one's situation. It involves much moving around and a lack of emotional and supportive contact with immediate family. A key site for social engagement is the street.

Other users of the street may not necessarily be considered homeless. While many young people use the street as the major source of social interaction and contact, not all of them are homeless; nor are they street kids (in the sense of being forced to spend most of their time around street-related activity). The nature of street-frequenting behaviour is, in fact, highly variable and involves a wide range of positive as well as negative experiences, depending on the immediate circumstances of the young person in question (Pe-Pua 1996).

For present purposes, the main concern is with those young people who are in marginalised social and economic situations, and who spend a large amount of their time on the street, including unemployed young people. It includes street-frequenting, non-English-speaking young people (see Pe-Pua 1996), young Indigenous street kids who suffer from unstable homes and uncertainties about their care-giving environment (Brady 1991), a sizeable proportion of young gay men, who often experience particular family difficulties related to coming out (Costigan 1996), and young people from a wide variety of social backgrounds (McDonald 1999).

At a descriptive level, many commentators have identified factors such as family conflict, sexual and physical abuse, substance abuse, and so on as the reasons for the street presence and/or homelessness of some young people (Burdekin 1989; House of Representatives Standing Committee on Community Affairs 1995). In addition, the behaviour of these young people has been scrutinised from the point of view of actions that put them at risk of serious health problems (for example, injecting drug use), and various attitudes have been noted that reinforce risk-taking behaviour (aggressive masculinity, for example).

While recognising the importance of describing the features of this group, it can be argued that addressing this social problem demands a response that places greater attention on the nature and operation of mainstream institutions (such as police practices, schooling, and social work) rather than on marginalised youth.

The presence of marginalised young people in the public domain is viewed by some as problematic for a range of reasons, including:

- lack of ability to purchase goods and services
- general attire and appearance
- begging and pestering behaviour is annoying
- constant reminder of inequality and poverty
- association with drugs and prostitution
- seen to be lazy, without discipline or drive to improve themselves
- potentially threatening because of dress and condition
- characterised as 'feral' children who live outside boundaries of normal citizens
- antisocial, anti-authority, and disrespectful
- dangerous, immoral, and unpredictable.

The notion of an urban youth underclass has been intertwined with conservative behavioural perspectives that essentially see such young people as social threats (Wyn & White 1997). Such a perspective focuses on the social deviance and apparent criminality associated with extensive use of the streets. The young people are portrayed as the problem, and the solution is usually framed in a highly coercive framework stressing law and order measures of some kind, such as youth curfews.

In fact, the evidence is that young people who live on the streets or use the streets extensively are usually victims of various kinds of personal harm or abuse (Halstead 1992). They are also more likely to feel threatened and to experience actual violence against their person because of where they spend most of their time and due to their lack of resources. Life on the street has been described in the following terms (Davis, Hatty & Burke 1995: 99): 'Being tough, being independent, minding your own business, never reporting crime and violence to the police, keeping your personal belongings with you at all times, being loyal to mates, and above all being "cool" and ever-vigilant are precautionary measures against ongoing predatory street behaviour.'

In this context, being streetwise means finding ways to cope with the violence and exploitation, and the sense of despair and isolation associated with the hardships of the street (see White 1990; McDonald 1999). Any crimes they commit tend to be for basic survival necessities or are associated with substance-related habits (which in turn usually stem from attempts to deal with traumatic life experiences). When it comes to public space issues, a central question always remains—where else can they go?

Youth street groups and cultures

Considerable media attention has been paid to the alleged problem of youth gangs in Western cities in recent years (see Klein et al. 2001). Confusions over the status of youth gangs in the Australian context stem in part from the lack of adequate conceptual tools to analyse youth group behaviour. Recent work in Canada provides a useful series of benchmarks, especially considering the many similarities in social structure and cultural life between the two countries. Based on work done in Vancouver, Gordon (1997) has developed a typology of group formations (see Gordon 1995, 1997) that consists of six categories:

- youth movements, which are social movements characterised by a distinctive mode of dress or other bodily adornments, a leisure-time preference, and other distinguishing features (for example, punk rockers)
- youth groups, which are comprised of small clusters of young people who hang out together in public places such as shopping centres (sometimes referred to as 'Mallies')
- criminal groups, which are small clusters of friends who band together, usually for a short period of time, to commit crime, primarily for financial gain (may contain young and not so young adults as well)
- wannabe groups, which include young people who band together in a loosely structured group primarily to engage in spontaneous social activity and exciting, impulsive, criminal activity, including collective violence against other groups of youths (territorial and use identifying markers of some kind)

▥ street gangs, which are groups of young people and young adults who band together to form a semi-structured organisation, the primary purpose of which is to engage in planned and profitable criminal behaviour or organised violence against rival street gangs (less visible but more permanent than other groups)

▥ criminal business organisations, which are groups that exhibit a formal structure and a high degree of sophistication, comprised mainly of adults; these groups engage in criminal activity primarily for economic reasons and almost invariably maintain a low profile (may have a name but are rarely visible).

What is known about street gangs in Australia seems to confirm that their actual, rather than presumed, existence is much less than popularly believed and that their activities are highly circumscribed in terms of violence or criminal activity directed at members of the general public (Collins et al. 2000; White et al. 1999; White 2002c, 2006a). Nevertheless, the image of gangs is a powerful one and has engendered varying kinds of social reactions. The social status and public perception of young people in groups very much influences the regulation of public space. Many groups of young people, some of which might be labelled gangs, tend to hang out in places like shopping centres. Difficulties in providing a precise or uniform definition of what a gang actually is, and the diversity of youth dress, language, and behaviour associated with specific subcultural forms (goths, punks), means that more often than not young people are treated as outsiders by commercial managers and authority figures on the basis of appearance, not solely on actual behaviour.

The combination of being bored and feeling unwelcome in such public domains can have a negative impact on the young people and make them resentful of the way in which they are always subject to scrutiny and social exclusion. This, in turn, can lead to various kinds of 'deviant' behaviour, as in the case of young people who play cat-and-mouse with security guards for the fun of it. It is unfortunate that the perception of gang membership may lead to exclusion or negative responses from authority figures, and that this in turn may itself generate gang-like behaviour on the part of the young people so affected.

To a certain extent, the concern about gangs is really a misunderstanding of the nature of youth subcultures, of how young people naturally associate with each other in groups, and of the material opportunities open to them to circulate and do things in particular places. The diversity of youth subcultural forms, especially the spectacular youth subcultures, has historically been a source of consternation among certain sections of the adult population (Hall & Jefferson 1976; Brake 1985; Stratton 1992; White 1993a, 1999b). It has also been associated with conflicts between different groups of young people and youth fearfulness of certain young people based on certain social and cultural affiliations (for example, homies, surfies, skinheads, punks). In most cases, the presence of identifiable groups is not the precursor to activity that is going to menace the community as a whole.

> To a certain extent, much of the concern about gangs is really a misunderstanding of the nature of youth subcultures, of how young people naturally associate with each other in groups, and of the material opportunities open to them to circulate and do things in particular places.

Still, the congregation of many different groups of young people from diverse social and cultural backgrounds does occasionally flare into street conflicts that range from name-calling through to more serious instances of personal harm. Antagonisms between groups of young people on the basis of race and ethnicity, for instance, have been noted around Australia and are reflected ideologically in moral panics over ethnic youth gangs and, materially, in the Cronulla beach riots of December 2005, which saw mob attacks on any youth of 'Middle Eastern appearance' (White 2006a; Poynting & Morgan 2007).

Violence against gay men and lesbians by groups of young men is also a significant social problem (Mason & Tomsen 1997). There is considerable evidence that violence against people who do not exhibit a strong adherence to heterosexual behaviour norms (regardless of actual personal sexual preferences) is above average compared with the rest of the population (Standing Committee on Social Issues 1995; Mason & Tomsen 1997; Mason 2002). In many cases young people are the targets and the perpetrators of this violence, much of which occurs in the public domain—on the street, in parks, and on beaches. Street violence of this nature can make young people in general feel unsafe and in need of protection when they venture out of their own homes and neighbourhoods.

One of the signal features of contemporary uses of public space by young people is the sheer diversity of groups and activities associated with the street. Street dancers still make their mark, but even so, much of the dance scene has moved inside to the clubs (Forrester 1993; Redhead 1997). Raves are mainstreamed and legalised, due in part to moral panics over drugs such as ecstasy and increasing middle-class youth involvement in the rave scene (Chan 1999). Meanwhile, hip hop becomes institutionalised and incorporated into the global commercial music industry, and breakdancing becomes a dance-floor competition that somehow transcends and leaves behind its gritty street origins.

Music and dance

Yet even in the midst of forces pressing for uniformity, conformity and safety, the street remains the haven for those who wish to resist and transgress the mainstream cultural norm. Hip hop lives differently here. It continues to reflect its roots in oppression and to give voice to the marginalised and dispossessed in many different national contexts. The suburbs of western Sydney thus see the appropriation of hip hop culture among many different ethnic minority youth (d'Souza & Iveson 1999). The beat—and the message—still resonate strongly among those who occupy the margins (Mitchell 2003).

Meanwhile, dance becomes a political act in its own right, at least in the hands of the FreeNRG counterculture (St John 2002). Technology meets politics meets pleasure, as the new technotribes of late capitalism challenge restrictions on public uses of space and the commodification of art. The task is to liberate space—physical, social, and spiritual—and this means taking back to the people what is seen to be rightfully theirs. It means organising, from the grassroots up, events, music, networks, and all forms of cultural production outside and/or in opposition to the dominant capitalist agenda.

Graffiti

So, too, graffiti continues to hold attractions for those who seek to be in a landscape that is so often hostile to their needs and, indeed, to their presence. Graffiti takes many different forms and is associated with different instrumental purposes—from political slogans to gang territoriality to artistic creation to identity tagging (White 2001). For some young people, the graffiti gang is a vital social connection in their lives. The graffiti experience represents an important 'identity-securing form of action', something that confirms who one is and their presence in the urban setting (McDonald 1999). The act of graffiti-ing is about making meaning; about constructing subjectivity that makes sense to the author. The marking of the surface is at one and the same time an ontological statement—I graffiti, therefore I exist. According to some writers, such activities are also intrinsically political. As Ferrell (1997: 22) puts it:

> Within relationships of power, inequality, and marginalization, the control of cultural space is contested: while powerful adults attempt to define and impose cultural space, less powerful young people attempt to unravel this imposition, to carve out their own spaces for shaping identity and taking some control over everyday life. For kids who work to create cultural space within dominant arrangements, this space may indeed be physical—a teenager's bedroom, an inner-city street corner—but almost always physical space is constructed as a relatively independent zone of identity through symbolic displays, stylized details, and ritualized activities.

In this analytical framework, the message is: I graffiti, therefore I resist. That to which resistance is directed is the increasing ways in which everyday life is being regulated and rationalised, from rules regarding how to dress and act in the local shopping centre through to what happens in the privacy of the bedroom (Presdee 2000). From the perspective of cultural criminology, vandalism, graffiti, drug use, and other types of ostensibly antisocial behaviour are best interpreted as meaningful attempts to transgress the ordinary and the given. In a world of standardised diversity and global conformities, it is exciting and pleasurable to break the rules, to push the boundaries, to engage in risky and risk-taking activities. Transgressions of this nature are one way in which the marginalised can attain a sense of identity and commonality in a world that already has turned its back on them (Hayward 2002).

Taking and making spaces of one's own is never a straightforward or simple social process. It involves adaptation to local conditions and environments, as when skateboarders reconceptualise the physical landscape of the city to best match their perceptions and uses of street furniture and building architecture (see Snow 1999). Somewhere to sit, a bench, is transformed into that which is skated on, over, or along. But this process also involves various types of social exclusion: I sit, therefore you cannot skate. I skate, therefore you cannot sit.

Transgression is never socially neutral. It involves different understandings of the environment and also involves potential conflicts of interest, not only between marginalised youth and powerful adults (see Ferrell, above), but among and between young people generally.

The dual character of street use, which may be good and bad for young people, is highlighted especially when the specific case of young women is considered.

Transgression is never socially neutral. It involves different understandings of the environment, but it also involves potential conflicts of interest, not only between marginalised youth and powerful adults, but among and between young people generally.

Young women and public space

The use of public spaces by young women in general is problematic, partly due to gender differences in how such spaces are socially constructed and partly because fear of victimisation has such a strong negative impact on how young women access and use public space. Young women and young men tend to do different kinds of things with their time. Several recent studies have provided an indication of the nature of these differences, and of the issues young women see as most important with regard to public space use.

A Melbourne study examined gender differences in the use of public space (White et al. 1997). Young people's perceptions of gender differences are summarised in Table 15.1.

TABLE 15.1 Young people's perceptions of gender differences in the activities of young men and women

Young men	Young women
Guys go out/do more	Girls stay home more
Guys play more sport	Girls more into shops/clothes
Guys do alcohol/drugs more	Girls talk more
Guys get into trouble more	

Source: adapted from White et al. 1997: 86.

The Melbourne research found that young women were perceived to have very different social interests from young men, and most of these tended to be seen in terms of traditional or conventional understandings of gender (for example, girls like shopping, boys like sports). Young people tended to see each other in terms of more passive categories for young women (for example, they like to talk) and expressive categories for young men (for example, they like to do things). This was reflected in various comments by the young people:

> Boys are more into sports. If they get bored they go and play basketball, footy or soccer. Us girls usually sit around and talk.

> Boys hang out in youth centres and play games like pinball and the girls do but not as much. Girls are less active—they just walk around the city and sit in one place.

Young people in rural locations have very similar perceptions of city space as being highly gendered in these ways. A recent study quotes one sixteen-year-old boy from a small fishing town, who commented:

> Boys are more into physical stuff, surfing and stuff, while girls are more into not physical stuff. Like just shopping. I reckon girls would fit in better in the city than in the country' (Kenway et al. 2006: 103).

Boys talk too, but again, there appears to be differences in how they interact with each other compared with the young women (White et al 1997):

> Guys sit around, watch TV, smoke. Guys talk a lot—too much and too loud. They aren't happy unless they've got all the little luxuries around them—food, drink, comfy seat—everything they want. Girls—it doesn't worry them. Guys laze around, all they're interested in is guys—the other guys. Girls run around more.

One of the most sustained and systematic examinations of how young women use and experience public space is provided by the Girls in Space project in Brisbane (Girls in Space

Consortia 1997), research that identified a range of factors that impact on young women's leisure practices. It also noted significant class and ethnic differences in how different groups of young women relate to leisure time and public space activities.

The general findings of this research were that young women had less leisure satisfaction than young men, they had more restrictions placed on their leisure time and options by parents, and that their activities were further restricted by young men's use and dominance of recreational spaces and facilities. As the research noted (Girls in Space Consortia 1997: 14):

> Young women interviewed in this study often discussed problems with young men dominating spaces and facilities. Many felt that entry into informal public spaces and use of facilities was often dependent upon the nature of their relationship with male users. For some young women, facilities were easier to access if young men who used those facilities were a part of their social network.

It was found that young women spend most of their recreational time indoors, and that the only spaces they felt any control over were their bedrooms and their playground territories at school. Research on girls' graffiti (Carrington 1989) reinforces the notion that certain women's-only spaces (in this case, railway station toilet blocks) are perceived as safe havens, while public space in general tends to be male-dominated.

The Brisbane research covered a range of issues and made a number of observations regarding young people's participation in public space (Girls in Space Consortia 1997: 28–29). These included the following:

- Young men currently dominate the use of youth-oriented public spaces and public facilities, tend to be highly skilled in the use of these spaces, and often feel a sense of ownership or control of these spaces.

- Networking plays an important role in the recreational lives of young women, and they are attracted to activities that provide them with opportunities to meet other people.

- Factors such as sexual harassment and other sexist behaviour, intolerance of difference, groups of drunk men, poor lighting, isolation, and mass media representations of female 'victims' impact upon young women's sense of personal safety in public spaces.

- Public transport does not adequately cater for young women's safety needs, particularly at night.

- Ethnic, socioeconomic, educational, and geographic backgrounds influence the experiences that young women have in public spaces, as indicated in racism being a problem for some young women, and lack of access to money preventing others from having greater access to safer recreational activities.

- The influence that parents/custodians have on girls' perceptions of and access to public spaces is considerable.

- Barriers to girls' access to public space may be influenced by diversity of people types and activity types within those spaces.

The research project concluded that:

Spaces that are designed with young women's personal safety needs as well as their aesthetic and social needs, are more likely to be utilised by young women. Young women in this study suggested that to better cater for their needs, public spaces needed to cater for their diversity of recreational and cultural activities from arts and sports based activity to less structured leisure activities such as talking with friends. Design strategies for public spaces may include functional solutions such as strategically placed seating areas, cheap food and drink and adequate lighting. The development of a 'female aesthetic' within design processes however, is also vital to the quality of the relationships that future female users will have with public spaces (Girls in Space Consortia 1997: 27).

There are clearly a number of issues here that need further investigation and consideration. Certainly one of the key issues pertaining to young women's use of public space is that of safety, an issue that deserves further discussion in its own right.

Public spaces, security, and safety issues

A survey of young people in Adelaide found that the following were the major safety issues for young people (Adelaide, City of 1997: 6):

- Harassment and/or violence is often triggered by issues of race/ethnicity.
- Young women feel particularly vulnerable, fearing sexual harassment and/or violence in public spaces.
- Intervention by police and security guards is sometimes inappropriate and/or inadequate.

Young people in other localities have also expressed concern over crime and violence and issues relating to safety and security (see White 1999a). For some the solution is to band together for protection. But, as a young man in Melbourne was to observe, this is then frequently tied back to the gangs phenomenon: 'The reason why a lot of people form gangs around here is like it tends to help them like if someone knows that they're in a gang it's less likely that they'll get hurt because a lot of times walking around at night you can get hurt for no reason' (quoted in White et al. 1997: 82). This indicates that sometimes issues of security and public safety may seem somewhat paradoxical: to be in a gang is to be safe, but to be in a gang engenders fear. Or, to feel secure is to not be in the presence of the police or private security guards but this may make others feel less safe than otherwise might have been the case.

The fear of crime and the development of appropriate security precautions is, as we have seen, a particularly sensitive and acute issue for young women. The Brisbane research on young women makes the observation that young women's 'perception of being "vulnerable" in public spaces is reinforced constantly by concerned parents and popular culture' (Girls in Space Consortia 1997: 16). The message is for young women to keep off the streets for the sake of their own personal safety. The testimony of young women themselves, together with academic research (see Painter 1992), confirms that women's fear of crime and harassment in some urban areas is not simply subjective perception—the risks are real.

The risks are real in another sense, as well. Sydney research has found that young Vietnamese women are often humiliated and alarmed by the specific nature of police intervention, particularly during strip searches (Maher et al. 1997: 40–41). There are important gender and ethnic issues here, ranging from the racialisation of street policing through to threats to the bodily integrity of the women who are targeted this way.

In response to the risks associated with being in public spaces, many young women use strategies of resignation (perceiving harassment as 'just stupid' and as part of being female) and avoidance (not going to certain areas at certain times). Networking (being with other people) and surveillance (being in areas of high visibility) are also strategies employed to ensure safety. Developing crime prevention strategies that open up options, rather than simply allowing young women to cope with restrictive opportunities and unpleasant situations, must be sensitive to the gendered nature of public space and the power relations associated with gender and sexuality in Australian society.

> Many young women use strategies of resignation (perceiving harassment as 'just stupid' and as part of being female) and avoidance (not going to certain areas at certain times). Networking (being with other people) and surveillance (being in areas of high visibility) are also strategies employed to ensure safety.

The intersections between gender, class, ethnicity, and race—as these pertain to safety issues—were also particularly evident in interviews with young Indigenous Australians (White 1999a). The most youth-friendly spaces for Indigenous young people were home and friends' places. These young people felt most comfortable and secure in places where they did not get hassled, where there were friendly people, friends were there, and there was lots to do.

In answer to a question about not feeling safe, the responses alluded to perceived threats posed by security and police officers, gender-related threats, prejudice, racism, and fights. One young man made the observation that: 'Young people want police to target drunks who hassle young people, have knives and cause stabbings. Instead, police hassle and target young people'. Another commented:

> Sometimes the refuge workers take us at night for a BBQ or something. I won't go out alone at night 'cos of the drinking and fights among older people. Sometimes my friends drink with them and I don't feel safe so I only go there in the daytime.

A young woman pointed out that:

> Young indigenous people hang out in 'tribes', which have names and a definite group identity. For example, I found that one particular group are really big bitches. I made them say sorry to one of my friends, 'cos they were picking on her all the time.

People felt safest when they were in a group. Significantly, a number of the young women raised the issue of threats and being fearful of groups of men—young and old, black and white, sober and drunk. They also spoke of actual forceful harassment and violence. From these accounts it is clear that how young (and old) people use public space has implications beyond that of simply signalling a form of transgression of the mainstream norms and rules. How and under what conditions these transgressions take place can have extremely hurtful and harmful effects. Racist graffiti, for example, is graffiti, but it is also so much more. Alienation and marginalisation may provide clues as to why certain individuals and groups engage with the urban environment in the ways they do but this does not excuse behaviour that may be oppressive of others.

Divergent uses of the street

Youth and public space issues can be summarised in relation to three broad trends:

- the efforts of young people to express their own sense of ownership and control without official intervention
- state attempts to suppress youth under the rubric of law and order and/or attempts to deal with the gang problem
- official attempts to include young people positively and actively in the construction and management of public spaces.

Underlying these trends is a sense of ambiguity, generated by the diversity of uses of public spaces and by the conflicts accompanying these uses. It needs to be emphasised that the three trends outlined here are simultaneous, although the emphasis or dominance of any one trend will vary according to local, regional, and national peculiarities. Their coexistence can sometimes surface as a series of practical paradoxes.

Modes of engagement of young people in public places

Youth agency and street life

- Youth music scenes, such as around the globe hip hop adaptations that shape cultural and physical spaces.
- Street machiners and car culture that involves the public parading and showing off of automobiles.
- Street dancers and the street as stage that involves public performance and exhibition of skills.
- Direct action politics that focus on music, political issues, and people power via appropriation of public spaces by large numbers of people.
- Anti-globalisation protests and social movement actions that involve large numbers of young people, such as Australian protests against the treatment of asylum seekers.
- Marking of the public landscape through graffiti art and other forms of graffiti production.
- Youth group formation and the sense of territory, usually perceived as gangs of young people who hang out together and who generally share common interests or identities.

Curtailing youth

- Offensive language provisions and public order policing, such as prosecutions for offensive language, which, in New South Wales, now outstrip prosecutions for offensive behaviour.
- Anti-weapons legislation that gives police greater powers to search people; the main targets for such searches and being told to move tending to be young people.

BOX 15.1

BOX 15.1

■ Anti-gang initiatives targeting groups of young people so that groups of, say, three or more young people can be told to disband.

■ Youth curfews, formal or informal, that are designed to limit young people's use of public spaces at designated times.

■ Street cleaning and zero tolerance policing; concerted campaigns to pick up young people and remove them from public places.

■ Laws allowing hoons' cars or stereos to be seized by police and confiscated, as in the case of anti-hooning legislation in a number of states and territories.

Youth participation as best practice

■ Specific projects and programs, such as documentation of youth-friendly spaces and youth-unfriendly spaces.

■ Strategic planning and public space development in the form of developing comprehensive, multifaceted responses by local government.

■ Direct youth involvement in planning for their own needs and in site development, particularly with respect to skateboard parks and recreational areas.

■ Urban design and planning guidelines developed specifically with young people in mind, as produced by the government departments dealing with urban affairs and planning.

■ Youth participation and youth policy initiatives at the local government level, now evident in many local council structures and processes.

■ Shopping centres adopting youth-friendly approaches through provision of youth services, supporting youth worker involvement, and adopting low-key inclusive management strategies.

Source: drawing upon White 2007c.

Consider an example that reflects developments in the Australian context. A major tension exists between the efforts of many local councils and private commercial ventures such as shopping centres to make public spaces more convivial and socially inclusive, and the efforts of state authorities to exclude particular users of public space under the rubric of community safety and effective law enforcement. Young people are at the fulcrum of this tension. On the one hand, they are being welcomed and offered a place at the community table through local council youth policies and initiatives and state government youth participation strategies; on the other, they are vilified and patronised and told to stay away until further notice (meaning, until their cashed-up adult years) through regulatory and law enforcement activity. Given this, is it any wonder, then, that, for many young people, public space issues will be dealt with in their way, by themselves, and on their own terms? But this, in turn, sets up an intervention dynamic insofar as expressions of youth agency are frequently met with concerted efforts by authority figures to clamp down on or to control the choices that young people make, often under the guise of fighting youth gangs or protecting young people from themselves.

Contesting public spaces

Recent studies (White et al. 1997; Presdee 2000; Hayward 2002) confirm that if legitimate access to amenities is limited and satisfaction with things to do lessened, then the likelihood of seeking illegitimate means to have fun and excitement is heightened. Research has also found that young people who engage in crime do so due to a combination of boredom and creating alternative ways to have fun and excitement, not for money. The general point here is that what young people do with their time and how they react to their local environment is circumscribed by the type and nature of amenities on offer and the resources upon which they can draw. When access to movie theatres, for instance, is low, the cost of entry is high, and the public transport system to get there is poor, it is not surprising that joy riding in someone else's car appears to be a reasonable and rational response to the situation (among other reasons for car theft).

> If legitimate access to amenities is limited and satisfaction with things to do lessened, then the likelihood of seeking illegitimate means to have fun and excitement is heightened.

Social differences in how young people use the street means that the street is also a site of conflict among and between young people themselves. Understanding how young people establish a public presence ought not to be conflated with approval of everything that young people do. As Cohen argued some three decades ago:

> Those same values of racism, sexism, chauvinism, compulsive masculinity and anti-intellectualism, the slightest traces of which are condemned in bourgeois culture, are treated with a deferential care, an exaggerated contextualization, when they appear in the subculture (Cohen 1973: xxvii).

Young people are not passive users of the street, nor are they reticent about establishing a public presence. In many different ways, and on different levels, young people have engaged directly in social processes that are implicated in significant social change. In responding to their environments, they have succeeded, as well, in transforming these environments. This is not always a conscious process, nor is it always intended to have the consequences that arise from certain types of activities.

From an analytical point of view, interesting questions regarding the public presence of young people revolve around issues of structure and agency. In contesting public spaces and using them to contest social issues, young people act according to diverse motives and in many different ways. There may be different types of resistance that help to explain particular actions and the formation of particular groups of young people that might include resistance to authority (such as police intervention), to rules (such as 'No dancing in the mall'), to lack of space or things to do (such as skateboarding on the street), to lack of opportunity (such as joyriding), and to established boundaries of behaviour (such as transgressing ordinary ways of dressing).

Notwithstanding its resurgent use within cultural criminology (see, for example, Ferrell 1997), the idea of resistance is conceptually somewhat problematic. Definitions of resistance, and how power and subjectivity are theorised, vary greatly depending on the analytical framework used to examine it (see Raby 2005). A key message is that how and why young people resist will vary greatly. So, too, the interpretation of these resistances will vary among social researchers. We see youth agency as always contingent upon consciousness of purpose, immediate and long-term objectives, and extent of organisation (see White & Wyn 1998). Indeed, for us, resistance is not always against

Resistance is not always against something; in some cases it may refer to the efforts of young people to be taken seriously, to be part of the mainstream.

something; in some cases it may refer to the efforts of young people to be taken seriously, to be part of the mainstream. In these cases, resistance is basically a fight for conformity, be it in relation to the acceptance of graffiti art as art or receiving respectful treatment at the hands of private security guards and the police.

One has to be aware that the actions of young people as they shape and are shaped by public spaces and cultural activities are always multidimensional. Change may be primarily within the individual or the group, or it may be within wider institutional structures. How change occurs may be intentional or the result of unintended consequences. Key questions here might include the following:

1 By doing what they do, are young people simply adapting to restrictions and oppressive interventions and thus exercising their agency in ways that give them a sense of their own creativity and freedom but do little to change the world around them, as in the case of spectacular subcultures?

2 Are young people engaging in a form of activity that will, through sheer weight of their numbers, lead to general changes in their surrounding environment, the expansion of commercial opportunities, and the routinisation of what were once seen as extraordinary activities, as in the case of skateboarding?

3 Will the activity lead to significant changes in the life chances and opportunities of young people and to improvements in their quality of life in general, because transgressive action such as taking back the streets is linked to a progressive politics and democratisation of public spaces, as in the case of illegal, free raves in public parks and streets?

4 Is the activity located within a particular, conscious, ideological framework, which in turn is linked to cross-generational concerns, whether these be of a right-wing or left-wing nature, and whether they be directed against institutions (for example, anti-capitalist movements) or groups (for example, white supremacist hate crime), as in the case of ecological movements, socialist alliances, and far-right mobilisations?

Summary

Young people are making their mark in public spaces in many different ways. The challenge for sociology of youth is to discern the many varieties of group formation, identity creation, and political orientation associated with ways of being on the street. Some forms of action may be seen as rebellious, as a response to heightened social regulation, as symptomatic of deep structural inequalities, or as just being fun. It is important that researchers do not romanticise the resistance, that they do not overstate the extent of agency being exercised, and that they do not inadvertently condone practices that in any other context would be considered antisocial and inappropriate.

How young people use public space is contingent upon access to resources and amenities, the construction of youth-friendly venues and areas, and the social relationships that are built on the street. As this chapter has demonstrated, different groups of young people use the street and other public venues in different ways. They also perceive the issues surrounding public space from a range of viewpoints. Issues of personal safety, for example, are not confined to older people. Young people, too, wish to have safe environments in which to socialise and move, and to be free from the threat of violence—whether from other young people, adults, or authority figures. Additionally, it needs to be recognised that specific groups of young people have specific needs. The discussion of young women, for example, provides some indication of the different experiences, perceptions, and wishes of these young people.

The struggle for meaning and place on the part of young people is a struggle very much intertwined with life on the street. The question we need to ask is how best to enhance and support youth agency in ways that do not exacerbate fear and insecurity among vulnerable groups of young people, or foster violent and self-destructive behaviours that do more harm than good. In other words, analysis of the street must, at some stage, be accompanied by an ethics of social transformation. This is an area that remains long overdue for sustained discussion and debate.

Questions for further exploration

1   What is public space and what is the relationship between public and private when it comes to the ownership, accessibility, and control over public spaces?

2   What are some examples of youth-specific and youth-friendly amenities in your neighbour-hood, or town, or city?

3   Public space, including the street, is made up of multiple users and multiple uses. Discuss.

4   Is the fear of crime just a problem for older people? Why? Why not? Is the fear justified?

5   What is resistance? Is it a useful concept when it comes to interpreting the actions of young people in public places?

REFERENCES

Adamson, C. 1998, 'Tribute, Turf, Honor and the American Street Gang: Patterns of Continuity and Change Since 1920', *Theoretical Criminology*, 2(1): 57–84.

Adelaide, City of 1997, *OutaSpace Youth Speak: Views and Proposals From a Forum on Young People's Access to Public Space in the City of Adelaide,* Adelaide: City of Adelaide.

Ainley, P. 1998, 'School Participation, Retention and Outcomes', in Dusseldorp Skills Forum, *Australia's Youth: Reality and Risk*, Sydney: Dusseldorp Skills Forum, pp. 51–65.

Alder, C., O'Connor, I., Warner, K. & White, R. 1992, *Perceptions of the Treatment of Juveniles in the Legal System*, Report for the National Youth Affairs Research Scheme, Hobart: Australian Clearinghouse for Youth Studies.

Andersen, J. 1999, 'Post-industrial Solidarity or Meritocracy', *Acta Sociologica*, 42(4): 375–85.

Andres, L. 1999, 'Multiple Life Sphere Participation by Young Adults', in W. Heinz (ed.), *From Education to Work: Cross-national Perspectives*, Cambridge: Cambridge University Press.

Anttila, T., Poikolainen, K., Uutela, A. & Lönnqvist, J. 2000, 'Structure and Determinants of Worrying among Adolescent Girls', *Journal of Youth Studies*, 3(1): 49–60.

Arthurson, K. & Jacobs, K. 2003, *Social Exclusion and Housing*, Melbourne: Australian Housing and Urban Research Institute.

Atkinson, L. & McDonald, D. 1995, 'Cannabis, the Law and Social Impacts in Australia', *Trends and Issues,* no. 48, Canberra: Australian Institute of Criminology.

Atkinson, S. & Nixon, H. 2005, 'Locating the Subject: Teens online @ ninemsm', *Discourse*, 26(6): 387–409.

Aumair, M. & Warren, I. 1994, 'Characteristics of Juvenile Gangs in Melbourne', *Youth Studies Australia*, 13(2): 40–44.

Australian Bureau of Statistics 1998a, *Family Characteristics*, cat. no. 4442.0, Canberra: Australian Bureau of Statistics (ABS).

—— 1998b, *A Guide to Major ABS Classifications, 1998*, cat. no. 1291.0, Canberra: Australian Standard Geographical Classification (ASGC).

—— 1998c, *Mental Health and Well-being Profile of Adults: Australia, 1997*, cat. no. 4326.0, Canberra: ABS.

—— 1999, *Household and Family Projections Australia 1996 to 2021*, cat. no. 4119.0, Canberra: ABS.

—— 2001, *Marriages and Divorces in Australia*, cat. no. 3310.0, Canberra: ABS.

—— 2002, *Census of Population and Housing: Selected Social and Housing Characteristics, Australia*, cat. no. 2015.0, Canberra: ABS.

—— 2002, *National Aboriginal and Torres Strait Islander Social Survey*, cat. no. 4714.0, Canberra: ABS.

—— 2003a, 'Measures of a knowledge-based economy and society, Australia', *Australia Now*, cat. no. 8146.0, Canberra: ABS.

—— 2003b, *Census 2001: Computer and Internet Use*, census paper no. 03/03, Canberra: ABS.

—— 2003c, *Household Telephone Connections, Queensland, October 2003*, cat. no. 8159.3, Canberra: ABS.

—— 2003d, *Household Use of Information Technology 2001–02*, cat. no. 8146.0, Canberra: ABS.

——2004, *Employee Earnings and Hours, Australia*, May, cat. no. 6306.0, Canberra: Commonwealth of Australia.

—— 2004, *Year Book Australia 2004*, 'Labour', cat. no. 1301.0, Canberra: Commonwealth of Australia.

—— 2005, *Australian Social Trends 2005*, cat. no. 4102.0, Canberra: Commonwealth of Australia.

—— and Australian Institute of Health and Welfare (AIHW) 2005, *The Health and Welfare of Australia's Aboriginal & Torres Strait Islander Peoples*, cat. no. 4704.0, Canberra: ABS and AIHW.

—— & National Youth Affairs Research Scheme (NYARS) 1993, *Australia's Young People*, Canberra: ABS.

Australian Council of Social Services (ACOSS) 2001, *Breaching the Safety Net: The harsh impact of social security penalties*, Sydney: ACOSS.

Australian Council of Trade Unions (ACTU) 2006, 'Kids Under 15 Years Old Are Signing Individual Contracts Under IR Laws', media release, Melbourne: ACTU, 19 October.

—— 2007, 'Women workers and low paid worst affected new research shows', media release, Melbourne: ACTU, 13 February.

Australian Housing and Urban Research Institute (AHURI), 2006, *Research & Policy Bulletin*, 82.

Australian Institute of Family Studies (AIFS) 2006, *Snapshots of Australian Families with Adolescents*, Melbourne: AIFS.

Australian Institute of Health and Welfare (AIHW) 1996, *Australia's Health*, Canberra: AIHW.

—— 1997, *Australia's Welfare 1997: Services and Assistance*, Canberra: AIHW.

—— 2002, *Australia's Children: Their Health and Well-being 2002*, Perth: AIHW.

—— 2003, *Australia's Young People: Their Health and Well-being 2003*, Canberra: AIHW.

Australian Psychological Society 2004, *Psychosocial aspects of mobile phone use among adolescents*, November, vol. 3.

Bagnall, N. (ed.) 2005, *Youth Transition in a Globalised Marketplace*, New York: Nova Publishers.

Ball, S. J. 2003, *Class Strategies in the Educational Market: The Middle Classes and Social Advantage*, London: RoutledgeFalmer.

——, Maguire, M. & Macrae, S. 2000a, 'Space, work and the "new urban economies"', *Journal of Youth Studies*, 3(3): 279–300.

—— 2000b, *Choice, Pathways and Transitions Post-16: New Youth, New Economies in the Global City*, London: RoutledgeFalmer.

Barry, M. 2006, *Youth Offending in Transition: The Search for Social Recognition*, London: Routledge.

Bartky, S. 1990, *Femininity and Domination: Studies in the Phenomenology of Oppression*, London: Routledge.

Basarin, H. & Basarin, V. 1993, *The Turks in Australia: Celebrating 25 Years Down Under*, Melbourne: Turquoise Publications.

Bauman, Z. 2004, *Identity: Conversations with Benedetto Vecchi*, Cambridge: Polity Press.

Bazemore, G. 1997, 'The "Community" in Community Justice: Issues, themes, and questions for the new neighbourhood sanctioning models', *Justice System Journal*, 19(2): 193–227.

—— & Walgrave, L. 1999a, 'Restorative Juvenile Justice: In search of fundamentals and an outline for systemic reform', in G. Bazemore and L. Walgrave (eds), *Restorative Juvenile Justice: Repairing the Harm of Youth Crime*, Monsey NY: Criminal Justice Press.

—— (eds), 1999b, *Restorative Juvenile Justice: Repairing the Harm of Youth Crime*, Monsey NY: Criminal Justice Press.

Beavis, C. & Charles, C. 2005, 'Challenging Notions of Gendered Play: Teenagers Playing the Sims', *Discourse*, 26(6): 355–67.

Beck, U. 1992, *Risk Society: Towards a New Modernity*, London: Sage.

—— & Beck-Gernsheim, E. 2002, *Individualization*, London: Sage.

—— & Lau, C. 2005, 'Second modernity as a research agenda: theoretical and empirical explorations in the "meta-change" of modern society', *British Journal of Sociology*, 56(4): 525–57.

Becker, H. 1963, *Outsiders: Studies in the Sociology of Deviance*, New York: Free Press.

Bennett, A. 2000, *Popular Music and Youth Culture, Music, Identity and Place*, Basingstoke: Macmillan.

Beresford, Q. & Omaji, P. 1996, *Rites of Passage: Aboriginal Youth, Crime and Justice*, Fremantle: Fremantle Arts Centre Press.

Bernard, T. J. 1992, *The Cycle of Juvenile Justice*, New York: Oxford University Press.

Bessant, J. & Hil, R. (eds) 1997, *Youth, Crime and the Media*, Hobart: Australian Clearinghouse for Youth Studies.

Bessant, J. & Watts, R. 1998, 'History, Myth-making and Young People in a Time of Change', *Family Matters*, 49: 5–10.

Bhatia, K. & Anderson, P. 1994, *An Overview of Aboriginal and Torres Strait Islander Health: Present Status and Future Trends*, Canberra, AIHW.

Bilchik, S. 1996, *Curfew: An Answer to Juvenile Delinquency and Victimization?*, Washington: Office of Juvenile Justice and Delinquency Prevention.

—— 1998, *Guide for Implementing the Balanced and Restorative Justice Model*, Washington: Office of Juvenile Justice and Delinquency Prevention.

Blackman, S. 2004, *Chilling Out: The cultural politics of substance consumption, youth and drug policy*, Milton Keynes: Open University Press.

—— 1998, 'The School: "Poxy Cupid!" An ethnographic and feminist account of a resistant female youth culture: the new wave girls', in T. Skelton and G. Valentine (eds), *Cool Places, Geographies of Youth Cultures*, London: Routledge.

Blackmore, J., Thomson, P. & Beckett, L. 2000, 'What's Happened to Social Justice Lately?', editorial, *Australian Educational Researcher*, 27: i–iii.

Blagg, H. 2000, *Crisis Intervention in Aboriginal Family Violence: Summary Report*, Canberra: Commonwealth of Australia.

—— 1998, 'Restorative Visions and Restorative Justice Practices: Conferencing, Ceremony and Reconciliation in Australia', *Current Issues in Criminal Justice*, 10(1): 5–14.

—— & Wilkie, M. 1995, *Young People & Police Powers*, Sydney: Australian Youth Foundation.

Boase, J. & Wellman, B. 2004, 'Personal Relationships: On and Off the Internet', in D. Perlman and A. Vangelisti (eds), *The Cambridge Handbook of Personal Relations*, New York: Cambridge University Press.

Boneva, B., Kraut, R. & Frohlich, D. 2001, 'Using E-mail for Personal Relationships: The Difference Gender Makes, *American Behavioral Scientist*, 44(3): 530–49.

Bordo, S. 1993, '*Unbearable Weight', Feminism, Western Culture and the Body*, Berkeley: University of California Press.

Boss, P., Edwards, S. & Pitman, S. 1995, *Profile of Young Australians: Facts, Figures and Issues*, Melbourne: Churchill Livingstone.

Botsman, P. 2000, 'Disability Policy: Rights or Social Investment', address to the closing plenary at the Australian Society for the Study of Intellectual Disability Conference, 9 September.

Bourdieu, P. 1984, *Distinction: A Social Critique of the Judgement of Taste*, London: Routledge.

—— 1990, *In Other Words: Essays Towards a Reflexive Sociology*, Cambridge: Polity Press.

—— & Passeron, J. C. 1977, *Reproduction in Education, Society and Culture*, London: Sage.

Brady, M. 1991, *The Health of Young Aborigines, A Report on the Health of Aborigines aged 12 to 25*, Hobart: Australian Clearinghouse for Youth Studies.

—— 1991, *The Health of Young Aborigines, Report for the National Youth Affairs Research Scheme*, Hobart: Australian Clearinghouse for Youth Studies.

—— 1994, *The Health of Young Aborigines*, Hobart: Australian Clearinghouse for Youth Studies.

—— 1985, 'Aboriginal Youth and the Juvenile Justice System', in A. Borowski & J. Murray (eds), *Juvenile Delinquency in Australia*, Sydney: Methuen.

—— 1993, 'Health Issues for Aboriginal Youth: Social and Cultural Factors Associated with Resilience', *Journal of Paediatric Child Health*, 29(supp. 1): 56–59.

Braithwaite, J. 1989, *Crime, Shame and Reintegration*, Cambridge: Cambridge University Press.

—— 1999, 'Restorative Justice: Assessing optimistic and pessimistic accounts', in M. Tonry (ed.), *Crime and Justice: A Review of Research*, vol. 25, Chicago: University of Chicago Press.

Brake, M. 1985, *Comparative Youth Culture*, London: Routledge & Kegan Paul.

Bray, J. R., 2000, *Social Indicators for Regional Australia*, policy research paper no. 8, Canberra: Department of Family and Community Services.

Brooks, R. 2006, 'Learning and work in the lives of young adults', *International Journal of Lifelong Education*, 25(3), 271–89.

Brown, D., Farrier, D., Egger, S. & McNamara, L. 2001, *Criminal Laws: Materials and commentary on criminal law and process in New South Wales*, Sydney: Federation Press.

Brown, W., Ball, K. & Powers, J. 1998, 'Is Life a Party for Young Women?', *ACHPER Healthy Lifestyles Journal*, 45(3): 21–26.

Bryan, D. 1994, 'Do We Really Want to be More Competitive?', *Green Left Weekly*, 20 July, pp. 16–17.

—— 1995, 'International Competitiveness: National and Class Agendas', *Journal of Australian Political Economy*, 35: 1–23.

Burbules, N. 2004, 'Rethinking the Virtual', *E-Learning*, 1(2): 162–83.

Burdekin, B. 1989, *Our Homeless Children: Report of the National Inquiry into Homeless Children* (Human Rights and Equal Opportunity Commission), Canberra: Australian Government Publishing Service (AGPS).

Burney, E. 2000, 'Ruling Out Trouble: Anti-social Behaviour and Housing Management', *Journal of Forensic Psychiatry*, 11(2): 268–73.

Butcher, M. & Thomas, M. 2003, 'Being in-between', in M. Butcher and M. Thomas (eds), *Ingenious: Emerging Youth Cultures in Urban Australia*, Sydney: Pluto Press.

Bynner, J. 2005, 'Rethinking the youth phase of the life course: the case for emerging adulthood?', *Journal of Youth Studies*, 8(4): 367–84.

Cain, M. 1994, *Juveniles in Detention. Special Needs Groups: Young women, Aboriginal and Indo-Chinese detainees*, Information and Evaluation Series no. 3, Sydney: New South Wales Department of Juvenile Justice.

—— 1996, *Recidivism of Juvenile Offenders in New South Wales*, Sydney: New South Wales Department of Juvenile Justice, Sydney.

Campbell, I. 1997, 'Beyond Unemployment: The challenge of increased precarious employment', *Just Policy*, 11: 4–20.

Canada, National Crime Prevention Council (NCPC) 1996, *Mobilizing Political Will and Community Responsibility to Prevent Youth Crime*, Ottawa: NCPC.

Canadian Labour Force Development Board (CLFDB) 1994, *Putting the Pieces Together: Toward a coherent transition system for Canada's labour force*, Ottawa: CLFDB.

Cantor C. H. & Coory M. 1993, 'Is There a Rural Suicide Problem?', *Australian Journal of Public Health*, 17(1): 382–84.

Carcach, C. 1997, 'Youth as Victims and Offenders of Homicide', *Trends and Issues in Crime and Criminal Justice*, 73, Canberra: Australian Institute of Criminology.

Carrington, K. 1989, 'Girls and Graffiti', *Cultural Studies*, 3(1): 89–100.

—— 1990, 'Aboriginal Girls and Juvenile Justice: What justice? White justice', *Journal for Social Justice Studies*, 3: 1–17.

Carrington, V. & Marsh, J. 2005, 'Digital Childhood and Youth: new texts, new literacies', *Discourse*, 26(6): 279–85.

Castells, M. 1989, *The Informational City: Informal technology, economic restructuring, and the urban–regional process*, Oxford: Blackwell.

Castles, S. 1996, 'The Racisms of Globalisation', in E. Vasta and S. Castles (eds), *The Teeth are Smiling: The persistence of racism in multicultural Australia*, Sydney: Allen & Unwin.

Catalano, R. & Hawkins, J. 1996, 'The Social Development Model: A theory of antisocial behaviour', in J. Hawkins (ed.), *Delinquency and Crime: Current Theories*, New York: Cambridge University Press.

Chan, C. & Cunneen, C. 2000, *Evaluation of the Implementation of the New South Wales Police Service Aboriginal Strategic Plan*, Sydney: Institute of Criminology, Sydney.

Chan, J. 1997, *Changing Police Culture: Policing in a Multicultural Society*, Melbourne: Cambridge University Press.

—— 1994, 'Policing Youth in "Ethnic" Communities: Is community policing the answer?', in R. White and C. Alder (eds), *The Police and Young People in Australia*, Melbourne: Cambridge University Press.

Chan, S. 1999, 'Bubbling Acid: Sydney's Techno Underground', in R. White (ed.), *Australian Youth Subcultures: On the margins and in the mainstream*, Hobart: Australian Clearinghouse for Youth Studies.

—— & Lee, H. 2006, 'Australians as Prosumers: How active are we?', paper presented at Digital Natives Conference, Melbourne: University of Melbourne.

Chapman, B., Weatherburn, D., Kapuscinski, C., Chilvers, M. & Roussel, S. 2002, 'Unemployment Duration, Schooling and Property Crime', *Crime and Justice Bulletin, Contemporary Issues in Crime and Justice*, 74, Sydney: New South Wales Bureau of Crime Statistics and Research.

Chatterton, P. & Hollands, R. 2003, *Urban Nightscapes: Youth Cultures, Pleasure Spaces and Corporate Power*, London: Routledge.

Chisholm, L. 1997, 'Initial Transitions Between Education, Training and Employment in Learning Society', *International Bulletin of Youth Research*, 15: 6–16.

Civics Expert Group 1994, '*Whereas the People …*', *Civics and Citizenship Education*, Canberra: AGPS.

Cody, D. 2006, 'Smoke Signals: Cannabis moral panics in the United States, Australia & Britain', Masters thesis of Criminology and Corrections, Hobart: School of Sociology and Social Work, University of Tasmania.

Cohen, P. 1997, *Rethinking the Youth Question*, London: Macmillan.

—— & Ainley, P. 2000, 'In the country of the blind?: Youth studies and cultural studies in Britain', *Journal of Youth Studies*, 3(1): 79–95.

Cohen, S. 1973, *Folk Devils and Moral Panics*, London: Paladin.

Collard, L. & Palmer, D. 2006, 'Kura, yeye, boorda, Nyungar wangkiny gnulla koorlangka: A conversation about working with Indigenous young people in the past, present and future', *Youth Studies Australia*, 25(4): 25–32.

Collins, C., Kenway, J. & McLeod, J. 2000, 'Gender Debates We Still Have to Have', *Australian Educational Researcher*, 27: 37–48.

Collins, J., Noble, G., Poynting, S. & Tabar, P. 2000, *Kebabs, Kids, Cops & Crime: Youth, ethnicity and crime*, Sydney: Pluto Press.

Commission on the Skills of the American Workforce 1990, *America's Choice: High skills or low wages!*, Rochester: Commission on the Skills of the American Workforce.

Commonwealth Department of Human Services and Health (DHSH) 1994, *Loddon–Mallee Region: Regional needs analysis*, Melbourne: Victorian State Office.

—— 1995, *The Health of Young Australians, A National Health Policy for Children and Young People*, Canberra: AGPS.

Commonwealth of Australia 1994, *Working Nation: Policies and Programs*, Canberra: AGPS.

Conger, Reuter & Conger 2000, 'The Role of Economic Pressure in the Lives of Parents and their Adolescents: The family stress model', in L. Crockett & R. Silbereisen (eds), *Negotiating Adolescence in Times of Social Change*, Cambridge: Cambridge University Press.

Connell, R. 1987, *Gender and Power*, Sydney: Allen & Unwin.

—— 1994, 'Poverty and Education', *Harvard Educational Review*, 64(2): 125–49.

—— 1995, *Masculinities*, Sydney: Allen & Unwin.

—— 2000a, *The Men and the Boys*, Sydney: Allen & Unwin.

—— 2002b, *Gender, Short Introductions,* Cambridge: Cambridge University Press.

Coorey, L. 1990, 'They Bash Wives in the Country Too', *Social Welfare Impact*, 20(2): 10.

Corrigan, P. 1979, *Schooling the Smash Street Kids*, London: Macmillan.

Costigan, G. 1996, 'The Cost of Coming Out', *The Big Issue*, 3: 29 July–11 August.

Coulton, C. 2003, 'Metropolitan Inequities and the Ecology of Work: Implications for welfare reform', *Social Service Review*, 77(2): 159–90.

Coumarelos, C. 1994, *Juvenile Offending: Predicting persistence and determining cost-effectiveness of interventions*, Sydney: New South Wales Bureau of Crime Statistics and Research.

Cowan, D., Pantazis, C. & Gilroy, R. 2001, 'Social Housing as Crime Control: An examination of the role of housing management in policing sex offenders', *Social & Legal Studies*, 10(4): 435–57.

Cowlishaw, G. 2006, 'Culturers of complaint: an ethnography of rural racial rivalry', *Journal of Sociology*, 42(4): 429–45.

Cox, E. 1997, 'Boys and Girls and the Costs of Gendered Behaviour', in *Gender Equity: A Framework for Australian Schools*, Canberra: Department of Employment, Education and Youth Affairs.

Crane, P. 2000, 'Young People and Public Space: Developing inclusive policy and practice', *Scottish Youth Issues Journal*, 1(1): 105–24.

Crowhurst, M. 1999, 'Working Against Heterosexism: Gay school experiences', in R. White (ed.), *Australian Youth Subcultures: On the margins and in the mainstream*, Hobart: Australian Clearinghouse for Youth Studies.

Cunneen, C. 1990a, *A Study of Aboriginal Juveniles and Police Violence*, Sydney: Human Rights and Equal Opportunity Commission.

—— 1990b, *Aboriginal–Police Relations in Redfern: With special reference to the 'police raid' of 8 February* 1990, Sydney: Human Rights and Equal Opportunity Commission.

—— 1994, 'Enforcing Genocide? Aboriginal Young People and the Police', in R. White, and C. Alder (eds), *The Police and Young People in Australia*, Melbourne: Cambridge University Press.

—— 2001, *Conflict, Politics and Crime. Aboriginal Communities and the Police*, Sydney: Allen & Unwin.

—— & McDonald, D. 1996, *Keeping Aboriginal and Torres Strait Islander People Out of Custody: An evaluation of the implementation of the recommendations of the Royal Commission into Aboriginal Deaths in Custody*, Canberra: Aboriginal and Torres Strait Islander Commission.

Cunneen, C. & Robb, T. 1987, *Criminal Justice in North-west New South Wales*, Sydney: New South Wales Bureau of Crime Statistics and Research.

Cunneen, C. & White, R. 1995, *Juvenile Justice: An Australian Perspective*, Melbourne: Oxford University Press.

—— 2002, *Juvenile Justice: Youth and Crime in Australia*, Melbourne: Oxford University Press.

—— 2006, 'Australia: Control, Containment or Empowerment?', in J. Muncie and B. Goldson (eds), *Comparative Youth Justice*, London: Sage.

—— 2007, *Juvenile Justice: Youth and Crime in Australia*, Melbourne: Oxford University Press.

D'Souza, M. & Iveson, K. 1999, 'Homies and Homebrewz: Hip hop in Sydney', in R. White (ed.), *Australian Youth Subcultures*, Hobart: Australian Clearinghouse for Youth Studies.

Daniel, A. & Cornwall, J. 1993, *A Lost Generation?*, Sydney: Australian Youth Foundation.

Davey, J., Davey, T. & Obst, P. 2002), 'Alcohol Consumption and Drug Use in a Sample of Australian University Students', *Youth Studies Australia*, 21(3): 25–32.

Davies, B. 1997, 'Constructing and Deconstructing Masculinities through Critical Literacy', *Gender and Education*, 9: 9–30.

—— 2004, 'Identity, abjection and otherness: creating the self, creating differences', *International Journal in Equity and Innovation in Early Childhood Education*, 2(1): 58–80.

Davis, M. 1990, *City of Quartz: Excavating the future in Los Angeles*, London: Vintage.

Davis, N., Hatty, S. & Burke, S. 1995, 'Rough Justice: Social Control and Resistance among Homeless Youth', in C. Simpson and R. Hil (eds), *Ways of Resistance: Social control and young people in Australia*, Sydney: Hale and Iremonger.

De Vaus, D. & Qu, L. 1998, 'Intergenerational Transfers Across the Life Course', *Family Matters*, 50: 27–30.

Deacon, B. 1983, *Social Policy and Socialism: The Struggle for Socialist Relations of Welfare*, London: Pluto Press.

Department of Education, Science and Training 2005, *Annual Report 2004–05*, Canberra: Commonwealth of Australia.

Department of Education, Training and Youth Affairs 1996, *National Report on Schooling in Australia*, Canberra: Commonwealth of Australia.

Department of Employment/Department of Education and Science 1991, *Education and Training for the 21st Century*, London: HMSO.

Developmental Crime Prevention Consortium 1999, *Pathways to Prevention: Developmental and Early Intervention Approaches to Crime in Australia*, Canberra: National Crime Prevention, Attorney-General's Department.

Dickenson, B. 2006, '"Warrior gene" more prevalent in New Zealand Maoris', *COSMOS* magazine, *Cosmos Online*, Wednesday 9 August, accessed 15 August 2006 at www.cosmosmagazine.com/node/535.

Dimitriadis, G. 2001, *Performing Identity/Performing Culture*, New York: Peter Lang.

Dixon, C. 1997, 'Pete's Tool: Identity and sex-play in the design and technology classroom', *Gender and Education*, 9(1): 89–104.

Dixon, D. 1998, 'Broken Windows, Zero Tolerance, and the New York Miracle', *Current Issues in Criminal Justice*, 10(1): 96–106.

Dolby, N. 2003, 'Popular Culture and Democratic Practice', *Harvard Educational Review*, 73(3): 258–83.

Donald, M., Dower, J., Lucke, J. & Raphael, B. 2000, *The Queensland Young People's Mental Health Survey*, Brisbane: University of Queensland.

du Bois-Reymond, M. 1998, '"I Don't Want to Commit Myself Yet." Young People's Life Concepts', *Journal of Youth Studies*, 1(1): 63–79.

Dudley, M., Waters, B., Kelk, N. & Howard, J. 1992, 'Youth Suicide in New South Wales: Urban–rural trends', *Medical Journal of Australia*, 156: 83–88.

Duff, C. 2003, 'Drugs and Youth Cultures: Is Australia experiencing the "normalisation" of adolescent drug use?', *Journal of Youth Studies*, 6(4): 433–46.

Duncan, G. 2000, 'Urban Pedagogies and the Celling of Adolescents of Color', *Social Justice*, 27(3): 29–42.

Dusseldorp Skills Forum 1998, *Australia's Youth: Reality and Risk*, Sydney: Dusseldorp Skills Forum.

—— 2004, *How young people are faring: Key indicators 2004: An update about the learning and work situation of young Australians*, Sydney: Dusseldorp Skills Forum.

—— 2006, *How Young People are Faring 2006 Key Indicators*, Sydney: Dusseldorp Skills Forum.

Dwyer, P. 1995, 'Disjunction between Pathways Policy and Student Outcomes: Experience of early school leavers', *Australian Journal of Education*, 39: 265–78.

—— 1996, *Opting Out: Early school leavers and the degeneration of youth policy*, Hobart: Australian Clearinghouse for Youth Studies.

—— & Wyn, J. 2001, *Youth, education and risk: Facing the future*, London: RoutledgeFalmer.

——1998, 'Post-compulsory Education Policy in Australia and Its Impact on Participant Pathways and Outcomes in the 1990s', *Journal of Education Policy* 13: 285–300.

Dwyer, P., Harwood, A., Costin, G., Landy, M., Towsty, D. & Wyn, J. 1999, *Combined Study and Work Paths in VET: Policy Implications and Analysis*, Leabrook: National Centre for Vocational Education Research.

Dwyer, P., Smith, G., Tyler, D. & Wyn, J. 2003, *Life-Patterns, Career Outcomes and Adult Choices*, Melbourne: Youth Research Centre.

Easthope, G. & White, R. 2006, 'Health and Well-being: How do young people see these concepts?', *Youth Studies Australia*, 25(1): 42–49.

Eckersley, R. 2001, 'Culture, Health and Well-being', in R. Eckersley, J. Dixon and B. Douglas (eds), *The Social Origins of Health and Well-being*, Cambridge: Cambridge University Press.

—— & Dear, K. 2002, 'Cultural Correlates of Youth Suicide', *Social Science and Medicine*, 55(11): 1898–906.

Education Victoria 1998, *Framework for Student Support Services in Victorian Government Schools: Support Materials*, Melbourne: Community Information Service, Department of Education.

Edwards, J., Oakley, R. & Carey, S. 1987, 'Street Life, Ethnicity and Social Policy', in B. Gaskell and R. Benewick (eds), *The Crowd in Contemporary Britain*, London: Sage.

Eldridge, M. & Grinter, R. 2001, 'Studying Text Messaging in Teenagers', paper presented at CHI 2001, Workshop # 1: Mobile communications: Understanding User, Adoption and Design, Philadelphia.

Elley, J. & Inglis, C. 1995, 'Ethnicity & Gender: The Two Worlds of Australian Turkish Youth', in C. Guerra and R. White (eds), *Ethnic Minority Youth in Australia*, Hobart: Australian Clearinghouse for Youth Studies.

Emslie, M. 1999, 'Coming Out or Staying In: Dilemmas of Young Lesbians and Gay Men', in R. White (ed.), *Australian Youth Subcultures: On the margins and in the mainstream*, Hobart: Australian Clearinghouse for Youth Studies.

Epstein, D. 1997, 'Boyz' Own Stories: Masculinities and sexualities in schools', *Gender and Education*, 9(1): 105–16.

Erikson, E. 1950, *Childhood and Society*, London: Imago.

European Commission 2007, *Youth in Action Programme 2007–13*, Brussels: European Commission.

Evans, K. 1995, 'Competence and Citizenship: Towards a complementary model (for times of critical social change)', *British Journal of Education and Work*, Autumn.

—— 2002, 'Taking control of their Lives? Agency in Young Adult Transitions in England and the New Germany', *Journal of Youth Studies*, 5(3): 245–69.

Eyre, L. 1997, 'Re-forming (Hetero)Sexuality Education', in L. Roman and L. Eyre (eds), *Dangerous Territories: Struggles for Difference and Equality*, New York: Routledge.

Fattore, T. (for New South Wales Commission for Children and Young People) 2005, *Children at Work*, Sydney: New South Wales Commission for Children and Young People.

Ferrell, J. 1997, 'Youth, Crime and Cultural Space', *Social Justice*, 24(4): 21–38.

Fontaine, E. & Kaymakci, Y. 1996, *I'm Turkish Australian*, Melbourne: Ethnic Youth Issues Network and the Australian Turkish Association.

Foote, P. 1993, 'Like, I'll Tell You What Happened from Experience … Perspectives on Italo-Australian youth gangs in Adelaide', in R. White (ed.), *Youth Subcultures: Theory, History and the Australian Experience*, Hobart: Australian Clearinghouse for Youth Studies.

Forrester, L. 1993, 'Youth-Generated Cultures in Western Sydney', in R. White (ed.), *Youth Subcultures: Theory, History and the Australian Experience,* Hobart: Australian Clearinghouse for Youth Studies.

Foster, J. 1995, 'Informal Social Control and Community Crime Prevention', *British Journal of Criminology*, 35(4): 563–83.

Foucault, M. 1991, 'Governmentality', in G. Burchell, C. Gorson and P. Miller (eds), *The Foucault Effect: Studies in governmental rationality*, Hemel Hempstead: Harvester Wheatsheaf.

Freeman, K. 1996, 'Young People and Crime', *Crime and Justice Bulletin*, 32, Sydney: New South Wales Bureau of Crime Statistics and Research.

Frost, L. 2003, 'Doing Bodies Differently? Gender, youth, appearance and damage', *Journal of Youth Studies*, 6(1): 53–70.

Funston, A. & MacNeill, K. 1999, 'Mobile Matters: young people and mobile phones', study conducted by the Communications Law Centre and Victoria University, retrieved 14 March 2005 from www.dcita.gov.au/crf/paper99/funston.html.

Furlong, A. & Cartmel, F. 1997, *Young People and Social Change: Individualisation and Risk in Late Modernity*, Buckingham: Open University Press.

— 2007, *Young People and Social Change: Individualisation and Risk in Late Modernity* (2nd edn.), Buckingham: Open University Press.

Furlong, A. & Kelly, P. 2005, 'The Brazilianization of youth transitions in Australia and the UK?', *Australian Journal of Social Issues*, 40(2): 207–25.

Fustenberg, F. F. & Cherlin, A. J. 1991, *Divided Families: What Happens to Children when Parents Part*, Cambridge MA: Harvard University Press.

Fyfe, I. & Wyn, J. 2007, 'Young Activists Making the News: The role of the media in youth political and civic engagement', in L. Saha, M. Print and K. Edwards, (eds), *Youth and Political Participation*, Rotterdam: Sense Publishers.

Gale, F., Bailey-Harris, R. & Wundersitz, J. 1990, *Aboriginal Youth and the Criminal Justice System*, Melbourne: Cambridge University Press.

Game, A. & Pringle, R. 1983, *Gender At Work*, Sydney: George Allen & Unwin.

Gatto, C. 1999, *European Drug Policy: Analysis and Case Studies*, San Francisco: NORML Foundation.

Geason, S. & Wilson, P. 1990, *Preventing Graffiti and Vandalism*, Canberra: Australian Institute of Criminology.

Gelsthorpe, L. 1999, 'Parents and Criminal Children', in A. Bainham, S. Day Sclater and M. Richards (eds), *What is a Parent? A socio-legal analysis*, Oxford: Hart.

Gere, C. 2002, *Digital Culture*, London: Reaktion Books.

Gibson, O. 2005, 'Young blog their way to a publishing revolution', *Guardian*, 7 October, p. 9.

Giddens, A. 1991, *Modernity and Self-Identity: Self and identity in the late modern age*, Oxford: Polity.

Gilbert, R. & Gilbert, P. 1998, *Masculinity Goes to School*, Sydney: Allen & Unwin.

Gilding, M. 2001, 'Changing Families in Australia 1901–2001', *Family Matters*, 60, Spring/Summer: 6–11.

Girls in Space Consortia 1997, *Phase 1 Report for the Girls in Space Consortia Research: A Project Investigating Young Women's Relationships to Public Space in Brisbane*, Brisbane: Backbone Youth Arts Inc.

Glenday, D. 1996, 'Mean Streets and Hard Time: Youth unemployment and crime', in G. M. O'Bireck (ed.), *Not a Kid Anymore: Canadian youth, crime and subcultures*, Toronto: Nelson Canada.

Gliksman, M. & Chen, J. 2001, 'Research Note: Changes in the juvenile crime incidence rate by gender in New South Wales, Australia, 1991/2 to 1996/7', *Australia and New Zealand Journal of Criminology*, 34(3): 302–09.

Goldson, B. & Jamieson, J. 2002, 'Youth Crime, the "Parenting Deficit" and State Intervention: A contextual critique', *Youth Justice*, 2(2): 82–99.

Goodall, H. 1990, 'Saving the Children', *Aboriginal Law Bulletin*, 2(44): 6–9.

Goodchild, B. & Cole, I. 2001, 'Social Balance and Mixed Neighbourhoods in Britain since 1979: A review of discourse and practice in social housing', *Environment and Planning D: Society and Space*, 19: 103–21.

Gordon, R. 1995, 'Street Gangs in Vancouver', in J. Creechan & R. Silverman (eds), *Canadian Delinquency*, Toronto: Prentice Hall.

—— 1997, 'Gangs in Vancouver', Justice/Immigration Domain Seminar, Ottawa, 27–28 February.

—— 2000, 'Criminal Business Organizations, Street Gangs and "Wanna-be" Groups: A Vancouver perspective', *Canadian Journal of Criminology*, January: 39–60.

Grabosky, P. 1999, 'Zero Tolerance Policing', *Trends & Issues in Crime and Criminal Justice*, 102, Canberra: Australian Institute of Criminology.

Graham, D. 1994, 'Note: Adolescent Suicide in the Australian Rural Recession', *Australian Journal of Social Issues*, 29(4): 407–11.

Gray, D. & Atkinson, D. 1990, *Review of Aboriginal Health Policy, Western Australia*, Perth: Community Health Research and Training Unit, Department of General Practice, University of Western Australia.

Graycar, A. & Jamrozik, A. 1989, *How Australians Live: Social policy in theory and practice*, Melbourne: Macmillan.

Green, A. 1995, 'The Changing Structure, Distribution and Spatial Segregation of the Unemployed and Economically Inactive in Great Britain', *Geoforum*, 26(4): 373–94.

Green, E. 1996, 'Rural Youth Suicide: The issue of male homosexuality', in G. Lawrence, K. Lyons and S. Momtaz (eds), *Social Change in Rural Australia*, Rockhampton: Rural Social and Economics Research Centre, Central Queensland University.

Greenberg, D. 1993, 'Delinquency and the Age Structure of Society', in D. Greenberg (ed.), *Crime and Capitalism: Readings in Marxist Criminology* (2nd edn), Philadelphia: Temple University Press.

Gregory, R. & Hunter, B. 1995, *The Macro Economy and the Growth of Ghettos and Urban Poverty in Australia*, discussion paper no. 325, Canberra: Centre for Economic Policy Research, Australian National University.

Guerra, C. 1991, *Young People, Social Justice and Multiculturalism*, Melbourne: Ethnic Youth Issues Network.

—— & White, R. (eds) 1995, *Ethnic Minority Youth in Australia: Challenges and myths*, Hobart: Australian Clearinghouse for Youth Studies.

Haapasalo, J. 2001, 'How do Young Offenders Describe their Parents?', *Legal and Criminological Psychology*, 6: 103–20.

Hage, G. 1998, *White Nation: Fantasies of White Supremacy in a Multicultural Society*, Sydney: Pluto Press.

Hall, S. & Jefferson, T. (eds) 1976, *Resistance Through Rituals: Youth Subcultures in Post-war Britain*, London: Hutchinson.

Halstead, B. 1992, *Young People as Victims of Violence*, Hobart: Australian Clearinghouse for Youth Studies.

Hannam, D. 2000, 'Learning Democracy is More than Just Learning about Democracy', *Connect*, 122, April: 4–6.

Harding, A., Kelly, S. & Bill, A. 2003, 'Income and Wealth of Generation X', *AMP–NATSEM Income and Wealth Report*, issue Issue 6, Income and Wealth of Generation X, Canberra: AMP/NATSEM.

Harding, R. & Maller, R. 1997, 'An Improved Methodology for Analyzing Age–Arrest Profiles: Application to a Western Australian offender population', *Journal of Quantitative Criminology*, 13(4): 349–72.

Harris, A. 2004, *Future Girl: Young women in the twenty-first century*, London: Routledge.

—— 1999, 'Is DIY DOA? Zines and the Revolution Grrrl style', in R. White (ed.), *Australian Youth Subcultures*, Hobart: Australian Clearinghouse for Youth Studies, pp. 84–93.

—— 2002, 'Young Australian Women: Circumstances and Aspirations', *Youth Studies Australia*, 21(4): 32–37.

—— 2001, 'Revisiting bedroom culture: New spaces for young women's politics', *Hecate*, 27(1): 128–39.

Harris, R. & Webb, D. 1987, *Welfare, Power and Juvenile Justice*, London: Tavistock.

Haworth, A. & Manzi, T. 1999, 'Managing the "Underclass": Interpreting the moral discourse of housing management', *Urban Studies*, 36(1): 153–65.

Hayden, C. & Martin, T. 1998 '"Safer Cities" and Exclusion from School', *Journal of Youth Studies*, 1(3): 315–32.

Hayward, K. 2002, 'The Vilification and Pleasures of Youthful Transgression', in J. Muncie, G. Hughes and E. McLaughlin (eds), *Youth Justice: Critical readings*, London: Sage.

Hazelhurst, K. (ed.) 1995, *Perceptions of Justice*, Aldershot: Avebury.

Healy, S. 1999, 'Generation X? Young People and Politics', in R. White (ed.), *Australian Youth Subcultures: On the Margins and In the Mainstream*, Hobart: Australian Clearinghouse for Youth Studies.

Hebdige, D. 1979, *Subculture: The meaning of style*, London: Methuen.

Heggen, K. & Dwyer, P. 1998, 'New Policies, New Options: Learning from changing student transitions at two ends of the world', *Journal of Research in Post-Compulsory Education*, 3(3): 261–77.

Heitmeyer, W. 2002, 'Have Cities Ceased to Function as "Integration Machines" for Young People?', in M. Tienda and W. J. Wilson (eds), *Youth in Cities: A Cross-National Perspective*, Cambridge: Cambridge University Press.

Hermer, J. & Mosher, J. 2002, *Disorderly People: Law and the politics of exclusion in Ontario*, Halifax: Fernwood Publishing.

Herrnstein, R. & Murray, C. 1994, *The Bell Curve*, New York: Basic Books.

Hicks, R. & Moh'd, A. 1995, 'Islam & Education: Muslim Youth Issues in a Remote North-western Town', in C. Guerra and R. White (eds), *Ethnic Minority Youth in Australia: Challenges & Myths*, Hobart: Australian Clearinghouse for Youth Studies.

Hil, R. & Fisher, L. 1994, 'Symbolising Panic: The Construction of a "Black Juvenile Crime Problem" in Queensland', *Socio-Legal Bulletin*, 13: 39–46.

Hillier, L., Dempsey, D., Harrison, L., Beale, L., Matthews, L. & Rosenthal, D. 1998, *Writing Themselves In: A national report on the sexuality, health and well-being of same-sex attracted young people*, monograph series no. 7, Melbourne: National Centre in HIV Social Research, Australian Research Centre in Sex, Health and Society, Faculty of Health Sciences, La Trobe University.

Hillier, L. Harrison, L. & Dempsey, D. 1999, 'Whatever Happened to Duty of Care? Same-sex attracted young people's stories of schooling and violence', *Melbourne Studies in Education Special Issue: Education and Sexualities*, (40)2: 59–74.

Hillier, L., Kuldas, C. & Horsley, P. 2001, *'It's just easier': the Internet as a safety-net for same sex attracted young people*, Melbourne: Australian Research Centre in Sex, Health and Society.

Hillier, L., Warr, D. & Haste, B. 1996, *The Rural Mural: Sexuality and Diversity in Rural Youth,* Centre for the Study of Sexually Transmissible Diseases, Melbourne: La Trobe University.

Hillman, K. & Macmillan, J. 2005, *Life Satisfaction of Young Australians: Relationships between further education, training and employment and general career satisfaction,* ACER research report no. 43, Melbourne: Australian Council for Educational Research.

Hirschfield, A. & Bowers, K. 1997, 'The Effect of Social Cohesion on Levels of Recorded Crime in Disadvantaged Areas', *Urban Studies*, 34(8): 1274–302.

Hobbs, S. & McKechnie, J. 1997, *Child Employment in Britain: A Social and Psychological Analysis*, Edinburgh: The Stationery Office.

Holdsworth, G. 2000, 'Leaving Home in Britain and Spain', *European Sociological Review*, 16: 201–22.

Hollands, R. 1995, *Friday Night, Saturday Night: Youth cultural identification in the post-industrial city*, Department of Social Policy, Newcastle Upon Tyne: University of Newcastle.

—— 2005, 'Rappin on the Reservation: Canadian Mohawk Youth's Hybrid Identities', *Sociological Research Online*, 9(3), retrieved from www.socresonline.org.uk/9/3/hollands.html.

Hopkins, S. 1999, 'The Art of "Girl Power": Femininity, feminism and youth culture in the 1990s', in R. White (ed.), *Australian Youth Subcultures*, Hobart: Australian Clearinghouse for Youth Studies.

House of Representatives Standing Committee on Community Affairs 1995, *A Report on Aspects of Youth Homelessness*, Canberra: AGPS.

Howard, J. & Zibert, E. 1990, 'Curious, Bored and Wanting to Feel Good: The drug use of detained young offenders', *Drug and Alcohol Review*, 9: 225–31.

Howe, N. & Strauss, W. 2000, *Millennials Rising: The Next Great Generation*, New York: Vintage.

Huff, R. (ed.), 1996, *Gangs in America* (2nd edn), Thousand Oaks CA: Sage.

Hughes, G. 1996, 'Strategies of Multi-Agency Crime Prevention and Community Safety in Contemporary Britain', *Studies on Crime & Crime Prevention*, 5(2): 221–44.

—— & Stone, W. 2003, *Family Change and Community Life, Exploring the Links*, Research Paper no. 32, Melbourne: AIFS.

Human Rights & Equal Opportunity Commission 1991, *Racist Violence: Report of the national inquiry into racist violence in Australia*, Canberra: AGPS.

Hunt, G., Evans, K. & Kares, F. 2007, 'Drug Use and Meanings of Risk and Pleasure', *Journal of Youth Studies*, 10(1): 73–96.

Hunter, B. 1998, 'Addressing Youth Unemployment: Re-examining social and locational disadvantage within Australian cities', *Urban Policy and Research*, 16(1): 47–58.

Iley, L. 1993, 'Life in the Past Lane', *Refractory Girl*, 46: 50–55.

Inglis, C. 1993, 'Turkish Youth and the Educational Rainbow', in R. Akcelic (ed.), *Turkish Youth in Australia*, Melbourne: Australian Turkish Friendship Society.

——, Elley, J. & Manderson, L. 1992, *Making Something of Myself: Educational Attainment and Social and Economic Mobility of Turkish-Australian Young People*, Canberra: Office of Multicultural Affairs.

Jackson, N. 2001, 'Understanding population ageing: a background', *Australian Social Policy*, Canberra: Department of Family and Community Services.

—— 2002, 'The Higher Education Contribution Scheme. A HECS on the family?', *Journal of Population Research and New Zealand Population Review*, 5: 105–19.

Jackson-Jacobs, C. 2004, 'Taking a Beating: The narrative gratifications of fighting as an underdog', in J. Ferrell, K. Hayward, W. Morrison and M. Presdee (eds), *Cultural Criminology Unleashed*, London: Glasshouse Press.

Jakubowicz, A. 1989, 'Social Justice and the Politics of Multiculturalism in Australia', *Social Justice*, 16(3): 69–86.

James, R. 2002, *Socio-economic Background and Higher Education Participation: An analysis of school students' aspirations and expectations*, Canberra: Commonwealth Department of Education, Science and Training.

——, Wyn, J., Baldwin, G., Hepworth, G., McInnis, C. & Stephanou, A. 1999, *Rural and Isolated School Students and their Higher Education Choices*, Canberra: National Board of Employment, Education and Training.

Jamrozik, A. 1998, 'Transformation in the Youth Labour Market: An empirical examination 1945–1996', in J. Bessant and S. Cook (eds), *Against the Odds: Young People and Work*, Hobart: Australian Clearinghouse for Youth Studies.

—— 2001, *Social Policy in the Post-Welfare State: Australians on the threshold of the 21st century*, Sydney: Pearson Education Australia.

——, Boland, C. & Urquhart, R. 1995, *Social Change and Cultural Transformation in Australia*, Melbourne: Cambridge University Press.

Jenkins, R. 1994, 'Rethinking Ethnicity: Identity, categorization and power', *Ethnic and Racial Studies*, 17(2): 197–223.

Jochelson, R. 1997, 'Aborigines and Public Order Legislation in New South Wales', *Crime and Justice Bulletin*, 34, NSW Bureau of Crime Statistics and Research.

Johnson, L. 1993, *The Modern Girl*, Sydney: Allen & Unwin.

Johnston, E. 1991, *National Report, Royal Commission into Aboriginal Deaths in Custody*, vols 1–5, Canberra: AGPS.

Jones, A. & Smyth, P. 1999, 'Social Exclusion: A new framework for social policy analysis?', *Just Policy*, 17: 11–20.

Jordan, B. 1996, *A Theory of Poverty and Social Exclusion*, Cambridge: Polity Press.

Junger-Tas, J. 1994, 'Delinquency in Thirteen Western Countries: Some preliminary conclusions', in J. Junger-Tas, G.-J. Terlouw and M. Klein (eds), *Delinquency Behavior Among Young People in the Western World: First results of the international self-report delinquency study*, Amsterdam: Kugler Publications.

Kehily, M. J. & Nayak, A. 1996, 'The Christmas Kiss: Sexuality, story-telling and schooling', *Curriculum Studies*, 4(2): 211–27.

Kelly, P. 2001, 'Youth at Risk. Processes of Individualisation and Responsibilisation in the Risk Society', *Discourse: Studies in the Cultural Politics of Education*, 22(1): 23–34.

—— 2006, 'The Entrepreneurial Self and "Youth at-risk": Exploring the horizons of identity in the twenty-first century', *Journal of Youth Studies*, 9(1): 17–32.

Kenway, J. & Fitzclarence, L. 1997, 'Masculinity, Violence and Schooling: Challenging "poisonous pedagogies"', *Gender and Education*, 9(1): 117–33.

Kenway, J., Kraack, A. & Hickey-Moody, A. 2006, *Masculinity Beyond the Metropolis*, Basingstoke: Palgrave Macmillan.

Klein, M., Kerner, H-J., Maxson, C. & Weitekamp, E. 2001, *The Eurogang Paradox: Street Gangs and Youth Groups in the US and Europe*, Dordrecht: Kluwer Academic Publishers.

Kulyk, Keefer, J. 2004, *Thieves, a novel of Katherine Mansfield*, Canada: Harper Perennial.

La Grange, T. 1996, 'Marking Up the City: The Problem of Urban Vandalism', in G. O'Bireck (ed.), *Not a Kid Anymore: Canadian youth, crime and subcultures*, Toronto: Nelson.

Lamb, S. 1994, 'Dropping Out of School in Australia: Recent Trends in Participation and Outcomes', *Youth and Society*, 26(2): 194–222.

Landt, J. & Scott, P. 1998, 'Youth Incomes', *Australia's Youth: Reality and risk*, Sydney: Dusseldorp Skills Forum.

Lantz, S. 2003, 'Sex, Work and Study: Students, Identity and Work in the 21st Century', unpublished PhD thesis, Melbourne: University of Melbourne.

—— 2005, 'Students Working in the Melbourne Sex Industry: Education, human capital and the changing patterns of the youth labour market', *Journal of Youth Studies*, 8(4): 385–402.

Lash, S. 2002, 'Foreword', in U. Beck and E. Beck-Gernsheim, *Individualization*, London: Sage.

Lawrence, G. & Williams, C. 1990, 'The Dynamics of Decline: Implications for Social Welfare Delivery in Rural Australia', in T. Cullen, P. Dunn and G. Lawrence (eds), *Rural Health and Welfare in Australia*, Bathurst: Charles Sturt University.

Lawrence, G., Lyons, K. & Momtaz, S. (eds) 1996, *Social Change in Rural Australia*, Rural Social and Economic Research Centre, Rockhampton: Central Queensland University.

Leccardi, C. & Ruspini, E. (eds) 2006, *New Youth? Young people, generations and family life*, Aldershot: Ashgate.

Lee, E. & Leets, L. 2002, 'Persuasive Storytelling by Hate Groups Online: Examining its effects on adolescents', *American Behavioral Scientist*, 45(6): 927–57.

Lee, M. 2006, 'Public dissent and government neglect: Isolating and excluding Macquarie Fields', *Current Issues in Criminal Justice*, 18(1): 32–50.

Lennings, C. 1996, 'Adolescents at Risk: Drug use and risk behaviour: Queensland and national data', *Youth Studies Australia*, 15(2): 29–36.

Lesko, N. 1996, 'Denaturalizing Adolescence: The politics of contemporary representations', *Youth & Society*, 28(2): 139–61.

Levine, D. 1994, 'The School-to-Work Opportunities Act: A flawed prescription for education reform', *Educational Foundations*, 8(3): 33–51.

Lien, P. et al. 2003, 'The Contours and Sources of Ethnic Identity Choices among Asian Americans', *Social Science Quarterly*, 84(2): 461–81.

Lincoln, R. & Wilson, P. 1994a, 'Questioning Crime Prevention: Towards a social development approach', *Transitions*, 3(3): 7–11.

—— 1994b, 'Aboriginal Offending: Patterns and causes', in D. Chappell and P. Wilson (eds), *The Australian Criminal Justice System: The mid 1990s*, Sydney: Butterworths.

Lindsay, J. 2004, 'Gender and Class in the Lives of Young Hairdressers: From serious to spectacular', *Journal of Youth Studies*, 7(3): 259–78.

Lingard, R. 1998, 'The Disadvantaged Schools Program: Caught between literacy and local management of schools', *International Journal of Inclusive Education*, 2(1): 1–14.

Lloyd, R. & Bill, A. 2004, *Australia Online: How Australians are using computers and the Internet 2001*, Canberra: Australian Census Analytic Program.

Loader, I. 1996, *Youth, Policing and Democracy*, London: Macmillan.

Loeber, R. & Farrington, D. (eds) 1998, *Serious & Violent Juvenile Offenders: Risk factors and successful interventions*, Thousand Oaks, CA: Sage.

Looker, D. & Dwyer, P. 1998, 'Education and Negotiated Reality: Complexities facing rural youth in the 1990s', *Journal of Youth Studies*, 1(1): 5–22.

Lovett, A. 1994, *A Survey of the Health Status of Homeless Young People in Victoria: Summary Report*, Melbourne: Centre for Adolescent Health, University of Melbourne.

Lucey, H. 1996, 'Transitions to Womanhood: Constructions of success and failure for middle and working class young women', paper presented at *British Youth Research: The new agenda* conference, Glasgow University, January.

Luther, S. S. & Becker, B. E. 2002, 'Privileged but Pressured? A Study of Affluent Youth', *Child Development* 72(5): 1593–610.

Lynch, M. & Ogilvie, E. 1999, 'Access to Amenities: The issue of ownership', *Youth Studies Australia*, 18(4): 17–21.

Lyons E. 1995, 'New Clients, Old Problems: Vietnamese young people's experiences with police', in C. Guerra and R. White (eds), *Ethnic Minority Youth in Australia*, Hobart: Australian Clearinghouse for Youth Studies.

MacDonald, R. 1998, 'Youth, Transitions and Social Exclusion: Some issues for youth research in the UK', *Journal of Youth Studies*, 1(2): 163–75.

—— 2006, 'Social Exclusion, Youth Transitions and Criminal Careers: Five critical reflections on "risk"', *Australian and New Zealand Journal of Criminology*, 39(3): 371–83.

Maher, L., Nguyen, T. & Le, T. 1999, 'Wall of Silence: Stories of Cabramatta street youth', in R. White (ed.), *Australian Youth Subcultures: On the margins and in the mainstream*, Hobart: Australian Clearinghouse for Youth Studies.

Maher, L., Dixon, D., Swift, W. & Nguyen, T. 1997, *Anh Hai: Young Asian Background People's Perceptions and Experiences of Policing*, Sydney: Faculty of Law Research Monograph Series, University of New South Wales.

Males, M. 1996, *The Scapegoat Generation: America's War on Adolescents*, Monroe ME: Common Courage Press.

Mallise, F. 2002, 'Government Vision and Policies', in M. Prior (ed.), *Investing in our Children, Developing a Research Agenda*, Canberra: Academy of the Social Sciences in Australia.

Mandel, E. 1968, *Marxist Economic Theory*, London: Merlin Press.

Marginson, S. 1999, *Young Adults in Higher Education, Australia's Young Adults: The deepening divide*, Sydney: Dusseldorp Skills Forum.

Martino, W. 1999, 'Disruptive Moments in the Education of Boys: Debating populist discourses on boys, schooling and masculinities', *Discourse*, 20(2): 298–94.

Marshall, J. 1999, *Zero Tolerance Policing*, information bulletin no. 9, Adelaide: Office of Crime Statistics, Attorney-General's Department.

Martino, W. & Pallota-Chiarolli, M. (eds) 2001, *Boys' Stuff: Boys talking about what matters*, Sydney: Allen & Unwin.

Mason, G. 2002, *The Spectacle of Violence: Homophobia, Gender and Knowledge*, London: Routledge.

—— & Tomsen, S. (eds) 1997, *Homophobic Violence*, Sydney: Hawkins Press.

McDonald, K. 1999, *Struggles for Subjectivity: Identity, action and youth experience*, Cambridge: Cambridge University Press.

—— 2006, *Global Movements: Action and Culture*, Malden: Blackwell.

McDonald, P. 1984, *Can the Family Survive?*, discussion paper no. 11, Melbourne: Australian Institute of Family Studies.

Ministerial Council on Education, Employment, Training and Youth Affairs (MCEETYA) 2000 *National Development Strategy*, Canberra: Commonwealth of Australia.

McKechnie, J. & Hobbs, S. 2002, 'Work by the Young: The economic activity of school-aged children', in M. Tienda and W. J. Wilson (eds), *Youth in Cities: A Cross-National Perspective*, Cambridge: Cambridge University Press.

McLaren, K. 2000, *Tough Is Not Enough—Getting Smart About Youth Crime: A Review of Research on What Works to Reduce Offending by Young People*, Wellington: Ministry of Youth Affairs.

McLean, S. 2005, '"It might be a scummy-arsed drug but it's a sick buzz": chroming and pleasure', *Contemporary Drug Problems*, 32, Summer: 295–318.

McLeod, J. & Yates, L. 2006, *Making Modern Lives: Subjectivity, schooling and social change*, Albany: State University of New York Press.

McNair, R., Dempsey, D., Wise, S. & Perlesz, A. 2002, 'Lesbian Parenting: Issues, strengths and challenges', *Family Matters*, 63, Spring/Summer: 40–53.

McRobbie, A. 1991, *Feminism and Youth Culture: From Jackie to Just Seventeen*, London: Macmillan.

Mellor, S., Kennedy, K. & Greenwood, L. 2002, *Citizenship and Democracy: Australian students' knowledge and beliefs*, Melbourne: Australian Council for Educational Research.

Merchant, G. 2005, 'Identity Involvement: Identity performance in children's digital writing', *Discourse*, 26(6): 301–14.

Milbourne, L., Macrae, S. & Maguire, M. 2003, 'Collaborative solutions of new policy problems: exploring multi-agency partnerships in education and health work', *Journal of Education Policy*, 18(1): 19–35.

Miles, S. 1998, *Consumerism—As a Way of Life*, London: Sage.

Miles, S., Cliff, D. & Burr, V. 1998, '"Fitting In and Sticking Out": Consumption, consumer meanings and the construction of young people's identities', *Journal of Youth Studies*, 1(1): 81–96.

Miller, J. G. 1996, *Search and Destroy: African-American Males in the Criminal Justice System*, New York: Cambridge University Press.

Mills, C. W. 1959, *The Sociological Imagination*, Oxford: Oxford University Press.

Milward, C. 1998, 'Later Life Parents Helping Adult Children', *Family Matters*, 50: 38–42.

Mission Australia 2004, *Mission Australia Youth Survey Results*, Melbourne: Mission Australia.

—— 2006, *National Youth Survey 2005: Rural and Regional Responses*, Melbourne: Mission Australia.

—— 2006, *The main concerns of young Australians: National Survey*, Melbourne: Mission Australia.

Misson, R. 1999, 'The Closet and the Classroom', *Melbourne Studies in Education Special Issue: Education and Sexualities*, (40)2: 89–104.

Mitchell, T. 2003, 'Australian Hip Hop as a Subculture', *Youth Studies Australia*, 22(2): 40–4.

Mizen, P. 2004, *The Changing State of Youth*, New York: Palgrave.

—— 2002, 'Putting the Politics Back into Youth Studies: Keynesianism, monetarism and the changing state of youth', *Journal of Youth Studies*, 5(1): 5–20.

——, Bolton, A. & Pole, C. 1999, 'School Age Workers: A critical review', *Work, Employment and Society*, 13(3).

Morris, L. & Irwin, S. 1992, 'Employment Histories and the Concept of the Underclass', *Sociology: The Journal of the British Sociological Association*, 26(3): 401–20.

Morrissey, M. 2006, 'The Australian state and Indigenous people 1990–2006', *Journal of Sociology*, 42(4): 347–54.

Moss, I. (for Human Rights and Equal Opportunity Commission) 1993, *State of the Nation: A Report on People of Non-English Speaking Backgrounds*, Canberra: AGPS.

Mounsey, S. 1997, 'Youth Offending in the Loddon Campaspe Region of Rural Victoria: A case study of the effect of "locality" upon juvenile crime and juvenile justice in "the country"', Honours thesis, Melbourne: Department of Criminology, University of Melbourne.

Muggleton, D. 2000, *Inside Subculture: The postmodern meaning of style*, Oxford: Berg.

Mukherjee, S. K. 1997a, 'The Dimensions of Juvenile Crime', in A. Borowski and I. O'Connor (eds), *Juvenile Crime, Justice and Corrections*, Sydney: Longman.

—— 1997b, 'Juvenile Crime: Overview of Changing Pattern', paper presented at the Australian Institute of Criminology Conference, 'Juvenile Crime and Juvenile Justice: Towards 2000 and Beyond', Adelaide, 26–27 June.

——, Carcach, C. & Higgins, K. 1997, *Juvenile Crime and Justice: Australia 1997*, Canberra: Australian Institute of Criminology.

Muncie, J. 1999, *Youth and Crime: A Critical Introduction*, London: Sage.

—— 2002, 'Policy Transfers and What Works: Some reflections on comparative youth justice', *Youth Justice*, 1(3): 27–35.

—— 2004, 'Youth Justice: Responsibilisation and Rights', in J. Roche, S. Tucker, R. Thomson and R. Flynn (eds), *Youth in Society: Contemporary Theory, Policy and Practice*, London: Sage, in association with The Open University.

—— 2005, 'The globalization of crime control—the case of youth and juvenile justice: Neo-liberalism, policy convergence and international conventions', *Theoretical Criminology*, 9(1): 35–64.

—— 2007, 'Youth Justice and the Governance of Young People: Global, International, National, and Local Contexts', in S. Venkatesh and R. Kassimir (eds), *Youth, Globalization and the Law*, Stanford: Stanford University Press.

—— & Goldson, B. 2006, 'States of Transition: Convergence and diversity in international youth justice', in J. Muncie and B. Goldson (eds), *Comparative Youth Justice*, London: Sage.

Murray, C. 1990, *The Emerging Underclass*, London: Institute of Economic Affairs.

National Health and Medical Research Council 1992, *Health Needs of Homeless Youth*, Canberra: AGPS.

National Inquiry into the Separation of Aboriginal and Torres Strait Islander Children from Their Families 1997, *Bringing Them Home*, Canberra: Commonwealth of Australia.

Nayak, A. 2003, 'Review symposium 2: generation, culture and society', *British Journal of Sociology of Education*, 24(4): 530–32.

New South Wales Law Reform Commission 2001, *Sentencing Young Offenders*, issues paper no. 19, Sydney: Law Reform Commission.

New South Wales Office of the Ombudsman 1994, *Race Relations and Our Police*, Sydney: Office of the Ombudsman.

—— 1999, *Policing Public Safety*, Sydney: Office of the Ombudsman.

New South Wales Peer Support Foundation 2006, *What's the problem: Issues of concern for young people*, Sydney: New South Wales-based Peer Support Foundation.

New Zealand Department of Corrections 2001, *About Time: Turning people away from a life of crime and reducing re-offending*, report from the Department of Corrections to the Minister of Corrections, Wellington.

New Zealand Ministry of Justice and Ministry of Social Development 2002, *Youth Offending Strategy*, Wellington: Ministry of Justice and Ministry of Social Development.

Noble G., Poynting S. & Tabar P. 1999, 'Lebanese Youth and Social Identity', in R. White (ed.), *Australian Youth Subcultures: On the margins and in the mainstream*, Hobart: Australian Clearinghouse for Youth Studies.

Norris, P. 2001, *Digital Divide: Civic engagement, information poverty and the internet worldwide*, Cambridge: Cambridge University Press.

Northern Territory Government 2006, *Building a Better Future for Young Territorians, Progress Report 2005–2006*, Darwin: Northern Territory Government.

Notarpietro-Clarke, C. 2007, 'Blackfella Beats and New Flows', *Arena Magazine*, February–March: 41–43.

O'Brien, S. 1999, 'Is the Future of Australian Feminism Feral?', in R. White (ed.), *Australian Youth Subcultures: On the margins and in the mainstream*, Hobart: Australian Clearinghouse for Youth Studies.

O'Connor, P. 2005, 'Local Embeddedness in a Global World: Young people's accounts', *Young*, 13(1): 9–25.

O'Regan, K. & Quigley, J. 1998, 'Where Youth Live: Economic effects of urban space on employment prospects', *Urban Studies*, 35(7): 1187–205.

Office of Juvenile Justice and Delinquency Prevention 2000, *OJJDP Statistical Briefing Book*, Office of Juvenile Justice and Delinquency Prevention, US Department of Justice, Washington, accessed at ojjdp.ncjrs. org/ojstatbb/html/qa253.html.

Office of Youth Affairs 2002, *Respect*, Melbourne: Victorian Government, Department of Education and Training.

Ogilvie, E. & Lynch, M. 1999, 'A Culture of Resistance: Adolescents in Detention', in R. White (ed.), *Australian Youth Subcultures: On the margins and in the mainstream*, Hobart: Australian Clearinghouse for Youth Studies.

—— & Bell, S. 2000, 'Gender and Official Statistics: The juvenile justice system in Queensland, 1998–1999', *Trends and Issues*, 162, Canberra: Australian Institute of Criminology.

Ogwang, T., Cox, L. & Saldanha, J. 2006, 'Paint on their lips: paint-sniffers, good citizens and public space in Brisbane', *Journal of Sociology*, 42(4): 412–28.

Open Family Australia 1996–97, *Logan City Public Space Initiative*, Brisbane and Melbourne: Open Family Australia.

Organisation for Economic Cooperation and Development (OECD) 1987, *Structural Adjustment and Economic Performance*, Paris: OECD.

—— 2001, *Knowledge and Skills for Life: First results from PISA 2000*, Paris: OECD.

—— 2002, *Education at a Glance 2002*, Paris: OECD.

Owen, D. 1996, 'The Young Active Citizen: Dilemmas and opportunities', *Youth Studies Australia*, 15(1).

Painter, K. 1992, 'Different Worlds: The spatial, temporal and social dimensions of female victimization', in D. Evans, N. Fyfe and D. Herbert (eds), *Crime, Policing and Place: Essays in environmental criminology*, London: Routledge.

Palmer, D. & Collard, L. 1993, 'Aboriginal Young People and Youth Subcultures', in R. White (ed.), *Youth Subcultures: Theory, history and the Australian experience*, Hobart: Australian Clearinghouse for Youth Studies.

Palmer, D. 1997, 'When Tolerance is Zero', *Alternative Law Journal*, 22(5): 232–36.

—— 1999, 'Talking about the Problems of Young Nyungars', in R. White (ed.), *Australian Youth Subcultures: On the margins and in the mainstream*, Hobart: Australian Clearinghouse for Youth Studies.

—— & Collard, L. 1998, '"… we cleared and built all that run": Nyungars, work and cultural incorporation', in J. Bessant & S. Cook (eds), *Against the Odds: Young people and work*, Hobart: Australian Clearinghouse for Youth Studies.

Paradies, Y. 2006, 'Beyond Black and White: Essentialism, hybridity and Indigeneity', *Journal of Sociology*, 42(4): 355–68.

Parker, H., Aldridge, J. & Measham, F. 1998, *Illegal Leisure: The normalization of adolescent drug use*, London: Routledge.

Payne, S. 1990, 'Aboriginal Women and the Criminal Justice System', *Aboriginal Law Bulletin*, 2(46): 9–11.

Pearson, N. 2001, 'Rebuilding Indigenous Communities', in P. Botsman and M. Latham (eds), *The Enabling State: People before bureaucracy*, Sydney: Pluto Press.

Pe-Pua, R. 1996, *'We're Just Like Other Kids!': Street-frequenting youth of non-English-speaking background*, Melbourne: Bureau of Immigration, Multicultural and Population Research.

—— 1999, 'Youth and Ethnicity: Images and constructions' in R. White (ed.), *Australian Youth Subcultures: On the margins and in the mainstream*, Hobart: Australian Clearinghouse for Youth Studies.

Perth, City of 1997, *Report of Findings: Youth forum*, Perth: City of Perth.

Pilcher, J. 1994, 'Mannheim's Sociology of Generations: An Undervalued Legacy', *British Journal of Sociology*, 45(3): 481–95.

Platt, A. 1977, *The Child Savers*, Chicago: University of Chicago Press.

Polk, K. & Schafer, W. 1972, *Schools and Delinquency*, Englewood Cliffs, Prentice-Hall.

Potas, I., Vining, A. & Wilson, P. 1990, *Young People and Crime: Costs and prevention*, Canberra: Australian Institute of Criminology.

Power, S. 2001, '"Joined-up Thinking"? Inter-agency partnerships in education action zones', in S. Riddell and L. Tett (eds), *Education, Social Justice and Inter-Agency Working: Joined up or Fractured Policy?*, London: RoutledgeFalmer.

Poynting, S. & Morgan, G. (eds) 2007, *Outrageous! Moral Panics in Australia*, Hobart: Australian Clearinghouse for Youth Studies.

Poynting S. 1999, 'When "Zero Tolerance" Looks Like Racial Intolerance: "Lebanese youth gangs", discrimination and resistance', *Current Issues in Criminal Justice*, 11(1): 74–78.

——, Noble G. & Tabar P. 2001, 'Middle Eastern Appearances: "Ethnic gangs", moral panic and media framing', *Australian and New Zealand Journal of Criminology*, 34(1): 67–90.

—— Noble, G., Tabar, P. & Collins, J. 2004, *Bin Laden in the Suburbs: Criminalising the Arab Other*, Sydney: Sydney Institute of Criminology.

Presdee, M. 2000, *Cultural Criminology and the Carnival of Crime*, London: Routledge.

—— 1984, 'Youth Unemployment and Young Women', *Radical Education Dossier*, 23: 4–7.

Preston, A. 1997, 'Where Are We Now with Human Capital Theory in Australia?', *Economic Record*, 73(220): 51–78.

Priday, E. 2006, 'Thinking About New Directions in Juvenile Justice: risk and cognitive behaviourism', *Current Issues in Criminal Justice*, 17(3): 413–30.

Prime Ministerial Youth Homelessness Taskforce 1996, *Report to the Prime Minister by the Prime Ministerial Youth Homelessness Taskforce on a Framework for the Youth Homelessness Pilot Program*, Canberra: AGPS.

Productivity Commission 1999, *Impact of Competition Policy and Reforms of Rural and Regional Australia*, report no. 8, Canberra: AusInfo.

Prout, A. 1999, 'Children—A suitable case for inclusion?', annual lecture, CPPR, King's College, London.

Pusey, M. 2007, 'The Changing Relationship between the Generations … It could even be good news?', *Youth Studies Australia*, 26(1): 9–16.

Putnins, A. 2001, *Substance Use By South Australian Young Offenders*, Office of Crime Statistics, information bulletin no.19, Adelaide: Attorney-General's Department.

Quixley, S. 1992, *Living, Learning and Working: The experiences of young people in rural and remote communities in Australia*, Canberra: National Youth Coalition for Housing.

Raby, R. 2005, 'What is Resistance?', *Journal of Youth Studies*, 8(2): 15–71.

Raffo, C. & Reeves, M. 1999, 'Youth, School-to-work Transitions and Social Exclusion—Individualised systems of social capital, situated learning and developments in the agency/structure debate', *Journal of Youth Studies*, 3(2): 147–56.

Raphael Reed, L. 1999, 'Troubling Boys and Disturbing Discourses on Masculinity and Schooling: A feminist exploration of current debates and interventions concerning boys in school', *Gender and Education*, 11(1): 93–110.

Rattansi, A. & Phoenix, A. 1997, 'Rethinking Youth Identities: Modernist and postmodernist frameworks', in J. Bynner, L. Chisholm and A. Furlong (eds), *Youth, Citizenship and Social Change in a European Context*, Aldershot: Ashgate.

Redhead, S. 1997, *Subculture to Clubcultures: An introduction to popular cultural studies*, Oxford: Blackwell.

—— (ed.) 1993, *Rave Off: Politics and deviance in contemporary youth culture*, Aldershot: Avebury.

Redman, P. & Mac an Ghaill, M. 1996, 'Schooling Sexualities: Heterosexual masculinities, schooling and the unconscious', *Discourse*, 17: 243–56.

Reiman, J. 1998, *The Rich Get Richer and the Poor Get Prison*, Boston: Allyn & Bacon.

Reiss, A. 1986, 'Why Are Communities Important in Understanding Crime?', in A. Reiss and M. Tonry (eds), *Communities and Crime*, Chicago: University of Chicago Press.

Reymond, M. 1998, 'I Don't Want to Commit Myself Yet: Young people's life concepts', *Journal of Youth Studies*, 1: 63–79.

Richardson, S. 2002, 'The Economics of Families and Children: A research agenda', in M. Prior (ed.), *Investing in our Children*, Canberra: Academy of the Social Sciences.

Roberts, K. 2007, 'Youth Transitions and Generations: A response to Wyn and Woodman', *Journal of Youth Studies*.

Robson M. 1991, 'Education in Rural Victoria is a Social Justice Issue', in C. Boylan (ed.), *What Does Social Justice Mean for Education in Rural Australia*, Wagga Wagga: Charles Sturt University.

Rodger, J. 1992, 'The Welfare State and Social Closure: Social Division and the "Underclass"', *Critical Social Policy*, 35: 45–63.

Roman, L. G. 1996, 'Spectacle in the Dark: Youth as Transgression, Display and Repression, *Educational Theory*, 46(1): 1–22.

Rudd, P. & Evans, K. 1998, 'Structure and Agency in Youth Transitions: Student experiences of vocational further education', *Journal of Youth Studies*, 1: 39–62.

Sampson, R. 1991, 'Linking the Micro- and Macro-Level Dimensions of Community Social Organisation', *Social Forces*, 70(1): 43–64.

—— 1993, 'The Community Context of Violent Crime', in W. Wilson (ed.), *Sociology and the Public Agenda*, Newbury Park: Sage.

——, Raudenbush, S. & Earls, F. 1997, 'Neighborhoods and Violent Crime: A multilevel study of collective efficacy', *Science*, 277: 918–24.

Sandercock, L. 1997, 'From Main Street to Fortress: The future of malls as public spaces—or—"shut up and shop"', *Just Policy*, 9: 27–34.

Sanderson, W. 2000, 'Andrew Mawson and the Community Action Network', Brisbane Institute, accessed at www.brisinst.org.au/resources/sanderson_wayne_can.html.

Sandor, D. & White, R. 1993, 'Police Powers Extended', *Alternative Law Journal*, 18(6): 299–300.

Santos, J. 2001, 'Down On The Corner: An analysis of gang-related anti-loitering laws', *Cardozo Law Review*, 22: 269–314.

Sawyer, M. et al. 2000, *The Mental Health of Young People in Australia*, Canberra: Mental Health and Special Programs Branch, Commonwealth Department of Health and Aged Care.

Schissel, B. 1997, *Blaming Children: Youth crime, moral panics and the politics of hate*, Halifax: Fernwood Publishing.

—— 2002, 'Youth Crime, Youth Justice, and the Politics of Marginalization', in B. Schissel and C. Brooks (eds), *Marginality & Condemnation: An introduction to critical criminology*, Halifax: Fernwood Publishing.

Schneider, J. 2000, 'The Increasing Financial Dependency of Young People on their Parents', *Journal of Youth Studies*, 3(1): 5–20.

—— & Stevenson, D. 1999, *The ambitious generation: America's teenagers: motivated but directionless*, New Haven: Yale University Press.

Senate Community Affairs References Committee 2004, *A Hand Up Not A Hand Out: Renewing the fight against poverty, Report on Poverty and Financial Hardship*, Canberra: Senate Printing Unit.

Sercombe, H. 1995, 'The Face of the Criminal is Aboriginal', in J. Bessant, K. Carrington and S. Cook, (eds), *Cultures of Crime and Violence: The Australian experience*, Melbourne: La Trobe University Press.

—— 1999, 'Boots, Gangs and Addictions: Youth subcultures and the media', in R. White (ed.), *Australian Youth Subcultures: On the margins and in the mainstream*, Hobart: Australian Clearinghouse for Youth Studies.

Seymour, J. 1988, *Dealing With Young Offenders*, Sydney: Law Book Company.

Sheahan, P. 2005, *Generation Y: Thriving and surviving with Generation Y at work*, Melbourne: Hardie Grant.

Shildrick, T. 2002, 'Young People, Illicit Drug Use and the Question of Normalization', *Journal of Youth Studies*, 5(1): 35–48.

Short, C. 1988, 'The Relationship between Youth and Adult Award Wages from 1930–1985', *Journal of Industrial Relations*, 30(4): 491–510.

Skeggs, B. 2005, 'The Re-Branding of Class: Propertising Culture', in F. Devine, M. Savage, J. Scott and R. Crompton (eds), *Rethinking Class: Culture, identities and lifestyle*, New York: Palgrave Macmillan.

Skelton, T. & Valentine, G. 1998, *Cool Places, Geographies of Youth Cultures*, London: Routledge.

Smandych, R., Lincoln, R. & Wilson, P. 1995, 'Towards a Cross-cultural Theory of Aboriginal Criminality', in K. Hazelhurst (ed.), *Perceptions of Justice*, Aldershot: Avebury.

Smart, D. 2002, 'Relationships, Marriage and Parenthood', *Family Matters*, 63: 28–35.

Smith, E. & Green, A. 2001, *School students' learning from their paid and unpaid work*, Adelaide: National Council for Vocational Education Research.

Smith, T. L., Smith, G. H., Boler, M., Kempton, M., Ormond, A., Chueh, H. & Waetford, R. 2002, '"Do you Guys Hate Aucklanders Too?" Youth: Voicing differences from the rural heartland', *Journal of Rural Studies*, 18: 179–80.

Smyth, J. & Hattam, R., with Cannon, J., Edwards, J., Wilson, N. & Wurst, S. 2004, *'Dropping Out', Drifting Off, Being Excluded: Becoming somebody without school*, New York: Peter Lang.

Snow, D. 1999, 'Skateboarders, Streets and Style', in R. White (ed.), *Australian Youth Subcultures: On the margins and in the mainstream*, Hobart: Australian Clearinghouse for Youth Studies.

Snowball, L. & Weatherburn, D. 2006, 'Indigenous over-representation in prison: The role of offender characteristics, *Contemporary Issues in Crime and Justice*, 99, Sydney: NSW Bureau of Crime Statistics and Research.

Spierings, J. 1995, *Young Australians in the Working Nation: A review of youth employment policies for the 1990s*, Social Justice Research Foundation Series 2, paper no. 1, Adelaide.

Spoehr, J. 1997, 'Alternatives to Despair—Reflections on the youth employment policy debate', *Australian Options*, 9, 2–6.

St John, G. (ed.) 2002, *FreeNRG: Notes from the edge of the dance floor*, Sydney: Pluto Press.

Standing Committee on Social Issues 1995, *A Report into Youth Violence in New South Wales*, Sydney: Legislative Council, Parliament of New South Wales.

Stanley, F. 2001, 'Centenary Article—Child health since Federation', in *2001 Year Book Australia*, Canberra.

—— 2002, 'A New Research Paradigm for Addressing Social Justice', in M. Prior (ed.), *Investing in our Children*, Canberra: Australian Academy of the Social Sciences, Canberra.

State Youth Affairs Councils and Networks 1992, *A Living Income: Income Support for Young People*, Sydney: Youth Action and Policy Association of New South Wales.

Stern, D., Bailey, T. & Merritt, D. 1997, *School-to-Work Policy Insights from Recent International Developments*, Berkeley: National Center for Research in Vocational Education.

Stevens K. & Mason D. 1992, 'Making Career Choices in Rural Western Australia', in C. Boylan (ed.), *Rural Education: In pursuit of excellence*, proceedings of the eighth Annual National Conference, Armidale.

Stokes H. & Tyler D. 1997, *Rethinking Inter-Agency Collaboration and Young People*, Melbourne: Language Australia and the Youth Research Centre, University of Melbourne.

—— 2003, 'Engaging Young People in School through the Arts', Melbourne: Youth Research Centre.

——, Wierenga, A. & Wyn, J. 2004, *Preparing for the Future and Living Now*, Melbourne: Youth Research Centre.

Stoller, R. J. 1968, 'On the Development of Masculinity and Femininity', *Sex and Gender*, vol. 1, London: The Hogarth Press.

Stratton, J. 1992, *The Young Ones: Working-Class Culture, Consumption and the Category of Youth*, Perth: Black Swan Press.

Superstein, D. 1994, 'Adolescents' Attitudes toward Their Schooling: The influence of encouragement and discouragement', *Individual Psychology*, 50(2): 183–91.

Sutton, A. & James, S. 1996, *Evaluation of Australian Drug Anti-Trafficking Law Enforcement*, Adelaide: National Police Research Unit.

Sweet, R. 1998, 'Youth: The rhetoric and the reality of the 1990s', in Dusseldorp Skills Forum, *Australia's Youth: Reality and Risk*, Sydney: Dusseldorp Skills Forum.

Tait, G. 1993, 'Re-assessing Street Kids: A critique of subculture theory', in R. White (ed.), *Youth Subcultures: Theory, history and the Australian experience*, Hobart: Australian Clearinghouse for Youth Studies.

Taylor, S. & Henry, M. 2000, 'Challenges for Equity Policy in Changing Contexts', *Australian Educational Researcher*, 27(3): 1–15.

Te Riele, K. & Wyn, J. 2005, 'Transformations in Youth Transitions in Australia', in N. Bagnall (ed.), *Youth Transitions in a Globalised Marketplace*, New York: Nova Science Publishers.

Teese, R. 2000, *Academic Success and Social Power*, Melbourne: Melbourne University Press.

—— & Polesel, J. 2003, *Undemocratic Schooling*, Melbourne: Melbourne University Press.

Teese, R., Davies, M., Charlton, M. & Polesel, J. 1995, *Who Wins at School? Girls and Boys in Australian Secondary Education*, Melbourne: Department of Education Policy and Management, University of Melbourne.

Tett, L. Crowther, J. & O'Hara, P. 2003, 'Collaborative partnerships in community education', *Journal of Education Policy*, 18(1): 37–51.

Thomson R. & Taylor, R. 2005, 'Between Cosmopolitanism and the Locals: Mobility as a resource in the transition to adulthood', *Young*, 13(1): 327–42.

Tjong, S., Weber, I. & Sternberg, J. 2003, 'Mobile Youth Culture: shaping telephone use in Australia and Singapore', paper presented at ANZCA 03 Conference, Brisbane, July.

Tonry, M. 1997, 'Ethnicity, Crime, and Immigration', in M. Tonry (ed.), *Ethnicity, Crime, and Immigration: Comparative and Cross-National Perspectives*, Chicago: University of Chicago Press.

Toohey, P. 2004, 'Gangsters' paradise', *The Bulletin*, 4 February.

Tressider, J. 1996, 'Perspectives on Adolescent Health in the 1990s', editorial, *Australian and New Zealand Journal of Public Health*, 20(3): 229–30.

——, Macaskill, P., Bennett, D. & Nutbeam, D. 1997, 'Health Risks and Behaviour of Out-of-School 16-year-olds in New South Wales', *Australian and New Zealand Journal of Public Health*, 21(2): 168–74.

Turrell G. & Mathers, C. 2000, 'Socioeconomic Status and Health in Australia', *Medical Journal of Australia*, 172: 434–8.

Twenge, J. M. 2006, *Generation Me*, New York: Free Press.

United Nations 1999, *Youth Participation Manual, Economic and Social Commission for Asia and the Pacific*, New York: United Nations.

Utting, D. 1996, *Reducing Criminality Among Young People: A Sample of Relevant Programmes in the United Kingdom*, Home Office Research Study 161, London: Home Office.

Vasta, E. 1995, 'Youth & Ethnicity: The second generation', in C. Guerra and R. White (eds), *Ethnic Minority Youth in Australia: Challenges & myths*, Hobart: Australian Clearinghouse for Youth Studies.

Vasta, E. & Castles, S. (eds) 1996, *The Teeth Are Smiling: The Persistence of Racism in Multicultural Australia*, Sydney: Allen & Unwin.

Venkatesh, S. & Kassimir, R. (eds) 2007, *Youth, Globalization, and the Law*, Stanford: Stanford University Press.

Vinson, T. 2004, *Community Adversity and Resilience: The distribution of social disadvantage in Victoria and New South Wales and the mediating role of social cohesion*, Melbourne: Ignatius Centre for Social Policy and Research, Jesuit Social Services.

——, Abela, M. & Hutka, R. 1997, *Making Ends Meet: A Study of Unemployed Young People Living in Sydney*, Uniya Research Report no. 1, Sydney: Uniya Jesuit Social Justice Centre.

Vromen, A. 2005, 'Young people, participation and Internet use', paper presented at Youth Electoral Study Workshop, Canberra.

Walby, S. 1994, 'Is Citizenship Gendered?', *Sociology*, 28(2): 379–95.

Walker, L. 1993, 'Girls, Schooling and Subcultures of Resistance', in R. White (ed.), *Youth Subcultures: Theory, history and the Australian experience*, Hobart: Australian Clearinghouse for Youth Studies.

—— 1999, 'Hydraulic Sexuality and Hegemonic Masculinity: Young working-class men and car culture', in R. White (ed.), *Australian youth subcultures*, Hobart: Australian Clearinghouse for Youth Studies.

Walkerdine, V. 1996, 'Subjectivity and Social Class: New directions for feminist psychology', *Feminism and Psychology*, 6(3): 355–60.

—— 2000, 'Feminist and Critical Perspectives on Educational Psychology', address to Committee on the Role and Status of Women, American Educational Research Association.

Walsh, T. 2004, 'Who is the "Public" in "Public Spaces"? A Queensland Perspective on poverty, homelessness and vagrancy', *Alternative Law Journal*, 29(1): 81–86.

Watson, L. 2003, *Lifelong Learning in Australia*, Canberra: Department of Education, Science and Training, Canberra.

Weatherburn, D. & Lind, B. 1998, 'Poverty, Parenting, Peers and Crime-Prone Neighbourhoods', *Trends and Issues in Crime and Criminal Justice*, 85, Canberra: Australian Institute of Criminology.

—— 2001, *Delinquent-Prone Communities*, Cambridge: Cambridge University Press.

Webster, S. & Nabigon, H. 1993, 'First nations empowerment in community based research', in P. Anisef and P. Axelrod (eds), *Transitions: Schooling and Employment in Canada*, Toronto: Thompson Educational.

West, P., Sweeting, H., Young, R. & Robins, M. 2006, 'A Material Paradox: Socioeconomic Status, Young People's Disposable Income and Consumer Culture', *Journal of Youth Studies*, 9(4): 437–62.

Weston, R. & Hughes, J. 1999, 'Family Forms—Family Wellbeing', *Family Matters*, 53: 14–20.

Weston, R. & Parker, R. 2002, 'Why is the Fertility Rate Falling? A discussion of the literature', *Family Matters*, 63: 6–13.

Weston, R., Stanton, D., Qu, L. & Soriano, G. 2001, 'Australian Families in Transition: Socio-demographic trends 1901–2001', *Family Matters*, 60: 12–23.

Wexler, P. 1992, *Becoming Somebody, Toward a Social Psychology of School*, London: The Falmer Press.

White, R. 1990, *No Space of Their Own: Young People and Social Control in Australia*, Melbourne: Cambridge University Press.

—— (ed.) 1993, *Youth Subcultures: Theory, history and the Australian experience*, Hobart: Australian Clearinghouse for Youth Studies.

—— (ed.) 1999, *Australian Youth Subcultures: On the Margins and in the Mainstream*, Hobart: Australian Clearinghouse for Youth Studies.

—— 1993a, 'Young People and the Policing of Community Space', *Australian and New Zealand Journal of Criminology*, 26(3): 207–18.

—— 1993b, 'Police Vidiots', *Alternative Law Journal*, 18(3): 109–12.

—— 1994, 'Street Life: Police practices and youth behaviour', in R. White and C. Alder (eds), *The Police and Young People in Australia*, Melbourne: Cambridge University Press.

—— 1996a, 'The Poverty of the Welfare State: Managing an underclass', in P. James (ed.), *The State in Question: Transformations of the Australian state*, Sydney: Allen & Unwin.

—— 1996b, 'Racism, Policing and Ethnic Youth Gangs', *Current Issues in Criminal Justice*, 7(3): 302–13.

—— 1996c, 'Schooling With A Future?', *Just Policy*, 5: 44–50.

—— 1996d, 'Ten Arguments Against Youth Curfews', *Youth Studies Australia*, 15(4): 28–30.

—— 1997a, 'Immigration, Nationalism and Anti-Asian Racism', in C. Cunneen, D. Fraser and S. Tomsen (eds), *Faces of Hate: Hate Crime in Australia*, Sydney: Hawkins Press.

—— 1997b, 'Young People, Waged Work and Exploitation', *Journal of Australian Political Economy*, 40: 61–79.

—— 1997c, 'Violence and Masculinity: The construction of criminality', *Arena Magazine*, December–January: 41–44.

—— 1998a, 'Globalisation and the Politics of Race', *Journal of Australian Political Economy*, 41: 37–63.

—— 1998b, 'The Health of Marginalised Young People and the Role of the General Practitioner. Challenging public health', *A Journal of Public Health and Health Promotion*, 2: 2–9.

—— 1998c, *Public Spaces for Young People: A guide to creative projects and positive strategies*, Sydney: Australian Youth Foundation and the National Campaign Against Violence and Crime.

—— 1999, *Hanging Out: Negotiating young people's use of public space*, Canberra: National Crime Prevention, Attorney-General's Department.

—— 2000, 'Social Justice, Community Building and Restorative Strategies', *Contemporary Justice Review*, 3(1): 55–72.

—— 2001, 'Graffiti, Crime Prevention and Cultural Space', *Current Issues in Criminal Justice*, 12(3): 253–68.

—— 2002, 'Youth Crime, Community Development, and Social Justice', in M. Tienda and W. J. Wilson (eds), *Youth in Cities: A cross-national perspective*, Cambridge: Cambridge University Press.

—— 2002a, 'Indigenous Young Australians, Criminal Justice and Offensive Language', *Journal of Youth Studies*, 5(1): 21–34.

—— 2002b, 'Understanding Youth Gangs', *Trends and Issues in Criminal Justice*, 237, Canberra: Australian Institute of Criminology.

—— 2002c, 'Early Intervention Models, Professional Practice and Workplace Environments', *Youth Studies Australia*, 21(4): 16–23.

—— 2003, 'Communities, Conferences and Restorative Social Justice', *Criminal Justice*, 3(2): 139–60.

—— 2006a, 'Youth Gang Research in Australia', in J. Short and L. Hughes (eds), *Studying Youth Gangs*, New York: AltaMira Press.

—— 2006b, 'Criminal Bodies? The physicality of violence', *NEXUS: Newsletter of the Australian Sociological Association*, 18(3): 20–21.

—— 2007a, 'Policing the Other: Lebanese Young People in a Climate of Conflict', in J. Jupp and J. Nieuwenhuysen, with E. Dawson (eds), *Social Cohesion in Australia*, Melbourne: Cambridge University Press.

—— 2007b, 'Paradoxes of Youth Participation: Political activism and youth disenchantment', in. L. Saha, M. Print and K. Edwards (eds), *Youth and Political Participation*, Rotterdam: Sense Publishers.

—— 2007c, 'Public Spaces, Consumption, and the Social Regulation of Young People', in S. Venkatesh and R. Kassimir (eds), *Youth, Globalization, and the Law*, Stanford: Stanford University Press.

—— & Alder, C. (eds) 1994, *The Police and Young People in Australia*, Melbourne: Cambridge University Press.

—— & Mason, R. 2006, 'Youth Gangs and Youth Violence: Charting the key dimensions', *Australian & New Zealand Journal of Criminology*, 39(1): 54–70.

—— & Perrone, S. 2001, 'Racism, Ethnicity and Hate Crime', *Communal/Plural*, 9(2): 161–81.

—— & van der Velden, J. 1995, 'Class and Criminality', *Social Justice*, 22(1): 51–74.

——, Aumair, M., Harris, A. & McDonnell, L. 1997, *Any Which Way You Can: Youth Livelihoods, Community Resources and Crime*, Sydney: Australian Youth Foundation.

——, Kosky, B. & Kosky, M. 2001, *MCS Shopping Centre Youth Project: A Youth-Friendly Approach to Shopping Centre Management*, Hobart: Australian Clearinghouse for Youth Studies.

——, Perrone, S., Guerra, C. & Lampugnani, R. 1999, *Ethnic Youth Gangs in Australia: Do they exist? (7 reports—Vietnamese, Latin American, Turkish, Somalian, Pacific Islander, Anglo-Australian, Summary)*, Melbourne: Australian Multicultural Foundation.

Whyte, W. F. 1943, *Street Corner Society: The social structure of an italian slum*, Chicago: Chicago University Press.

Wierenga, A. 2003, *Sharing a New Story: Young People in Decision-making*, Melbourne: Australian Youth Research Centre and Foundation for Young Australians.

—— 1999, 'Imagines Trajectories: Local culture and social identity', in R. White (ed.), *Australian Youth Subcultures: On the Margins and In the Mainstream*, Hobart: Australian Clearinghouse for Youth Studies.

—— 2001, 'Making A Life', PhD thesis, Hobart: School of Sociology & Social Work, University of Tasmania.

—— 2008, *Young People Making a Life*, Basingstoke: Palgrave Macmillan.

——, Wyn, J., Glover, S. & Meade, M. 2003, *Application of Enabling State Principles in the Delivery of Youth Services*, Melbourne: Youth Research Centre.

Willis, E. 1977, *Learning to Labour: How Working Class Boys Get Working Class Jobs*, Farnborough: Saxon House.

—— 2004, *The Sociological Quest*, 4th edn, Sydney: Allen & Unwin.

Willis, P. 2003, 'Foot Soldiers of Modernity: The dialectics of cultural consumption and the 21st century school', *Harvard Educational Review*, 73(2): 390–415.

Willis, S. 1998, 'Teens at Work, Negotiating the Jobless Future' in J. Austin and M. N. Willard, *Generations of Youth: Youth Subcultures and History in 20th Century America*, New York: New York University Press.

Wilson, B. & Wyn, J. 1987, *Shaping Futures*, Sydney: Allen & Unwin.

Wilson, P. & Arnold, J. 1986, *Street Kids: Australia's Alienated Youth*, Melbourne: Collins Dove.

Wilson, W. J. 1996, *When Work Disappears*, New York: Knopf.

Winter, I. 1995, *Young People Living on the Urban Fringe*, National Youth Affairs Research Scheme Report, Hobart: Australian Clearinghouse for Youth Studies.

Wood, R. T. 2003, 'The Straightedge Youth Sub-Culture: Observations on the Complexity of Sub-Cultural Identity', *Journal of Youth Studies*, 6(1): 33–52.

Wooden, F. 1997, *Youth Access Audit: 6 Month Progress Report*, Melton: Melton Shire Council.

Wooden, M. 1996, 'The Youth Labour Market: Characteristics and Trends', *Australian Bulletin of Labour*, 22(2): 137–60.

—— & Van den Heuvel, A. 1999, *The Labour Market for Young Adults, Australia's Young Adults: The Deepening Divide*, Sydney: Dusseldorp Skills Forum.

Woodman, D. 2004, 'Responsibility and Time for Escape: The meaning of well-being to young Australians, *Melbourne Journal of Politics*, 29: 82–95.

Wright Mills, C. 1959, *The Sociological Imagination*, New York: Oxford University Press.

Wright, J. & Burrows, L. 2004, '"Being Healthy": The discursive construction of health in New Zealand children's responses to the National Education Monitoring Project', *Discourse: Studies in the cultural politics of education*, 25(2): 11–30.

Wyn, J. 2000, 'The Postmodern Girl: Education, "success" and the construction of girls' identities', in J. McLeod and K. Malone (eds), *Researching Youth*, Hobart: Australian Clearinghouse for Youth Studies.

—— 2004, 'Becoming Adult in the 2000s: new transitions and new careers', *Family Matters*, 68 (Winter): 4–10.

—— 2006 'What *is* happening to "adolescence"? Growing up in changing times', in J. A. Vadeboncoeur, and L. P. Stevens (eds) (2005), *Re/Constructing the 'Adolescent': Sign, Symbol and Body*, New York: Peter Lang.

—— 2007, 'Generation and Class: Young people's new, diverse patterns of life and their implications for participation in civic society', *International Journal of Children's Rights*, 15: 1–16.

—— & Dwyer, P. 1999, 'New Directions in Research on Youth in Transition', *Journal of Youth Studies*, 2: 5–21.

—— & Dwyer, P. 2000, 'New Patterns of Youth Transition in Education', *International Social Science Journal*, 164: 147–59.

—— & Lamb, S. 1996, 'Early School Leaving in Australia: Issues for Education and Training Policy', *Journal of Education Policy*, 11(12): 259–68.

—— & White, R. 1997, *Rethinking Youth*, Sydney: Allen & Unwin.

—— & White, R. 1998, 'Young People, Social Problems and Australian Youth Studies', *Journal of Youth Studies*, 1(1): 23–38.

—— & White, R. 2000, 'Negotiating Social Change: The paradox of youth', *Youth and Society*, 32(2): 165–83.

—— & Woodman, D. 2006, 'Generation, Youth and Social Change in Australia', *Journal of Youth Studies*, 9(5): 495–514.

—— & Woodman, D. 2007, 'Researching Youth in a Context of Social Change: A Reply to Roberts', *Journal of Youth Studies*, forthcoming.

——, Semmens, B., Falk, I. & Guenther, J. 2001, *Education for Rural Development in Australia 1945–2001*, working paper 22, Melbourne: Youth Research Centre.

——, Stokes, H. & Stafford, J. 1998, *Young People Living in Rural Australia in the 1990s*, Research Report 16, Melbourne: Youth Research Centre, University of Melbourne.

Yang, C. C. 2000, 'The use of the Internet among academic gay communities in Taiwan: An exploratory study', *Information, Communication & Society*, 3(2): 153–72.

Yates, L. 1997, 'Gender Equity and the Boys Debate: What sort of challenge is it?', *British Journal of Sociology of Education*, 18(3): 337–47.

—— 2000, 'In What Sense is "Class" Still a Useful Concept?', paper presented at American Educational Research Association Annual Conference Symposium *Reinventing Youth at the Turn of the Century*, New Orleans, 23–28 September.

—— & McLeod, J. 2000, 'Social Justice and the Middle', *Australian Educational Researcher* 27: 59–78.

Ybarra, M. & Mitchell, K. 2004, 'Youth engaging in online harassment: associations with caregiver–child relationships, Internet use, and personal characteristics', *Journal of Adolescence*, 27: 319–36.

Youdell, D. 2006, *Impossible Bodies, Impossible Selves: Exclusions and student subjectivities*, Dordrecht: Springer.

Young, I. 1990, *Justice and the Politics of Difference*, Princeton: Princeton University Press.

Young, K. 2004, 'Internet Addiction: A new clinical phenomenon and its consequences', *American Behavioural Scientist*, 48(4): 402–15.

Zelinka, S. 1995, 'Ethnic Minority Young People', in C. Guerra and R. White (eds), *Ethnic Minority Youth in Australia*, Hobart: Australian Clearinghouse for Youth Studies.

INDEX